ECONOMIC INTERDEPENDENCE
IN UKRAINIAN-RUSSIAN RELATIONS

SUNY series in Global Politics
James N. Rosenau, editor

Economic Interdependence in Ukrainian-Russian Relations

Paul J. D'Anieri

STATE UNIVERSITY OF NEW YORK PRESS

Published by
State University of New York Press, Albany

For information, address State University of New York Press,
State University Plaza, Albany, NY, 12246

Production by Cathleen Collins
Marketing by Dana Yanulavich

Library of Congress Cataloging in Publication Data

D'Anieri, Paul J., 1965–
    Economic interdependence in Ukrainian-Russian relations / Paul J.
D'Anieri.
       p.   cm. — (SUNY series in global politics)
    Includes bibliographical references and index.
    ISBN 0-7914-4245-4 (alk. paper). —ISBN 0-7914-4246-2 (pbk. :
alk. paper)
       1. Economic security—Ukraine.   2. Ukraine-Economic
conditions—1991–   3. Ukraine—Foreign economic relations—Russia
(Federation)   4. Russia (Federation)—Foreign economic relations—
Ukraine.   I. Title.   II. Series.
HC340.19.D36   1999
337.470477—dc21   98-45360
                                                              CIP

10   9   8   7   6   5   4   3   2   1

Contents

Acknowledgments

When the Soviet Union dissolved, it took many research agendas with it. At the same time, it opened up a plethora of new issues that are only now beginning to be addressed. For me as a scholar of international politics, the notion of creating a whole new group of states where there had previously been just one was intriguing. The question that immediately arose was "How are these new states going to get along with one another?" Before long it became clear that expectations concerning future arrangements in the region diverged widely. Much of the research at the time, and since, has focused on Russia. As the largest of the former Soviet states, and the recognized successor to the Soviet Union, Russia is the most important for the region and the west. At the same time, however, it seemed to me that the reaction of the smaller states to Russian policies would be crucial in determining the future of the region, and that while Russia could set the agenda, it could not unilaterally implement its will. In this context, it seems likely that Ukraine's response to its independence and to Russian policies will play a key role in the region's future. The need to understand Ukraine's dilemmas and its responses prompted this project.

Much of my initial research on the problem was completed in 1993–1994 while I was on a Fulbright Grant at L'viv State University in Ukraine. I am grateful to CIES for the Fulbright Grant and to the University of Kansas for granting me leave. The people and scholars of L'viv were incredibly helpful. Markian Mal'skiy and his colleagues at the Faculty of International Relations provided a congenial atmosphere to teach and study. The International Relations Department, and its head, Volodymyr Kyrylych, were indispensable in taking care of all necessary bureaucratic arrangements. The scholars at the Geneza Research Institue, and Ihor Markov in particular, allowed me to participate in all of their activities, and provided useful feedback on early drafts of the theoretical framework. Yevhen Hlibovitsky provided research assistance. On a personal level, I am deeply indebted to Professor Roman Ciapalo of Loras College, and to his cousins, Ihor and Halla Ciapalo of L'viv, who be-friended me and looked after me during what was in many respects a long and difficult year.

Both before my trip to Ukraine and after my return, I received generous support from the University of Kansas General research fund for additional research and writing. Marc Nordberg provided thorough and indefatigable research assistance, and made useful comments on early drafts of the empiri-cal chapters. Trisha Hobson provided additional research assistance. The Russian and East European studies program at Kansas, and its director, Pro-fessor Maria Carlson, have been unstinting in moral and material support. Many of the ideas expressed in the book were worked out at presentations at the REES brown-bag series.

In the summer of 1996, I was able to return to Kiev for follow-up re-search. This trip was funded by a grant from the International Research and Exchanges Board. Anna Abdulakh of the Kiev Mohyla Academy set up many of the initial contacts that made that trip fruitful. Scholars in the Department of Politology of the Kiev Mohyla Academy, Institute for World Economy and International Relations at the Ukrainian Academy of Sciences, and Institute of the History of Ukraine at the Ukrainian Academy of Sciences were very helpful, spending a great deal of time assisting me in assembling and inter-preting the data I had collected. I am also grateful to the Kiev Mohyla Acad-emy for allowing me access to their libraries and to the Abdulakh family for its hospitality.

For this second trip to Ukraine, I am especially grateful to my wife Laura who did not belabor the fact that I had promised to help her clean out the garage that month. In many ways much more significant than that, her pa-tience and encouragement have made this book possible. Our children, Jacey, Zachary, and Lily, have been a much-appreciated distraction from the seri-ousness of academic life. I regret that numerous frog-catching expeditions were postponed to allow the completion of this project.

Finally, I owe a profound debt to my parents, to whom I dedicate this book. I will not embarrass them by enumerating the reasons, but they have put up with a lot and deserve a great deal of credit.

The flaws that remain are mine alone.

Part I

Introduction and Conceptual Framework

1

Introduction

Ukraine's Dilemma

> Future historians, looking back at the former Soviet Union
> in the late twentieth century, may well conclude that the
> fate of Ukraine dominated the quest for stability in the re-
> gion. They may even speak of the "Ukrainian question" as
> the organizing problem of the period. By this they could
> mean one of two things: either Ukraine succeeded in estab-
> lishing its independence and helped to reorganize Eurasia
> on the basis of viable nation-states, not empire; or Ukraine
> will have become the sick young man of Europe, absorbing
> the attention and efforts of Russia and the other powers to
> the detriment of reform and regional stability.
> —Sherman W. Garnett, "The Ukranian Question
> and the Future of Russia"

The expansion of NATO to the borders of Ukraine will increase the importance to the west of an independent and stable Ukraine. At the same
time, it will likely increase Russia's desire to reassert its dominance over the
former Soviet states. Ukraine is therefore becoming even more important
than Garnett estimates, for its stability will likely influence not just East Central Europe, but the entire post–Cold War order between the West and Russia. If a newly expanded NATO is not to find itself face to face across the
Polish-Ukrainian and Hungarian-Ukrainian borders with a Russia reasserting
its great power status, Ukraine will have to remain sufficiently independent of
Russia to resist the stationing of Russia's troops on it soil. Ukraine clearly has
the political desire to remain independent of Russia. It is unclear, however, if
Ukraine has the economic wherewithal to back up its political goals. Economic statecraft—the manipulation of trade for the purposes of state—will
play a crucial role in this relationship.

Eight years after gaining its independence from the Soviet Union,
Ukraine's independence remains on shaky economic footing. While complete

reabsorption into Russia seems unlikely, a renewed subordination is not only possible, but is indeed advocated by many Russian leaders and even some Ukrainians. In early 1996, the Russian Council on Foreign and Defense Policy proposed to rein-tegrate much of the former Soviet Union using Russia's inherent economic dominance,[1] and the secretary of the Ukrainian National Security Council called for "renewed union" in the Commonwealth of Independent States (CIS).[2] The centrifugal forces unleashed in 1991 have weakened, and gravity seems to be bringing Russia's former satellites closer and closer to the "center."

Ukraine and Ukrainians are caught between two forces, one driving them from Russia and another pulling them closer, yet they are not simply at the mercy of these forces; Ukraine's choices will be decisive in determining relations between the two states. Ukraine is driven away from Russia by the nationalist desire to achieve full sovereignty and genuine independence, and by memories of mistreatment under Russian/Soviet rule. Simultaneously, however, Ukraine is pulled toward Russia by economic factors. Events have discredited the belief that Ukraine's economy would thrive when separated from Russia's, and many believe that the only hope for Ukraine to reform its economy and prosper lies in closer ties with Russia. Therein lies Ukraine's dilemma, for many fear that to pursue prosperity through closer ties with Russia would jeopardize Ukraine's independence. Unless Ukraine is able to resolve the tensions inherent in its interdependence with Russia, it will be unable to play the stabilizing role that is increasingly being foisted on it by NATO's eastward expansion and Russia's determination to resist.

This dilemma between closer economic ties and complete political independence is the fundamental question in the international politics of the former Soviet Union, and nowhere is it more important than between Russia and Ukraine, the two most powerful successors to the Soviet Union. The future of Russian-Ukrainian relations will depend largely on how Ukraine views the dilemma between maintaining its political autonomy and gaining the economic benefits of integration with Russia. That is the fundamental question addressed in this book: *How is Ukraine pursuing an economically beneficial relationship with a Russia that is also perceived to be the primary threat to Ukraine's independence?*

After a period in 1991 and early 1992 when Ukraine hurriedly broke ties with Russia and scorned the new CIS, and when Russia seemed content to let its former possessions go their own way, both trends have dramatically changed. The profound problems that have accompanied Ukrainian independence have fueled debate over the ideal extent of separation from Russia. At the same time, Russia has reasserted itself in the region, and seeks at least the role of first among equals in a strong CIS and perhaps a regathering of the territory of the former Soviet Union. Ukrainian-Russian relations are still highly malleable, and will remain that way for some time. The early post–Soviet years will likely be as formative for the Russian-Ukrainian relationship as the immediate post–World War II years were for U.S.-Soviet relations. By examining the development of the relationship to this point, we can see the nature of the difficult predicament that is emerging.

The relationship between trade and power is one of the oldest issues in both the study and the practice of international politics, but the horns of this dilemma are particularly sharp for the non-Russian successors to the Soviet Union. Economically, Ukraine is in a tailspin, with GDP undergoing massive decline, and social unrest increasing as a result. While many experts expected Ukraine to be the most prosperous of the former Soviet states, it has instead become synonymous with economic catastrophe. From independence through December 1993, Ukrainian living standards dropped 80 percent.[3] It is difficult to quantify how much of this tailspin is due to the breakup of the Soviet Union (or how much would be restored by renewing integration with Russia), but there is no doubt that the collapsed Soviet Union left behind not only a devastated Ukrainian economy, but one largely dependent on Russia.

The power side of the dilemma is perhaps even more acute. While most treatments of interdependence, especially those concerned with the advanced Western economies, treat the major economic threat to "security" as the threat to domestic economic security (i.e., prosperity), the threat to Ukraine is much greater. For Ukraine in its dealings with Russia, the basic independence of the state is threatened on several fronts. First, Ukraine's territorial integrity has been threatened by secessionist movements in Eastern Ukraine and Crimea, which are directly linked to the question of economic relations with Russia. "A rise in living standards would automatically lead to a decline in separatist sentiments among the Russian-speaking population of the Donets Basin and Luhansk and would eliminate any social basis for propaganda among Ukraine's Russians in favor of reconstituting the empire."[4] Russia's ability to injure Ukraine's economy creates a serious threat to Ukrainian stability. Second, pressure to join the CIS threatens reduced sovereignty, which Ukraine has come to view as primary goal. Finally, bilateral cooperation, if it follows the form of deals worked out between Russia and other successor states, threatens Ukraine's right to administer its own economy.

Ukraine thus faces an old problem (security vs. prosperity) in very new circumstances (the remains of the Soviet economic structure). The trend in world trade in recent decades has been toward economic integration, especially on the regional level. The doctrine and policy of free trade have replaced older views, such as mercantilism and economic nationalism, which focused on the effects international trade has on national power. For Ukraine, both the older realist and newer liberal doctrines are relevant, because it faces the problems of economic interdependence as well as the threat of economic coercion. Ukraine has struggled, therefore, to combine elements of a nationalist economic strategy, which focuses on security, with elements of a free-trade strategy focusing on economic efficiency. While the potential benefits of economic integration in the former Soviet Union are easy to see, so are the political costs in terms of vulnerability to external pressure.

The Security Situation

All of the non-Russian successor states fear the possibility that Russia will seek to rebuild its empire. One can debate Russian intentions (though there is increasing consensus, both within and outside Russia), but the fear that other states feel is real and is a powerful force in the politics of the region. The perception that Russia seeks to reassert its dominance in the region has increased since 1993, when the momentum of democratization seemed to wane in the face of renewed conservative vigor. As the dust from the August 1991 coup settled, the Yeltsin government made common cause with Ukraine in finishing off Mikhail Gorbachev and the Soviet Union. At that time Yeltsin and Foreign Minister Andrei Kozyrev pursued a Western-oriented foreign policy to supplement domestic political and economic reform. As conservative opinion reasserted itself in Russia in 1993, however, a new view became dominant: Russia must control the former Soviet Union politically, even if it does not actually retake the territory. The isolation and then replacement of foreign minister Kozyrev symbolized the changed line. Claims concerning Crimea, intervention in Georgia and Moldova, and the war in Chechnya have reinforced the notion that Russia is serious in its intention to renew its regional dominance.

The most obvious fear, but the least likely eventuality, is Russian invasion. While Russia might be able to conquer former Soviet territory, it is unlikely to do so, because the costs would be enormous and the benefits uncertain. Military action would mean a renewal of the Cold War that Russia could not sustain economically. More pragmatically, the performance of Russian troops in Chechnya creates doubts about both the capability and the will of the Russian military. The fact that Russian military invasion is not the primary threat to Ukraine's security was acknowledged by Ukrainian leaders when they decided to surrender the country's nuclear arsenal. Not only is Russian invasion unlikely, but Ukraine cannot hope to deter Russia by engaging in an arms race, which Ukraine cannot win.

The less obvious, but more genuine, danger to Ukraine is of Russia using means other than overt invasion to regain control. Among such means are fomenting rebellions within neighboring states until Russian troops are required to put them down,[5] or using the threat of economic chaos and ensuing social unrest to induce the former republics to play according to Russia's rules. Russia's economic size, and the dependencies built up during the Soviet era, mean that Russia can cause immense damage to its neighbors' economies at relatively little cost to itself. This is what happened to Ukraine, during the "energy war" of 1993–1994.)

It is this last possibility, the use of Russian economic power, that concerns the other states as they contemplate the economic problems caused by disintegration and the possibility of reintegration. Economically Russia has the means to employ a great deal of pressure.[6] Historically it has viewed the former Soviet states as Russian territory. And currently its leaders, not significantly less than their opposition, voice the desire to reassert Russia's dominant role in the region. There is now wide consensus among Russian political elites that reintegration of at least some of the former Soviet Union—on Russia's terms—should be pursued.[7] The notion of a Russian "Monroe Doctrine," first advanced in 1992 by Evgenii Ambartsumov, chair of the Supreme Soviet's committee on Foreign Affairs and Foreign Economic Relations, has gained adherents over time.[8] This desire for integration, and the potential use of economic means to accomplish that goal, was stated most clearly in May 1996, when *Nezavisimaya Gazeta* published a report by Russia's Council on Defense and Foreign Policy (the Russian equivalent of the Council on Foreign Relations), advocating reintegration of the former Soviet Union and laying out a strategy for accomplishing it.[9] This combination of factors creates a unity of economic and security concerns for Ukraine—the primary threat to the country's independence stems from its economic dependence on Russia.

The Trade Situation

Economics constitutes a potentially powerful lever of influence in the region because of a combination of deep interdependence and high political sensitivity due to increased economic hardship. At the time of the breakup of the Soviet Union, the economies of the republics were more deeply integrated than those of the countries of the European Community.[10] Breaking such a single economy into 15 separate economies, and doing it overnight with no planning, has led to immense dislocation in each of the successor economies.[11] There are numerous benefits provided by economic integration, and the successor states have given up those benefits for political independence.[12] Some of the more important economic benefits of integration (and corresponding problems of disintegration) are free trade, common currency, and common fiscal and economic policies.

Free trade, according to the theory of comparative advantage, maximizes overall efficiency of an economy by ensuring that each component of the economy produces that at which it is comparatively most efficient. Trade in

Free Trade

the Soviet Union was not free, and therefore was not determined by comparative advantage, but the successors could hope to gain such efficiency by implementation of free trade agreements. Moreover, the concentrated nature of
the Soviet economy means that an increase in trade barriers will be especially
disruptive.

A common currency makes it possible for producers in different countries
to trade without the need to exchange currencies. For countries with convert-
ible currencies, trade is hindered by the uncertainty over the future of exchange rates. For this reason, establishment of a common currency has been
a major goal of the European Union (EU). For countries with nonconvertible
currencies, and no centralized clearing system, trade is limited to the amount
of available hard currency (which usually is very little) or must be conducted
on barter terms. Monetary disintegration has been one of the major economic
setbacks of the collapse of the Soviet Union, and one for which a cure does not
appear imminent.

Common fiscal policies reduce the potential for one state's fiscal policy to
have adverse effects on the rest. Common economic laws ensure that products
made for one market can be sold in another, and they help eliminate the nontariff barriers to trade that are increasingly problematic in world trade. One of
the major goals of the Maastricht treaty in the European Union and of NAFTA
was to create common laws to reduce nontariff barriers to trade. Similarly, the
Group of Seven states have sought to coordinate macroeconomic policies to
promote stability and avoid mutually canceling policies. To facilitate the adoption of common laws, the states of the EU have delegated more and more law-
making power to central EU institutions, an example that the former Soviet
republics, having just escaped central control, are loath to emulate.

These three issues are the main focus of all debates on economic integration. For the successor states, however, the problem of splitting the Soviet
economy is compounded by the legacy of the command economy. In the Soviet Union, the economies of the individual republics were completely sub-
jugated to the needs of the entire union, as determined by central planners in
Moscow. This led to four effects that make the breakup of the Soviet economy
particularly disruptive, completely apart from the fact that Soviet rule left all
these economies in shambles.

First, industry in the Soviet Union was highly concentrated, such that for
many products, there was a single manufacturer for the entire Soviet Union.
Besides creating problems for domestic efforts to create free markets, this concentration exacerbates the effects of disruptions of trade. Second, while the
command economy was aimed at some type of overall efficiency, it was not
aimed at efficiency as determined by comparative advantage. Now the successors must cope not only with new barriers to trade, but with creating an entirely new composition of trade, based on market forces and comparative

advantage, rather than on central planning. Third, the command system created some extraordinary dependencies within the system that have enormous effects when turned into international dependencies. The best example is that of oil. Not only were most republics dependent on Russian oil, but they received the oil at an artificially low price due to subsidies, and their industries were built on the assumption of cheap oil. With the collapse of the Soviet Union, states such as Ukraine not only have to figure out where to get their oil, but they have to readjust their consumption patterns to deal with the new reality of paying world market prices in hard currency. Fourth, the system placed Moscow at the hub of the economy, with all other parts of the economy connected to each other largely through Russia. This provided control for the central organs of the Soviet Union, and now it provides leverage for Russia.[13]

Alternatives to Interdependence with Russia

Ukraine's dilemmas are acute in large part because it has found it difficult to orient its trade away from Russia and to find external security partners. In the short term, Ukraine has not been able to redirect trade away from Russia, and its ability to do so in the long term will affect its ability to maintain its independence. Similarly, Ukraine's inability to gain outside support against Russia has constrained its options, but its increasing importance in the eyes of the United States has improved Ukraine's position considerably.

One option to is to integrate or align with partners less threatening than Russia. Ukraine (as well as the Baltics) have looked toward Western Europe, but neither the EU nor NATO appears to be set to bring in post-Soviet states, and even trade with the EU is difficult due to the EU's external trade barriers.[14] The Baltics states have been much more welcome in Western Europe due to historical ties, geographic proximity, rapid reform, and small economies, which make their exports little threat in the EU. Nor have Ukraine's postcommunist neighbors in Central Europe been eager to join with Ukraine in an alliance against Russia or even a trading bloc. Both economically and politically, they are casting their future with the EU and NATO, where their prospects are good. All four of Ukraine's western neighbors (Poland, Slovakia, Hungary, and Romania) have been leading candidates for early NATO admission. Although only Poland and Hungary seem likely to be accepted in the first round of expansion, Romania and Slovakia have high hopes for the next round, far ahead of Ukraine. The central European states have shunned security cooperation with Ukraine out of fear both of antagonizing Russia and complicating NATO accession.[15] Ukraine has had little success in its efforts to promote "Baltic to Black Sea" cooperation among the states to the west of Russia. A final option is to create a regional bloc within the former Soviet Union excluding Russia.

There are signs of emerging cooperation between Ukraine, Georgia, and Azerbaijan,[16] but it is difficult to build economic cooperation excluding Russia, because Russia is the hub connecting the other economies. They have a lot less to offer each other than Russia has to offer all of them.[17] Ukraine has met with success in one area, improving political relations with the United States.

The United States has made preservation of Ukraine's independence an important foreign policy goal, thus providing some ease of mind for Ukrainian leaders. Economically, however, the same problems remain: U.S. and European markets remain protected against Ukraine's most competetive exports. To the extent that U.S. political concern leads to substantial Ukrainian links with western economies, Ukraine's dilemmas will become less acute. There is little reason, however, to expect this to happen in the short term. The discussion that follows, therefore, views Ukraine's policy problems in the context of continuing high economic interdependence with Russia.

Four Dilemmas

What happens between Russia and Ukraine will be determined as much by what Russia and other states do as by what Ukraine does. Studying Ukraine's reaction to Russian pressure is vital, however, because it is Ukraine that faces the difficult choices. There is much less uncertainty involved in Russian policy, and much less to be learned, because Russia does not face the same dilemma that Ukraine does. Russia, as the most powerful state in the region, and the largest economy, does not have to fear that it will be dominated by any of its partners. It can agree to cooperate knowing that while certain aspects of its economy are at stake, its independence is not. For this reason Russia has been able to focus solely on the economic costs and benefits of integration while not being threatened by the power effects. For Russia, the choices are considerably less complicated.

For Ukraine, however, cooperation creates serious threats as well as potential benefits, and it must weigh these two in arriving at a "Russia policy." In doing so, Ukraine must confront four dilemmas that are inherent in problems of interdependence, both in policy and practice. Ukraine will not be able to resolve any of the four dilemmas; rather it must make a series of trade-offs. The choices that it makes will reflect Ukraine's political priorities as well as the constraints imposed by the external situation and Ukraine's domestic politics. The wisdom with which Ukraine makes these choices, and the success with which it implements the resulting policies, will determine whether Ukraine will succeed in becoming a prosperous and genuinely independent state, or whether the state will be ruined economically or fall back into Russia's grasp, as it has after several previous attempts at independence.

First, Ukraine must decide whether it will attempt to resist Russian power, that is to "balance," or to come to an accommodation, to "bandwagon."[18] Many theorists of international politics argue that the economic leadership of a hegemon is beneficial to hegemon and small state alike because it enables the resolution of collective action problems, such as tariff wars, which otherwise decrease economic efficiency for all.[19] Ukraine must decide whether the traditional rule of opposing superior power or the newer view of the benevolence of economic hegemony is more applicable to its situation. It appears that Ukraine, while unwilling to submit to Russian hegemony, is unable to effectively oppose Russian power. If so, Ukraine must find some other policy option.

Second, Ukraine must answer for itself a fundamental question in debates about trade and interdependence: to what extent does achievement of economic efficiency endanger political autonomy. Many expected that, because the Soviet Union exploited Ukraine, severing economic ties would make Ukraine both more independent and more prosperous. This has turned out to be untrue. Ukraine must now decide what degree of vulnerability it is willing to endure for a given increase in economic efficiency. Even the leading theorist of free trade, Adam Smith, cautioned that "defense is of much more importance than opulence,"[20] but Ukraine found the economic disruption that resulted from a nationalist economic strategy intolerable. Domestic resentment over the effects of the breakup posed as much threat to the state as Russian aggression. Ukraine has struggled to find a strategy that will ensure Ukraine's domestic satisfaction at a minimum level of dependence on Russia.

Third, Ukraine faces a somewhat paradoxical threat between sovereignty and autonomy, where autonomy is the state's ability to get what it wants, and sovereignty is simply the ability to make its own decisions (even if the state cannot get what it wants). Because it focuses so much on its sovereignty, Ukraine has been unwilling to delegate authority to any CIS body. Doing so, while maintaining *de jure* sovereignty, may also mean that Ukraine must face Russia alone, rather than in concert with ten other states to help counter Russia's power. Moreover, participation in the CIS would make Ukraine's trade relations with Russia subject to rules, rather than only to bargaining power, an arena in which Ukraine has a decided disadvantage.

Fourth, Ukraine must resolve for itself a debate about international institutions: Do international institutions serve to constrain the most powerful states by "tying them down," as many liberal international relations theorists (and supporters of the EU) have argued, or are international institutions the instruments through which powerful states control the weak, as realist and

Marxist theories argue? Will the CIS constrain Russian power by tying it down with institutional procedures and dilute it by giving it only one vote out of twelve, or will it empower Russia by taking sovereignty from other states and giving it to an institution that Russia will dominate by sheer virtue of its size?

Theoretical Questions

Ukraine's dilemmas in its relations with Russia raise a of series of theoretical questions for students of international politics. Theoretically, this book raises more question than it answers, and the primary theoretical goal is to examine the relationship between existing theories of international political economy and this very new situation. Such an examination is fruitful both for understanding the case and for improving the theories. There is no attempt formally to "test" a particular hypothesis. Rather the goal is to develop an initial conceptual understanding of the problem that will provide a basis both for analysis of the practical issues and for future theorizing on the problem.

Because the situation that Ukraine faces is not different in its essence than the problems of other economically weak states in an interdependent world economy, the theories that have been used to explain international cooperation elsewhere should apply here as well. Concepts from the general literature on international political economy are very useful in understanding this particular case, but as will be explored in more detail in the conclusion, the Ukrainian-Russian relationship presents several anomalies from the perspective of international relations theory. These anomalies provide an impetus for refinement of the theories and some indication of how that might be done.

In an era that many are seeing as the triumph of liberalism, what happens among the former Soviet states is an important test case. Conditions here are somewhat challenging to liberal theory, so if Ukraine and Russia are able to implement the liberal vision, the model's relevance beyond the advanced industrial states will be shown. If, however, Russian-Ukrainian relations turn out to be more defined by the realist politics of the past, then we must wonder about the applicability of the liberal model beyond the advanced industrial states.

This case is potentially an important one for liberal theory more broadly. Some contend that the success of the European Community was due above all to the fact that the members were politically unified by the Soviet threat and protected by U.S. security commitments to Europe. Clearly, security is a major concern in Russian-Ukrainian relations. If they manage deep cooperation, without Russia dominating Ukraine, there will be an important case to show that economic cooperation does not depend on the prior alleviation of security concerns.

More broadly, the predominance of security concerns and power politics indicates that a realist framework is appropriate, and Albert Hirschman's realist treatment of German economic policy in the interwar years provides a conceptual template for much of the analysis. The conflictual nature of Russian-Ukrainian relations despite the immense economic incentive to cooperate forces us to ask whether rather than spreading to the entire world after the Cold War, the liberal vision will remain contained in Western Europe. But here too there are significant problems: Ukraine has found that, in its relations with Russia, the military realm is much less important to its security than is the economic realm. This contradicts a tenet of many (but not all) realist theories that "clubs are trumps."

Finally, this case raises a fundamental question about theories of international institutions. One prominent line of argument finds that international institutions tend to bind their most powerful actors with rules, and thus contribute to the autonomy of small states. A second approach finds that the powerful use such institutions to extend their control over the weak. In the case of the EU, it appears that the former argument is true, but Ukraine is convinced that the CIS would lead to Russian dominance. It seems likely that both arguments are correct, and the question then is in what conditions do international institutions constrain potential hegemons and in what conditions do they empower them? Answering this contingent question would provide a more fruitful line of research than the current sterile debate over whether institutions "matter," and the implications for policy would be much more relevant.

The Ukraine–Russia relationship has important implications for the other former Soviet states, for Central Europe, and for the West. For Ukraine, the stakes in its economic relations with Russia are somewhat clear: What will be the nature of its relationship with Russia, and the degree of its independence? A number of outcomes are possible, but there is little doubt, on the one hand, that if Russia applies significant pressure, and Ukraine handles it badly, Ukraine could again lose much of its independence. On the other hand, Ukraine has the potential to be not only an independent state in the region, but an important actor in world politics.

For Russia, the stakes may be equally high, but in a way that is less obvious. Russia's relations with Ukraine will, in the opinion of many, determine whether Russia will be a nation-state or an empire. At stake is not simply Russia's international position, but its domestic political system. Vladimir Lukin, formerly ambassador to the United States and later chair of the Foreign Relations Committee in the Russian Duma, states: "The starting point for any discussion about the interests of Russia has to be a discussion about Russia itself. What kind of country are we talking about—territorially, politically, ideologically?"[21] Similarly, Sergei Stankevich asserts: "The practice of our foreign policy . . . will help Russia become Russia."[22] If so, Russian relations with Ukraine will be crucial, as Zbigniew Brzezinski has pointed out: "It cannot be stressed strongly enough that without Ukraine, Russia ceases to be an empire, but with Ukraine suborned and then subordinated, Russia automatically becomes an empire."[23] Ukraine's pivotal role in defining the identity of the surrounding states was shown following the coup when both Mikhail Gorbachev and Boris Yeltsin asserted that a continued union without Ukraine was unthinkable. Ukraine is vital to rebuilding a Russian sphere of influence not only in historical and conceptual terms, but geopolitically as well, because as long as it exists there will be a significant check on Russian power in the region. Ukraine's status is important to Russia domestically because, many believe, Russia cannot be both an empire and a democracy. The measures that would be required for reestablishment of dominance over Ukraine, and the domestic groups privileged by it (i.e., the military and nationalists) would likely mean an end to democracy within Russia. For this reason, many Russian democrats and reformers have opposed attempts to reintegrate Ukraine. Even if it could be done, they argue, the results would be disastrous for development of a modern Russian state. From this perspective, Ukraine may be saving not only itself as it resists Russian pressure, but Russian democracy as well.

Ukraine's policy toward Russia may prove a bellwether for other republics in their relations with Russia for two reasons. First, Ukraine was viewed at the time of independence as having an excellent chance of succeeding independently, due to its economic strength, its proximity to the West, and its intense determination to be independent. If Ukraine cannot maintain its independence, or can do so only through economic ruin, other republics my see the challenge as insurmountable, and submit to Russian hegemony. Second, because of its size and status, if Ukraine joins Russia in some type of economic union, the pressure on other republics to do so will increase immensely. Smaller states that have resisted Russian hegemony, such as Moldova, Georgia, and Azerbaijan, have some hope of succeeding as long there is significant opposition to Russian dominance. Ukraine's independent course not only puts a check on the momentum of Russian imperial sentiment, but also prevents the total isolation of smaller states that would also remain outside Russia's orbit.

For other Central European states, especially those states that border Ukraine (Poland, Slovakia, Hungary, Moldova, and Romania) the stakes are equally high. If recent deals negotiated with other republics, notably Belarus, are indicative, a significant reassertion of Russian influence in Ukraine would entail the right to place Russian troops on Ukraine's western borders.[24] Such an occurrence would critically change the security outlook for the bordering states.[25] Faced with Russian troops on their borders, and NATO's unwillingness to commit to their protection, these states would likely feel it necessary to undertake massive military expansion. Such military expansion would have significant economic costs, which could derail economic and in turn political reform in the region. Alternatively they too could submit to renewed Russian hegemony.

As NATO expands to include Poland, the Czech Republic, and Hungary, the fate of Ukraine becomes more important for western security. Both Hungary and Poland share borders with Ukraine, and so will NATO when it includes those two states. If Ukraine falls back into the Russian sphere, we could again find NATO troops facing Russian forces across a lengthy frontier. As NATO moves to Ukraine's borders, only continued Ukrainian independence stands in the way of renewed confrontation. NATO expansion, however, seems likely to increase Russian pressure on its western neighbors. NATO expansion, therefore, will likely make Ukraine more important and more pressured at the same time. The west has so far succeeded in preventing its disagreements with Russia from deteriorating into a second cold war, but this balancing act would be considerably more difficult if important western interests such as Poland and Hungary were again under Russian pressure. Moreover, for those who consider Ukraine to be an essential buffer zone between Russia and Germany, the movement of Ukraine into the Russian orbit would create greater fear in Germany, potentially leading to a German decision to attain nuclear weapons and a new Russo-German rivalry.[26] Whether one envisions Ukraine as a barrier, bridge, or buffer zone between Russia and the West, its existence as a state independent of Russia is perhaps "the most significant geostrategic development in Europe" since World War II.[27]

Findings

The most significant finding of the book is that because Ukraine has above all sought to preserve its *de jure* sovereignty, it remains, somewhat paradoxically, in a situation where its genuine autonomy remains vulnerable to Russian economic pressure. Ukraine originally sought to increase its autonomy from Russia by implementing a nationalist economic strategy in early 1992, deliberately breaking trade ties. The consequences for Ukraine's economy were catastrophic. As domestic unrest over the economic situation, and pressure to reestablish economic ties with Russia increased, Ukraine moved to restore much of the lost trade. While this policy shifted, however, Ukraine stuck steadfastly to its refusal to compromise its sovereignty in any way. The result is that Ukraine once again has a large amount of trade with Russia, and the trade is carried on bilaterally and without any institutionalized rules. Ukraine therefore remains highly vulnerable to Russian economic pressure, and there is nothing to prevent a repetition of the "energy war" of 1993–1994, when Russian cuts in energy deliveries crippled Ukraine's economy. In the short term, Ukraine has stabilized the situation, in part by healing some of the domestic divisions that prevented it from developing a coherent economic strategy. This stability may continue, but Ukraine remains vulnerable.

Three other findings are worthy of emphasis here. First, Ukraine has come to recognize that the struggle to remain independent will be played out in the economic rather than the political realm. It is telling that Ukraine was willing to surrender its nuclear weapons, the so-called absolute weapon, but unwilling to sell its gas pipelines to Russia despite immense pressure. Nuclear weapons were seen as an unusable asset in an arena where actual conflict was unlikely. The gas pipelines are a crucial asset in an arena where the two countries were fighting brutally for nearly two years.

Second, the amount of hardship that could be introduced into the Ukrainian economy by Russia's reduction of energy supplies was staggering, but was matched by the resilience and determination of the Ukrainian people. While some Ukrainians advocated that Ukraine make the necessary concessions to restore energy supplies, more saw Russian policy as an indicator of Russian hostility and became even more determined to resist. During the winter of 1993–1994, Ukraine nearly came to a standstill, but in the end Russia tired of inflicting damage before Ukraine tired of receiving it. Perhaps because Ukraine has been the ground for catastrophe so frequently this century, it was difficult for Russia to present something that Ukraine could not endure.

Third, while Ukraine's economic vulnerability is due largely to factors outside Ukraine, its inability to deal with it effectively has largely been the result of Ukraine's internal divisions. Ukraine's populace is divided by region, by support for reform, and by degree of nationalism. These divisions have strictly constrained the policy options open to Ukrainian leaders. It is extremely difficult to find an economic policy satisfactory both to eastern Ukrainians who are particularly tied to Russia economically, and western Ukrainian nationalists, who seek to break ties with Russia and turn instead westward. Leaders have almost no freedom of action. Moreover, the state itself is badly divided institutionally. Power at the top of the Ukrainian state has been so spread out that no one is able successfully to advance and implement an economic strategy. The result has been that even within the narrow constraints imposed by external and societal factors, the state has often been incapable of making policy. Revisions of institutional arrangements in 1995 partially alleviated this problem, and the long-overdue adoption in June 1996 of a new constitution may do so further. The success in practice of the new consititution will be as important to Ukraine's foreign policy as to its domestic policy.

More broadly, this case shows above all that realpolitik is alive and well in the former Soviet Union. Because Ukraine's problem concerns how to trade off autonomy and prosperity in an interdependent international political economy, liberal theory seems a natural fit, and indeed liberal theory is quite useful in explaining the pressures that Ukraine faces economically. However, Ukraine's fixation on its sovereignty, which is a driving force in its policies, has no place in liberal international theory, which either views sovereignty as irrelevant or takes it for granted. The essential role played by security fears in this story tends to confirm the argument that security must be established before cooperation on the liberal model can take over. Ukrainian-Russian economic relations are a matter of survival, not just prosperity, for Ukraine. And the exertion of power has been the most important way of resolving disputes in the relationship. In this respect, the politics of the former Soviet Union remain fundamentally different from those of the advanced industrial states.

Overview of the Book

This introduction has sketched the main themes of the dilemma faced by Ukraine in dealing with Russia. The following two chapters examine these themes more closely. Chapter 2 focuses on the Ukrainian-Russian relationship in general, beginning with a brief overview of history, which gives some idea of how Russians view Ukraine and why Ukraine tends to be nervous about agreements with Russia. It then covers in more detail the events surrounding Ukraine's independence in 1991, and relations between the two countries since that time. An assessment of Russia's intentions toward Ukraine and other former Soviet states shows that, even if Russia is not as aggressive as its spokesmen sometimes imply, Ukraine has legitimate reason to fear for its independence. A review of Ukrainian views toward ties with Russia shows that after a near unanimous vote for independence in 1991, Ukraine then became badly divided, with those favoring much closer ties gaining the upper hand in 1994, and some favoring complete reintegration. The chapter concludes with a discussion of some of the outstanding disputes in the relationship that have exacerbated the mutual distrust and fear that already existed.

Chapter 3 turns from the empirical to the theoretical, discussing different approaches to the problems Ukraine and Russia face. While Ukraine's economic problems are captured by interdependence theory, their political consequences require the use of realist concepts. Borrowing from Albert Hirschman's classic study of economic vulnerability and political power, a framework for understanding the international political economy of the former Soviet Union is developed. The sources and remedies of economic vulnerability are explored in detail. The key to this discussion is that a given level of interdependence does not lead to a fixed degree of vulnerability. The challenge for small states is to minimize the vulnerability for the level of interdependence that they see as necessary for prosperity. Ukraine's situation creates a series of trade-offs between three fundamental goals: autonomy, prosperity, and sovereignty. After examining the theoretical nature of these three trade-offs, the chapter closes by showing how they are linked to the issue studies that follow.

The second part of the book addresses the specifics of Russian-Ukrainian interaction to assess how Ukraine is making its choices and what the implications are. Four of the most important issues in the relationship are covered, as is the effect of Ukraine's domestic political situation on its economic strategy. These chapters constitute the empirical heart of the study.

Chapter 4 investigates what has been perhaps the most important concrete issue between the two states: energy supplies. Ukraine is heavily dependent on Russia for its oil and natural gas, and dependent on Russian subsidies to pay for it. Russia no longer has any reason to subsidize Ukraine, but has found Ukraine's dependence very useful, and has not hesitated to link energy supplies to other outstanding issues. The "energy war" of 1993–1994 justified the fears of Ukrainian nationalists who had argued that Russia would use economic ties to undermine Ukrainian independence, but it equally highlighted how devastated the Ukrainian economy would be if ties to Russia were completely cut. This chapter sets the stage for those that follow by showing just how high the stakes are for Ukraine.

Chapter 5 addresses the questions of currency and trade relations, which some see as the most crucial problems in the future of international trade in the region. Due to the nature of the Soviet economy, normal trade dependencies were exaggerated. Free trade between Russia and Ukraine ended with the collapse of the Soviet Union, and the use of common currency ended in 1992. In order to establish its independence, Ukraine adopted an economic plan in early 1992 that deliberately cut ties with Russia. Ukraine's economy, already in a tailspin, was further injured by the barriers to access to key supplies and markets. Because these effects were felt more heavily in eastern Ukraine, the trade problems have exacerbated Ukraine's regional tensions. The breakdown of trade and the difficulty of conducting trade with non-convertible currencies have been ongoing problems, and no solution appears imminent. These problems have most directly prompted pressure in Ukraine for closer ties with Russia. By 1994, Ukraine underwent a significant shift politically, and reversed its policy of economic isolation. As it again trades heavily with Russia, the issue of multilateral cooperation has become more important, and it is the focus of the following chapter.

Chapter 6 broadens the perspective to the question of the future and nature of the Commonwealth of Independent States. The CIS is a fundamental problem, because it involves surrendering the power to make decisions and the re-creation of a "center" reminiscent to some of the Soviet Union. The CIS seemed dead immediately after its birth, but since 1993 has revived, such that

Ukraine is now one of the few former Soviet states withholding unconditional membership. Ukraine's most consistently held value in its foreign economic policy has been the preservation of its sovereignty, and regulating trade by means of the CIS has been out of the question. When trade was reduced to a low level, this was not a significant problem, but as trade ties have again increased, so has the need for some type of mechanism to coordinate these ties. Ukraine's refusal to coordinate trade policies multilaterally not only limits the amount of trade that can take place, but also leaves trade measures to be determined through bargaining power, where Ukraine is weak. The desire to trade with Russia and the refusal to create institutions to govern that trade constitute a contradiction that Ukraine has yet to resolve.

Chapter 7 most explicitly links economic and security issues in its discussion of the role of economic pressure in the Ukrainian decision to surrender its nuclear weapons. The case provides a paradox in comparison to the other issues discussed: If Ukraine is frightened for its security, the last thing it should want to do is give away the potential security guarantee of nuclear weapons. Yet it did so while remaining recalcitrant on seemingly less crucial issues such as the economic union. After a phase in which Ukraine believed it had to counter Russian military power, Ukrainian leaders came to the conclusion that this was simply not possible. There was no way Ukraine could succeed in a nuclear arms race with Russia. Moreover, it became clear that the threat to Ukraine came primarily in the economic realm, a threat which, due to Western concern, was exacerbated by nuclear weapons. Ukraine's policy on nuclear weapons is significant in that it shows Ukraine's slow recognition that the economic threats to its security were at least as important as the military threats. In turn, Ukrainian leaders have recognized the importance of domestic reform for the country's security.

Chapter 8 discusses the role of Ukrainian domestic politics in Ukrainian policy toward Russia. Divisions in Ukrainian society have left leaders little room for maneuver, and divisions in Ukraine's state structure have made formulation and implementation of a coherent policy nearly impossible. The constraints on Ukrainian policy due to Ukrainian domestic politics are nearly as important as those due to Russian pressure, and between these two sets of constraints, Ukrainian policy has been immobile for much of the period in question. The long-overdue adoption of a post-Soviet constitution in 1996 promises to sort out Ukraine's institutional situation, but it remains unclear whether the Ukrainian state is agile enough to maneuver through the difficulties inherent in its international situation.

Finally, Chapter 9 returns to the questions raised in the first chapter to draw some conclusions concerning how Ukraine has dealt with its dilemmas, why it has take certain approaches, and what the outlook is for the future of

Russian-Ukrainian relations. The book ends with a discussion of the role of traditional power politics in the modern era, where the view from the former Soviet Union is quite sobering.

On the one hand, that Ukraine has weathered the storms of the early independence years leads to the impression that the worst is behind and that independence is now secured. On the other hand, the conditions that created Ukraine's difficulties—economic vulnerability, Russia's desire for increased influence, and a divided society—remain. The dilemmas examined in this book are likely to be the defining issues in Ukrainian-Russian relations for some time to come. The priorities that have been established, the policies that have been adopted in pursuit of those priorities, and the results of those policies therefore offer important lessons for Ukraine and the other states of the region. The main aims of this study are to identify the forces at work and to show what are likely to be the crucial factors in Ukraine's ongoing struggle for independence. Whether Ukraine will survive as a fully independent state, or return to some sort of subjugation is not yet determined. In that sense one can at this stage make only general predictions about eventual outcomes, for despite the length of this study, it covers only the first act in what will likely be a much longer drama.

2

Ukraine and Russia
Past and Present

For Russia and Ukraine, both struggling to redefine their
statehood, nationhood, and interests, the experience of the
post-1945 world is often perceived as less relevant than
what happened in 1918, in 1654, or even as far back as the
tenth century.

—John Morrison, "Pereyaslav and After:
The Russian-Ukrainian Relationship"

The histories of Russia and Ukraine have been intertwined since the rise
of Kiev-Rus in the tenth century, and have left the two states a full agenda
of contentious issues. The historical legacy includes the frequent Russian at-
titude that Ukraine is not a genuinely separate nation, and a widespread
Ukrainian mistrust of Russian intentions, as well as deep economic and social
connections between the two states, which are making separation more difficult. With the collapse of the Soviet Union and Ukrainian independence in
1991, debates over the nature of the relationship took on a very practical significance. The first years of the post-Soviet era have been tumultuous within
both states, with economic collapse in Ukraine and near-civil war in Russia,
and between them, as the two states try to figure out what their goals are, to
what extent they are compatible, and how they might achieve them.

Embedded in the acrimony that characterizes Russian-Ukrainian relations is a paradox: Historically, linguistically, culturally—and in many "mixed
marriages"—the two peoples and states seem quite similar, if not indistin-
guishable. Yet that similarity, far from guaranteeing good relations, has led to
a battle over national identity. Precisely because the two states share so much,
there is much to dispute, and because many see little difference between the
two peoples, Ukrainian nationalists in particular need to assert the different-
ness and separateness of Ukraine and Russia. History and accompanying disputes over national identity lie beneath much of the conflict between Russia

21

and Ukraine, and some understanding of the history of the two states is necessary to understanding why Ukrainian independence is today so important for many Ukrainians and so irksome to many Russians.

Russian-Ukrainian Relations to 1917

Russia and Ukraine both trace their origins to the state of Kievan Rus that emerged on the banks of the Dnipro in the tenth century and adopted Christianity before falling to internal division and Mongol attacks in the fourteenth century.[1] There remain significant differences in interpreting the legacy of Kievan Rus.[2] The traditional Russian interpretation is that the state that began in Kiev was transferred, via Vladimir, to Moscow, such that modern Russia is the heir to Kievan Rus, and that Ukraine is part of Russia. Ukrainian nationalists, however, contend that the torch was passed via Volhynia and Galicia to modern Ukraine, and that modern Russia originated separately in Muscovy. The Soviet version, which argued that Russia, Belarus, and Ukraine all originated in Kievan Rus, fit well with the doctrine that the three peoples were really one, and justified the common rule of all three from Moscow.

> This controversy over the question of who are the legitimate heirs to the Kievan tradition—the Russians or the Ukrainians—which has continued to the present day, has had a profound impact on the development of the cultural perception, historical awareness, modern national conciousness, and the national mythology of the intelligentsias and even common people of the two sides involved.[3]

The tracing of modern Russia's roots to Kiev helps explain why Russian nationalists feel so strongly that Ukraine is an important part of Russia. Nikolai Travkin, founder of the Democratic Party of Russia, states:

> For Russia and Ukraine alike, Kiev is our common home, the source of our common language, common religion, and common culture. We share a common value system. Every Russian understands these fundamental facts. No matter how history proceeds—how presidents and parliaments behave—a Ukrainian will always be a Russian's closest friend. In the development of Russia's foreign policy, then, these cultural considerations must stand on an equal footing with economic principles.[4]

While Russia and Ukraine both trace their origins to Kievan Rus, significant differences emerged in later development. After the collapse of Kievan Rus and the retreat of the Mongols, Muscovy slowly emerged as the power center of Russia, and under the Tsars built one of the most powerful and autocratic states in the world. Meanwhile Ukraine found itself on the frontiers of more powerful actors—Lithuania, Poland, Russia, the Ottoman Empire, and the Austrian Empire—and was unable to establish its independence as others fought over its territory. While Russia's history became the history of a dominant state, Ukraine's became that of a dominated people without a state.

In the mid-seventeenth century the Ukrainian Cossacks, under the leadership of Bohdan Khmelnytsky, attempted to repel the Russians and Poles and create an independent state. In order to protect the new state from Poland, however, Khmelnytsky sought an alliance with the Russian Tsar in the Treaty of Pereiaslav (1654). The result was not the expulsion of the Poles from western Ukraine, but the subjugation of the nascent Ukrainian state to the Russian Tsar, who interpreted the treaty as putting Ukraine under his authority. A second attempt under Petro Doroshenko also failed, and a final attempt at Ukrainian Cossack independence failed when Peter the Great defeated the forces of the Cossack leader Ivan Mazepa and King Charles XII of Sweden at the battle of Poltava in 1709. Ukrainian self-rule was eliminated entirely under Catherine the Great later in the eighteenth century. Ukraine remained divided between Russia and Poland.

These distant events have left important marks on Ukrainian-Russian relations today. The exploits of the Cossacks have become an important part of Ukrainian national identity and a symbol for Ukrainian nationalists, providing a tradition of independent and democratic government to view as an important precedent.[5] More concretely, Ukraine remained split between Russia and Poland (and then the Austrian Empire) from that time until 1939, such that the two parts of the country developed under very different circumstances. In many ways, Ukraine itself has two histories, which are the basis for much of the regional political divisions that plague Ukraine today (see chapter 8).

Most important, perhaps, the Treaty of Pereiaslav has become a powerful symbol in Ukrainian attitudes toward treaties with Moscow today. While Russia regarded the Treaty as a voluntary decision by Ukraine to (re-)join Russia, Ukrainians then and since have argued that Russia cynically used a military alliance to conquer Ukraine, as Hrushevsky argues: "What [the Ukrainians] wanted was aid in their struggle for independence from Poland and freedom from the landlords, but Muscovy appeared to look upon Ukraine as a new territorial aquisition for herself, over which she gained complete control."[6] Whose interpretation is correct is probably impossible to say.[7] The more important point is that Ukrainians today view those events as reason to be very cautious about signing any sort of agreement with Russia.[8] At the same time, Russians view 1654 as the date of the "unification" of Russia with Ukraine, the importance of which was marked by Khrushchev in his transfer of the Crimea to Ukraine on the 300th anniversary of Pereiaslav in 1954.

Under Russian rule, eastern Ukraine was subject to the autocracy of the Tsar, which included the imposition of serfdom, abolished only in 1861, and the banning of writing in the Ukrainian language. Meanwhile, western Ukraine was occupied mostly by Poland and then the Austro-Hungarian Empire, and looked toward Warsaw and Vienna rather than Moscow. While not benevolent from the Ukrainian perspective, Polish and Austrian rule was considerably more liberal politically and less repressive of the Ukrainian nation. "While Russians were imposing serfdom on the Left Bank, Austrians were dismantling it in western Ukraine."[9] It is difficult to overestimate the impact today of the different developmental paths of the two parts of Ukraine. Economic, political, social, and cultural traditions were vastly different in the Russian and Austrian empires, and the result today is a Ukrainian population with a dual personality.

From Revolution to Gorbachev

As World War I ended, the Austrian and Russian Empires, which controlled the two halves of Ukraine, collapsed, and Ukrainians found it necessary to build a state of their own.[10] In 1917, Ukrainian national democrats formed the Ukrainian People's Republic, but found it necessary to sign a peace with Germany and Austria when the Bolsheviks invaded in early 1918.[11] After the Treaty of Brest-Litovsk, Germany installed a puppet regime under Pavlo Skoropadsky, but he proved exceedingly unpopular, and the national democrats returned to power in after Germany withdrew in December 1918. They were again unable to consolidate power in the chaos of war and collapsing empire. In the Austrian part of Ukraine, the Western Ukrainian Republic was declared in L'viv in October 1918, but was defeated by Polish troops the following month.[12] In 1919, six different armies operated on Ukrainian territory: Ukrainian, Polish, Bolshevik, White, Entente (French and Greek), and Anarchist.[13] After another attempt to build a Ukrainian state failed, this one led by Simon Petliura, the Bolsheviks took over in 1920. The ensuing war with Poland left Ukraine divided as before, with Poland retaining that part of western Ukraine which had previously been linked to it under the Austro-Hungarian Empire.[14]

The Bolsheviks promised Ukraine autonomy in order to gain support during the civil war, and when the war with Poland ended, there were two treaties, one between Poland and Soviet Russia and another between Poland the Ukrainian S.S.R.[15] Soon, however, Moscow began to reduce the authority of the Ukrainian government. The first step was an agreement under which Russia would represent Ukraine at the Genoa Conference in 1922. The second step was the Soviet Constitution adopted in December of 1922, which "took the form of a treaty among the several states," thus seemingly confirming their sovereignty.[16] In fact, the independence of the Ukrainian government was steadily eroded during the centralization and collectivization in the late 1920s, and then eliminated altogether. As with the Treaty of Pereiaslav, the Union Treaty of 1922 is viewed by many Ukrainians today as a reason to be leery of treaties with Russia even when Ukrainian sovereignty seems guaranteed.

Soviet rule in Eastern Ukraine had several effects on Ukrainian-Russian relations besides the well-known consequences of Soviet system: industrialization, inefficiency, and environmental ruin. First, under the Soviets a Ukrainian political elite, which had been suppressed by Russia much earlier, was reestablished. The 1920s was a period of Ukrainian cultural and political renaissance. After consolidating power, however, Stalin decided to crush both Ukrainian nationalism and peasant resistance to collectivization. In the early thirties, the Ukrainian communist leadership was purged to remove all those with nationalist tendencies, and policies focusing on Ukraine, such as Ukrainian-language education, were eliminated. Then, to finish off Ukrainian nationalism as well as resistance to collectivization, the Soviets created an artificial famine in the early 1930s, requisitioning all the grain from the villages, so that none was left to feed the peasants, leaving as many as six million Ukrainians dead,[17] a holocaust that has not been forgotten by Ukrainians today. The decimation of the Ukrainian population was followed by an influx of Russians into eastern Ukraine, which helps account for the heavy Russian population there today.

In 1939, Stalin agreed with Hitler to partition Poland once more, and in invading Eastern Poland/Western Ukraine on 28 September, Stalin reunited Ukraine for the first time in centuries. He promptly instituted a terror among the west Ukrainian intellectuals and nationalists, which to this day are the most vigorously anti-Russian. Stalin's brutal policy toward Ukraine was partially responsible for many Ukrainians greeting the German army as a liberator in the summer of 1940—Metropolitan Andrei Sheptyts'kyi of L'viv stated: "We greet the victorious German Army as a deliverer from the enemy."[18] While two million Ukrainians fought in the Red Army in World War II, another 220,000 fought with the Germans.[19] Following the defeat of Germany, western Ukrainian nationalists continued to fight a guerrilla war for independence, and were not completely supressed until the early 1950s.[20] A related result of World War II is that Stalin deported the Tatars from Crimea, because he felt they were too sympathetic to Germany's cause. This deportation and the subsequent influx of Russians made the Crimea the most heavily Russified region of Ukraine.

This contested history, characterized both by separateness and togetherness, has left a complex legacy for the current era. Two general issues emerge from the past. First, there is the unresolved ethnographic/national identity question: Are Ukrainians and Russians one people or two? For our purposes, the question is more important than the answer, because to question Ukrainian distinctiveness is to some extent to question the justification for a separate state[21].

Because Ukraine's distinctiveness is fundamentally questioned by many, the Ukrainian state and Ukrainian sovereignty become vehicles for asserting that distinctiveness, and some separateness of Ukraine's interests from Russia is necessary for that assertion. That Ukraine is a new state and has only begun to consolidate its statehood make these issues even more important. This fixation on sovereignty and seperateness plays a key role the choices Ukraine makes in dealing with its interdependence with Russia. Second, contemporary relations are complicated by the "lessons" learned from past interactions. Can Ukraine trust Russia? Some cite the long history of dominance as evidence that Russia simply cannot tolerate an independent Ukraine, and therefore constitutes a signficant threat. For them, the 1654 Treaty of Pereiaslav and the 1922 Union Treaty seem particularly relevant to future cooperation. For others, the history of joint interaction and cultural similarity promise continued friendship, which is only reinforced by economic ties. Ukraine's internal debate over relations with Russia mirrors debates over the historical legacy. Historical interaction does not determine future interaction, but it does color perceptions of contemporary problems. In particular, disputes over identity and "lessons" of history prompt many Ukrainians today to put a high priority on sovereignty.

The Path to Independence

By the early 1990s, the Soviet Empire was crumbling as the Russian Empire had before it, and again Ukraine somewhat unexpectedly found the opportunity and the necessity to create an independent state.[22] This time, they were more successful than previously, at least in the short term. The long-term independence of Ukraine is still uncertain.

When Mikhail Gorbachev came to power in 1985, it was clear that the Soviet system needed reform if it was not to fall ever further behind the West. By taking economic measures that created more chaos than reform, and political measures that allowed people to act on their dissatisfaction, Gorbachev doomed the Soviet Union. The fatal blow to the Soviet Union was the aborted coup attempt of August 1991, but Ukraine and other republics had already taken significant steps toward independence. The groundwork for Republic independence was laid beginning with Gorbachev's decrees on decentralization in July 1986 and July 1987, which aimed at increasing the authority and accountability of the republics.[23] This decentralization was part of Gorbachev's strategy of improving economic performance by taking decisions out of the hands of the the middle-level bureaucrats that dominated under the Brezhnev system. The policy of complete economic autonomy for the republics was introduced at the nineteenth Party Conference in 1988, though the intent was that the republics would pursue centrally set Unionwide goals.[24]

Gorbachev's *glasnost* permitted dissent, and in many of the Republics, led by the Baltics, the combination of freedom of speech and increased autonomy fueled organized national independence movements. Ukrainian nationalists openly organized in the form of Rukh, led by Vyacheslav Chornovil, in 1989. In March 1990 Rukh gained one-third of the seats in elections to the Verkhovna Rada.[25] When longtime Ukrainain leader and Communist loyalist Volodymyr Scherbytsky was dismissed, the Ukrainian Communist Party split into pro- and antiperestroika factions. The leader of the reformers, Leonid Kravchuk, allied himself with the nationalists in order to defeat his rival, Stanislav Hurenko. Kravchuk's cooptation of the nationalist agenda was essential in his subsequent success, but has been a mixed blessing for nationalists.

The devolution of authority from Moscow to the republics continued in 1990. The law "On the Fundamentals of Economic Union Between the USSR and the Union and Autonomous Republics," adopted in April 1990, specified the division of authority between Union and Republic institutions, and prohibited interrepublic trade discrimination.[26] It took effect at the beginning of 1991, but by then events in the republics had rendered it irrelevant. Following the Ukrainian declaration of sovereignty on 16 July 1990, which "included all the prerogatives one would expect of an independent state, but . . . also implied loose membership in a reorganized USSR,"[27] the demands of Ukrainian nationalists escalated from reform to independence.[28] Even at this stage, however, independence was not seen as imminent. Dmytro Pavlychko, head of the Taras Shevchenko Ukrainian Language Society and later a prominent nationalist spokesman on foreign affairs in the parliament, said in August 1990 that "an immediate seccesion from the Soviet Union is, first of all, impossible. . . . We are not yet mature enough as a people for complete independence. There are many Russified Ukrainians; there are many who will view such a step negatively."[29]

Ukrainian nationalists, and Rukh in particular, made the tactical decision, however, to make their agenda compatible with national-oriented communists, in order that Ukrainian independence would not again be foiled by divisions within the country.[30] In particular, they called for an independent Ukraine without necessarily calling for the ouster of the existing elites, a move that has had important repercussions since independence. Ukraine became independent, but with a political and economic system that was essentially Soviet and a well-entrenched Soviet bureaucratic apparatus. Supporting nationalist goals became the best way for Kravchuk and other elites to retain power, and supporting the elite became the best way for the nationalists to pursue independence.

In early 1991, the focus of the sovereignty/independence debate shifted to the proposed Union Treaty. In March, a referendum on the Union demonstrated somewhat contradictory opinion in Ukraine: 70 percent supported some type of Union while 80 percent supported Ukrainian "sovereignty."[31] An agreement was reached in April that would have created a much-weakened union, but just before it was to be signed in August, the failed coup and its aftermath ended any real chance to preserve the Soviet Union. Ukraine again found that circumstances dictated that it declare independence, whether it was ready or not, and it did so on 24 August 1991.[32]

Independent Ukraine and Russia: The First Years

In the weeks following Ukraine's declaration of independence on 24 August, 1991, debate continued over the relationship between the Soviet Union, Russia, and the other eleven ex-Soviet states (the Baltics having previously declared independence). Originally, some sort of union was envisioned, and in early October a "Draft Treaty on Economic Union" was signed by eight republics, including Russia and Ukraine, while others stated their intention to sign later.[33] The draft treaty was modeled on the European Community's 1957 Treaty of Rome, and in some ways envisioned more central coordination of economic policies than the Draft Union Treaty that had provoked the coup attempt. However, despite constant meetings and statements of intentions to cooperate, the republics were unable to come to any concrete measures. Russia began to implement economic reform unilaterally, which undermined any attempts at cooperation. In November, Russia took control of the Soviet Vneshekonombank (Bank of Foreign Trade) and all its assets, and spent all the hard currency, including that in accounts of the republics and their enterprises, to service foreign debt.[34]

Ukraine's overwhelming support for independence in the 1 December 1991 referendum signaled the birth of an independent Ukraine and the death of the Soviet Union. Overall, more than 70 percent of Ukrainians voted for independence. Significantly, a majority voted for independence in every region including eastern Ukraine and Crimea, though the percentage in favor was much lower in Crimea (54%) than in the nationalist west, where nearly 95 percent voted for independence. Simultaneously, Leonid Kravchuk, the party ideologist turned nationalist, easily defeated Rukh leader Vyacheslav Chornovil to become Ukraine's first president. Russian leader Boris Yeltsin stated that Russia would respect the results of the independence vote, while western leaders vacillated between recognizing the outcome and continuing to support Soviet unity.

If the Ukrainian independence vote finally killed the Soviet Union, the creation of the CIS was the funeral. On 8 December, Kravchuk, Yeltsin, and Belarusian leader Stanislau Shushkevich met outside Brest and agreed to create the Commonwealth of Independent States, and, in so doing, annul the Union Treaty of 1922, the legal basis for the Soviet Union. From the beginning, however, the CIS has been plagued by the contradictory goals of its members. Ukraine regarded the CIS agreement more than anything as a divorce decree, a means of legally dissolving the Soviet Union. Russia has sought a much stronger Commonwealth, something of a weakened union with Moscow at the center—but under Russian rather than Soviet control. Russia waited several months, for example, to begin building its own armed forces separate from those of the CIS. For both states, however, no clear set of intentions or goals existed at this time. Having cooperated to destroy the Soviet Union, they had given little thought about what to do next.

Ukrainian-Russian relations since 1991 can be divided into three phases. The first was the continued dismantling of Soviet structures, which proceeded into 1992, when Russia finally created its own Ministry of Defense. During this period of time, the main question for debate was just how strong the CIS would be. Russia, having helped destroy the Soviet Union, was now interested in maintaining as much central control as possible, but despite its desire to see a robust Commonwealth, Russia was no more willing than other states to coordinate economic policies. Russia's rapid liberalization in early 1992 left the region's other states behind, accelerating economic and political fragmentation in the region. Ukraine, still undergoing nationalist euphoria, asserted its independence in every way possible. By mid-1992, the Soviet Union had been dismantled, and the CIS had been rendered ineffective, at least in the short term. Ukraine got its way in this period, but the region remained in flux.

The second period, from mid-1992 until the Ukrainian presidential elections in 1994, was defined by the collapse of the economies in both countries, and the threat of significant civil disturbance. The economic collapse had started even prior to the breakup of the Soviet Union, but in the first months of independence was overshadowed by the tumult of state-building. Ukraine had the more severe economic collapse, and Russia had the more severe political upheaval. The key question in relations between the two states at this time was whether Ukraine's economic woes, and the accompanying regional division, would force Ukraine into some type of renewed union with Russia. Various analysts predicted secession and civil war in Ukraine, and many Ukrainians advocated economic union with Russia, even if that meant Russian dominance. Whereas in the first period the needs of nationalism were given priority over economics, in this period many in Ukraine insisted on a reversal of these priorities. The pro-union sentiment was much stronger in eastern and southern Ukraine than in the west, contributing to regional tension.

Ukraine's economic policy in the first year of independence was characterized as much by the desire to assert its independence from Russia as by the need to reform the economy (see Chapter 5). The neglect of reform and severing of ties with Russia have both proven devastating to the Ukrainian economy, which has seen its GDP drop by more than 20 percent per year since independence. Many in Ukraine, especially in the east and south, attribute the drastic drop in the standard of living to the disruption of ties with Russia. The crash of the economy is the dominant problem in Ukraine, and many see renewed ties with Russia as the easiest cure.

> One of the most widespread arguments for independence had been that, by eliminating Moscow's exploitation, independence would materially improve the lot of Ukraine's inhabitants. This view was strengthened by the traditional stereotype of "rich Ukraine," a land blessed with an abundance of resources, that would bloom if properly treated. Many who voted for independence did so in the expectation that it would raise their standard of living. But that did not happen; the economic situation continued to worsen, and by early 1993, it was catastrophic.[35]

This question of priorities defined the campaigns for the Ukrainaian Parliament (the Verkhovna Rada) and the Presidency in the first half of 1994. Leonid Kuchma, the former Prime Minister, ran on a platform focusing on economic prosperity, and on increasing ties with Russia. Kravchuk continued his formula of uniting nationalist themes with political conservatism, and ran against any union with Russia. Kuchma won in a vote that split largely on regional lines.[36] After the election, however, Kuchma stated clearly that increased cooperation with Russia would not be pursued to the detriment of Ukrainian sovereignty. Instead, by pushing the economic reform that Kravchuk had avoided, he hoped to improve Ukraine's economy without becoming more reliant on Russia. At the same time, the end of Russia's honeymoon with the West gave Ukraine increased importance to Western governments. Ukraine's role shifted from that of an unwanted complication and potential destabilizer to that of potential counterweight to a resurgent Russia. This renewed geopolitical importance, combined with Kuchma's implementation of reform, allowed Ukraine to receive significant IMF and World Bank aid that had previously been denied it.

In the current, third phase, of post-Soviet politics, Ukraine and Russia are figuring out how to deal with one another as independent states. It has become clear to most in Russia that Ukraine will not soon be reintegrated into Russia.

It has become equally clear in Ukraine that Ukraine cannot simply turn its back on Russia: it still depends on Russia too much. The third phase then will determine what the nature of the relationship between the two states will be. Put differently, it will determine the extent to which Ukrainian economic dependence on Russia will curtail Ukrainian autonomy, even as Ukraine's existence as a state is solidified.

Some explicitly argue that increased economic ties will undermine Ukraine's independence. Political power in Ukraine shifted from the west to the east, from the nationalists to conservatives, in 1994. And while political power has shifted from the nationalist west to the Russified east, there is no evidence that Ukrainian independence and sovereignty are being removed from the agenda, even if economic welfare is being added as a goal. Many Ukrainians still believe that the less interdependent Ukraine is with Russia, the better off it is.

At the same time, Russia has increased its efforts to build some sort of economic and political union in the space of the former Soviet Union. In the months after the coup, and even after the formation of the CIS, Russian policy was predicated on the continuation of some type of union, especially in military affairs. The realization that such a union would not exist has contributed, along with a resurgence of Russian conservative political forces, to a Russian foreign policy that is much more assertive in four ways: First, Russia's goals have expanded following the rapid contraction of the Soviet role in international politics. Both regionally and globally, Russia has enunciated a larger foreign policy agenda, from its right to a role in Yugoslavia, to NATO policy in Central Europe, to the rights of Russians in the "near abroad." Second, Russia increasingly claims a special status in the region as a great power and as the successor to the Soviet Union and special rights to intervene in the region on issues in which it takes an interest. Third, it has more stridently sought political and economic union agreements, with many conservatives openly calling for a new Soviet Union. Fourth, it has more openly employed threats—of economic measures, of military intervention, and of foment of civil unrest—in order achieve its goals.

The first three years of the post-Soviet era were characterized by disarray. Relationships between the new states have been sorted out slowly. Domestic politics have been chaotic in all the new states, though in varying degrees. The economic collapse has been bewildering. Since mid-1994, however, the situation has become more stable in that it has become more clear what the key problems are and in what parameters they must be addressed. The domestic political situation has now stabilized in both Ukraine and Russia. In Russia, after dissolving the Parliament in 1993, the Yeltsin government has instituted a semidemocratic government, and the opposition has drawn its lines clearly. The situation is still fluid, but uncertainty now centers on the outcome of elections, not on their taking place. In Ukraine, the moment of national euphoria is well past, and the uneventful transfer of power after the 1994 elections indicates that democracy has taken firm root there. Economically, problems continue unabated, but a clearer view of what the problems are and how they might be addressed is emerging. The government is finally (and cautiously) embarking on the path of economic reform, though the fate of reform in Ukraine remains uncertain.

Issues of Contention

The agenda between the two states has also taken form. The primary item on it is the extent to which Ukraine will be politically independent of Russia. Most of the practical issues such as Crimea and the Black Sea Fleet, nuclear weapons, and the status of Russians and the Russian language in Ukraine, come back to this larger question: Are the two states equals, or does Russia have some special status? The substance of these issues is not the primary focus of this book. Instead, the book focuses more broadly on the means by which many of these issues may be resolved—economic statecraft. There is, for example, no chapter on the Crimea, despite the importance of this issue, and the chapter on nuclear weapons focuses on the interaction between economic and military security, not on the substance of the issue itself. The issues are important as the objects often at stake in the application of economic pressure.

From the moment of the collapse of the Soviet Union, Russian authorities have been concerned with the rights of the twenty-five million Russians living outside Russia's borders. Russia's frequent statements concerning its willingness to intervene to protect these individuals' rights have been controversial in the region and around the world. The issue has been most difficult in the Baltic states, where the Russians are recent arrivals, are viewed as colonists, and have consequently been subjected to citizenship laws that make it difficult for them to become citizens in their adopted lands. In response, Russia has made a series of military threats, including delaying the withdrawal of Russian troops from the region.

With approximately twelve million Russians, concentrated in the eastern oblasts and Crimea, Ukraine is potentially the source for major conflict over the rights of Russians.[37] The situation is potentially exacerbated by the fact that to many Russians, eastern Ukraine and Crimea are really Russian territory (they were controlled by Russia for more than two centuries until 1991). However, the potential for violent conflict here has yet to be realized, and there are no signs that this will be the issue over which the two states fight, in part because Ukraine has taken a much more inclusive approach to its Russians than the Baltic states have. There are no language requirements for citizenship. And while Ukrainian nationalists have insisted on having only Ukrainian as an "official" language, Russian has been adopted as a second "state" language, in deference to the Russian minority as well as the reality that much government business is carried out in Russian. The government newspaper, *Holos Ukrainy*, for example, is published in a Russian edition as well as Ukrainian. Moreover, attempts by nationalists to make Ukrainian language the mandatory language of instruction throughout the country have been rebuffed. Most of the measures that have offended Russians elsewhere have not been adopted in Ukraine, not so much because of the threat of Russian intervention, but because of domestic opposition. As is true with Kazakhstan, Russia has little complaint about the treatment of Russians in Ukraine.

However, concerns have remained, and Ukraine's refusal to enact a law enabling Russians there to have dual Ukrainian-Russian citizenship was the major obstacle to the signing of a long-negotiated treaty of friendship (finally signed in May 1997). Ukraine has opposed the measure because a significant portion of citizens in some regions might then be subjects of Russia as well as Ukraine. Such status would, it is feared, allow Russia to claim a role in matters regarding these people, thus increasing its influence in Ukraine, and its ability to claim a legitimate right to interfere. Boris Yeltsin repeatedly refused to visit Kiev or sign the treaty in the absense of such a law, but finally gave in.

The debate over Crimea, and the related conflict over the Black Sea Fleet are surrogates for the larger question of the relations between the two states, and absent that problem, would probably be resolved. The dispute over the Black Sea Fleet is one part of the larger question of who will control Crimea which itself will symbolically indicate the relationship between the two states.[38]

The fleet itself is not militarily significant. Although ships from the fleet did oppose the U.S. Sixth Fleet in the Mediterranean during the Cold War, it was never relied on for this purpose, as passage through the Turkish Straits could never be guaranteed during hostilities.[39] Thus it is more important in a regional and symbolic role than in genuine power projection. Moreover, while it is composed of some 350 major vessels, and nearly 900 total ships—roughly 20 percent of the former Soviet Navy, the fleet itself is obsolete and rapidly deteriorating.[40]

Ukraine initially demanded that the fleet be split equally, and that Russia find its own base for its half. If accepted this even split would codify Ukraine's sovereign equality with Russia. The relocation of Russian ships away from Sevastopol, the Fleet's traditional base in Crimea, would reinforce Ukrainian sovereignty over the most disputed city on the peninsula. Russia, on the other hand, seeks an uneven division of the fleet, to force recognition of Russia's superior status in the region. Ukraine has been willing to sell much of its half of the fleet to Russia, conceding the practical issue while maintaining its right as an equal successor to the Soviet Union.

Dividing the fleet is not nearly as contentious, however, as the status of Sevastopol, the fleet's base. Practically, Sevastopol is the only port on the Black Sea deep enough for the fleet's largest ships.[41] The fleet, and its base at Sevastopol, play an important part in the history of the Russian empire. The real issue, however, is whether Russia will have a permanent military base on Ukrainian soil. An agreement on the Fleet issue was apparently reached in early 1995. The two sides agreed that Russia would obttain the majority of the fleet, and that Russia would lease Sevastopol to base its fleet, but there was no agreement on crucial details. Russia has sought a long (99-year) lease, separate facilities from the Ukrainian fleet, and the right to base troops onshore. Ukraine seeks a short (7-year) lease, basing of Ukrainian ships alongside Russian vessels, and a minimal Russian presence.[42] Essentially Russia seeks a permanent sovereign presence, while Ukraine seeks a temporary agreement to facilitate complete Russian withdrawal. The settlement finally reached in May 1997 gives Russia a twenty-year lease, effectively putting the issue aside for the time being.

The larger debate over who rightfully should control Crimea has been convoluted, driven largely by misinformation, and ultimately unprofitable. Russia's claim stems from the fact that Russia seized the land from the Tatars at the end of the eighteenth century, and that it was never part of Ukraine. Ukraine's claim stems from the geographical and economic connection of Ukraine and Crimea, which was the main reason for Moscow's decision to transfer the region to Ukrainian administration in 1954, and from the fact that at the time of independence, Crimea was, *de facto* and *de jure*, part of Ukraine.[43]

Crimea is important both strategically, for its position in the Black Sea, and economically. It is a major agricultural region, and is more temperate than other parts of Ukraine or Russia. It is equally important economically for its shipping industries, based in Sevastopol. And finally, it has been a traditional center of tourism due to its warm weather, mountains, and beaches. Indeed, many argue that the major driving force in the conflict over the region is not international politics, but control over privatization, which will be immensely profitable not only to the controlling state, but the controlling individuals.[44] Thus the Crimean legislature and President began battling each other, rather than Kiev, in 1994, primarily over who would control privatization.[45]

A majority of Crimeans voted for Ukrainian independence in 1991, but sentiment shifted as relations with Russia were severed and the Ukrainian economy plunged compared to Russia's. At the same time, nationalists in Russia began claiming the territory for Russia. While the Russian parliament has laid claim to the city of Sevastopol, and debated annulling the 1954 transfer of Crimea, Yeltsin and the government have been careful not to inflame the situation. A battle over Crimea would weaken the hand of Russian reformers, throw the region into turmoil, and endanger relations with the west. The Kiev government has been equally assiduous in avoiding open conflict in the region, repeatedly refusing calls by nationalists to introduce presidential rule in Crimea, while annulling those moves by the Crimean legislature deemed contrary to Ukraine's constitution. It is this perception that a military resolution of conflicts between Russia and Ukraine would be catastrophic for both sides that has shifted the main focus of pressure to the economic realm. Russia has nothing to gain by military confrontation with Ukraine, but it may gain many of its goals without such confrontation, if Ukraine is sufficiently dependent on Russia economically. The nature of this connection is explored in detail in the following chapter.

Assessing Russian Intentions

In dealing with a powerful neighbor, a state's leaders must be concerned with both the capabilities of that state and its intentions. U.S. dominance in the West was tolerated much more willingly than was Soviet hegemony in the East, in large part because the United States was perceived as having benign intentions.[46] As much of the Cold War era was spent speculating about Soviet intentions, much of the post–Cold War period has been spent assessing Russian intentions. This is true in particular for Russia's neighbors, which are most vulnerable should Russia seek to expand. The question is especially important for our subject, economic interdependence and security relations. How one evaluates Russia's intentions is crucial for how one evaluates the various plans for economic cooperation and integration, as well as the dangers of interdependence.

Assessing Russian intentions, however, is problematical for two reasons. First, there are wide differences in how observers view Russia. In Ukraine, many Galicians can remember being part of Poland, and viewing Soviet troops as invaders in 1939, while many in the east have been linked to Russia for generations. They naturally have different perspectives. For the political scientist, there are underlying theoretical issues in interpreting Russian acts and statements. Is today's Russia a continuation of Soviet Russia, Tsarist Russia, or both—with all their imperial aims? If so, the last several centuries may provide important insight into Russian motivations—hence the frequent citation in Ukraine of the Treaty of Pereiaslav. Or is post–Soviet Russia an entirely new phenomenon, whose fundamental characteristics remain to be seen?

More bothersome still is the question of which Russian leaders to listen to. There is no consensus within Russia concerning what Russia's aims in the region are or should be. Since the collapse of the Soviet Union, Russia has been struggling to define its identity, including its role in the region. Is the bombast of Vladimir Zhirinovsky some indicator of Russian intentions? Is it true, as many in the region say, that "what is on Zhrinovsky's tongue is on Kozyrev's mind"? On the one hand, to some extent, what "Russia's" intentions are will depend on who runs Russia, itself difficult to predict. On the other hand, there seems to be a consensus emerging around an assertive, but not deliberately aggressive, policy in the former Soviet Union. This basic consensus leads Russia's neighbors to wonder whether there is much substantive difference between Kozyrev's repeated assertions that Russia will use its military to protect Russians in the "near abroad"[47] and Zhirinovsky's promise that: "the Russian army will march over Ukraine, eliminating everything it in its way, and will deploy its garrisons everywhere it meets resistance."[48]

Despite these problems, there is a fair amount of agreement among scholars over the main competing schools of thought in Russian foreign policy. Karen Dawisha and Bruce Parrott have outlined three competing views in Russia of Russia's role in the world and in the region. The most Western-oriented group of democratic and market reformers have adopted an "Atlanticist" position, which is pro-Western and benign in the region. A second group supports domestic reform, but views Russia as a global and regional Great Power, and insists that Russia must predominate in the region. A third group, the Russian imperialists, laments the collapse of the Soviet Union and seeks to expand the borders of the Russian state.[49]

The Atlanticist school of thought would base Russian foreign policy on its underlying domestic goal: successful economic reform. In order to reform the Russian economy, Russia needs good relations with its neighbors and with the West for three reasons. First, aid from the West is essential for reform in Russia, and such aid will be forthcoming only to the extent that Russia and the West remain on good terms. Second, integration into Western economic structures is necessary for trade and investment. Third, getting Russia's state budget in order requires controlling military expenditures. Only by reducing threats from abroad is this possible. A genuine and lasting end to the Cold War and a lack of any new rivalries is essential to the goal of rapid economic and political reform.

Regarding the "near abroad," Russia's most serious reformers would adopt a policy based strictly on advantageous trade. They would not spend money or resources trying to dominate the region, and they would not continue to subsidize energy sources. In that respect, their policies would be in the short term a major problem for Ukraine and the others dependent on Russian oil and gas. In sum this position is politically one of benign neglect, and economically one of self-interest. In the early months of independence, this policy seemed to have considerable support in the government. Foreign Minister Andrei Kozyrev, and to a lesser extent Boris Yeltsin, focused on making Russia appear unthreatening to the world. The view was never unchallenged, and by 1993, it was under increasing attack from nationalists of various stripes, and has since lost any influence it had in the government, just as the most liberal individuals, such as Kozyrev and Yegor Gaidar, have lost their positions. It appears unlikely that this view will return to prominence soon, because there is still pressure for even more conservative foreign policy, and because the groups that support a pro-Western policy have very little support in Russian politics today.

The "Great Power" perspective has become almost a political consensus in Russia. If Yeltsin and Kozyrev started off in the first group, Yeltsin is now firmly in this middle group, and Kozyrev has been replaced. This group supported the collapse of the Soviet Union, and indeed was the driving force behind it. And it supports economic and political reform in the country, though in a more limited way than the first group. But for them, foreign policy does not simply serve domestic goals.[50] There is a separate goal internationally—power, influence, and prestige—that requires Russia's assertion of its traditional great power status. For these people, Russia has always been a great power, and must continue to be one. While the first group seeks a complete break with the past, this group seeks continuity with the past in many ways, often focusing on the Russian Empire rather than on the Soviet era for inspiration. By great power status, these people mean that Russia should have an active role in world affairs, that its approval should be required for major international decisions (especially in Europe) and that the former Soviet Union (and perhaps Central Europe) should be considered a Russian sphere of interest.

The "great power" position has manifested itself in some of Russia's most significant foreign policy moves since 1991. Much of the debate over NATO expansion has concerned the contention that Russia has the right, as a great power, to veto any decision so important to it. Similarly, Russian policy on Yugoslavia has been based in part on the simple insistence that Russia have a role. In the former Soviet Union, this view does not advocate an end to the independence of the other successor states, but does insist on their submission to Russian hegemony. Russia is to be the organizer of the region, and is to have the right to dispatch troops abroad for mutual defense, for settlement of domestic conflicts, and to protect Russian speakers.[51] It is also to organize the region's economy, so that mutually profitable trade can be carried out. The "Strategy for Russia," devised by by the Foreign and Defense Policy Council, a group of high Russian government officials and foreign policy elites, advocated a policy "not to restore with some modification the situation that existed before the disintegration of the USSR, but to modernize these relations in a way advantageous for Russia, whereby it will retain many advantages of its former geostrategic position and at the same time create for itself a much more advantageous economic position in the new commonwealth of states."[52] More broadly, the "Kozyrev" doctrine in has been described as a Russian Monroe doctrine, "according to which the entire territory of the former Soviet union would be the exclusive sphere of Russia's influence."[53] Regarding Ukraine, this group has focused on bringing Ukraine back into Russia not through force, but by using economic pressure to weaken Ukrainian independence.[54]

Unlike the great power advocates, the Russian imperialists lament the dissolution of the Soviet Union and seek the expansion of Russian territory, if not to include all the former Soviet Union, at least the "Russian" lands of Belarus, Ukraine, and Northern Kazakhstan. Thus the Duma announced in January 1995, its intention to review the Belavezha agreement that dissolved the Soviet Union and created the CIS, to reconsider whether the dissolution of the USSR was appropriate.[55] The group consists of many disparate elements, including unreformed communists and extreme Russian nationalists, that do not share many other views. For these individuals, Russia should not merely dominate in the region, but reassert its complete political control. Vladimir Zhirinovsky has made the most widely quoted remarks in this regard, but there are many adherents of this view who are less outrageous.

Russian intentions are becoming easier to assess in part because there seems to be a growing consensus within Russia itself in favor of the "great power" view. The Atlanticist view simply has been discredited. The imperialist position has more potential to become influential, but suffers from two problems. First, its supporters, who range from Zhirinovsky on the far right to Zyuganov on the far left, do not agree on much else, and are unlikely to be sufficiently unified to take over foreign policy, even if they do pull it in their direction. Second, even if such individuals did come to power, it would be difficult to pursue their objectives within prevailing international and domestic constraints. The important overall point is that the debate has shifted noticeably. For the year or so after the collapse of the Soviet Union, the debate was between the Atlanticists and the great power advocates. Since then, it has been between the great power advocates and the imperialists, and there is consensus on the goal of "reintegrating" the former Soviet Union. Boris Yeltsin made reintegration Russia's primary goal in the region in a September 1995 decree on strategy toward the CIS, and his 1996 election platform made reintegration Russia's "main foreign policy priority."[56] An observer of the 1995 campaign for the Russian Duma commented that "all parties and movements consider it obligatory to mention the reintegration of the former USSR territory in their foreign policy programs."[57]

Russia's unwillingness to fully accept Ukraine's independence was shown in the negotiations on a "friendship and cooperation" treaty between the two states. Russia refused to "recognize state borders," offering instead to "respect" borders, as long as the word "state" was left out.[58] Russian actions throughout the former Soviet Union also indicate that while military attack is unlikely, a variety of types of pressure will be brought to bear in pursuit of Russian predominance. Trade measures have been used both as carrots (continued subsidies of various types) and sticks (complete cutoffs) to cajole partners into political arrangements Russia considers favorable. The economic union negotiations between Russia and Belarus throughout 1994 provide only one example. Russia has also somewhat transparently supported rebellion in Georgia in order to make Georgia choose between asking Russia for help and suffering division. Similar leverage has been applied on Azerbaijan, through support of Armenia in the conflict over Nagorno-Karabakh.[59] Both Georgia and Azerbaijan initially rejected membership in the CIS, but have been compelled to reconsider. Finally, Russia has sought in international fora such as the UN and the Organization for Security and Cooperation in Europe (OSCE) to have its role as arbiter of disputes in the region legitimated by the international community. Russian actions thus run parallel to Russian leaders' statements of their goals. They have not actively tried to reintegrate territory of the former Soviet Union, even when, in the case of Abkhazia, doing so would have been relatively easy. But they have stated an intention of dominating the politics and economics of the region, and they have pursued that goal.

Saying that Russia seeks to dominate the former Soviet Union leaves many questions unanswered. How vigorously Russia will pursue its goals, and what means it will apply in pursuing them, remains to be seen, and may vary with the political winds within Russia itself. Moreover, this desire for dominance may wane as the severity of Russia's own problems and the permanance of Soviet collapse become more clear. However, the issue for Ukraine and the other successor states is relatively clear: while outright military invasion is not a likely scenario in the near future, economic pressure of various types will be likely.[60] The great power Russians have stated their intention to use economic leverage to force political recognition of Russia's predominance, and have acted on that intention. The foreign policy challenge for Ukraine, therefore, is how to prevent economic dependence from leading to political suzerainty.

Determining Ukrainian Priorities

To decide how it will deal with its dependence on Russia, Ukraine first needs to decide what its own priorities are and how they relate to one another. Only then can it decide how to pursue them. The issue in Ukraine has boiled down to two key values: the desire to be independent of Russia and the desire to prosper economically. Those two goals are not necessarily contradictory, but they are widely perceived to be, and at least in the short term trade disruption will decrease efficiency. The debate to some extent reflects the east-west debate within the country. While all Ukrainians seek prosperity and almost all support independence, there is much disagreement over how much prosperity should be sacrificed in pursuit of economic independence. For nationalists, who reside primarily in the area of western Ukraine linked to Russia only since 1939, independence is worth a very high price indeed, and clearly stands above prosperity as a priority. For those, especially in the east, who view Russia and Ukraine as less distinct, or who are linked economically with Russia, independence is desirable, but not at any cost.

Bridging this gap has been one of the main challenges in Ukrainian domestic politics, and driving a wedge in it has been one of the main tactics in Russian foreign policy. When Leonid Kravchuk was elected President in Ukraine's first election in 1991, he successfully bridged the gap between nationalists and communists. Ukraine's first economic policy satisfied communists by implementing almost no reform, and it pleased nationalists by breaking ties with Russia. This clever mixture led rapidly to economic chaos in the country. The debate shifted from communism versus nationalism to economic isolation versus integration with Russia. After winning the Presidency in 1994, Leonid Kuchma bridged the gap in a different way—pleasing eastern Ukrainians with a promise of tighter integration with Russia while reassuring nationalists that Ukrainian sovereignty would not be sacrificed.

This debate is still in progress on several fronts. First, while Kuchma has reached a compromise, there is by no means consensus in Ukraine, and Ukrainian attitudes about key trade-offs are liable to shift. A survey conducted in May 1997 showed that 44 percent of Ukrainians favored joining the Russian-Belarusian union, while only 32 percent opposed it (and 24% were undecided).[61] Second, as will be demonstrated in the following chapter, it is not so easy to protect Ukrainian independence while cooperating economically with Russia. Third, Ukraine's domestic economic situation, and thus its international vulnerability, are highly dependent on the success of economic and political reform, which have only just begun.

The issues raised in this chapter, which are the legacy of a millennium of interaction as well as the last few years of upheaval, concern the fundamental relationship between Russia and Ukraine. Will the two countries reunite, as some have advocated, and as Belarus is contemplating? Will Ukraine finally consent to being subject to a Russian sphere of influence, if its *de facto* sovereignty is assured? Will the two states be separate, independent actors, cooperating with each other as sovereign equals? Will they be locked in militarized rivalry?

These questions are being slowly worked through in Russian-Ukrainian relations. Neither the Ukrainian hope of complete sovereign equality nor the Russian imperialist hope of reunion seem realistic outcomes. But there is much variation between these two extremes. The contention of this book is that these questions will be resolved largely in the realm of economic statecraft—that is, the manipulation of trade for the purposes of state. This chapter has discussed the past and its influence on the present situation in the two states. The rest of the book is concerned with showing how the decisions made in the present time will influence Russian-Ukrainian relations—and by extension European and world security—for many years to come.

3

Trade and Power in International Politics

The Dilemmas of Interdependence

> The choice between economic independence and economic
> efficiency is the most important dilemma.
> —Volodymyr Sidenko, "Economic
> Independence or Economic Efficiency"

The relationship between economic interdependence and political power has been at the heart of the study of international politics for centuries. From mercantilism to liberalism to Marxism, theories of international politics have explored the connection between "power" and "plenty," as Jacob Viner put it.[1] The basic questions concern the effects of different international trading arrangements on two essential state goals: domestic prosperity and international power. A third goal, sovereignty, is critical to understanding the situation in the FSU, even if it can be taken for granted elsewhere. The discussion focuses on extending an existing body of concepts and theories to the new situation that we find in the former Soviet Union.

Most recent discussions of interdependence have focused on how international institutions are created to help states deal with their considerable economic interdependence.[2] This discussion has made significant theoretical advances in recent years, but has been applied in a limited fashion, almost exclusively to the European Union and to the advanced industrial states more broadly. In doing so, it has focused on groups in which the basic independence and sovereignty of the states are unquestioned, and among whom the primary challenge to security comes not from within the group, but externally, from the Soviet Union.[3] Keohane and Nye, for example, premise their seminal analysis on the assumption that domestic welfare is the dominant goal of states.[4]

For Ukraine and the other non-Russian states of the former Soviet Union, the situation is somewhat different. Their independence and sovereignty are

43

very new and shaky institutions, and cannot be taken for granted. Ukrainian President Kuchma said in 1994: "Ukraine has not yet attained real independence. In 1991, it created only the skeleton of a soverign state, and over the last three years, has been unable to fill it with real content."[5] While the new states are confronted with the need for open trade advocated in liberal trade theory, they also recognize that "liberalism can be given priority only if the provision of security is taken for granted."[6] Russia and many western states have questioned the legitimacy, viability, and even the desirability of the new states' independence. Because the independence and sovereignty of these states cannot be taken for granted, Russia's economic leverage becomes a threat not only to domestic economic security, but to security in the traditional sense—the survival of the state. In this way, more traditional realist theories of international political economy remain relevant for the former Soviet Union. In particular, Albert Hirschman's account of German penetration of Eastern Europe in the interwar years demonstrates how economic interdependence can be manipulated for the purposes of power politics.[7] The FSU shares both the need for cooperation that characterizes modern Western Europe and the potential for coercion that characterized the interwar period. The overarching goal of this chapter, therefore, is to draw from a wide range of approaches a set of concepts necessary to probe the international political economy of the former Soviet Union.

This theoretical approach will be developed through four more specific tasks: First, three key concepts—interdependence, autonomy, and sovereignty— are clarified. Second, the chapter examines the roots of economic vulnerability, drawing from the literature on international political economy. This discussion highlights the links between economic interdependence and power politics, and examines the ways in which state policies can increase or decrease economic vulnerability. Third, the chapter explores three broad dilemmas created by Ukraine's economic vulnerability. This section specifically addresses the question What is at stake in Ukraine's dependence on Russia? Fourth, it shows how the theoretical problems outlined here are linked to the very practical concerns discussed in the second section of the book.

Interdependence, Autonomy, and Sovereignty

Three of the main concepts involved in discussions of modern political economy are interdependence, autonomy, and sovereignty, and each is key to relations between Ukraine and Russia. Interdependence indicates not only intereaction between economies, but the effects of one economy on another. In this case, the effect that concerns us most is economic vulnerability. Such vulnerability endangers not only prosperity, but also autonomy and sovereignty. These latter two concepts, while similar, are conceptually distinct, and in fact are sometimes in tension with one another in situations of economic interdependence. An examination of interdependence, autonomy, and sovereignty provide the foundation for understanding the problems Ukraine faces.

Interdependence

Interdependence is often defined simply as the interaction of two or more economies, and is customarily measured by the amount of trade between the economies. The word *interdependence*, however, implies not only that two economies interact, but that they have important effects on one another, which simply discussing the amount of trade does not represent.[8] Therefore, most political analyses of interdependence focus on two aspects of the problem: sensitivity and vulnerability.[9] *Sensitivity* is defined by Keohane and Nye as the amount change in one state's economy caused by a given amount of change in another's.[10] The question is not how much two states trade, but rather the effect that changes in one economy produce in the other. For example, what is the effect in Ukraine of a rise in the price of meat in Russia? Simply knowing the amount of trade in meat between the two states does not answer this second question. High mutual sensitivity motivates states to coordinate their economic activities, so they do not engage in policies that are mutually defeating, and much of the study of interdependence in recent years has focused on how states that are mutually sensitive coordinate their policies.

Vulnerability is the cost to a state of offsetting such change emanating from abroad.[11] This second aspect of interdependence concerns us most, because it lends itself to manipulation by states to apply political pressure.[12] Only if the cost of adjustment is high need the state concern itself with its interdependence. In the Ukrainian-Russian relationship, Russia is sensitive to changes in the prices of Ukrainian agricultural products, because it imports a lot of such products from Ukraine. It is vulnerable, however, only to the extent that reacting to an increase in the price of Ukrainian produce would be costly. This relies on two further factors: the extent to which a product is indispensable, and the extent to which it can be replaced through other suppliers. Sensitivity in items that are not basic necessities (such as fur coats) or are easily obtained elsewhere (grain) do not create vulnerability. This has been underscored both by the difficulties in implementing effective economic sanctions and by the difficulty in creating sellers' cartels for items other than oil. When the price of coffee was raised, importing countries simply consumed much less coffee. "Quantitatively, interdependence tightens as parties depend on one another for larger supplies of goods and services; qualitatively, inter-dependence tightens as countries depend on one another for more important goods and services that would be harder to get elsewhere."[13]

In assessing vulnerability, the key question is how hard is it to adjust to a cutoff in trade. What opportunities for increased welfare are given up when trade is severed, either through choice or through another state's action? David Baldwin defines interdependence in terms of the costs of alternative polices. Similarly for Hirschman, the gains from trade represent the cost of *not* doing trade, and hence the state's vulnerability to a cutoff.[14] Interdependence is the opportunity cost of autarky.[15] Or as James Caporaso puts it, "Dependence provides a direct measure of the costs of breaking a relationship and substituting for it a new one."[16]

Interdependence implies a mutual relationship: two states are dependent on one another. It does not necessarily follow, however, that the two states are equally or symmetrically dependent on one another, even though this is often assumed in literature on the subject. Symmetrical interdependence requires coordination of policies, but does not create the potential for coercion, because any injurious action can be reciprocated. When interdependence is asymmetrical, however, one state needs trade more than the other. A cutoff of trade, therefore, will hurt the vulnerable economy more, giving it a greater incentive to take measures to avoid such a cutoff. International politics is defined not simply by interdependence, but by asymmetric interdependence (or dependence). Asymmetric interdependence has important implications for states' autonomy, and is the defining characteristic of Ukrainian-Russian relations.

Autonomy and Sovereignty

Sovereignty and autonomy are often equated in studies of international relations, and international institutions are therefore often seen as challenging states' sovereignty and autonomy.[17] However, autonomy and sovereignty are distinct concepts, and the difference between them is crucial, for as we will see below, sovereignty and autonomy are conflicting goals in some circumstances. While many definitions are offered for these two concepts, we will focus on sovereignty in the somewhat narrow meaning as the authority to take a decision, and on autonomy in the more practical sense of the ability to control one's own fate.

Autonomy essentially means "self-governance." "Autonomous states make their own decisions with respect to international and domestic problems."[18] In making these decisions, the autonomous state need not take into account the wishes of other states. In that sense, autonomy is the opposite of interdependence. Sovereignty is "the formal ability of countries . . . to make their own decisions, but not necessarily to achieve their own objectives."[19] The difference between sovereignty and autonomy therefore is that sovereignty is a narrow concept basically referring to the acknowledged authority to make decisions, as opposed to having them delegated to some higher or lower authority. The modern state is sovereign because it has superior authority over substate actors, and has no superior whom it is committed to obey. In contrast, autonomy assumes some (but not absolute) ability to make decisions, but denotes in addition the ability to act contrary to the wishes of others, and the ability to make decisions that are not simply negated by the actions of others. More practically, it means to have a significant range of options.

Sovereignty and autonomy often go together: the state that is sovereign is often free to make choices autonomously. But in some cases they do not. A state can be sovereign but not autonomous if it is able to make its own decisions, but has its options severely constrained by the ability of other states to foil its policies or impose high costs on them. This was true in the case of the Warsaw Pact states, which were legally sovereign, but had very little real autonomy. It is true to a lesser extent of all interdependent states, where one state's tariffs can easily be counteracted by another's. Conversely, many regions of Russia today lack sovereignty, but have a great deal of autonomy to order their affairs. Thus while sovereignty refers to the acknowledged authority to make choices, autonomy refers to the actual ability to make choices. Autonomy can therefore be identified with *de facto* sovereignty, in contrast with *de jure* sovereignty. For Ukraine in its relationship with Russia, the distinction is significant because on some issues, pursuing an increase in sovereignty may lead to some reduction in autonomy. That is, Ukraine may be able to increase its authority to choose only by reducing the options to choose from. This trade-off constitutes an important dilemma for Ukraine.

Economic Dependence and Political Leverage

Asymmetric interdependence (or dependence) is of paramount importance in international politics. Robert Gilpin states:

> The interdependence of national economies creates economic power, defined as the capacity of one state to damage another through the interruption of commercial and financial relations. The attempts to create and to escape from such dependency relationships constitute an important aspect of international relations in the modern era.[20]

Therefore the degree of symmetry of interdependence has much more import for many states than the aggregate amount of interaction. This point is often missed in analyses that imply that a high level of interaction will make conflict between states costly and therefore less likely. This is true only when the high level of interaction is needed equally by the two sides.[21] When a high degree of trade is needed more by one side than another, power accrues to the side that needs it less, and coercion and conflict are possible.

States in the modern world therefore face a difficult dilemma: the complexity of modern economies means that there are large economic gains possible from specialization and trade. Moreover, one of the defining characteristics of modern politics is that states are held responsible for the economic welfare of their citizens. Specialization and trade, however, are certain to create vulnerability for some states, and power for others. Indeed, it is the very fact that states gain so much from trade that makes the threat of a cutoff dangerous to them, and useful to their adversaries as a tool of coercion. The trick for states therefore is to gain the benefits of exchange while maximizing their autonomy (minimizing their vulnerability).[22] States therefore pursue economic security, or passive economic power: the invulnerability to economic coercion.[23]

As Hirschman argues, the relationship between trade and autonomy is contingent on the structure of foreign trade; that is the composition of trade, the partners chosen, and their relative vulnerabilities.[24] Because this relationship is contingent, it can be manipulated, and Hirschman emphasizes that static analysis is insufficient to ascertain which side will prevail in a conflict.[25] Economic power is not static. It can be increased (or countered) through certain policies. Moreover, will and skill in applying and resisting power are important in determining outcomes. While some determinants of vulnerability are essentially fixed (the overall size of a state's GNP), others, such as its trading partners, may be subject to policy. Hirschman's seminal work on trade coercion shows how Germany, given a relatively favorable power position to begin with, was able to structure trade relations in Eastern Europe in the interwar years to make the governments of the region highly vulnerable to embargo and therefore easy to manipulate politically. It is therefore possible for the relationship between power and wealth to be greatly altered without changing the basic fact of interdependence. The small European states, for example, are as economically dependent on trade as third world states, but they have managed to maintain much more autonomy.[26] It is therefore necessary to elaborate the conditions that affect economic vulnerability.

Conditions that Affect Economic Vulnerability

While the case of interwar Germany was an extreme one, the potential for coercion is inherent in international trade. The questions for Ukraine and the other former Soviet states are: first, how disadvantageous is their position structurally, and second, what can be done to minimize their vulnerability to coercion. Several of the structural determinants of vulnerability are difficult to manipulate, but others are more subject to a strategy of economic autonomy. Here we address nine basic factors that can alter the degree of economic vulnerability in a relationship. The following chapters address the ways in which Russia and Ukraine have used these strategies against each other.

Relative Size of the Economies

The simplest determinant of economic vulnerability is the relative size of the economies involved, a fact noted by economists as far back Adam Smith.[27] The direct reason is that any amount of trade between two states will be a bigger *proportion* of trade and GNP for the smaller state than for the larger one. It was the size of Germany's economy relative to the small Eastern European states that provided the foundation for economic penetration,[28] and it is the size of Russia's economy relative to its partners that makes a cutoff in trade inherently less damaging to Russia than to others. For this reason Katzenstein argues that for the small state, the problem is not interdependence, but dependence.[29]

The size of a state's economy is difficult to alter dramatically in the short term, and in this sense there is no direct strategy to overcome the size problem for small states. But other strategies can be undertaken. One that is difficult politically is for small states to band together to form a united front against larger states (see the following discussion of multilateralism). More simply, states can, to whatever extent possible, redirect their trade from large states to smaller states. To Hirschman, this is an "elementary principle."[30] If a state can trade as much as possible with other small states, its vulnerability will be reduced, because its partners will be injured by a cutoff as much as it will be. Conversely the largest state can maximize its leverage by directing trade toward smaller states. Obviously the potential to do this is limited by the ability to find small state partners who can supply the same goods, markets, or both that the large one can.

This potential strategy creates interesting possibilities for Ukraine, given its intermediate position in the GNP hierarchy of the former Soviet Union. Ukraine's GNP at the time of the breakup was approximately one-third that of Russia. In this respect, Ukraine has been on the losing side of the size principle. However, Ukraine's GNP is roughly four times as large as that of the next largest economy, Kazakhstan. If Ukraine could shift trade from Russia to other republics, it would move from a very unfavorable position to a very favorable one. Or by shifting trade toward Central and Western Europe,

Ukraine could decrease its vulnerability to Russia. This possibility was immediately recognized following independence. The problem has been in finding other states that can provide what Russia does, and that have some corresponding need from Ukraine to make trade economically desirable. In many cases, such a shift in trade incurs some cost in efficiency and prosperity. Moreover, the problem for Ukraine is not just that Russia is much larger than Ukraine, but that Russia is much larger than most of Ukraine's potential alternative partners, and can use its influence on them to prevent a restructuring of trade.

Bilateral versus Multilateral Trading

Related to the issue of size is the question of the form of international trade, and whether trade agreements are worked out bilaterally or multilaterally. As discussed above, one way of circumventing the size problem is for small states to band together. In a multilateral trading system, where rules for trade (i.e., tariffs) are negotiated multilaterally, the power of the large state is somewhat diluted. Conversely in bilateral trade, the power of the large state is maximized over each of the smaller ones; and it can follow a policy of "divide and conquer," playing the small states off against one another. Zbigniew Brzezinski's classic study of the Soviet bloc showed how Moscow used bilateral ties to dominate the smaller states of the region.[31] Many international political economists have found that it is the extreme vulnerability of bilateral trading that makes international regimes acceptable to small states, even at the cost of some sovereignty.[32] Thus Joseph Grieco contends that the EU serves the interests of it smallest members by "binding" Germany and preventing it from exploiting them bilaterally.[33] Hirschman finds that strict bilateralism was an important part of Germany's strategy in Eastern Europe, and Roman Szporluk argues that Josef Stalin opposed the formation of a Balkan confederation following World War II precisely in order to facilitate Soviet coercion of the individual states.[34]

This finding implies that membership in the CIS and a strengthening of that organization would help make the smaller states, including Ukraine, less vulnerable to Russian coercion. This clearly has been Kazakhstan's strategy, and while Ukraine has decried Russian pressure to join the CIS, Kazakh leaders have criticized Russia for trying to dominate bilaterally. Clearly Ukraine has not found the potential benefits of multilateral trading sufficient to overcome its other objections to the CIS. Explaining why this is so is one of the purposes of this book.

The Number of Trading Partners

Because vulnerability is dependent on the amount of damage a potential opponent inflicts by cutting trade, concentration of trade increases the potential for coercion. The greater the portion of state A's trade that is conducted with state B, the greater the potential for state B to coerce state A. As the state increases its number of trading partners for a fixed amount of trade, it decreases the damage that any one of its partners can do, in effect diluting the potential for injury.[35] Studies of economic sanctions have shown that the conditions under which economic coercion works are limited to cases where either the sanctioning state controls a large portion of trade with the target, or can convince other trading partners to go along. A widespread response to the oil crisis of 1973, which was essentially an attempt at using economic vulnerability politically, was for industrialized states to diversify their sources of oil, so that a unity of all their suppliers became less likely. The powerful state seeking to increase its ability to coerce will undertake to retain a large role in the trade composition of its smaller partners. One way to do this is through offering preferential terms of trade (see below). Again, the strategy for the small state is to diversify its trade composition, which may mean foregoing the cheapest sources of goods, the most lucrative markets, and more generally, the best trading relationship from the perspective of domestic prosperity.[36]

The Identity of Trading Partners

States contemplating the distribution of trade must consider not only the amount of trade with various partners, but the identity of their trading partners and the potential that they will attempt to use any vulnerability against a weaker state.[37] To be dependent on a partner that is distant and disinterested in coercion is safer than to be dependent on a neighbor who has objectives that might be furthered through coercion. Concentration of trade is not of equal importance among all partners; it is of greater concern with those by whom the state feels threatened. This somewhat self-evident assertion is important for trade politics in the former Soviet Union. The problem for the small states is not simply that they are very dependent on another, but that they are dependent on another state whose intentions toward them they do not trust. As was shown in the previous chapter, there is good reason for Ukraine to believe that vulnerability to Russia will be exploited, and therefore increased incentive to reduce that vulnerability.

It is therefore possible to reduce the danger of being coerced without reducing dependence, by shifting trade toward states who are unlikely to use the dependence coercively. For this reason, most of the successors have been much more willing to integrate with the EU than the CIS. They perceive that dependence on the EU countries is unlikely to be exploited. Indeed, much of Ukraine's strategy for economic security has consisted of shifting trade ties from Russia to more benign partners, especially those in the West. Again, however, shifting one's trade is easier said than done, and is often costly. While much hope was placed in trade with the EU, that arena has been largely closed off, because the most competetive Ukrainian goods—notably agricultural products and steel—are considered "sensitive goods" by the EU, and are hence subject to special restrictions. Similarly, Ukrainian steel exports to the United States have been hampered by antidumping measures.[38] Ukrainian efforts to shift some of its oil dependence to alternative suppliers are hampered by the increased expense involved in transporting oil from more distant shores.

The Importance of the Goods Traded

As was discussed above, vulnerability is created only to the extent that the goods being traded (or the markets under consideration) are important.[39] This problem is particularly relevant in the Ukrainian-Russian relationship, where two of the primary commodities traded have been oil and gas. The issue will be treated in detail in the following chapter, but it is sufficient here to say that Ukraine's problems stem in large part from the fact that it is immensely dependent on Russia for commodities without which its economy simply cannot function. Energy is not the only issue where this is so: Ukraine is heavily dependent on Russian markets as outlets for industry that employs much of its population, and is much more dependent on Russia than Russia is on it.[40]

There are several ways to reduce the importance of a given good or market, but none is simple. One is to develop an indigenous capacity for the good in question. A traditional strategy of preserving autonomy has been to remain self-sufficient in the key areas of economics and military production. Thus many states subsidize their agriculture to preserve domestic capacity even though cheaper supplies may be available abroad. Similarly the United States has dedicated considerable money to maintaining a domestic semiconductor industry. Following the OPEC oil boycott, many states moved to increase domestic exploration and production. Ukraine's ability to do this varies with the industry in question: On the one hand, Ukraine's energy sources are somewhat depleted, and it is unlikely that domestic consumption will make up for lost exports to Russia; on the other hand, Ukraine may be able to develop domestic supplies of some intermediate products that formerly came from Russia.

A second way to reduce the importance of a good is to reduce the amount that one needs—that is, to become more efficient. Or one can shift production out of the industries that are most reliant on the key supply. Following the 1973 oil boycott, the United States and many other states implemented domestic conservation measures that significantly reduced demand. As chapter 4 shows, Ukraine has sought to shut down some of the most inefficient industrial consumers of energy, and to pass more of the cost of energy on to consumers, to increase their incentive to reduce consumption.

The Availability of Substitutes

When an alternate supplier (or easily substitutable product) is available, the state need not be so concerned about a cutoff. The main tensions in world trade today concern not limited access to materials, but limited access to markets, because alternative markets are often more difficult to find than alternative suppliers.[41] This is the source of the U.S. leverage over Japan. The significance of the availability of substitutes is demonstrated by the Ukrainian-Russian relationship: The two main products exchanged between the two states traditionally have been food (from Ukraine) and energy (from Russia). Both of these goods are essential to the recipient's economy. Many believed, therefore, that Ukraine would have an effective counterlever against Russian pressure on oil.

However, while the two states are both highly dependent on their imports, it is much easier for Russia to find substitutes for Ukrainian grain than for Ukraine to find substitutes for Russian oil. The basic reason is the structure of the world market for agricultural products, which is consistently in a state of surplus supply. Many states subsidize agricultural exports in order to prop up their domestic agricultural sectors. No state needs to subsidize oil sales to find buyers. Not only is it easy for Russia to find alternate suppliers of grain, it will be hard for Ukraine to find alternate buyers in a glutted (and highly protected) world market. The different availability of substitutes makes Ukraine's dependence on Russian oil much more important than Russia's dependence on Ukrainian grain.[42]

The Terms of Trade

The terms of trade, because they largely determine how the gains from trade are divided, play an important role in determining vulnerability. The more a state gains through trade, the more it stands to lose if that trade ceases. Since the terms of trade are negotiable, it is possible to manipulate them to one's advantage. By granting a partner favorable terms of trade, the state can increase the vulnerability of its partner. This is one area in which the interests of prosperity and autonomy conflict. Prosperity requires getting the best deal possible—that is, buying a good at the lowest possible price. The better the deal, however, the more one loses if it falls through. Vulnerability increases and autonomy decreases correspondingly.[43]

Terms of trade can easily be manipulated by powerful states seeking to increase their leverage. By selling key commodities at below-market prices (or granting special market access) the cost to the target state of breaking the relationship can be increased, and so can the political concessions required for a maintenance of the relationship. This tactic has been most noticeable in the FSU in Russia's continued willingness to sell oil at below market prices,[44] but was also seen in the terms for currency negotiated in the aborted Russian-Belarussian economic union in 1994. For the target state, particularly difficult dilemmas are created. If a partner offers very advantageous terms of trade, it would be difficult to turn them down: can Ukraine or any other state say to Russia: "We insist on paying a higher price for your oil"? Clearly this would be difficult, and would directly contradict domestic economic interests. But establishing the favorable relationship, and building one's economy on the assumption of favorable treatment, creates vulnerability, because the favorable conditions are easily revoked.[45] The advantages of giving one's partner generous terms of trade may explain what John Morrison calls the "paradox of the CIS": "Russia seeks to continue, at great cost, an organization which seems largely to give subsidies to other republics, while Ukraine, the largest beneficiary of Russian subsidies, has tried to destroy the CIS or escape from it."[46]

Transit Trade

Hirschman asserts that one of the best tools for building economic power is transit trade, by which he means the transit of goods across a state's territory, where the state in question is neither the producer nor the consumer of the good.[47] Transit trade makes both the supplying state and the consuming state dependent on the transit state's facilities, and makes both vulnerable to a blockage of transit. Moreover, because the transit state is neither the producer nor the consumer, the cost to it of disrupting the transaction is likely to be relatively low.

Transit trade provides Ukraine with its most effective means of counterpressure against Russia.[48] Russian oil and natural gas travel through Ukrainian pipelines to hard-currency customers in western Europe. Ukraine can threaten to close those pipelines, injuring both the Russian companies and the European consumers, at the cost only of foregoing the transit fees. The main means to reducing this type of vulnerability is the development of alternate transit routes. Russia therefore seeks to build pipelines through Belarus or to purchase the Ukrainian pipelines. Because Ukraine is located closer to western Europe, and has excellent port facilities on the Black Sea, it is not subject to significant pressure from Russia in this regard. Ukraine depends on supplies that come from Russia, not through Russia.)

Strength of the State Domestically

Finally, it is important to note that the domestic strength of the state is an important determinant of how much autonomy is reduced by dependence.[49] Studies of the small western European states show that the strength of their states allows them to be autonomous in the face of dependence. Somewhat simplified, the argument is that corporatist states, with highly centralized decisionmaking, provide the state sufficient agility adjust to economic shocks from outside. By facilitating shifts from noncompetitive industries, and compensating those most disadvantaged by new conditions, such states are able weather international economic storms relatively smoothly. In short, they retain a large degree of ability to substitute one composition of trade for another. They therefore reduce their vulnerability for a given level of dependence.[50]

(Creating a stronger state, more able to negotiate between domestic economic woes and international vulnerability, has been one of the main issues in Ukraine's attempt to deal with its vulnerability. For example, it has been difficult to close industries that waste scarce energy supplies even though the industries are unprofitable, because the state cannot withstand the pressures from the workers who would be laid off. Similarly, it has been difficult to reduce consumption by ending the subsidies on energy supplies. Chapter 8 shows in detail how the divisions in Ukraine's state and society have made the state very weak, and consequently unable to adopt a strategy to cope with economic dependence.)

State strength is important in the state's ability to wield, as well as to resist, economic power. Any attempt at sanctions will likely be opposed by the industries it will hurt most, as was the case when U.S. farmers opposed a boycott on grain sales to the Soviet Union in 1980. While Russia's state is quite weak in many areas, it has proven strong in controlling sectors of the economy that are essential to foreign policy goals. Most notable is the gas industry, where the Soviet gas monopoly remains under the control of the Russian government. It cannot, therefore, provide a significant barrier to the state decision to subsidize gas supplies or cut them altogether.[51]

To summarize, a given level of interdependence does not lead to a fixed degree of vulnerability. Instead, vulnerability is contingent not only on the amount and asymmetry of interdependence, but also on the way that trade is structured. A variety of factors, such as the size of the states, the ability to find alternate partners, and the skill and strength of the government, can increase or decrease the vulnerability and autonomy of a state. Hirschman concludes that the goal of the state concerned with economic power is "to make the interruption of trade of much graver concern to its trading partner than to itself."[51] Ukraine finds the interruption of trade of much graver concern to itself than to its primary trading partner, Russia. Ukraine is not merely dependent on Russia for a variety of goods and markets that are key to its prosperity, it is dependent in such a way that makes it highly vulnerable: it trades with Russia for essential goods (and markets), Russia's size makes it inherently powerful, Russia's intentions are suspect, Ukraine has few cheap substitutes, and it is unable to mobilize its society to reduce vulnerability. Economic vulnerability, the potential effects of it, and the costs of overcoming it are crucial issues for Ukraine today.

Three Trade-offs

In most cases reduction in vulnerability comes at some cost in other goals, because gains from trade inherently create vulnerability.[53] Finding less powerful trading partners may mean higher prices. Developing indigenous capacities entails diverted investment and inefficiency. Because maximizing economic efficiency requires trading with the most profitable partners regardless of political concerns, this goal inevitably collides with that of maximizing autonomy. More broadly, three key goals for Ukraine (autonomy, prosperity, and sovereignty) are in tension with one another, leading to three trade-offs (prosperity versus autonomy, prosperity versus sovereignty, and autonomy versus sovereignty).[54] These tradeoffs are inherent in Ukraine's situation, and indeed in international politics, as E. H. Carr noted in discussing the Versailles system: "The self-determination of the small nations is incompatible with unbridled economic power and complete economic interdependence."[55]

All states seek prosperity for their society, and in the current era, provision for domestic welfare has become one of the key responsibilities of national governments. Among the industrialized market economies, maintenance of prosperity is a key indicator of the effectiveness of governments. Robert Keohane therefore identifies the problem created by interdependence as one of effectiveness: the more a state's economy is subject to pressures beyond that state's borders, the more difficult it is for the government to be effective.[56]

A second goal pursued by states is autonomy, which has already been defined in some detail. States desire to be able to govern their affairs without taking the policies of other states into account. Interdependence creates a tension between autonomy and prosperity, and this tension is exacerbated when interdependence becomes highly asymmetrical. A third goal states seek is sovereignty. In some ways sovereignty—the recognition by other states of the right of a given state to control a given territory—is the most fundamental goal of states. Discussions of international cooperation based on liberal economic theory tend to see sovereignty as an irrational obstacle to economic efficiency. However, as Harry G. Johnson points out, sovereignty and its trappings, as well as some degree of self-sufficiency, are important state goals, and cannot be termed "irrational."[57] The important point is not to judge states' goals, but to understand the implications of them.

Sovereignty is one of states' most fundamental goals, but by itself it does not do much for a state practically. While sovereignty is jealously guarded when threatened, without autonomy it does not confer genuine control over one's fate, and without effective government, does not guarantee prosperity to the state in question. However, the weaker the state in terms of autonomy, the more important sovereignty is likely to become: Jackson and Rosberg have shown that having one's sovereignty recognized formally by the international community can help states persist even when those states lack the basic characteristics of "empirical statehood," that is *de facto* sovereignty, or autonomy.[58] This is particularly important for the states of the former Soviet Union: Their sovereignty is new and fragile. It was admitted only reluctantly by Russia and by the world community, and many doubt these states' ability to maintain it. Moreover, Russia has not yet fully accepted it, and has at least some thoughts of trying to end it. These states, and especially Ukraine, whose struggle for sovereignty is more than 300 years old, are particularly concerned with asserting and safeguarding their sovereignty.

Prosperity versus Autonomy

The potential for interdependence to lead to power for one state and vulnerability for another creates a trade-off for some states between prosperity and autonomy. Traditional mercantilist theory equated wealth with power, and focusing on the balance of trade, saw gains in one state's wealth/power as losses for its partner.[59] Adam Smith's advance was not to question the relationship between wealth and power, but to show that trade was not a zero-sum game, and that both societies could become wealthier (and gain absolute power) simultaneously. He contrasted economic relations with political and military relations, arguing that while in the former both sides could gain simultaneously, in the latter they could not. The implication was that certain trade arrangements might be beneficial on economic grounds, but counterproductive for national security. Thus Smith defended protectionism in key sectors, including the Navigation Acts, stating that "defense is of more importance than opulence."[60]

The trade-off between autonomy and prosperity, which Smith called defense and opulence, occurs even in cases of symmetrical interdependence, because with a large degree of mutual dependence, domestic economies are heavily influenced by events and policies over which their governments have no control. This is the tension focused on in the vast majority of literature on interdependence, and it applies to the former Soviet Union.[61] However, the tension between prosperity and autonomy takes on an added dimension in situations where interdependence between two states is asymmetrical. As described in detail above, asymmetric interdependence creates the possibility for manipulation and coercion that does not exist with symmetric interdependence. The danger is increased not only because this interdependence can be purposefully manipulated, but also because it is easily linked to issues that transcend economics, including security, as Hirschman's analysis of German economic diplomacy demonstrates.

The vulnerable state therefore has a choice: It can maximize economic efficiency and prosperity by trading with the more powerful state, as liberal theory emphasizes. Doing so, however, leaves the state vulnerable to implicit or explicit coercion, the focus of realist approaches: If the more powerful state is not happy, it can injure the weaker at comparatively low cost to itself. Thus Keohane and Nye argue that for the state whose dominant goal is economic welfare, "interdependence restricts autonomy."[62]

The dependent state can preserve its autonomy—its insulation from the policies of other states—by reducing the interaction that leaves it vulnerable. The policy of economic isolation was advocated historically by theorists such as Rousseau and Fichte, and today by Ukrainian nationalists.[63] The state can simply do without the goods (or markets) provided by the partner, or it can find alternatives, either abroad or at home. If substitution is easy, then the dependence was not high in the first place. But if substitution is difficult, economic efficiency and prosperity will suffer from isolation. Autarky, comes at immense opportunity cost in terms of forgone benefits of trade. "For most countries . . . , the advantages of international involvement and the sheer impossibility of insulating themselves from the vicissitudes of international politics make autarky an unattractive strategy."[64] By cutting much trade with Russia for the sake of autonomy, Ukraine found significant sectors of its economy injured. To some extent, such a policy simply means injuring one's self to prevent others from threatening to do so. The state and society pay a heavy price for autarky.[65] Prosperity, therefore, is the opportunity cost payed for autonomy. The state seeking greater autonomy must, in an interdependent world, accept decreased prosperity. Keohane and Nye summarize the problem: "From the foreign-policy standpoint, the problem facing individual governments is how to benefit from international exchange while maintaining as much autonomy as possible."[66] Caporaso sees the problem similarly: "How much global involvement should a state foster and how much vulnerability and loss of autonomy is a state willing to suffer?"[67]

Prosperity versus Sovereignty

In much the same way that interdependence creates a trade-off between prosperity and autonomy, it creates a trade-off between prosperity and sovereignty. The trade-off between prosperity and sovereignty occurs because free trade is limited by a variety of nontariff barriers inherent in different legal and economic systems. Even after tariffs are removed, different labor, environmental, and other laws create barriers to trade, and therefore economic inefficiency. Thus the European Community has found it necessary to homogenize an increasing portion of states' domestic laws in order to promote efficiency and prosperity. Similarly, the United States under the Articles of Confederation found trade greatly hampered by the variety of economic laws. The interstate commerce clause of the Constitution was an effort to remove such inefficiency, but it also removed the states' sovereignty on certain trade matters.

Even a group as dedicated to integration as the EU has found this trade-off hard to make, as the slow progress and constant opposition to integration have shown. Having removed almost all other barriers to trade, the EU found the existence of different currencies a barrier to trade, and the establishment of a single currency was planned. While such a single currency would greatly decrease transaction costs, it would also remove the ability of states to govern their economies through monetary policy. When integration goes this far, the cost to sovereignty of increased prosperity can be quite high.

In the former Soviet Union, the same story is told in reverse. There, states with no sovereignty had a high degree of integration. When each state became independent, the goal of sovereignty was served, but the proliferation of different currencies and economic regimes has thrown trade into chaos, and production and standards of living have crashed.

The trade-off occurs when states consider means to increasing trade efficiency. Coordination of domestic economic policies is essential to efficient trade under high interdependence. To the extent that the necesary measures are not complex, coordination can occur on an ad hoc basis, as in the G-7 coordination of macroeconomic policies. But deeper coordination, such as that pursued in the European Union (and sometimes in the CIS), requires allowing supranational bodies to have some say over the types of laws and policies one can enact. Delegating decision making authority to such supranational bodies represents a reduction of the individual states' sovereignty. Thus many of the former Soviet states have resisted cooperating through the CIS because they fear that it threatens their sovereignty. Similarly, one of the objections raised in the United States to the new World Trade Organization is that membership would reduce U.S. sovereignty, particularly through the invalidation of laws viewed as barriers to trade.

If the pursuit of prosperity through trade and specialization passes a somewhat basic level, further prosperity can be attained only through decreases in sovereignty. Stanley Hoffman characterizes integration as "a process that devalues sovereignty, gradually brings about the demise of the nation-state, and leads to new foci of loyalty and authority."[68] It is precisely these results that many states fear from integration. In refusing to integrate, however, they place constraints on how efficient their trade can be, and therefore on how prosperous they can be. For the state concerned only with prosperity, hypothesized by much of the literature on interdependence, such a trade-off does not occur. But for those concerned with sovereignty, the trade-off is significant.

Autonomy versus Sovereignty

The first two trade-offs (prosperity vs. autonomy and prosperity vs. sovereignty) follow straightforwardly from economic theory. The third trade-off, that between autonomy and sovereignty, is somewhat paradoxical, because it seems that autonomy and sovereignty are so similar that they must largely co-vary. However, for economically vulnerable states (as for militarily vulnerable states), greater autonomy can be pursued at the expense of some sovereignty; and a defense of sovereignty can lead to decreased autonomy.

The trade-off becomes clear when one considers relations with international organizations. In the military realm, a small state (such as Norway) may increase its ability to resist threats from a powerful neighbor (such as the Soviet Union) if it joins with other states in an alliance (such as NATO). Joining an effective alliance, however, requires coordinating defense and foreign policies with other states, and decreases the state's sovereignty to make its own decisions. Thus military alliances involve an increase in autonomy at the expense of a decrease in sovereignty.

The same principle works in a more complicated way in economic organizations. A small state may increase its autonomy vis-à-vis strong trading partners by surrendering some of its autonomy to an international economic organization.[69] The increase in autonomy arises from two different characteristics of international organizations. First, they are multilateral, and may therefore alter the power relations between weak and strong. Second, they operate according to rules, which may constrain the largest power from using its power arbitrarily.

It is widely argued that in bilateral trade relations, the power of the strong over the weak is maximized.[70] Taken together, the small states may not be nearly as vulnerable as any of them are individually. Thus multilateral organizations may overcome the divide and conquer strategy of the largest and instead allow balancing by the weaker states. In the CIS, for example, Russia's population and GNP are roughly half of the whole. This imbalance is problematic, but perhaps not as problematic as the imbalance any of the individual states would have with Russia. Ukraine, the second largest of the successors, has roughly one-third the population of Russia and an even smaller share of GNP.

International organizations may protect the weak not only by diluting the power of strong states, but also by shifting the basis of outcomes from bargaining power to rules. In the absence of rules, power is the arbiter of disputes. In this realm the small state cannot succeed, and sovereignty loses its import.[71] In international organizations, decisions are made according to rules. By getting large states to agree to such rules, the small states can insulate themselves from their power. Keohane and Nye assert that "Small states often welcome international regimes as barriers to arbitrary abuse of power by the strong,"[72] and Krasner contends that the GATT has made it harder for any single state to exercise leverage over others.[73] Creating effective international institutions, however, requires small and large states alike to delegate some decision-making authority—sovereignty—to the institution.

Small states may be willing to surrender sovereignty to multilateral institutions, because absent greater autonomy, sovereignty can become "an empty shell."[74] Thus states cannot protect their independence simply by preserving *de jure* sovereignty. They face a trade-off between sovereignty and autonomy, between the ability to make one's own decisions, and the ability to have a meaningful range of options.[75] The small state dealing with the large in terms of power may retain the ability to make a formal decision, but if the alternatives are set out by the larger state, the smaller may not have much choice at all. By joining international organizations, the small state can hope, by giving up some sovereignty, to face a more palatable range of alternatives. Donald Puchala argues that international institutions actually enhance the sovereignty of small states because institutions tend to respect sovereignty, whereas power politics does not.[76]

This is the dilemma faced by the small states of Western Europe, and by the small states of the CIS, who hope to assert their newly established statehood by refusing to delegate sovereignty to international organizations. Maintaining sovereignty does not maintain these states' independence, broadly construed. The large degree of economic dependence on Russia, especially in the energy sphere, means that Russia has the ability to coerce the other states on a wide variety of issues. Ukraine, for example, has retained its sovereignty, but this might simply mean sovereignty to decide between doing what Russia wants and having energy supplies reduced. Some therefore assert that economic integration will actually increase Ukraine's independence.[77] As Hirschman argues, it is impossible to prevent states from using foreign trade coercively without severely restricting sovereignty.[78]

Exactly how much autonomy can be gained by joining international organizations depends on the decision rules of the organization. If decision-making is shifted from the realm of raw power to that of majority voting and one-state-one-vote, small states can find themselves transformed from weakness to a situation where individually they have as much power as the large states, and collectively they have more. For this reason voting rules have been a main axis of conflict in the debate over the CIS. There is a conflict of interest between the largest state, which wishes to maintain the ability to take advantage of its economic power, and the smaller states, who wish to gain influence through voting power.

It is not certain that international organizations will constrain the power of the largest members. Indeed, the opposite is possible, as the Warsaw Treaty and Comecon demonstrated. Some, therefore, fear that international organizations will empower the strong more than the weak, and that along with eroding small states' sovereignty, will erode their autonomy. For example, some fear that German influence on a common European currency might enable it to increase its influence on other members of the EU.[79]

Whether international organizations increase or decrease the power of the weak is theoretically unclear, and probably depends on the specifics of the institutions created. Figuring out what effect an organization would have on autonomy is a critical question for the vulnerable state seeking to guard its autonomy. The uncertain effects of greater integration are one of the main barriers to further cooperation between Ukraine and Russia. The unfortunate examples of the treaty of Pereiaslav and the 1922 Union Treaty make it difficult for many Ukrainians to believe that an economic union will not lead to renewed Russian dominance.[80] Statements by some Russians that such a result is precisely their intention makes the matter even worse.

There are therefore two distinct ways in which the potential trade-off between sovereignty and autonomy presents difficulties for Ukrainian policy. First, as a newly sovereign state, Ukraine values its sovereignty highly, and must ask how much precious sovereignty is worth surrendering for increased political autonomy. Second, Ukraine must assess any proposed institutions to see whether they would actually increase autonomy, or decrease it. Ukraine might be willing to sacrifice some sovereignty for increased autonomy, but it wants to be sure not to surrender sovereignty only to find that its autonomy has been reduced as a result.

These dilemmas have been developed here in terms of general theoretical principles of international political economy, but they have very practical relevance for the political economy of the former Soviet Union. When Ukraine chose to assert its autonomy in early 1992 by breaking trade ties with Russia, it chose to privilege autonomy over prosperity. Leonid Kravchuk's reluctant admission the following year that some form of economic union was necessary signaled a rethinking of the trade-off between these two values. Russia's threat in September 1993 to cut the supply of gas to Ukraine if it did not agree to sell the Black Sea Fleet to Russia, and Ukraine's refusal, demonstrated the political effects of economic vulnerability, and also Ukraine's choice to assert its sovereignty rather than assuring its prosperity. Ukraine's steadfast resistance to participate in any CIS agreements that create new international institutions, or that do not allow Ukraine a veto, demonstrates Ukraine's commitment to preserving its sovereignty at the cost of increased autonomy and prosperity. These three dilemmas are not the only ones that characterize Ukraine's economic relations with Russia, but they are the defining ones, and they assert themselves in all of the major issues of Ukrainian-Russia economic relations.

The Dilemmas and the Cases

The following three chapters concern three particularly important areas of Ukrainian-Russian relations where the dangers of interdependence are clear and these three dilemmas play themselves out.

Ukraine's dependence on Russia for energy is discussed in chapter 4. Energy dependence is significant because it most powerfully demonstrates Ukraine's economic vulnerability. Ukraine's economy simply cannot function without the oil and gas supplied by Russia. This vulnerability has been converted to a direct challenge to Ukraine's autonomy and prosperity, in the form of Russian threats to cut the supply if certain political concessions are not made. Ukraine's dilemma has been that to have any chance of prosperity, it must remain in a position of meager autonomy. Ukraine's reliance on Russian energy supplies, more than any other single factor, makes a strategy of economy isolation—which would maximize autonomy—completely untenable because of the welfare costs. However, Russia's energy leverage is not unlimited, and Ukraine has striven to find ways to reduce the effectiveness of that leverage. Moreover, Russia's play of the "energy card" has clarified for Ukrainian leaders the dangers inherent in reliance on Moscow.

The breakdown of trade with Russia (chapter 5), partially intentional, has been the broadest source of strain on the Ukrainian economy, and one of the most divisive internally, due to the concentration of its effects in Eastern Ukraine. The breakdown is not so much a case of explicit coercion, as with energy vulnerability, but rather a case where trade and prosperity require increased international cooperation. Here, prosperity conflicts with autonomy and sovereignty, one or both of which must be sacrificed in some form to keep the economy from collapsing.

Having decided to trade with Russia to prevent economic collapse, Ukraine has had to decide which aspects of trade should be regulated internationally, and how this should be done. Bilateral agreements with Russia have preserved Ukrainian sovereignty, but they are not the most efficient means, and therefore sacrifice some prosperity. Moreover, they keep Ukraine in a very disadvantageous bargaining position, which limits autonomy. The primary alternative presented has been the CIS (chapter 6), and the CIS remains a crucial issue because it engages these fundamental goals. A strong CIS, which could promote multilateral economic coordination, would help remedy many of the problems of the trade breakdown. Moreover, it might allow Ukraine to join together with other states to increase their bargaining leverage vis-à-vis Russia, thus augmenting autonomy as well as prosperity. A strong CIS has two potential costs to weigh against the potential gains in prosperity and autonomy. First, an effective CIS would entail a diminution of all members' sovereignty. Second, if not constructed carefully, the CIS could prove disastrous for the smaller states: if it does not constrain Russia's ability to wield its power, it could diminish autonomy and prosperity as well, thus representing a simultaneous decline in all three goals. Both of these costs have mitigated against Ukrainian participation in a strong CIS: Ukrainian leaders are extremely skeptical that the organization will really augment prosperity and autonomy in return for a sacrifice of some sovereignty. And even if they are convinced of this, they are still not sure that they would want to make the sacrifice of sovereignty.

Ukrainian policy has evolved since independence in three ways. First, the dilemmas themselves have been clarified as the dust from the collapse of the Soviet Union has settled. Originally, for example, Ukrainian leaders acted as though sovereignty and autonomy would covary, until breaking ties with Russia left the economy so weak that Russia found it easy to make demands. Second, Ukrainian priorities have evolved and been clarified: sovereignty, while still an important goal of Ukrainian leaders, no longer is held to be untouchable. Third, the Ukrainian domestic situation has changed, and the severity of Ukraine's vulnerability has changed accordingly: as Ukraine's domestic divisions have narrowed to some extent, the governement has been more able to adopt an economic strategy.

Conclusion

The history of international political economy is characterized by states' efforts to maximize both their economic wealth and their political power. It is virtually impossible to trade in such a way that does not create vulnerability and therefore create some threat to state autonomy. The more vulnerable the state is, the larger the trade-offs between autonomy, prosperity, and sovereignty. Because most contemporary analyses of interdependence focus on the advanced industrial states, and take state sovereignty for granted, they present relatively straightforward tradeoffs between autonomy and prosperity, and show how western states have secured tolerable amounts of both. The situation in the former Soviet Union is considerably less tractable for the small states. The extreme vulnerability, the high priority on sovereignty, the high level of threat perception, and the chaotic state of the economies preclude an easy resolution of the dilemmas of interdependence.

Ukraine spent its first three years of independence discovering the seriousness of its economic and political predicament and is now trying to develop a solution that provides acceptable levels of autonomy, prosperity, and sovereignty. It is not clear what this solution might be. More significantly, it is not yet clear that such a solution exists. If a solution does not exist, or cannot be found, the future of Ukraine's statehood is in doubt, and so in turn is the emerging political order in post–Cold War Europe.

Part II

Issues

4

The Energy War, 1993–1994

The existence of Ukraine as a sovereign European state is
directly connected with the solution of the problem of energy
in all the basic sectors of the economy.
—Volodymyr Diukov, "Shchob vyity z enerhetichnoi kryzy"

No single issue has demonstrated the danger created by Ukraine's vulnerability to Russia more vividly than its reliance on Russia for much of its
energy supply. Because Ukraine depends on Russia for the energy that runs its
economy, a cutoff would be devastating. The Russian government is aware of
this, and has worked to maintain and increase the dependency, as well as to exploit it. On several occasions, the Russian government has explicitly threatened
an energy cutoff if Ukraine does not submit to the Russian position on various
issues. Implicitly, the issue pervades every facet of the Russian-Ukrainian relationship. It became explicit during the "energy war" of 1993–1994, when Russia actively tried to use Ukraine's energy dependence to force submission on
several outstanding issues. While Ukraine has, since 1996, been increasingly
able to pay for its energy supplies, the latent threat of a cutoff remains, and energy continues to be an important national security concern for Ukraine.

Energy politics are crucial to the issues of dependence and autonomy discussed in this book for three related reasons. First, energy is a crucial sector of
the economy in which Ukraine is highly dependent on supplies from Russia.
Ukraine's economy is highly vulnerable to energy shortages, because much of
the economy is energy intensive.[1] Second, therefore, energy highlights the
perceived dangers of a large degree of economic dependence on Russia. Third,
energy dependency has in fact been used by Russia to attempt to persuade
Ukraine to give way on a whole range of issues. In energy, therefore, Ukrainian fears about interdependence with Russia have already been realized.

The energy relationship shows most clearly how vulnerability creates a
trade-off between autonomy and prosperity for Ukraine. Ukraine's economy
would suffer tremendously from a cutoff of Russian energy sources. Russian

energy comes at below-world-market prices, credit terms have often been liberal, and other supplies are not readily available. In a strictly economic sense, the energy trade with Russia is highly beneficial to Ukraine. This benefit, however, is a political liability, because it can so easily be removed, at a comparatively small cost to Russia. In terms of the criteria laid out in the previous chapter, the energy trade provides a powerful lever for Russia to use to influence Ukraine's policies.

This lever, however, has had only limited success in forcing change in Ukrainian government policy, for a number of reasons. One has been that Ukraine has largely been willing to sacrifice its prosperity rather than meet Russia's terms for steady energy supplies. Another has been that Russia has hesitated to employ the lever to its fullest extent—an all-out embargo. A third has been the Russian desire to hold the weapon in reserve for the future. Ukraine, therefore, has so far been able to resist submitting to Russian demands without seeing its energy supplies completely cut. Indeed, one notable result of Russian attempts to threaten Ukraine with an energy cutoff has been a stiffening of the Ukrainian government's resolve. While Ukraine has never directly caved in to Russian demands, the damage to Ukraine's economy by reduced gas supplies has been significant, and the indirect effects on Ukraine's policy are noticeable. Ukraine's isolationist economic policy has been moderated, and Ukrainian nationalism has lost is dominant role in the country's policy making. A weakening in enthusiasm for independence may also be attributable in part to the hardship incurred by the "energy war."

This chapter examines the problems created by Ukraine's energy vulnerability and Russian attempts to exploit that vulnerability. It then focuses on Ukraine's responses to these trade-offs, and explores why Ukraine has so far been able to avoid the worst potential outcomes. This issue demonstrates the leverage that results from dependence as well as the limits to that leverage, and it shows the high cost in prosperity Ukraine paid to preserve its autonomy.

The International Politics of Oil

Since oil became the lifeblood of industry (and war) in the early twentieth century, control of its supply and transport has been a key issue in international politics, and the struggle over oil has been both a means and an end in many of the major conflicts of the century.[2] In World War II, the need for a secure supply of oil was a driving force behind Japanese expansion into Southeast Asia and eventually the war with the United States. It was equally important in Germany's war aims first in Eastern Europe, and then in the drive toward the Caucasus in the Soviet Union, and in the end shortage of oil seriously hampered the German war effort. More recently, the prospect of Iraq substantially increasing its control over Persian Gulf oil was an important factor in U.S. determination to dislodge Iraq from Kuwait in 1990–1991.

Oil has been important not simply as the fuel of war, however. The reliance of modern industry on petroleum has meant that oil can also be used, without recourse to war, to injure other states' economies. The rise of OPEC, and in particular the oil embargo of 1973, demonstrated that even powerful countries could be severely injured if their oil supplies were disrupted. Following that boycott, many oil-importing industrial states adapted national security strategies for energy, involving diversifying sources, building up reserves, and decreasing reliance on petroleum. These are the types of problems confronted by Ukraine today, though it is much less able to adjust than more prosperous and advanced states.

Nor is the use of energy leverage new to Russian strategy. In the late 1950s, the Soviet Union began exporting oil to the West and quickly became a significant player in the world market. In addition to providing a much needed source of income, the Soviet role in the energy market was intended to provide leverage over Western customers. By 1960, the Soviet Union had become the second largest oil producer in the world (after the United States). The issue of vulnerability was raised in the 1980s with the building of a pipeline to bring Soviet natural gas to customers in Western Europe. The Reagan administration strongly opposed the pipeline, contending that it would make Western Europe dependent on Soviet gas, and therefore subject to Soviet coercion. Neither the fact of Ukraine's energy dependence nor the political problems created by it is unique in international politics. As we shall see, however, Ukraine's case of energy vulnerability is particularly acute, and Ukraine is poorly equipped economically and politically to maneuver its way out of the corner in which it finds itself.

The Soviet Legacy

Ukraine has the reputation of being a land of great natural wealth, and while that may have been true once, decades of Soviet economic policies have left Ukraine today deeply dependent on imported petroleum. It is unclear whether Soviet policy was intended to foster that dependence, or if it was coincidental, but especially in the Brezhnev era, Soviet energy policy "became increasingly disadvantageous from the Ukrainian standpoint."[3] For our purposes, however, the result is most important. Soviet energy policy created the current Ukrainian dependence in three important ways. First, under the Soviet system, the Ukrainian economy became very reliant on energy-intensive sectors, such as ferrous metallurgy, petroleum refining, and chemical and building-material industries. These three sectors accounted for 23 percent of final energy consumption in 1980.[4] The energy consumption of these industries is exacerbated by the fact that their capital stock is obsolete and inefficient. In the 1980s, it took 60 percent more energy to produce a ton of steel in Ukraine than in Japan.[5]

Second, and related, in the Soviet Union the petroleum industry was heavily subsidized. Because energy was artificially cheap, consumption patterns were built up, and capital allocated, in a way that was perhaps rational given cheap energy, but is extremely irrational in terms of world market prices. For example, portions of industries could exist at great distances from each other, because with subsidized oil, transportation of components was cheap. Similarly, with energy cheap and capital scarce, it did not pay to invest in technology to increase energy efficiency. Because of the artificially low price of energy, Ukraine used much more energy than it would have otherwise. Even the agriculture sector in Ukraine was structured on the assumption of cheap fuel for transport. With supplies insecure and prices rising after the collapse of the Soviet Union, Ukraine has consumption patterns and capital stock that are inappropriate to the new conditions.

Third, in the Soviet system, Ukraine's considerable indigenous supplies of energy were extensively depleted. The rich Donbas coal mines have produced approximately 8.4 billion tons so far, but easily minable deposits have been exhausted.[6] Ukraine's three petroleum producing regions have been exhausted, in part because development of Siberian deposits took longer than expected. The remaining reserves are in deep and scattered pockets.[7] In addition to the energy problems created by resource depletion, Ukraine is faced with the politically touchy issue of closing the mines, which are inefficient but employ a large and politically active labor force.

The results of these three trends have been decisive. Ukraine, which as late as 1970 had a small overall energy surplus, had a 42 percent net energy deficit by 1988. "No other region or republic has seen its energy position change more rapidly for the worse than Ukraine."[8] The belief that Ukraine was being exploited economically was a driving force behind Ukraine's declarations of sovereignty in 1990 and of independence in 1991, but Ukraine gained control of its natural resources after most of them had already been extracted and consumed.

Ukraine's Current Energy Situation

The legacy of Soviet planning is a Ukraine that is in deep trouble in the energy sphere. "Among the large republics, Ukraine is in the most difficult situation because of its rapidly falling coal production, shrinking electric power generation capacity, and its need to import large amounts of increasingly expensive oil and gas."[9] Vulnerability aside, the expense in adjusting to market prices for energy would be immensely disruptive to the economy. It has been estimated that simply raising the prices of Russian raw material to world levels would cause the transfer of 30 percent of Ukraine's GDP to Russia.[10] "This is one reason why stagflation occurred in Ukraine just as it did in OECD countries in the 1970s following the OPEC oil price increases."[11] The need to import energy from a potential adversary adds an international political dimension to an already bleak domestic picture. The problem has assumed two important parts for Ukraine and Russia. First, energy dependence makes Ukraine vulnerable to an embargo. Second, Ukraine has on several occasions, most notably in 1994, accumulated massive debts to Russia for its energy imports.

Ukraine must import a significant portion of its energy supplies, and nearly all of these imports must come from Russia.[12] In 1991, Ukraine's total fossil fuel consumption (oil, coal, and gas), amounted to 202 million tons of oil equivalent (MTOE).[13] Of this, 110 MTOE, or over 50 percent, was imported. An exact breakdown of suppliers is unavailable, but the vast majority of the gas, and virtually all the oil and coal, comes from Russia, with some gas coming from Turkmenistan.[14] Overall, Ukraine imports more than two-thirds of its fossil fuels.[15] In aggregate terms, therefore, the dependence on Russia is massive.

Broken down into sectors, the dependence becomes even more problematic, because it is concentrated in two crucial fuels: oil and natural gas. In 1991 Ukraine imported about 90 percent of the oil it consumed (49 MTOE of 54 MTOE), as well as about 77 percent of its gas (69 MTOE of 89 MTOE).[16] It was a small net exporter of coal (8 MTOE)[17] and electricity.[18]

In order to assess Ukraine's vulnerability, we need to know not only how much fuel it imports, but also what role the fuels play in the economy. Of Ukraine's overall energy needs, 26 percent are accounted for by oil, 35 percent by gas, 34 percent by coal, and 4 percent by nuclear and hydro.[19] Gas and oil, which together account for 61 percent of Ukraine's energy, are the areas in which it is so dependent on Russia. Perhaps the single most important statistic is that Ukraine depends on Russia for 40 percent of its overall energy needs.[20]

When Russia chooses to reduces gas and oil deliveries, or simply to raise prices, the consequences in Ukraine are immense.[21] Because Ukrainian industries were built on the presumption of cheap fuel, the rise in prices has made many of their products too expensive to be profitable. The lack of revenue to these enterprises has resulted either in unemployment, or various substitutes for it, such as worker furloughs or the nonpayment of wages. It also has resulted in a series of severe austerity measures, in which industries were simply closed, buildings were not heated, streets were dark, and television broadcasts curtailed. Unrest among the Ukrainian population and the dissatisfaction with the government have been the natural results. To the extent that Moscow has deliberately manipulated the supply and price of energy, it has been in the hope that the hardship would cause Ukrainians to rethink the wisdom of their sharp break with Russia. By mid-1994 that strategy seemed to be working. Thus Russia can pressure the Ukrainian directly, by convincing leaders that the country cannot withstand reduced supplies, and indirectly, by reducing the living standards of the people, and hence their enthusiasm for the government and perhaps even for independence.

At the level of international politics, Ukraine's energy trade with Russia has yielded two types of threats that Russia can apply, although both rely to some extent on the threat of a cutoff. First, because Russia continues to supply a huge share of Ukraine's energy needs, it can manipulate the supply. It can do so either by reducing deliveries (or even stopping them altogether) or by changing the price. Price can work either as a carrot or a stick: On the one hand, non-Russian republics were told that refusal to participate in certain CIS functions would result in a raising of prices to world levels, with payment in hard currency required and no credit available; on the other hand, continued subsidies, and sometimes even increased subsidies, have been offered to those who would conform with Moscow's preferred order in the region. For example, a lowering of Russian oil prices to Belarus has been a part of negotiations over economic union between the two states.[22]

Second, Ukraine's inability to pay for all the gas and oil it consumes, coupled with Russian willingness to extend credit, has led to the accumulation of a massive debt. By early 1994, Ukrainian debt to Russia was estimated at $2 billion.[23] Much of this was owed by the Ukrainian government to the Russian gas monopoly, Gazprom, for natural gas, and the debt was subsequently converted into state debt between Russia and Ukraine. Russia has threatened to call in the debt if political demands are not met, and, conversely, has offered to forgive part or all of the debt in return for certain assets (most notably the Black Sea Fleet, nuclear weapons, or Ukrainian gas pipelines). As this debt rises, however, it may turn into a political asset for Ukraine, because if Russian policies injure Ukrainian too much, Ukraine will be unable to pay it back.[24]

It is important to recognize, however, that when Russia has raised prices or cut supplies, it has not necessarily done so in an effort to coerce Ukraine. A rise in prices to world levels is necessary in both states as a part of economic reform, and rising fuel prices have caused much disruption in Russia as well as in Ukraine. Gazprom has threatened to cut gas deliveries to Russia's own regions in order to force overdue payments.[25] Had Russia followed the dictates of "shock therapy" and immediately moved to world market prices, the effects on Ukraine would have been even more devastating. Similarly, Russian threats to Ukraine and other republics have sometimes been necessary to get the customers to pay their overdue bills.[26]

As noted in the previous chapter, however, it is precisely by offering more beneficial terms than are available on the world market that the powerful state can create vulnerability. If Russia had immediately gone to world market prices, the domestic effects in Ukraine would have been catastrophic, but the international political effects would have been marginal.[27] By maintaining favorable supply conditions, Russia—intentionally or otherwise—created for itself a powerful lever. For our purposes it is less important to debate Russian motivations than to examine how this vulnerability has been dealt with in practice. After an initial phase in which the main stated reason for gas cutoffs was the nonpayment for previous deliveries, the energy supply and debt issues have become increasingly linked to unrelated political questions.

Russian Energy Firms and the Russian Government

At this point, a digression into the links between energy firms and the Russian government is necessary. Given the fissiparous nature of Russian politics, and the weakness of the Russian government, how is it possible that the Russian government can force powerful firms such as Gazprom and Lukoil to do its bidding in relations with Ukraine? The murky nature of Russian politics and business make it impossible to say exactly how energy firms relate to the government, but there is clear evidence that they work in concert in the arena of foreign policy.[28] That evidence comes in six categories: statements by leaders, the personal links between government and energy concerns, government ownership of stakes in the firms, the government's role in international energy contracts, and the government's ability in many areas to make even the largest firms to work toward government goals. Most significant, there is considerable direct evidence of the Russian government successfully using the energy firms in foreign policy.

The first indication that the government is behind threats of cutoffs and actual cutoffs, even when carried out by firms that appear to have been privatized, is the statements by top officials such as Boris Yeltsin and Vice-Premier Mikhail Poltoranin indicating a desire to use the energy lever for the purpose of promoting reintegration.[29] One possible conduit for such coordination is the number of oil and gas officials prominent in the Russian government, which has prompted the observation that "Gazprom management and the Russian government are so closely intertwined that it is difficult to say which is controlling the other."[30] Yeltsin's former Prime Minister, Viktor Chernomyrdin, was former director of Gazprom, and reputedly holds a large block of stock. Moreover, even after the firms were privatized, the Russian government has continued to hold considerable stakes in them, in many cases remaining the largest stakeholder. For example, the state holds the largest share of Gazprom's stock, and even after the oil industry was restructured, controlling interest remained with the Ministry of Fuel and Energy.[31] As of mid-1997, Aleksandr Kazakov, Yeltsin's first deputy chief of staff, was chair of the Board of Directors of Gazprom, and five of the board's eleven directors represented the state.[32] Particularly during the key events described in this chapter (from 1993–1994), the Russian government was able to control these industries through the most direct form: ownership. "Although Russia's energy enterprises were nominally privatized, the government remained their largest shareholder. Thus, state interests always entered into negotiations between Russia and its smaller neighbors."[33]

It is possible, however, that with privatization, the potential for such coercion would decrease. However, the links between government and energy firms remain tight, and the government continues to play a large role in what those firms do. The government is able to have its way with the firms not only through personal ties, but through the incentives it can offer, particularly in tax breaks.[34] Thus it is possible that despite generating $30 billion in hard currency exports in 1995, Russian energy firms are among the biggest tax debtors to the government.[35] Moreover, in privatizing the firms to a narrow circle of banks and large investors at cut-rate prices, the government has created a certain indebtedness among the new owners. Evidence of the state's continued ability to control the industry is the persistence of government price controls to keep prices down. The same type of control occurs for foreign policy goals: "When the government, for strategic reasons, makes decisions that impose costs on energy producers, the latter expect compensation when it comes to export policy, prices, and taxes."[36]

More concretely, because the government retains control on export licenses, which are crucial in a time when hard currency is scarce and domestic customers rarely pay their bills, companies out of favor with the government can potentially be ruined. As Hirschman argues, the state does not need to control or own business to use it for political purposes: it need only control the ability to export and import. Apparently energy firms have opposed allocation of pipeline access through competetive tender, finding it more profitable to make deals with the state than to compete on price. The result is a powerful state lever.

Despite privatization, the Russian government has also been involved in the energy industry as a negotiator. In 1994 Ukraine and Russia signed a treaty agreeing that transit tariffs on pipelines could be raised only by government-level agreement. The agreement clearly presupposes the governments' ability to regulate the relevant firms accordingly. In 1995, Mobil signed its deal to export Russian oil not with the relevant Russian firm, but with Prime Minister Chernomyrdin.

All this evidence is compelling but circumstantial. The "smoking gun" is provided by several public cases of linkage that substantiate the Russian government's ability to use energy for foreign policy. In the case of the Massandra summit, described below, Gazprom cut gas deliveries immediately prior to the summit. More significantly, the Russian government offered to erase Ukraine's gas debt in return for concessions on security issues. How could the government cancel a debt owed to Gazprom? It is unclear, but we must assume that the government would either pay Gazprom the sum owed, or compensate it in some other way. The 1996 "zero option" agreement between Russia and Belarus included an elimination of Belarus's debt to Gazprom, for which Gazprom was not directly compensated by the government. The government did, however, negotiate on Gazprom's behalf duty-free transport across Belarus.[37]

In sum, while the exact nature of the relationship between Russia's energy firms and its government is not clear, it appears that they work together for the mutual benefit of both. The government uses its political and diplomatic muscle to help energy firms gain concessions in other countries, particularly in the former Soviet Union. The energy firms help the government put pressure on the same states. We need not conclude that the government completely controls the energy firms, or that there is never dispute over the best policies, or resistance to cooperating with the government's plans. The cases of joint action by the government and the energy firms, most importantly Gazprom, are numerous and significant enough to pose a problem for the Ukrainian government and its citizens.

Russian Attempts at Coercion

The problem of paying for Russian oil and gas (and, to a lesser extent, for Turkmen gas) has plagued Ukraine almost since independence. After the various republics declared sovereignty in 1990, agreements were worked out to continue trade in 1991 at 1990 levels. But in the first two months of Ukrainian independence (December 1991–January 1992) Russian oil supplies to Ukraine fell short of Ukrainian needs by 600,000 tons.[38] Shortages of supply have continued to the present day, and Ukraine's inability to pay even for those supplies which it did receive has been equally problematical. The first emergency for Ukraine came in February 1992 when Prime Minister Vitold Fokin rushed to Turkmenistan to plead with the Turkmen government not to raise the price of gas tenfold or cut off supplies to debtors, as planned.[39] The following month, Fokin went to Moscow on a similar mission.[40]

To this point the story was a traditional one of economic interdependence: events in one economy (liberalization of fuel prices) produce shocks in other economies (higher prices in Ukraine). Russia was not necessarily raising prices (or cutting supplies) to Ukraine in an attempt to undermine Ukraine's independence. The price rise in particular can be attributed to the Russian domestic economic reform plan, which emphasized liberalizing prices to enable market forces to work. Since the price of oil is determined by the world market, this meant raising Russian domestic prices to equal what the products could be sold for abroad. Russia has in fact not brought domestic prices up to the world level, but it has consistently reduced subsidies, both domestically and to its FSU customers. The natural result, then, of Russia's reform plan, is that the price of oil and gas to Ukraine would increase. The decrease in supply is harder to explain, but at least initially, there was no hard evidence of coercion (of which Ukrainian officials routinely accused Russia), but merely of disruption following the collapse of the Union. The decline in oil deliveries may be linked to the drop in Russian oil production in recent years.[41]

By early 1993, however, the energy issue became explicitly linked to political matters, as Russia linked the continuation of fuel deliveries to Ukraine to Ukrainian concessions on the ongoing issue of repaying the debts of the old Soviet Union. The linkage was made explicit by the Russian ambassador to Ukraine, Leonid Smolyakov, in a press conference 5 February 1993, and repeated by Deputy Prime Minister Alexandr Shokin on 8 February.[42] Energy supplies became a main tool in Russia's efforts to order the former Soviet Union, and softening the potential blow from an energy cutoff has been a central theme in Ukraine's foreign and domestic politics. By September 1993, Russia was explicitly demanding major political concessions in return for continued supply, while Ukraine resisted. Through the spring of 1994, energy politics was the major front in an increasingly hostile relationship. This phase of overt coercion lasted until autumn 1994, when the situation was stabilized to some degree. Ukraine's energy vulnerability remains, as does the latent threat of coercion, so the issue remains an important one.

The Massandra Summit

The linkage between energy dependence and political pressure came to the fore at the Massandra summit in early September 1993. The summit, in the Crimean resort of Massandra, was aimed at resolving two issues: the Black Sea Fleet and Ukraine's nuclear disarmament. A week before the summit,

Gazprom cut its supply of gas to Ukraine by 25 percent, citing Ukrainian non-payment as the reason. At Massandra, Russian negotiators caught the Ukrainian delegation off guard by proposing a cancellation of Ukrainian gas debt in return for full control of the Black Sea Fleet and the surrender of Ukraine's nuclear warheads. If Ukraine did not agree, the Russians said, gas supplies would be halted. The Ukrainian leadership apparently agreed to the deal, but denied this when word of the sale of the Black Sea Fleet caused an uproar in the Verkhovna Rada and the country.[43]

The significant point in this summit was that the Russian government explicitly linked the issues of energy supply and debt to issues that were basically unrelated, and cut to the heart of Ukraine's national security. As Kravchuk described the meeting:

> In the Crimea [Massandra], it was said in no uncertain terms . . . that if Ukraine did not find the means to settle its debt and make payments for energy carriers, that are due now, Russia would be forced to suspend oil and gas deliveries to Ukraine entirely. This was said in no uncertain terms, rather than hinted at. . . . This was the situation the delegations had to work in.[44]

Yeltsin's version of events was similar, though expressed more gently.[45] This represented a more assertive Russian policy, and highlighted to Ukrainian diplomats (who accused Russia of "economic diktat") the vulnerability to economic pressure not only of Ukraine's economy, but of the whole range of Ukraine's political and security interests. If Russia could use the energy card to force Ukraine to cave in on the Black Sea Fleet, it could force concessions on nearly any other issue. The point was further underscored in November 1993, when *Izvestiya* cited unnamed officials in the Russian Foreign Ministry as saying Russia might bring economic pressure to bear on Ukraine to surrender its nuclear weapons.[46]

Russia intended to present Ukraine with a deal it could not refuse. It was somewhat unthinkable what chaos would ensue if the gas were turned off. Industry would halt, as would generation of electricity that relied on gas. People would be unable to cook their food, heat water, or heat their apartments. Civil disorder and the collapse of the state might follow. Given this prospect, Kravchuk did what the Russian negotiators expected, accepting "economic realities," including the reliance of Ukraine's economy on Russian energy, the massive debt, and the inability of Ukraine to come up with the cash necessary to pay the debt. For him, selling "part" of the Black Sea Fleet to Russia was a necessary, if unpleasant, solution. "We had to act on the basis of realism. Suppose we had slammed the door and left. The gas would have been turned off and there would have been nothing else left to do."[47] "If we were rich," he said, "we would be talking differently."[48] Nationalist parliamentarian Dmytro Pavlychko criticized the agreement, but accepted that Russia's use of the energy lever made compromise necessary. Socialist Party leader Oleksandr Moroz was equally realistic: "The danger (for Ukraine) is not having a Russian base on its territory, it is having bad relations with Russia."[49]

Many Ukrainians, however, refused to be "realistic," and in fact there was little debate in Ukraine concerning how to deal with the matter. There was an uproar as parliamentarians from across the political spectrum accused Kravchuk of selling out Ukrainian interests and even of treason. Kravchuk found little support for his position, because even those who advocated closer ties with Russia objected to Russia's heavy-handed methods. Allowing Ukraine to be pressured in this way was "capitulationism," and not to be tolerated. Kravchuk backpedaled furiously and laboriously asserted that the agreements were discussed, but not actually signed (the evidence appeared otherwise) and that they had to be ratified by parliament in any event. This was clearly not going to happen.

The Massandra agreements were never implemented; indeed, it was never resolved what exactly had been agreed on. However, they had an important impact in Ukrainian policy toward energy dependence in the coming months: they stiffened Ukrainian resolve by convincing many Ukrainians of Russia's unfriendly intentions and put the issue of energy dependence more seriously on the political agenda. Prior to Massandra, Ukraine used two methods to attain the energy necessary for its economy. The first method was begging suppliers not to cut Ukraine off. This was moderately successful for a time, but Yeltsin's Massandra ultimatum made it clear that the costs in political terms could be high. And while the Massandra threat was not immediately carried out, it remained possible to do so at any time. Second, Ukraine had explored alternative suppliers, particularly in the Middle East, but this had proved unpromising, especially in the short term.

Massandra forced Ukraine to face squarely the trade-off between autonomy and prosperity. It also helped create the political will in Ukraine to adopt more drastic measures. By October 1993, the energy crisis had forced the closure of half of Kiev's industrial enterprises,[50] and the coldest November in fifty years helped force the issue for Ukraine. Through the winter of 1993–1994, most public buildings were not heated, most streetlights were turned out, and Ukrainian television began operating on a reduced schedule in order to conserve energy. Gas for heat of residences was maintained in most places, but many industries were idled through the winter.[51] Ukraine's refusal to give in to Russia's demand had a very high domestic price. Russia's hard line made clear the trade-off between autonomy and prosperity, and Ukrainians chose autonomy at a very high cost to prosperity.

The Attempt to Control Ukrainian Pipelines

In early 1994, Russia shifted the focus of its energy offensive, seeking owner-ship of Ukrainian gas and oil facilities rather than political concessions. This policy, discussed first in October 1993,[52] became the focus of talks in March and April of 1994. There appear to be four reasons for the shift in Russian aims. First, the policy of linking oil supplies to the Black Sea Fleet did not work. Ukraine refused to give in, and Russia was unwilling to carry out the threat. Second, the trilateral nuclear weapons agreement of January 1994 re-moved the need to use energy supplies to cajole Ukraine on that issue, though indications are that promises of below-world-price energy sales and debt can-cellation played a significant, if not crucial part, in that deal.[53] Third, and per-haps most important, Ukraine's pipelines and storage facilities provided the one element of Ukrainian leverage in the energy relationship: If Russia cut off supplies to Ukraine, Ukraine could stop transporting Russian natural gas to the rest of Europe, eliminating a major source of hard currency revenue. Finally, Russia was undertaking a broad program in the spring of 1994 to increase its control in the oil and gas industry of the former Soviet Union, in which Ukrainian facilities played only one part.[54] Ukrainian pipelines and storage facilities were important both as sources of revenue and as levers of control.

By February 1994, Ukraine's debt to Russia for natural gas reached a tril-lion rubles, and Gazprom again began reducing the supply of gas to Ukraine.[55] By the beginning of March, the supply of gas to Ukraine from Russia was down to one-fifth the normal level, and a meeting was set for 10 March to re-solve the crisis.[56] Russian officials emphasized that full payment in cash was expected on 10 March, though property rights to Ukrainian pipelines would be accepted as a substitute.[57] By this time Ukrainian debt to Russia was $1 bil-lion for gas, and $3.2 billion for energy overall.[58] Ukraine was flexing what muscles it had, allegedly siphoning off gas from the pipelines that served West-ern Europe. A senior Ukrainian official denied that Ukraine was siphoning gas, but threatened that Ukraine might have to do so if its own supplies were cut.[59] At the 10 March meeting, Ukrainian Vice-Prime Minister Valentyn Landyk agreed that in return for the resumption of gas supplies from Russia, Ukraine would pay the debt accrued already in 1994 in rubles or hard cur-rency, and pay half of the debt from 1993 in cash and the other half by trans-ferring ownership in Ukrainian gas facilities. In particular, it was agreed that Gazprom would obtain a majority stake (51%) in the pipelines crossing Ukraine.[60]

If implemented, the deal would have removed Ukraine's primary means of deterring a complete cutoff. That danger, combined with resistance in

Ukraine to surrendering sovereignty over any national asset, prompted Ukrainian nationalists to oppose this deal as vigorously they had the Massandra agreement. It is impossible to know whether control of Ukrainian pipelines would have enabled Russia to return to coercion on vital political issues (the Black Sea Fleet was still in limbo) or whether it would simply have made it easier for Gazprom to force payment, but after Massandra, Ukrainians were not willing to find out.

The details of the deal were to be finalized on 10 April, and Gazprom stated its intention to cut supplies on that date if payment was not made.[61] In the meantime, Gazprom continued to threaten a cutoff, and repeatedly complained that Ukraine had paid only a portion of the $100 million installment due by 1 April. Moreover, Ukraine had not yet even made a list of the specific enterprises in which Gazprom was to gain an interest, and accusations of siphoning continued.[62] On 1 April, Landyk reported that Ukraine had paid the first installment on time. He also announced that no more than 30 percent of the Ukrainian company controlling gas and oil facilities would be sold to Gazprom, foiling any plan to gain control of it. Alluding to opposition from nationalists, he said that "nobody can accuse us of selling off Ukraine."[63]

Even after the 10 April deadline, however, the deal was not finalized, primarily because the Ukrainian side refused to make concrete commitments on which facilities it would transfer to Russia.[64] Due to Ukraine's complete lack of economic reform, the entities under consideration had not yet been privatized into joint-stock companies, so there was no way to sell shares in them. Subsequent privatization initiatives in the Ukrainian energy sector in 1995 exempted the pipelines and storage facilities from privatization in order to prevent their control by Gazprom.[65]

The facilities still had not been privatized by August 1994. By this time, Russia seems to have given up hope of gaining control of them, and an agreement was reached to allow Gazprom to sign direct contracts with customers in Ukraine. This would perhaps facilitate cutting off customers without involving the Ukrainian government, which would serve Gazprom's interest and take the Ukrainian government out of a difficult position, but it is unclear if this was implemented or with what result (in early 1995, Gazprom was still trying to trade debt for an interest in Ukrainian gas facilities, and Ukraine was still refusing[66]). Finally, in November 1995, the Ukrainian Verkhovna Rada passed by an overwhelming vote (263–5), a resolution prohibiting the privatization of the oil and gas industries, ending any possibility that Gazprom could buy shares. Energy committee Chairman Olexandr Kozhushko stated: "Defending national interests and reducing energy dependency on former Soviet republics which are exporting nations form the foundation of Ukraine's further development."[67] Perhaps because Ukraine was by this time more prompt in paying its bills, there was no significant Russian reaction.

Beginning in 1994, the situation slowly stabilized, though it remains on the agenda (in mid-1997, there were still sporadic gas cutoffs due to nonpayment of bills). Three factors account for the ebbing of the energy war. First, with assistance from Western lending institutions and through domestic conservation, Ukraine has been much more prompt in paying its bills, eliminating both the economic incentive and the political justification for a cutoff. By September 1995, Ukraine was paying Russia on time for gas deliveries, though a sizable debt from earlier supplies remained.[68] By the end of 1996, Ukraine had paid for 95 percent of its debt to Gazprom for that year, and the Ukrainian government said it would not permit Ukrainian enterprises to incur new debts.[69] Ukraine has learned that Russia will reduce gas supplies if Ukraine does not pay for its gas. Second, Russia has learned that Ukraine will not make significant sacrifices either on political issues or in transferring ownership of gas facilities in order to restore the supply. It would rather shut down its industries. And third, Russia is unwilling to take the drastic step of completely cutting off energy supplies to Ukraine. However, a resumption of tough tactics remains possible, and even after the energy war had subsided somewhat, Russia continued to link a permanent resolution of the energy issue to Ukrainian willingness to give in on the Black Sea Fleet.[70]

Ukraine's Responses

Initially, Ukraine's strategy toward energy dependence was part of its broader strategy of economic independence from Russia: it would simply find other trading partners. As this proved unrealistic, and Russian pressure increased, Ukraine pursued a series of other measures, including finding alternate domestic energy sources, reducing consumption, and threatening retaliation on other issues. None of these responses has been sufficient to solve the problem, but together they have, in the short term, allowed Ukraine to receive Russian energy without making extreme concessions. Ukraine could not avoid the dilemma between autonomy and prosperity, but it was able to avert the worst: a complete energy embargo or capitulation to Russian demands.

Alternate Supplies

Ukraine's initial strategy was to buy its oil and gas from Iran, in effect heeding Hirschman's advice to diversify trade and to trade with nonhostile partners. The plan ran into two major obstacles. First, Middle East suppliers wanted payment on normal terms—in hard currency and in cash, though Ukraine's economic collapse has left it with little hard currency. The alternative, therefore was barter, which has been used in many deals with other former Soviet Republics to circumvent the problems of currency inconvertibility. To the extent that potential suppliers were willing to accept barter deals, a second problem was the lack of infrastructure necessary to transport Middle Eastern oil and gas to Ukraine. While ambitious plans for a pipeline from Iran to Azerbaijan to serve Ukraine were announced in early 1992,[71] little real progress was made, nor could such sources be counted on in the short term in any event.[72] The idea of relying on Iran rather than Russia was characterized by Ukrainian energy officials as "utopia."[73] Similarly, talks with the United Arab Emirates in October 1994 could not surmount the obstacles of infrastructure, hard currency, and the inability of Ukraine's refineries to process "heavy" oil.[74] In early 1994, Ukraine was attempting to negotiate oil deals with Nigeria, Croatia, Iran, India, and Vietnam but has been unable to find a reliable alternative to Russia. In late 1996, Ukraine negotiated gas agreements with Uzbekistan and Kazakhstan, though that gas must still travel through Russia, and was negotiating with Azerbaijan over oil, in hopes of shipping it across Georgia to the Black Sea, circumventing Russia completely.[75]

The search for alternative suppliers will no doubt continue, and the expansion of existing oil terminals at the ports of Odessa and Mykolaiv is aimed at overcoming the need to rely on pipelines, which are subject to the politics of every state they pass through.[76] The hard currency requirements will continue to make such deals problematic, however, which is why Russia's willingness to trade for rubles and at subsidized prices made it such an attractive supplier. Moreover, Russia has shown its determination to keep Ukraine dependent, threatening to raise its prices to the world level if Ukraine bought oil from Iran at world prices.[77]

An additional problem with finding alternate suppliers is Russia's continuing subsidy of oil and gas shipments to Ukraine. As Hirschman notes, one way to increase a state's dependence is to offer it favorable terms of trade. Russia's subsidy of energy supplies to Ukraine is as much a legacy of Soviet energy policy as a deliberate attempt to foster dependence. The effect, however, is that Ukraine would see its energy costs rise dramatically if it shifted to other suppliers. In the first quarter of 1995, the average price of oil sold by Russia to the United States and Europe was $110 per ton. To CIS states, the price was only $78.80 per ton, a subsidy of nearly 30 percent. Similarly, Ukraine was paying $50 per thousand cubic meters of natural gas, rather than the world price of $80 dollars per thousand cubic meters.[78] Leonid Minin, the Deputy Minister of Economics, clearly understood this problem: "Any oil or gas that comes to us [from suppliers other than Russia] will always be more expensive than Russian oil or gas, which comes through pipelines."[79] It is important, however, not to overestimate the extent of the subsidy. Because agreements to sell energy to Ukraine at below market prices were accompanied by provisions for Russia to transport oil and gas across Ukraine at below market prices, the dollar prices paid by Ukraine underestimate the actual cost. As the price paid for Russian oil approaches world market levels, some of the disincentive to finding alternate suppliers will be removed, though infrastructure problems remain.

Alternate Domestic Sources

Traditionally, Ukraine had plentiful domestic sources of energy, but this is no longer the case. In part in response to Russian pressure, exploration has increased in Ukraine in areas where oil and gas has been extracted previously, but it remains uncertain whether reserves will prove sufficient to significantly resolve the problem. To promote exploration, especially off the Black Sea coast, the government formed a new company, Ukrshelfneftohaz, in 1996 as part of $4 billion plan to increase domestic gas and oil production. Nonetheless, gas output in Ukraine actually dropped slightly from 1995 to 1996.[80]

A more promising means for Ukraine to reduce its dependence, especially in electricity generation, is nuclear power, the same method Japan and France used to reduce dependence on imported oil following the oil shocks of the 1970s. In 1994 Ukrainian nuclear power plants were operating at 111 percent of capacity to offset some of the shortfall from other sources, and the contribution of nuclear power to Ukraine's electricity generation rose from 26 percent in 1990 to 40 percent in early 1994.[81] In 1993, a World Bank/International Energy Agency study showed that upgrading of nuclear facilities is Ukraine's most economically promising alternative to gas consumption.[82]

However, there are immense political problems with this plan as well, stemming from the domestic and international legacy of the Chernobyl disaster. Many argue that Chernobyl was a crucial event in the reawakening of Ukrainian nationalism in the late 1980s, and it still has powerful repercussions in the country. In the remaining reactors at Chernobyl, as well as at other nuclear power stations, Ukraine uses the graphite-moderated reactors that are considered inherently dangerous. Moreover, one unit at Chernobyl was damaged in the 1986 accident but has remained running. As a result, while Ukraine has hoped to rely more on nuclear power to reduce dependence on Russia, Western European states have tried to persuade Ukraine to close the remaining reactors at Chernobyl. Like the Russians, though perhaps more benevolently, they have employed economic pressure, making promises to shut down Chernobyl a condition for economic aid and membership in Western European organizations. In December 1995, Ukraine signed an agreement with the G-7 and the EU to close Chernobyl with financial support from those organizations. Moreover, a cutoff of nuclear fuel deliveries from Russia in early

1994[83] showed that even nuclear power did not increase self-sufficiency, though the Trilateral nuclear agreement should provide an additional guarantee of nuclear fuel. Nuclear power, therefore, is not a politically practical solution to Ukraine's dependence.

Conservation

One of the main responses in the west to the oil shocks of the 1970s was reduced consumption, and in this realm the potential is significant. Conservation can be pursued both through reduced consumption, and through increased efficiency.[84] In the short term, the massive inefficiency of Ukrainian industry, which accounts for 70 percent of the Russian gas used in Ukraine, exacerbates its dependence on Russia.[85] In the longer term, it offers one avenue to reduce that dependence. By implementing efficiency measures, Ukraine could save 40–50 percent of the energy used in 1990 by the year 2000.[86] Due to this potential, and to decreased consumption due to economic downturn, it is estimated that Ukraine will consume no more energy in 2000 than it did in 1990.[87] Simply increasing the efficiency of Ukrainian oil refineries to Western efficiency levels would save one-third of Ukraine's crude oil.[88] This will not reduce the need for imports, but could at least stabilize the situation. Two significant barriers impede implemention of the needed measures. First, increasing efficiency requires replacement of old, inefficient capital stock with modern equipment. This in turn will require significant investment, for which Ukraine does not have the money. The outlook for foreign investment in such projects is not good. Second, the requisite economic restructuring will be disruptive to an already chaotic economy, and one can expect stiff political resistance to the needed measures. Closing down an inefficient factory will be opposed by all those employed there as well as local politicians. In any event, while increasing efficiency remains an option for the future, it could not be implemented quickly in the crisis of 1993–1994.

Reducing consumption (without increased efficiency) is a second route to reducing energy needs. In the short term, this has been done crudely: by closing factories, curtailing operation of certain public services, and not heating buildings. In the longer term, reductions can be induced by removing the subsidies that remain from the Soviet system. In 1993, the Ukrainian government subsidized electricity consumption by 90 percent, eliminating the incentive to conserve and draining the state treasury. In early 1995, the domestic Ukrainian price of gas was $2 per thousand cubic meters, compared with a world market price of $80.[89] By making commercial and residential consumers pay market prices for the energy they consume, significant incentives for conservation can be created, especially in an economy where poverty is so widespread.[90]

The first plans to do this were laid following the Massandra summit, but serious measures were not taken for another six months.[91] Gas supplies were cut to 2,300 delinquent enterprises in May 1994.[92] In August 1994, when threats of a cutoff due to nonpayment were again raised, Ukrainian enterprises owed the state $320 million in gas bills that the government could not collect.[93] In January 1995, Ukrainian deputy minister for energy and electricity Oleksii Sheberstov reported the bankruptcy of the Ukrainian energy ministry, blaming it on nonpayment of bills. Of 32 trillion karbovantsy owed by the ministry to suppliers (mostly Russia) 20 trillion was owed it by Ukrainian consumers.[94] In September 1995, Deputy Prime Minister Vasyl Yevtukhov reported that 8,000 firms had been cut off due to lack of payments.[95] In the first eleven months of 1996, over 20,000 Ukrainian enterprises had their gas supplies cut for lack of payment.[96]

Decreasing subsidies will likely spur further private efficiency measures, as well as raising an estimate $30 million per month.[97] Again here, there are political barriers. Suddenly raising prices to world-market levels would make it impossible for many Ukrainians, especially those on pensions, to heat their apartments or cook, and would cause significant turmoil. Nonetheless, Economics Minister Roman Shpek announced plans in May 1995 to increase domestic prices to $60 per thousand cubic meters by September of that year (from the previous price of only $2).[98] There are also barriers in infrastructure: many enterprises and residences in Ukraine have no gas meters, because under the Soviet system, consumers bills were not determined by the amount of gas consumed. In order to rationalize the system, a massive investment in gas meters is required.[99]

The government has, however, slowly lowered subsidies to business, and become increasingly insistent that commercial consumers pay their bills or be cut off. By decreasing the government subsidy, the government not only decreases consumption, but has more money to pay for the gas that is consumed. These measures seemed to succeed in the short term, and in the first five months of 1995 Ukraine was able to reduce its debt to Gazprom by $330 million, largely through payment of $280 million in currency, which was possible in part because of reduced domestic consumption.[100] The government has also tried to get out of the business of being middleman between Russia's Gazprom and Ukraine's insolvent firms. Doing so would remove the government's responsibility to domestic consumers for cutoffs and remove its responsibility to Gazprom for the debts accrued. It has also sought to end the practice of guaranteeing its firms' debts, which gave the firms little incentive to pay their bills.[101] Thus in early 1996, the government authorized firms other than Ukrhazprom to negotiate deals with Gazprom, though Gazprom subsequently refused to deal with anyone other than the Ukrainian government.[102]

The general lack of reform in the Ukrainian economy also contributes to the problem. Most fundamentally, creating transparency in energy pricing and placing the costs of energy consumption directly on consumers would help bring revenue in line with costs. A lack of hard currency earnings also plagues Ukraine's ability to purchase foreign energy. Ukraine's biggest source of hard currency was agricultural exports, but the government's policy of propping up the value of the currency discouraged exports. In late 1993, Ukraine's hard currency earnings were estimated to be about 10 percent of the cost of its energy imports.[103]

Counterthreats

The bargaining over energy supplies has helped clarify the nature of interdependence between the two states in this area, and made it clear that while Russia can apply a great deal of pressure on Ukraine, the pressure is not without cost to Russia. It has also become clear that Ukraine has a few cards that it can play in response. Russia is not completely free to cut off supplies to Ukraine, because doing so would have significant negative consequences for the Russian industries involved. Moreover, the transportation of Russian gas via Ukrainian pipelines to Western Europe makes Russia vulnerable to being cut off from its best customers. Third, a drastic move such as an energy embargo would have justified a Ukrainian refusal to continue the nuclear disarmament process, endangering a fundamental Russian (as well as European and American) foreign policy aim. With the Ukrainian nuclear disarmament process now complete, that deterrent to Russian coercion has been removed.

Russia has found that the threat to cut energy supplies, like many threats, is most useful when it does not actually have to be carried out. Russia's political leverage stems from the fact that it can make Ukraine's future much more difficult. Once it actually carries out its threats, however, the ability to hurt Ukraine is used up, and the lever of influence disappears. Russia can threaten to call in Ukraine's gas debt if Ukraine does not submit on other issues. However, if it does, it can no longer use the threat. Similarly, Russia can threaten to cut energy supplies or end subsidies, but once it does so, it has no more leverage. Thus Russia found that once it actually called in the debt, Ukraine had no reason to give in to Russian demands on the Black Sea Fleet.[104] In the previous chapter it was shown that leverage is built through giving one's partner favorable terms of trade. As long as those terms obtain, there is leverage in threatening to end them, but if the threat is carried out, and the favorable terms ended, that means of influence is largely exhausted. This explains why Russia has gradually decreased the supply, then reinstated it, and then reduced it again. Russia must try to make its power felt without using it up.

A second barrier to Russia carrying out its threats has been the damage it would cause in the domestic gas and oil industries. While Russia overall will not suffer nearly as much as Ukraine from a cutoff in trade, powerful industries in Russia would. A decline in demand for Russian gas, due to the collapse of the post-Soviet economies and to decreased demand in Western Europe, has made maintenance of markets in the former Soviet republics essential.[105] Ukraine, which receives approximately 25 percent of all Russian energy exports, is an important market. While oil deliveries to countries outside the FSU increased by 20 percent in 1993, revenue from those sales dropped by $4 billion over 1992 due to falling prices.[106] It was extremely difficult to maintain revenues in an industry that is one of Russia's main sources of income. Moreover, problems in the Russian energy industry make a cutoff problematic for technical reasons. Because Russia has limited facilities to store unsold gas, it must either sell the gas or close wells and lay off workers. While Russia was trying to step up the threat of a cutoff of energy in early 1994, the Russian state company in charge of selling oil in the Former Soviet Union, Transneft, found itself forced to actually increase oil shipments to Ukraine and Belarus, because of the insolvency of many of domestic customers and the inability to transport the oil elsewhere.[107] At the same time, Lukoil, Russia's largest oil company, froze the domestic price of crude oil because low demand had forced it to close numerous wells and run up a surplus in storage of 1.5 million tons of oil.[108] In the first three quarters of 1994, Ukraine actually received 55 percent more gas than was contracted for, despite the repeated cutoffs early in the year.[109] The Russian state gas company, Gazprom, has increasingly pursued its goal of revenue and market building rather than the Foreign Ministry's goal of political influence. Particularly since Gazprom's director Viktor Chernomyrdin became Prime Minister, the Foreign Ministry has been unable to prevail in this debate.[110]

In addition, while Ukraine is highly dependent on Russian oil and gas sources, interdependence in the broader context of the oil and gas industries is more symmetrical. Chaos in the Ukrainian economy will reverberate in Russia:

> Adequate energy availability in Ukraine is critical for Russian and other FSU energy production. This is because Ukrainian factories supply key metallurgical and chemical products and machinery throughout the FSU, with the coal, petroleum and gas industry being important consumers. Most FSU coal-mining equipment, and the bulk of steel pipes, for example, are produced in Ukraine. . . . Paying world prices for oil and gas from Russia . . . would devastate Ukraine's economy, severely damaging that of Russia in turn.[111]

The broader interdependence between the two economies also means Russian measures that result in the closing of Ukrainian industries will rebound to injure Russian industries as well. Such damage would only be a fraction of that imposed on Ukraine, but given Russia's equally fragile domestic economic and political situations, these costs cannot be ignored. "After all, instability and chaos in Ukraine make conducting democratic changes in Russia extremely difficult and will boomerang against Russia's still somewhat weak statehood."[112]

As noted in the previous chapter, Ukraine's one area of economic leverage over Russia also concerns energy, and stems from the transit trade of Russian oil and gas via Ukraine to Western Europe through the ironically named *Druzhba* [friendship] pipeline.[113] The pipelines cannot be moved, and in the short term, Russia has no other means to ship gas to western Europe.[114] Because Russian gas shipments to Western Europe, a significant source of hard currency revenue, are carried through Ukraine in the same pipelines that supply Ukraine, Russia cannot actually cut the supply to Ukraine without cutting off its Western customers as well[115] (hence the Russian effort to gain control over these pipelines). Moreover, because Ukraine owed so much money to Gazprom, gas was being shipped across Ukraine at nominal rates until late 1996, giving Gazprom more incentive not to disturb the relationship.[116] Ukraine cannot take the decision to cutoff the supply to Western Europe lightly, because it badly needs the support of those states; but in order for Russia to supply them, it cannot cut off the supply to Ukraine, even if Ukraine has to siphon off some of the supply intended for Western Europe and claim it as its own. There have been several instances already where local authorities in Ukraine have done just that.

If Russia is able to purchase control of the pipelines and storage facilities, it would make it much more difficult for Ukraine to take gas intended for Western Europe—Ukraine would have to expropriate the pipelines back from Gazprom, which would be much more difficult politically than simply taking the gas that Ukraine claims it is entitled to. Similarly, if Russia goes ahead with its plan to build an alternate pipeline through Belarus, which is much more amenable to Russian dominance, Ukraine will no longer have this lever.[117] The expense that Russia is willing to go through to build an alternate pipeline indicates how powerful Ukraine's lever is, and the time it will take to build it indicates that Russia is taking the long view regarding energy politics in the region.

Ukraine has been able to make counterthreats other than cutting off gas shipments to Western Europe. Ukrainian President Kravchuk, who was in Washington, DC, in early March 1994 as the gas situation was reaching a showdown, stated that Ukraine's fulfillment of its pledge to transfer its nuclear weapons to Russia would be endangered by Russian economic pressure on Ukraine: "Fulfillment of all agreements, including agreements on nuclear commitments, is possible only if the economy works. If tomorrow factories come to a halt in Ukraine, and this is a reality if there is no gas, what carrying out of commitments can be spoken of?"[118]

This threat seems to have been a powerful one. First, it would not be difficult technically or politically to carry it out. In international legal terms, a gas cutoff would probably not justify reneging on disarmament agreements, but in terms of political legitimacy, many would regard the cutoff as a hostile act, and a refusal to continue disarmament as a reasonable countermove. Second, achieving a nonnuclear Ukraine is perhaps Russia's highest foreign policy goal; and having nearly achieved it, Russian leaders did not want to reopen the debate by pushing other issues too hard, especially since time was on Russia's side. Now that the weapons have all been removed from Ukraine, this counterthreat is no longer available, though it played a role at the height of energy war in early 1994.

International Assistance

Ukraine's ability to reduce its energy arrears to Russia in 1995 and 1996, and to begin paying for current supplies, has depended in large part on assistance from the international financial community. Beginning in 1994, the United States became increasingly concerned that Ukraine would be unable to remain independent of Russia, and has stepped in to help with the energy crisis. First, it has made Ukraine the third largest recipient of bilateral U.S. aid (surpassing Russia, and remaining behind Israel and Egypt). Second, it has prodded the IMF to help Ukraine restructure its energy debts, despite the fact that Ukraine seems unable to meet IMF fiscal and monetary targets. Third, it has pressured Russia and Turkmenistan, Ukraine's two largest energy suppliers, to reschedule Ukraine's energy debt, first at the end of 1994, and then again after new debts were accrued in early 1995.[119] Together, these arrangements helped Ukraine eliminate its arrears by the end of 1995.

Ukraine has therefore found a variety of methods to minimize the impact of Russian energy threats. In the short term, Ukraine simply accepted reduced energy consumption, making the trade-off between autonomy and prosperity in favor of autonomy. The medium-term threat of retaliation—by cutting off transit of Russian gas to Western Europe, by ceasing the nuclear disarmament process, or both—has helped moderate Russian demands. In the long term, however, the ability to use these counterthreats will likely erode (or already has eroded, in the case of nuclear weapons), and Ukraine's position will weaken. Ukraine will need to adopt strategies of conservation and to find alternate suppliers to overcome its energy dependence.

Economic Repercussions in Ukraine

While Ukraine never had to suffer a complete energy embargo from Russia, it endured extremely difficult conditions, especially in the winter of 1993–1994, because of the reduced energy supplies. The energy shortage rippled throughout the economy as well as throughout Ukraine's political situation. It is difficult to quantify the effects of reduced consumption, but the immediate effects can be enumerated. Moreover, we can see (but not prove) a link between the energy war and the shift away from nationalism in the Ukrainian elections of 1994.

Already in March 1992, the Odessa and Lisichansk oil refineries shut down due to a shortage of oil, and in May the fuel situation in Dnipropetrovsk was "critical."[120] Electric power generation was also affected, declining 6 percent in the first half of 1993 due to the shortage of oil. The situation worsened considerably when the Russian and Ukrainian power grids were separated in November 1993. Ukraine could produce only 42 percent of the needed electricity. At this point the decision to curtail television broadcasting was made.[121]

Fuel shortages devastated Ukrainian agriculture, which should have been the strongest sector in the economy. Here as in heavy industry, the system was predicated on cheap energy, and became obsolete in a world of market pricing.[122] In Donetsk oblast, in the spring of 1992, farmers had only 1,700 of the 20,000 tons of fuel needed to complete the spring sowing. The fall harvest that year was similarly hampered by the lack of fuel to run machinery. In Poltava region 2,000 hectares of sugar beets were left unharvested.[123] In 1993, Crimea reported similar problems with the wheat harvest, and in July Luhansk Oblast declared a state of emergency due to the lack of oil.[124] The problems in agriculture were then transmitted to consumers' food prices. An oil price rise in September 1992 was expected to increase food prices by 50 percent.[125]

In addition to reduced television hours, Ukrainians suffered from reduced heating through the winter of 1993–1994. In November 1993, the Energy Ministry warned of an "Armenian winter."[126] In residences with centrally controlled heating, heat was shut off half a month early to conserve energy,[127] and many public buildings were heated minimally throughout the winter. In Odessa, 45 percent of industrial enterprises as well as some schools were closed, and conditions were compared to those of the immediate postwar years.[128]

Political Repercussions in Ukraine

These economic effects of the energy spread to the political system as well. Throughout Ukraine, the high costs of autonomy moderated somewhat enthusiasm for a complete break with Russia. In the 1994 elections, which directly followed the "gas war," a much more pro-Russian parliament was elected, and Leonid Kuchma was elected president, campaigning for an economic union with Russia (though he changed his line after the election).

Russia's energy policy could achieve its goals either by convincing the Ukrainian government to alter its policies or by creating popular dissatisfaction with the government and with independence. While President Kravchuk seemed convinced on several occasions to give in rather than face an energy embargo, he was never able to follow through, because the rest of the government opposed such a policy. While promises on future energy supplies seem to have played a role in sealing the Trilateral nuclear agreement in January 1994, they were probably not the driving consideration even there (see chapter 7). Eventually, Kravchuk followed the lead of the Verkhovna Rada and took a more belligerent line in response to Russian pressure. In that respect, the policy failed.

At the broader societal level, however, the policy may have achieved its objectives, even if this did not translate into immediate policy change. By increasing the hardship of independence, the energy shortage sapped the enthusiasm of at least some Ukrainians for independence. And by undermining Kravchuk, the policy made it more likely that a more pro-Russian president would be elected. It seems likely, though it is difficult to prove, that the energy war helped cause a massive shift of the Ukrainian political spectrum in the first half of 1994.[129]

The most telling evidence of a political shift in Ukrainian politics was the position in the political spectrum of Leonid Kravchuk. In December 1991, when Kravchuk was elected president, he was the candidate of the moderates and conservatives, as befitted his position as speaker of the Soviet-era Verkhovna Rada. The nationalist candidate was Rukh leader Vyacheslav Chornovil, who came in second in the election with 24 percent of the vote.[130] Many nationalists continued to oppose Kravchuk through the end of 1993. But by the time Presidential elections were held in June and July 1994, the nationalists were firmly behind Kravchuk, as the best possible candidate to save Ukraine. In the run-off between Kravchuk and Kuchma, Kravchuk won 90 percent of the votes in the western regions that had been the stronghold of Rukh and the independence movement.

Rukh did not run a candidate in 1994, and Chornovil found himself after the election lamenting Kravchuk's loss and proclaiming that he had done everything possible to help him.[131] In 1991, Kravchuk received 90 percent of the vote in Eastern Oblasts, and less than 10 percent in west. By 1994, he received 90 percent in the west, and less than 20 percent in the east.[132] In 1991, Vyacheslav Chornovil received 90 percent of the vote in many western oblasts, and by 1994 the nationalists could not even field a presidential candidate, calculating that Kravchuk was the best they could hope for. The Ukrainian political spectrum shifted significantly to the East, to conservatism, and toward Russia.[133]

It is hard to say how much of this shift was due to reduced supplies of fuel as opposed to Ukraine's other economic problems, but the hardships imposed during the shortage undoubtedly played a major role.[134] The links between energy shortages and Ukrainian politics were alluded to by a Ukrainian spokesman in early 1992: "The facts indicate that Russia is keeping Ukraine on starvation rations by not fulfilling its treaty obligations with regard to energy carriers in full . . . This is helping to increase social tension to a certain extent."[135] Several factors point to the link between the energy war and Ukraine's political shift. First, Russia intended to undermine support for Ukrainian independence, either directly through pressure on the government or indirectly by injuring the economy. Second, many Ukrainians believed that closer relations with Russia would solve many economic problems. Third, at least in the case of Kravchuk's dealings on the Massandra summit, agreeing to move closer to Russia was directly related to fear of the alternatives. Similarly, a common theme in Kuchma's campaign rhetoric was the need for closer ties with Russia. Relations with Russia, not reform, was the issue that Kuchma used to dominate eastern and southern Ukraine.[136] Fourth, Russia made it clear that economic union would assure continued supplies of subsidized fuel. This has been a cornerstone of negotiations over Russian-Belarussian union agreements. Finally, Russian leaders voiced satisfaction when Kuchma was elected president, clearly believing (as did everyone else) that he would move Ukraine back into Russia's orbit.

While Russia was never willing to completely cut fuel supplies to Ukraine, its reduction of deliveries had a major impact on Ukraine economically and politically. Ukraine's choice of enduring domestic hardship rather than giving in to Russian demands confirmed this effect. The long-term effects of the policy are yet unknown, but the short-term effects satisfied Russian goals in many ways. While Ukraine did not cave in to pressure, its citizens and politicians were persuaded that Ukraine needed Russia. A major political shift toward pro-Russian groups in Ukraine was effected. Therefore, Russia's policy was partially successful, and Ukraine was only partially able to resist the pressure, despite its impressive capacity to endure hardship. For this reason, Ukraine's energy vulnerability continues to be an issue for both states. If Russia decides that Kuchma is too independence-minded, the threats could begin anew. More significantly for Ukraine, it now must make all of its foreign policy decisions—including those involving NATO and the United States—knowing that Russia can make life as difficult for any future Ukrainian government as it did for Kravchuk's.

Conclusions

Energy is the economic sector that demonstrates most clearly the problem of Ukrainian economic dependence on Russia, and Ukraine's response to Russian pressure in this sector provides important insight into how Ukraine is facing the dilemmas elaborated in the previous chapter. Above all, it shows how determined Ukraine is to maintain its autonomy, even when domestic prosperity suffers significantly. In the period from September 1993 to April 1994, Ukraine repeatedly decided to cut its consumption of energy, forcing the closure of many industries in an already-reeling economy, rather than transfer ownership of Ukrainian assets, whether they be ships of the Black Sea Fleet, nuclear warheads, or gas transport facilities.

It would seem that such a policy could not be maintained in the face of growing domestic unrest over the economic collapse, but it has been. The seriousness of the trade-off, as perceived in Ukraine, was emphasized by Kravchuk, who stated that without a solution, "You will arrive in the evening at home and want to cook something to eat and there will be no gas."[137] Yet Ukraine could not pay, and did not significantly compromise. Indeed, it seems that the issue has made many Ukrainians even more resistant to Russia, as Russia's tactics were perceived as heavy-handed, and served only to convince many Ukrainians that they really do have something to fear from Russia.[138]

The "energy war" between Russia and Ukraine, and Ukraine's ongoing energy dependence, illuminate several important facets of the international political economy in the region: First, economic interdependence in the former Soviet Union is not merely a matter of states battling over wealth, but of states' fundamental independence. Economic interdependence has much higher stakes here than it does among the advanced industrial states. In most "trade wars," the primary value at stake is the domestic employment levels in the two states, and related economic issues. In this case, the independence and sovereignty of Ukraine are in question—and are in fact the *crucial* question, in Russian-Ukrainian relations. Because Russia has not only the means to bring Ukraine's economy to its knees, but also the desire of curtailing Ukrainian independence, economic interdependence in this region takes on a national security dimension much more strongly than elsewhere. Vladimir Selianov, national security adviser to President Kravchuk, acknowledged the problem stating:

> The economic security of the country is becoming the basis of national security as whole. . . . We now interpret economic security . . . as a state of the national economic system, free from the threat of any destructive action that could completely or partially disrupt the efficient material sustenance of the Ukrainian people and society.[139]

The energy issue highlights in particular the fact that in this relationship, the problem of interdependence is only partially one of coordinating policies, as is discussed in the following chapter. It is equally a problem of coercion, as argued by Hirschman.

Second, as Ukraine slowly finds its feet as an independent state, the experience of the energy war has been a vital learning experience. Like most such experiences, it has been painful. In particular, Ukraine has learned that economic isolation from Russia, while ideal to some nationalists, is not really possible in the near future. Moreover, it may not be desirable, even if it were possible. Ukraine has also learned that economic weakness threatens its independence, perhaps more than does any military threat. In fact, it seems that Ukraine was so recalcitrant in caving in on energy, while being willing to surrender its nuclear weapons, because its leaders perceive economic coercion to be a more immediate threat to its national security than military attack.[140]

The notion that isolation would remove Russia's ability to injure Ukraine ignored the fact that such isolation also weakened the economy to the point where Ukraine was an easy target for economic coercion. If interdependence is thought of as the cost of isolation, then isolation from Russia does not really end interdependence, it merely pays the cost. Reducing interdependence requires changing the Ukrainian economy structurally, and it is no coincidence that following the energy war, the Ukrainian Parliament and President, despite being allegedly more conservative than their predecessors, have begun serious reform of the economy.

Third, for the student of the region's politics, Ukraine's reaction to energy reductions shows how committed the Ukrainian government is to its independence, despite the misgivings of some of the populace.[141] Ukraine perceives autonomy and sovereignty to be more fundamental goals than prosperity, and feels that these fundamental goals are endangered. Higher priority of sovereignty and autonomy was shown by Ukraine's willingness to watch the economy grind to a halt, and its citizens literally shiver, rather than give in to Russian demands. This contrasts with some other former Soviet republics, most notably Belarus, which has signed an economic union agreement with Russia that curtails its sovereignty in the hope of easing its economic crisis. It remains to be seen whether, as Ukraine reforms its economy and becomes more democratic, it will be less able to sacrifice prosperity to other goals. Similarly, it remains to be seen whether, as the Ukrainian-Russian relationship evolves, Russian acceptance of Ukrainian independence will make Russia less likely to exploit Ukraine's vulnerability.

It is also unclear whether Ukraine could withstand a more protracted energy war. While Russia is not invulnerable, it could presumably prevail in an energy war of attrition. So far, it has been unwilling to wage such a war, perhaps because it does not want to completely destabilize its neighbor. Ukrainian resistance has made a quick and easy victory impossible. While the energy war has cooled off for the time being, Ukrainian leaders know that as long as it is so dependent on Russian energy, the threat remains. Moreover, it has become clear that even if Ukraine has resolved where it stands on this particular dilemma, it has other dilemmas of interdependence to contend with as well.

5

Trade and Currency

Fragmentation and Integration

A deprivation of economic freedom will lead to a deprivation
of political freedom.
——Valerii Kalyniuk, "Dohovir Ukrainy rospne
i bona vzhe nykoly ne voskresne"

Russia is our strategic partner number one, including in economic relations
——O. S. Samodurov, "Z Nashym Stratehichnym Partnerom"

As Ukraine asserted its independence from Moscow in the late 1980s, the
main economic issues were economic performance and the benefits of
decentralization. Gorbachev's reformers as well as Ukrainian nationalists
believed that decentralization of administration from Moscow to the republics would facilitate improved economic performance. For Ukrainians, an
added goal of increased autonomy was improving the distribution of the gains
from trade, to keep more of Ukraine's wealth at home and reduce Moscow's
exploitation.

When the Soviet Union collapsed in 1991, the range of possible economic
relationships between Russia and Ukraine was greatly expanded. It was now
possible to imagine, as some Ukrainian nationalists did, that economic relations
between the two states would be largely severed, reducing Russia's exploitation
of Ukraine and the potential for future coercion. It was equally possible to retain the status quo levels and patterns of interdependence, as was envisioned by
the first treaty for economic cooperation advanced following the coup.

The fundamental question raised by this new freedom of choice was: To
what extent should the Ukrainian economy be interdependent with that of
Russia? A second question that follows from the first is: To the extent that the
two are interdependent, what institutions or methods shall be used to manage

97

that interdependence? Both questions involve economic and political goals and means, and their interaction. This chapter focuses on the first question: How much and what type of interdependence did Ukraine seek? The next chapter addresses the second, focusing on the role of the CIS as an international economic organization.

This chapter begins with a discussion of the collapse of the Soviet Union and the problems it has created for the economies of the two states. The second section elaborates on a series of competing arguments concerning the best arrangement of interdependence, and highlights the political and economic dilemmas involved. The third section will discuss in some detail the actual problems confronted by Ukrainian policy makers, and the evolution of Ukrainian policies. The conclusion will assess Ukraine's evolving policy on the level of interdependence with Russia.

The most fundamental theme running through this story is the trade-off between prosperity and autonomy. Initially, many Ukrainians believed that there was no trade-off between these two goals; that ending interaction with Moscow would both increase prosperity and assert Ukraine's autonomy. Conventional trade theory, however, finds that isolation decreases prosperity, and this was found to be true for Ukraine, leading to a debate over which goal was more important. Nationalist political economists as far back as Friederich List and Alexander Hamilton have advocated that the state isolate itself from potential enemies in order to prevent interdependence from being used for coercion, and this sentiment has driven the arguments of Ukrainian nationalists. As shown in the last chapter, the politics of energy confirmed nationalists' fears that interdependence would endanger autonomy. Ukraine's first economic plan in early 1992 deliberately isolated Ukraine's economy from that of Russia.

Less nationalist Ukrainians, including some reformers as well as conservatives, have asserted the necessity of maintaining ties with Russia in order to maintain prosperity. The issue was the central debate in the presidential elections in 1994, and that year signaled the end of the dominance of the nationalist position. The continuation of two problems, fear of Russia and economic collapse, ensures that this debate will remain a critical one in Ukrainian politics and in Ukrainian-Russian relations. Ukraine will no longer pursue separation without regard to the economic cost, but it will continue to make the preservation of Ukrainian autonomy a criterion by which all economic agreements will be evaluated.

The Economic Fragmentation of the Soviet Union: Aspirations and Reality

Perhaps the most difficult aspect of Ukrainian independence has been coming to grips with the reality of economic collapse, which has diverged so far from expectations. By ending communism and breaking away from Russia, Ukrainians expected to become more prosperous rapidly. The last chapter showed that Ukrainian energy supplies had been transferred to other parts of the Soviet Union. Similarly, as "the breadbasket of the Soviet Union," much of Ukraine's agricultural output was also transferred to other republics. However, by the end of the 1980s, subsidies in other areas—most notably energy—meant that in the aggregate Ukraine was actually being subsidized (it was gaining more in underpriced resources than it was losing in underpriced food and other outputs), and would suffer a substantial terms-of-trade loss in shifting to world market prices in its trade with the other former Soviet states.[1] Ukraine was substantially dependent on Russia, but there has been disagreement concerning how best to deal with that situation.

The impression that Ukraine was exploited under the Soviet Union was shared by economists as well as politicians and citizens. Volodimir Bandera compares the transfer of Ukrainian wealth to Russia with transfers from France to Prussia after the Franco-Prussian war, from Germany to the Allies from 1924–1932, and from East Germany to the Soviet Union in the postwar decades, and asserts that Ukraine suffered the greatest loss, measured as share of GNP. "The historical evidence shows that for well over half a century, at least 10 percent of Ukraine's national output has been given up annually."[2] Other scholars viewed Ukraine's relation to Russia as that of an "internal colony."[3] From this perspective it made sense that, by breaking ties with Russia, Ukraine's exploitation would end, and its citizens would end up better off. Moreover, because the division of labor created under the Soviet Union was not driven by comparative advantage, it is not clear that continuing that division is economically efficient. "It is thus likely that a large part of trade in manufactures among the 15 states is trade diversion and will vanish in the long run without preferential treatment."[4]

Despite these assertions about the long term, the dominant opinion in Ukraine and among many economists is that in the short term Ukraine will be injured by rapidly breaking ties with Russia.[5] There are two basic reasons: the disruption of a rapid shift and the lack of alternative trade partners. Theorists as well as practitioners have contended that, whatever the inefficiencies and inequalities of the Soviet trading system, dismantling it willy-nilly would create massive disruption and increase, rather than decrease, inefficiency.[6] While many agree on the long-term need to reduce Ukraine's dependence on Russia, the view remains widespread that quick movement toward that goal would lead to short-term chaos. Moreover, while those advocating a shift of trade away from Russia have assumed increasing ties with other partners, these have been slow to develop.

Separate Currencies

A national currency is one of the hallmarks of the independent state. Currency is important not only as a symbol, but as an important tool of economic policy. Monetary policy has been one of the main foci of reform in the former Communist states, and as Keynes pointed out, nothing destroys a country's economy more rapidly than an unstable currency. There have been two reasons to establish separate currencies in the former Soviet Union. First is national sovereignty: "The creation of the national economy requires the introduction of a national monetary unit."[7] For this reason, establishment of a Ukrainian currency has been nonnegotiable for Ukrainian nationalists, and was planned even before Ukraine declared independence.[8] More prosaically, implement by states of different monetary policies requires separate currencies. This tension is visible in the debate over a single currency in the EU. The fundamental problem in establishing a single currency is the difference in monetary policies sought by the members: Germany, which fears above all inflation, insists on an extremely tight monetary policy, while others, worried more about stimulating economic growth and employment than inflation, desire to use monetary policy to that end. With separate currencies, the policy dispute need not be resolved.

But there are also good economic reasons to establish separate currencies, in particular involving "moral hazard."[9] When several states share a currency, and each has its own monetary policy, each state has an incentive to conduct an inflationary policy. This problem was evident in the months after the Soviet collapse. By emitting rubles through credits to its enterprises, Ukraine adds to the money supply, pushing the value of the currency down and inflation up. While these inflationary costs are shared by all other users of the common currency, the benefits of that currency emission accrue only to Ukraine, which established the credit.[10] Every other member of the union has the same incentive, and inflation therefore tends to get out of control. There are only two solutions. The first is to establish strong central control over monetary policy, tightly constraining the separate states' right to have distinct monetary policies. The other solution is to abandon the single currency. With multiple currencies, moral hazard no longer occurs, because the state that emits inflationary credit and reaps the benefits also incurs all the costs, since other states do not use that currency.[11]

Maintaining a single currency would not leave the individual states much maneuverability economically, for it would require coordinating tax systems, agreeing on the size and financing of budget deficits, unifying VAT rates and import/export duties, and constraining local government actions within states.[12] Because the first scenario, strong regulation, was viewed as politically unrealistic, many observers of the FSU have advocated the second, separate currencies.

Many economists as well as politicians, however, have opposed the second scenario, and argued that the economic costs are so high that a political solution must be found to allow implementation of a single currency. The main reason to oppose separate currencies is the effect on trade, and by extension, on overall economic performance. Separate currencies make trade more difficult to carry out and less efficient even among states with strong currencies. Among states with inconvertible currencies, such as the former Soviet states, it makes trade nearly impossible.[13] Trade is obstructed by the need to exchange currencies as well as by the uncertainty created by large fluctuations in the relative values of the currencies. Moreover, without some effective clearing mechanism, a surplus in current account with one state cannot be used to offset a deficit with another, nor can a surplus in one period be used to offset a deficit in another.[14] Under such conditions, trade is limited to the "double coincidence of wants."[15] Barry Eichengreen estimates that this condition would reduce trade in the region by 25 percent and combined GNP by 7 percent.[16] If that estimate is correct, one-half to one-third of the economic downturn in Ukraine is due to currency problems alone. As Havrylyshyn and Williamson point out, the only way to reconcile the trade benefits of a single currency and the stabilization benefits of separate currencies is to have multiple currencies but with strong central control. This solution, however, collides head-on with a third goal: sovereignty.

Trade Barriers

A second area in which economic disintegration threatens to reduce prosperity is through trade barriers. This too is a problem with which the advanced capitalist states are quite familiar, for the focus of international economic politics since World War II has been the campaign to decrease tariffs and then nontariff barriers to trade through mechanisms such as the GATT, and more recently, the World Trade Organization. As disputes between the United States and Japan, and between the United States and the EU demonstrate, however, these problems are not easily resolved even for states with much in common and little fear of one another.

In the former Soviet Union, two opposite problems have arisen. The first concerns the scarcity of many consumer products and raw materials. In order to preserve domestic supplies of critical commodities, governments have enacted export bans. In other areas, the opposite problem occurs: there is insufficient demand for products, causing enterprises to go bankrupt and unemployment to rise. In these areas, states have sought to raise barriers to imports (this is the problem normally seen in the West). Import and export bans make each state worse off in the aggregate by limiting free trade and preventing specialization and efficiency, but they tend to persist because of collective action problems. And as will be discussed below, their effects tend to ripple through highly interlinked economies such as those of the FSU.

Contradictory Economic Policies

A third problem created by fragmentation is contradictory economic policies. The nature of interdependence, even when it is symmetrical, is that events in one economy have effects in others. In such a situation, to have separate but interdependent economies makes it possible for governments to undertake policies that cancel each other out. This is true not only in tariffs, but throughout economies, and it makes it difficult for states to control their economies. This problem is the one most often focused on in discussions of interdependence. An example is that a state undertaking an anti-inflationary monetary policy can have that undermined by inflationary policies in trading partners. Or two states that seek to boost exports through currency devaluation will cancel each others' moves. More broadly, to the extent that states have differing regulations, it makes it harder to treat them as one market, and if products have to be differentiated for different markets, economies of scale are lost.

These problems of fragmented economies are fundamental to international trade anywhere, and integration efforts such as NAFTA and the Single European Act have aimed at overcoming them. But at precisely the same time that North America and Western Europe have been seeking to overcome these barriers, states of the FSU, and Ukraine in particular, have been throwing them up. The situation is made much more dire, however, by the peculiar nature of the Soviet economic system, which was not based on markets. The characteristics of the Soviet economy have a negative synergy with the effects of fragmentation, exaggerating the problems created.

First, industry in the Soviet Union was highly concentrated, such that for many products, there was a single manufacturer for the entire Soviet Union.[17] Just as liberal trade theory argues that specialization leads to economies of scale, Soviet planners sought economies of scale by building massive factories that produced large portions of the Union's need for a given output.[18] The fixation with economies of scale was exacerbated by the systematic underpricing of transportation, which separated related industries by great distances, and set the stage for crippling bottlenecks to spread through the economy, as shortages of one intermediate product lead to shortages in those it is used to make.[19] Besides creating problems for domestic efforts to create free markets, this concentration exacerbates the effects of trade barriers.[20]

A few examples illustrate the severity of the problem: In machine building, 87 percent of product groups were produced by a single producer for the entire union.[21] In chemicals the share of products made by a single producer was 47 percent, and in metallurgy 28 percent. Overall, the IMF estimates that 30–40 percent of industrial output in the Soviet Union was produced by monopolies.[22] To a much greater degree than in other regional groupings, events in one republic will have repercussions in the other states. When an export quota in Ukraine prevents shipping of certain parts or commodities to Russia, the Russian factories using those products must shut down. Delivery of their products then ceases, not only to Russia and Ukraine, but to the whole region, crippling production of other products, as the effect reverberates throughout the region.

Second, while the command economy was aimed at some type of overall efficiency, it was not aimed at efficiency as determined by comparative advantage.[23] Now the successors must cope not only with new barriers to trade, but with creating an entirely new composition of trade, based on market forces and comparative advantage, rather than on central planning. Much of the deviation from comparative advantage can be accounted for by the drive for economies of scale, but other factors were at work as well. For example, the absence of market pricing meant that Ukraine built up enormous industries in which, due to its lack of oil and gas, it does not genuinely have comparative advantage.

Some see this bizarre division of labor as reason to discount the need to continue trade: "It is impossible to argue logically about why and how the republic should specialize internationally when its apparent losses of trade surpluses and incomprehensible terms of trade render the gains from trade quite dubious."[24] Others contend that, "However irrational [trade relations] may be, their overnight discontinuance would lead to complete collapse of the economy."[25] The solution, they say, is not to sever the trade ties that have built up over decades, but to gradually adjust from the structure built by the Soviets to that dictated by market forces and free trade. This debate has been at the heart of Ukrainian policy concerning trade with Russia and Ukrainian security.

Third, the command system created some extraordinary dependencies within the system, which have dramatic effects when turned into international dependencies. The best example is that of energy. Not only were most republics dependent on Russian energy, but they received it at an artificially low price due to subsidies, and their industries were built on the assumption of cheap energy. With the collapse of the Soviet Union, states such as Ukraine not only have to figure out where to get their oil, but they have to readjust their consumption patterns to deal with the new reality of paying world-market prices in hard currency.[26] The specialization discussed above, however, means that all the states are dependent on each other for crucial products, making it very easy for them to inflict economic harm on one another, intentionally or otherwise.

Fourth, the system placed Moscow at the hub of the economy, with all other parts of the economy connected to each other largely through Russia. This provided control for the central organs of the Communist party, and now it provides leverage for the Russian government. More than 50 percent of the Soviet Union's expenditures went through Moscow.[27] Because so much trade is conducted through Russia, trade ties with Russia have a large impact on ties with third states within the region. It will take time to reroute trade flows.

Fifth, with very few exceptions, the products of post-Soviet industries are not competetive in other markets, such as Western Europe. Ironically, the EU's "free market" is closed to those Ukrainian products that could compete successfully, such as agriculture and steel. The absence of other outlets for production "dooms the newly emerged states to a common economic life for the foreseeable future. Political leaders may try to escape this, but their ambitions will not be satisfied during the lifetime of this generation."[28] Thus Alexander Granberg contends that there really are not distinct national economies in the region: "The degree of integration of the Soviet economic space is such that it is difficult to isolate relatively autonomous and homogeneous regional (or local) markets within it. The boundaries of markets are quite fuzzy and do not correspond to the frontiers of national or other economic units."[29]

The Collapse of Trade and the Collapse of the Economies

In the event, many Ukrainian citizens and leaders have been very hesitant to heed these signs that separation of economies will lead to economic collapse, for two reasons. First, the arguments strongly contradict their experience: "The unfortunate experience of the Ukrainian economy within the Russian Empire and its successor the USSR is incomparably more important for the Ukrainian population than any possible theoretical advantages associated with a future association with Moscow."[30] This point of view tended to deny the trade-off between autonomy and prosperity. Second, concerns with their economic sovereignty prompted many to view the disruption of trade as the necessary cost of genuine independence. Working from the theoretical arguments laid out in chapter 3, and the experience with energy discussed in chapter 4, they simply believe that Ukraine is better off alone even if it is costly. This point of view recognizes the trade-off between prosperity and sovereignty, and chooses to give priority to sovereignty.

Even if the costs of fragmentation are high, there are perceived political benefits. Establishing barriers to trade has the advantage of appeasing domestic groups who are injured by international competition. By diminishing the overall amount of trade between two states, it reduces vulnerability and makes economic coercion more difficult. And because a state's economy is then less affected by external factors, it improves the state's control over its own economy. Thus while fragmentation of the Soviet Union threatened decreased efficiency, it promised increased national autonomy, and to some was seen as beneficial in that respect.

The experience of the first few years of independence has established two basic facts. First, Ukraine's economy has obviously been significantly injured by the break of ties with Russia and the other former Soviet republics. Second, while this has apparently led many to question their desire for economic separation (implying they did not believe in the trade-off between autonomy and prosperity, and do not want to surrender prosperity for autonomy) others have remained steadfast that Ukraine must not make its renewed prosperity dependent on cooperating with Russia, because doing so will erode the state's autonomy.

Reliable data on economic trends in the region are difficult to come by, and it is therefore impossible to quantify the changes that have taken place in the amount and composition of trade since independence. Because Russia and Ukraine had no border controls at the time of Ukraine's independence, there is no way to measure trade since that time. Much economic activity is unreported, because it happens in the "gray market" and is not ever observed by the governments. For example, while the European Union reported $1.7 billion worth of exports to Ukraine in 1994, Ukraine reported only $900 million worth, indicating that Ukrainian reporting is off by nearly half.[31] Some basic information is available, however, and two general observations can safely be made. First, economic output crashed in all the economies by 15–20 percent annually in the first three years of independence (1991–1994). The most recent figures indicate that Ukraine's GDP continued to fall by 10 percent in the first 9 months of 1996.[32] Second, economists estimate that 50–80 percent of the decline in output is a result of the collapse of trade.[33] It is impossible to precisely quantify the portion of the decline in output that is due to the breakup of the Soviet Union as opposed to the domestic problems of reform (and nonreform) that plague the economies. It is worth noting that output was falling even before the collapse of the Soviet Union. Due to Ukraine's lack of a monetary system, it is difficult even to assess its trade balance, which according to Grigori Yavlinsky, the Ukrainian government does not know.[34] While precise quantification is not possible, a qualitative assessment, based on anecdotal evidence as well as trade statistics, makes it clear that the breakdown in trade is contributing substantially to the overall economic downturn in the FSU, and in Ukraine in particular, as Barry Eichengreen states.[35] Ukraine was much more dependent on its trade with Russia than vice versa, which is typical of a small state trading with a large one. In 1992, Russia accounted for 60.7 percent of Ukraine's exports while Ukraine accounted for only 16.7 percent of Russia's.[36] Ukraine continues to be highly dependent on trade with Russia. In 1994, 39 percent of Ukraine's exports were to Russia and 30 percent of its imports came from Russia, and for 1995 the corresponding figures were 42 percent and 50 percent.[37] Both as a supplier and as a market, Ukraine needs trade with Russia.

Ukrainian Trade Policy: Autonomy and Prosperity

The collapse in Ukrainian-Russian trade was fully intended by most of the Ukrainian leadership. After the legacy of Soviet rule, and the inability of Ukraine and Russia to cooperate in the early days of independence, Ukraine enacted an economic program in early 1992 explicitly aimed at breaking trade ties with Russia. At this point, Ukraine chose to privilege autonomy over prosperity, though it seems that few realized how high the price would be. As the Ukrainian economy descended ever deeper into chaos, however, there has been a reassessment, and Ukraine is currently attempting to rebuild many of the links that were previously severed. "The story of Ukrainian economic strategy since 1991 is largely a chronicle of the struggle of the exponents of the [nationalist] school of thought against recalcitrant economic realities."[38]

From the Coup to the Commonwealth

Following Ukraine's declaration of independence in August 1991, there was great uncertainty regarding relations between Ukraine and Russia, as there was among all the former republics. In the short term, establishing a separate Ukrainian economy was not on the government's agenda. Indeed, the opposite was true, as Ukraine and Russia undertook to assure each other that previous arrangements would continue to operate until some new ones could be made. In October 1991, Kravchuk stated: "For us, the Union with Russia is a cornerstone of Ukraine's policy. . . . Contacts with Russia are our long-term and far-sighted principal policy. This is our history, our roots, and we have to take this into account."[39] Thus the original plan for fuel deliveries for 1992 was simply to continue them at their 1991 levels. Political arrangements were another matter, as Ukraine prepared for its independence referendum in December and anticipated complete political independence from Russia. At this stage the tension between political and economic independence recieved little attention from most Ukrainian leaders.

The nationalist opposition, however, already had different priorities. When Prime Minister Vitold Fokin asked for additional time to formulate a draft economic plan in October 1991, he cited the need to first complete economic agreements with Russia and the other republics. "This was like pouring oil on the fire: A demand was heard for the government's immediate resignation,"[40] and nationalist deputies issued a call not to enter into any relations with whatever union might persist. A compromise was reached, according to which ties with other republics were allowed as long as they were exclusively economic. And while Kravchuk continued to advocate economic ties with Russia, he explained that by this he meant "mutually profitable trade and cooperation with other sovereign states," but not a single market in which "absolutely everything is unified and identical."[41]

Even at this early stage, however, the political separation of the states overflowed into the economic arena. Most notable in this realm were steps taken by Ukraine to assure sufficient food and commodity supplies in the republic (a ban on oil exports was enacted in September).[42] The export limits enacted not only created problems for Russian consumers, but created an excuse for Russia to retaliate. In this way, trade barriers were hastily erected with no clear rationale (other than to provide opportunities for those who could evade them to get rich). At this point, however, the motivation was still short-term welfare rather than establishing economic autonomy. During this period, the different economic interests of the two states became clarified in a series of disputes over the disposition of Soviet assets, and the notion of economic coordination eroded as each state, in attempting to deal with the economic chaos, succumbed to the temptation to act unilaterally when common measures could not be agreed on. When Ukraine confirmed its independence at the beginning of December 1991, hopes of reconstructing some type of union were dashed, but there were still no official plans to disjoin the two economies. In his first address to the Rada after his election as president and the success of the independence referendum, Kravchuk named "integration of Ukraine's economy with the economy of the former Union states" one of "our first steps in the area of economics."[43] The Commonwealth treaty promised coordinated economic policies, even if it created no real mechanism for reaching or implementing such policies.

December 1991 was perhaps the crucial month for the early history of Ukrainian-Russian trade relations, because at this point interdependence became a major problem for Ukrainian policy makers, and the first real incentives for economic isolation were laid. The previous disputes over the disposition of Soviet assets undermined Russian standing among Ukrainian leaders, but did not provide a reason to separate. The dispute over implementation of reform went a long way in convincing the Kravchuk administration of the need to cut ties with Russia.

While Russia was advocating an economic union in late 1991, it was also planning to adopt an economic reform package, which Kravchuk and his administration were not ready to do, in part because they had less time than the Russian Federation to lay plans and in part because they were much more conservative in their politics, and much less enthusiastic about reform. Russia announced in the fall of 1991 its intention to free prices as of 2 January 1992, but Ukraine was preoccupied with its upcoming referendum and did not react until December.[44] Ukraine acknowledged the need to reform to some extent, and the need to coordinate polices, but was entirely unprepared, and Prime

Minister Fokin asked Russia to delay the price liberalization for two weeks so Ukraine could implement the appropriate policies. The Russian government refused, for reasons that are unclear. Perhaps they did not want to negotiate reform policies for fear that conservatives in other republics would insist on watering them down. The Ukrainian leadership accused Russia of not living up to its previous commitments to coordinate economic policies.[45]

The links between the economies, however, meant that whether Ukraine was ready or not, it would have to deal with Russia's liberalization. Two broad problems were created, one in trade and one in currency. First, higher prices in Russia created a flight of goods from Ukraine to Russia, and corresponding shortages and price rises in Ukraine. Second, the higher prices in Ukraine created a shortage of currency.[46] Ukrainian First Deputy Prime Minister Konstantin Masik complained:

> Our view was not taken into account even though a majority of republics supported us. Representatives of Russia were firm in the decision to introduce free prices as of January 2, giving us no time to resolve the numerous problems. . . . In 24 hours we have to work out for the president, the Supreme Soviet [Verkhovna Rada] and the Government of the Ukraine methods to protect the population.[47]

When Russia went ahead and freed prices at the beginning of January, neighboring economies were thrown into turmoil. In Ukraine, the retail price index increased by over 400 percent in January 1992.[48] Goods, and food in particular, flowed from the other republics to Russia, where prices were now higher. The other states had two choices: they could either free prices, so that their prices would rise to match those in Russia, and the incentive to export would decrease, or they could prohibit exports of crucial goods. Ukraine did some of both. In anticipation of the drain on goods, Ukraine (as did Moldova, Kyrgyzstan, and Belarus) freed its prices on many commodities at the same time Russia did.[49] It also prohibited exports of some foodstuffs. The process continued throughout 1992, as Ukraine had to free the prices of more and more goods to stem the flow of goods out of the country.[50] In addition to freeing prices, Ukraine instituted export controls, which were later raised by Russia as well.[51]

The liberalization of prices created a second problem, in monetary liquidity. With the drastic increase in prices, there was no longer enough currency in Ukraine to facilitate trade.[52] While Ukraine could issue ruble credits to industries on paper, the only facilities to actually print more currency were in Russia. Having followed Russia (more or less) in price liberalization, the other economies found themselves in a massive currency shortage. Russia sought to tighten the money supply in large part to offset the inflationary pressures created by other republics, which were leading to a drain of resources from Russia,[53] and increased its share of currency emissions from two-thirds under the Soviet Union to 80 percent in 1992.[54] Aleksandr Yemelyanov, first deputy chairman of the Government Economic Council of Ukraine complained: "Welcoming the Minsk accords, we thought we did away with the dictate of the center. We did do away with administrative dictate, but the economic one remained. It is in the hands of those who own the money-printing machine."[55] Kravchuk as well became less sanguine about economic relations with Russia: "Our dependence on Russia is dependence on the ruble . . . The ruble zone forces us to move away from Russia."[56] Because currency was not forthcoming, Ukraine began to introduce "coupons" in January 1992.[57] These coupons were basically substitute temporary rubles, used so that workers could be paid and could buy food when there was insufficient supply of genuine rubles.[58] In March, Ukrainian workers began receiving 75 percent of their salaries in coupons and 25 percent in direct deposit to banks, so that the government did not need rubles to pay them.[59] As it turned out, these coupons were the precursors of a separate currency in Ukraine, but this was not the manner in which Ukraine had hoped to introduce its currency. After more than four years of extremely high inflation and irresponsible monetary policy, Ukraine finally stabilized the *karbovanets'* and then replaced it with the *hryvnya* in September 1996.

From the perspective of economic reform, Russia may have been doing some of the other republics a favor by forcing them to embark on a price liberalization that most other leaders had neither the desire nor the domestic strength to implement on their own. In Ukraine, however, Russia's unilateral measures were interpreted differently by many. These measures demonstrated that Ukraine's deep interdependence with Russia meant that Ukraine was not in fact free to do what it pleased in its domestic economy. It could not really choose its own pace of reform, and could not choose when to establish its own currency. Having established Ukrainian sovereignty at the beginning of December, Ukraine's leaders were dismayed to find out at the end of the month how little *de jure* sovereignty really amounted to in conditions of deep interdependence. The desire to establish economic autonomy commensurate with Ukraine's juridical sovereignty drove Ukrainian policy in the following months.

The Policy of Economic Isolation

In March 1992, the Verkhovna Rada reacted to Russian unilateralism and pressure from Ukrainian nationalists, adopting a measure on "Fundamentals of National Economic Policy." The policy provided for little domestic reform and focused instead on establishing economic independence from Russia, including a plan for a separate currency and a rapid departure from the ruble zone, barriers on imports from Russia, and a refocus of exports toward western markets.[60]

The plan for economic isolation was supported by three distinct groups in Ukraine: the *nomenklatura*, the nationalists, and the national communists.[61] This strange coincidence of interests had coalesced at the time of independence, with the nationalists agreeing to allow the communists and *nomenklatura* to retain power in return for their support for independence. They had in common not only a focus on nationalism and fear of Russia, but a lack of enthusiasm for reform. While the nationalists' views on reform varied, in any case reform was a secondary issue to independence. The *nomenklatura* opposed anything that would endanger their privileged positions, and the national communists shared the nationalists' fear of Russia and the *nomenklatura's* opposition to reform.

From the nationalist perspective, Ukrainian independence (and even reform) could be achieved only in isolation from Russia, for three reasons. First, Russia would use any connections to reassert its domination of Ukraine, as it had in the past, and as it seemed to be doing with reform programs and with energy. Second, instability in Russian society and economy would be more likely to overflow into Ukraine if the two economies were connected. Again, recent experience with prices seemed to bear this out, although Russia's economy turned out to be more stable than Ukraine's, and it never experienced the same levels of inflation. For those who supported reform, there was a third reason: Many Ukrainians, especially in the west, believed at this point that western Ukraine's historical experience with liberalism would lead to speedy reform, and that connection with Russia would only slow down the process.[62] In May 1992, Rukh advocated withdrawal from the CIS on the grounds that the CIS hindered economic development.[63] For those who believed the first two arguments, the efficiency costs of isolation were an acceptable price to pay for independence. For those who believed the third, there was no cost of isolation. One nationalist advocated a "great wall of China" between Ukraine and Russia.[64]

In contrast with this, the top priorities of the "New Ukraine" movement were halting Ukraine's economic collapse and reforming the economy. Their views have coincided largely with those of western analysts, focusing on the costs of breaking such deep interdependence. These politicians argued that trade with Russia was crucial to the economy, and that reform could not proceed without it. Leonid Kuchma played a prominent role in this group, which provided an early (but largely unnoticed) indication that he was not simply interested in closer relations with Russia for their own sake, but rather as a means to reform. Another prominent member, Vladimir Lanovyi, was economics minister until he was dismissed for being too reformist.

The economic plan focused on independence rather than reform, and was based on the contention (in Kravchuk's words) that:

> at a time when Ukraine has become an independent state and the Union center has ceased to exist, our economy continues to be managed from afar. . . . In practice Ukraine has not taken, indeed has not been able to take, any serious independent decisions on the economy. . . . Ukraine's complete dependence on the existing integration in the two states' economies, Russia's usurpation of functions bequeathed by Union financial, banking, and other systems, and its monopoly on ruble printing facilities across the whole ruble area— all of these things place our economy in a very difficult position, which is growing steadily worse.[65]

The program contained four main policies:[66] First, it called for the establishment of a Ukrainian currency and a rapid exit from the ruble zone. This policy was based both on the recent and ongoing experience with currency shortages, and on the nationalist desire to have a Ukrainian currency for its symbolic value. Second, it called for a restriction on imports from Russia, in order to reduce Ukraine's vulnerability. Third, it called for a reorientation of exports to other, less imposing states of the FSU and the west. Fourth, it envisioned using Ukraine's economic power to negotiate favorable deals where possible, by taking advantage of its monopoly position on certain goods and the large amount of transit through Ukraine: "The structural reform policy should include: . . . the exploitation of Ukraine's monopoly in producing certain types of products when forming relations . . . with states in the ruble zone; [and] the introduction of a system of payment for freight transported through Ukraine's territory."[67] These last three items are exactly what Hirschman advocates for a state trying to reduce its vulnerability.

The New Ukraine bloc criticized the plan, asserting (correctly as it turned out) that cutting ties with Russia would decimate Ukraine's economy. A rally in Donetsk to oppose the program, sponsored by the Socialist party, drew 3,000 people. "Kravchuk and his team are being led by Rukh, which is heading towards the withdrawal from the Commonwealth of Independent States. This would have disastrous consequences for the Ukrainian economy and for our region, and would further destabilize the political climate in the republic."[68] At this time, however, the nationalists were still ascendant, and the pro-integration forces, who were associated with the communists, were discredited and had not yet been resuscitated. The reformers alone were unable to stem the tide of economic nationalism in the country. Moreover, it was clear that the nationalists were willing to accept some economic cost: "We must realize that the achievement of balance will inevitably entail a fall in deliveries of scarce goods purchased from Russia and other CIS countries, which in turn will lead to a reduction in production volumes, temporary unemployment, and a fall in income for workers at a number of enterprises."[69] The separation was initiated immediately and formalized at the beginning of 1993, when Ukraine set up customs control at its borders with Russia and Belarus.[70]

As predicted by many, economic isolation from Russia proved catastrophic for Ukraine's economy. The severing of trade ties, combined with the nearly complete absence of economic reform, and the energy problems described previously, paralyzed what remained of the Ukrainian economy. It has been estimated that 67 percent of Ukraine's final production is accounted for by inputs from Russia,[71] and while Ukraine's policy of isolation did not completely stop trade, it did significantly restrict it. Figures on Ukrainian foreign trade are unreliable, but it is clear that trade with Russia fell in 1991 and 1992, and by mid-1993 had "hit rock-bottom."[72] Anecdotal evidence abounds of factories in Ukraine going idle because some key component from Russia could no longer be received, or because a key market in Russia was no longer available. Lack of access to markets was cited along with the energy shortage as the main reasons for the 31.2 percent decline in industrial output in the first three quarters of 1994.[73]

Eastern Ukraine, which was more tightly connected to Russia, both because of its geographical proximity and its heavy industrial concentration, was hit especially hard by the severance of trade. The regional disparity in the impact of the trade restrictions facilitated the emergence of the regional division in Ukraine, never far from the surface, as a major political issue.

The Establishment of the Ukrainian Currency

As was discussed briefly above, Ukraine found it necessary to introduce a pseudocurrency of "coupons" in January 1992. Two problems provided the immediate impetus for the introduction of a separate currency.[74] First, Russia controlled the only presses capable of producing ruble notes, and was unwilling or unable to emit sufficient currency to preserve liquidity as the prices of goods rose. There simply was not enough currency to go around, and several republics, including Ukraine, felt compelled to issue "coupons"—supplementary currencies—long before they were ready to actually create individual currencies. Second, as long as fifteen republics were using one currency, there was a great incentive for each republic to issue credits to failing industries. Doing so was inflationary, but the inflation caused by one state's credit emissions would be spread among all fifteen republics. There was a classic collective action problem regarding credit emission and inflation.[75] Thus the European Bank for Reconstruction and Development advised in February of 1993 that the former Soviet states not attempt to maintain the ruble zone.[76] But having fifteen separate currencies created its own problems, especially since all were being ravaged by inflation.[77] With no convertibility of currencies, interrepublic trade was limited either to barter or hard currency transactions, which created yet another jolt to the economies.

Ukraine's coupons did not immediately become the *de facto* currency of the country, because in the short term Ukraine had made no preparations for establishing a currency and because the ruble continued to circulate. Negotiations over a central currency, and over clearing mechanisms for individual currencies, were carried out almost constantly, but as time went on, establishing the coupon, or *karbovanets'*, as the official currency became the only tenable policy. The story of the currency is much the same as that for trade levels: a mixture of nationalist sentiment and intractable problems in coordinating policies with Russia convinced Ukrainian leaders that they had to take a course that inevitably undercut their republic's prosperity.

In May 1992, the leaders of the CIS states met at Tashkent to institute common monetary and fiscal policies in order to end the ruinous emission of ruble credits by all the republics. Russia made a significant concession by agreeing to consensus decision making, rather than weighted voting. However, short-term exigencies led all of the states to breach the agreement.[78] The energy issue was relevant here as well, with Yegor Gaidar stating in May 1992 that Ukraine would have to pay for Russian energy in hard currency if it left the ruble zone.[79] By August 1992, the *karbovanets'* accounted for 97 percent of official cash transactions in Ukraine, and on 12 November Kravchuk decreed that the ruble would no longer be used, effectively removing Ukraine from the ruble zone.

The introduction of a separate currency further disrupted Ukrainian-Russian trade.[80] Because Russian firms had no use for *karbovantsy*, Ukrainian firms could not simply pay for goods from Russia as they had previously. They either had to find a source of rubles or dollars, both of which were in short supply, or they had to barter. These limitations were exacerbated by the instability of the two currencies. Because the values of the currencies were so volatile, contracts to exchange a given amount of goods for a given price could not be made, because one never knew how much a given amount of currency would actually be worth. Contrary to the view of Ukrainian nationalists, the *Economist* opined that the collapse of the ruble zone was "good news for Russia, but potentially disastrous for other republics," because the ruble zone had served as a mechanism for the transfer of Russian wealth to the others, and encouraged others to export their inflation to Russia.[81]

The introduction of the *karbovanets'* also had important effects in Ukraine's domestic economy. Because the currency was introduced as a hasty reaction to Russian reform, little preparation was made. Most notably, Ukraine was unable to back the *karbovanets'* with a hard currency, as most of the successful currency reforms in the former communist states have done. The introduction of the *karbovanets'* was essentially an unsupported currency emission, and it had the expected effects. The value of the currency plummeted, from 5,000 to the dollar in September 1993 to 140,000 in June 1994, to 180,000 in June 1996. Ukraine endured hyperinflation for much of 1993. Savings and investment have been nearly nonexistent, because they are quickly wiped out by inflation. The only people who have benefited have been currency speculators and corrupt officials, who were able to buy goods with government loans, sell the goods abroad for hard currency, then pay back the loans in grossly devalued *karbovantsy*. Inflation, and the accompanying decline in standards of living, have been problems that have angered even nationalist Ukrainians. In this realm, as well as in trade, severing ties with Russia had catastrophic effects on economic efficiency and prosperity.

In the fall of 1996, the establishment of a separate Ukrainian currency was finally completed with the long-delayed introduction of the *hryvnya*. The Ukrainian government delayed introducing the new currency until the karbovanets' had been stabilized, and until funding from the IMF made it possible to introduce the currency in a noninflationary way. But while the inflation problem has been dealt with to some extent, the exchange problem remains: Trade between Ukraine and Russia is inhibited by the uncertainty of currency fluctuations of two weak currencies. There remain no reliable mechanisms for clearing currency transactions between the two states, and the dollar remains crucial to trade in the region.

In one significant way, the successful introduction of the *hryvnya* represents a step toward economic independence from Russia: the main gauge for the value of the currency, and for Ukrainian monetary policy, is not the Russian ruble, but the U.S. dollar. After a shaky start in which the *hryvnya* lost 5.2 percent of its value in October 1996, the government was able to stabilize the currency, and in May 1997, the Central Bank of Ukraine announced it would defend the *hryvnya* to keep it within a band of 1.7–1.9 dollars.[82] This technical point has not only major implications for the stability of Ukraine's economy, but also shows that Ukrainian monetary policy has been successfully delinked from Russian policy.

The Reassessment

"Rarely can misguided policies and mismanagement have led so quickly to a country's collapse."[83] As the Ukrainian economy continued to crash in 1993, domestic opposition to Kravchuk's policy of isolation increased. By 1995, talk of the need to separate the economies had largely been replaced by discussions of the need to maintain the deep connections between the two economies.

There was talk of secession not only in Crimea, but in Donetsk Oblast' in eastern Ukraine, and such talk was linked directly to the severance of ties with Russia. Residents of eastern regions lamented the "abnormality of relations between the neighboring oblasts of Ukraine and Russia," including the fact that local phone lines had been cut, so that calls to neighboring cities had to go through Kiev and Moscow, and called for the "liquidation of artificially created barriers."[84] Local governments in Kharkiv and Luhansk negotiated association treaties directly with neighboring Russian cities such as Belgorod. The goal was "to restore the traditional, above all, economic ties."[85] It is significant that these movements did not protest Ukrainian independence per se (over 70 percent of Donetskites had voted for independence), but rather the severing of economic ties. In March 1994, the Donetsk regional council called a referendum, to coincide with parliamentary elections, on closer ties with Russia, including dual citizenship, Russian as a second language, and Ukrainian membership in the CIS Economic Union.[86] Ninety percent favored joining the union.[87]

Russia's continuing advocacy of some sort of economic union provided a focal point for those who had disagreed all along with the strategy of isolation, including Leonid Kuchma. As Prime Minister, he tried not only to implement reform, an effort never endorsed by Kravchuk and foiled by the Verkhovna Rada, but also to negotiate an economic agreement with Russia to reestablish many of the ties that had previously existed. As early as February 1993 he stated that ending Ukraine's economic conflict with Russia was his top priority.[88] He was opposed in this effort by nationalists, who continued to believe that Ukraine's economic downturn was not sufficient reason to return to the Russian sphere.[89] Kuchma's resignation was finally accepted in 1993, after he had signed an economic union agreement and infuriated the nationalists in parliament.

Kravchuk recognized early in 1993 that he had misjudged Ukraine's economic position, admitting that "we obviously overestimated the potential of our economy. We overlooked the fact that it was structurally incomplete. . . . It took us too long to realize how much the monetary system of Ukraine depends on the money issue policy of the Central Bank of Russia."[90] But the political forces with which he had cast his lot made it difficult for him to change course. The national communists were opposed to domestic reform, as were Kravchuk's supporters in "the party of power," the administrators who would retain their communist-era positions and privileges only as long as genuine change was forestalled. And the western Ukrainian nationalists opposed any renewal of trade ties with Russia. As he did on the energy issue, Kravchuk tended to give in to reality, and agree to closer relations with Russia, only to back off and toe the nationalist line when pressed. Because his nationalist credentials were so weak, he did not have the political capital with that group that would allow him to make a small move back toward Russia while guarantee-ing that it would not go too far. Essentially he took a passive role, allowing Kuchma to try to solve the problem and incur the wrath of parliament.

In July 1993, Kuchma signed an economic union agreement with Russia and Belarus to reverse some of the damage of economic isolation. The treaty's language on why such an arrangement was necessary indicated a very differ-ent assessment of the situation than had prevailed previously: "The interests of the states dictate the necessity of preserving a single economic area where in conditions of market relations production will effectively develop, goods, services, and capital will move freely."[91] The plan was broadened in Septem-ber 1993 into the CIS Economic Union, modeled on the early stages of the European Community.[92] The treaty envisioned integration in the areas of pro-duction, investment, trade, credit, and currency, most of the areas in which the earlier Ukrainian plan had severed ties. However, the time in Ukraine had not yet come, and Kuchma and the treaty were attacked. While the CIS Economic Union progressed, Ukraine's part in it diminished. Speaker of the Verkhovna Rada Ivan Plyushch found the agreement "absolutely unacceptable," viewing it as "an attempt to restore not only a single economic space, but also a single state administration."[93] Again the crucial issue was sovereignty: Ukraine re-fused to be bound by any measure to which it did not explicitly agree. Any co-ordination proceeded with Ukraine retaining an effective veto power, or simply not participating in programs with which it had problems. The Eco-nomic Union represented greater willingness to accept the reality of interde-pendence, but also emphasized the barriers to significant cooperation or integration.

From the summer of 1993 through 1995, the issue of reestablishing ties between the Russian and Ukrainian economies topped the political agenda in Ukraine, with those who favored increased ties, led by Kuchma, having in-creasing success against the nationalist/isolationist position. Kravchuk vacil-lated on the problem, expressing his support for economic union by stating that he might sign the agreement and then let the Verkhovna Rada decide whether to ratify it. "[T]oday not a single state of the former Soviet Union will be able to solve the crisis unless we create a common economic space and a common market within the CIS."[94] Kravchuk seemed to be motivated by a newly found realism. In presenting a new plan for economic recovery in No-vember 1993, he advocated "strengthening advantageous economic coopera-tion with CIS countries, and above all with the economy of Russia," though he did not dwell on the point.[95] His commitment to renewing ties with Rus-sia remained much weaker than his rhetoric.

The shortage of energy supplies through the winter of 1993–1994, and the steady decline of the economy during that period raised pressure for some-thing to be done, and Ukrainians increasingly viewed the breakup of the Soviet Union as at least in part responsible for their troubles. The relationship with Russia was the primary issue in the Ukrainian presidential election in June and July 1994. Kuchma, with his support based in the East, ran advocating an economic union with Russia, while Kravchuk moved further to the western/nationalist position, which viewed economic union as a sellout of Ukrainian sovereignty. Kuchma's victory reflected not only a crucial shift in political power away from nationalists and the west and toward eastern Ukraine, but a fundamental reassessment of Ukraine's policy of isolating itself from the Russian economy.

By backing off from economic isolation, some of the collapse in trade was immediately reversible. Import and export quotas were cut in May and June 1993, and in August 1993 the government eliminated VAT and excise taxes on trade with other CIS countries. Export incentives and trade liberalization, enacted by Kuchma, including the lifting of central control of prices and foreign trade, ending fixed exchange rates, and lowering taxes, helped increase exports 40 percent and imports 27.6 percent in 1994, and in the first three quarters of that year, Ukraine amassed a trade surplus of a billion dollars.[96]

Why did nationalist leaders oppose reestablishing ties even after the economy crashed? Most fundamentally, as nationalists, many of them saw Russia as a greater evil than poverty. After 300 years under Russian dominance, a period of extreme difficulty was seen as a reasonable price for establishing genuine independence. It is also worth noting that compared to what Ukraine had been through earlier in the century, including being the battleground for two world wars and the target of Stalin's famine, the current problems were not unprecedented. Ukrainians considered themselves survivors, and this period was no different. Also, it was still possible to convince ones self that Ukraine's economic downturn was not the result of cutting ties with Russia, but of the ties with Russia that still remained. At the same time that dissatisfaction over the economy was reaching a crescendo, in the fall of 1993, Russia was using a heavy hand in trying to gain control of the Black Sea Fleet. This convinced some that it was worth any price to stay clear of Russia, and convinced even moderates that Ukraine's independence was in danger, and that Ukraine had to be very careful in restoring economic ties with Russia.

Finally, for those nationalists who supported reform it was plausible to argue (because it is almost certainly true) that reintegration with Russia was no substitute for genuine economic reform, and that reform, not reintegration, should be the focus. As early as May 1992, Rukh had asserted that relations with Russia were only a part of Ukraine's economic problems, and that serious domestic reform was a prerequisite for prosperity under any circumstances. "The Congress believes that to a large extent the economic crisis is due to the incompetent and clumsy actions of the government, which, far from taking effective measures to alleviate the consequences of Russia's economic policy, has worsened the crisis through its own actions."[97] Chornovil stated in early 1994 that "the cause of poverty is not in independence and not in the cutting of ties, but in the leadership."[98] While Kravchuk supported the Union treaty, he warned, "If there are people who think that after this everything will be cheaper, and Ukraine will get cheap oil, gas, and timber, this is nothing but another illusion. We must forget it."[99] More recently, President Kuchma has pursued economic reform with much greater vigor than any economic agreement with Russia, in a seeming reversal of the expectations when he was elected.

Kuchma and Interdependence

As was discussed in the previous chapter, the election of Leonid Kuchma in 1994 signaled a shift in the Ukrainian political spectrum. In his inauguration address, Kuchma demonstrated his priorities: "Ukrainian statehood cannot be an end in itself . . . A state that is incapable of defending its citizens from spiritual and material impoverishment is worth nothing."[100]

> Ukraine's vitally important national interests are concentrated on this territory of the former Soviet Union now. These are also sources of necessary goods, raw materials, and energy-carriers. It is the most realistically accessible market for the products of Ukrainian producers. . . . Ukraine's self-isolation and its voluntary refusal to campaign vigorously for its own interests in the Euro-Asian space was a serious political mistake, which caused great damage, above all to the national economy. . . . In this context the normalization of relations with Russia, our strategic partner, is of principal significance. The signing of a comprehensive and broad treaty on economic cooperation with the Russian Federation, whose preparation is practically complete, could become the first step in this direction.[101]

However, the shift in Ukraine's Russia policy has not been nearly as great as expected. Kuchma's policies as president have resembled more the views that he advocated prior to becoming Prime Minister in 1992 than those he espoused on the campaign trail, which were quite effective in winning the election. In particular, he has sought increased economic ties with Russia, but as a concomitant to economic reform, not as a goal in itself or as a substitute for reform. Contrary to expectations, Kuchma stated shortly after his election that he would not involve Ukraine in any new central structure, rejecting anything that would "limit our sovereignty.[102] At the same time, he has courted the West in general, and the IMF in particular, and finally inaugurated economic reform.

While Kuchma has rejected the nationalist belief that ties with Russia must be severed, he has supported their position on avoiding an economic union with Russia, a dramatic change from his earlier stance. While this policy is perhaps aimed at placating Ukrainian nationalists, those forces will continue to need placating. The shift toward Russia that was expected to follow Kuchma's election has not materialized. If Kuchma is able to reform Ukraine's economy, he may be able to reduce Ukraine's economic vulnerability while leaving connections with Russia intact.

Kuchma has succeeded where Kravchuk failed in part because he has been more determined to reform the economy. Two other factors were equally significant in his ability to actually do what he hoped. The first was the political shift in the country, which meant that there was a clear majority in favor of closer ties—indeed many hoped he would go further. The second was that unlike Kravchuk, he owed nothing to the nationalists for his election, and therefore had nothing to lose by alienating them, as long as he did not push them to revolt. Indeed, many in the west were so bitterly opposed to Kuchma's election that he could not alienate them further. This worked to his advantage. Not only did he have nothing to lose by increasing ties with Russia, but by not going nearly as far as the more alarmist nationalists feared or the communists hoped, he was able to increase ties with Russia while pleasantly surprising his most bitter opponents. The political opportunity structure in Ukraine therefore allowed Kuchma possibilities that Kravchuk did not have, and Kuchma navigated this environment shrewdly. "The president told the left wing to abandon all hopes for restoration of the Soviet Union; the nationalists—not to even think about the previous course toward artificial self-isolation and forcibly breaking ties with Russia."[103] Debates in Ukraine now concern how best to structure trade with Russia, and how Ukraine should position itself between Russia and the west. That Ukraine needs to trade with Russia and will continue to do so is no longer seriously debated.[104]

Conclusion

Whatever misconceptions about interdependence and prosperity existed in 1991 have since been dispelled. Ukraine was not being economically exploited by Russia, but was in fact receiving substantial transfers, especially in energy. Ukraine was not being held back from reform by Russia, in fact the opposite was true. Ukraine's prosperity was not injured by its ties with Russia, even if its independence was. And Ukraine could not simply redirect trade from Russia to the West, due to a combination of shoddy Ukrainian goods and Western protectionism. Economic isolation was exceedingly costly for Ukraine, but the question remained whether it was worth it to solidify the state's independence.

It is important to separate two broad issues involved in trade and currency cooperation between Ukraine and Russia. The first issue is a practical one: the level of interdependence between the two economies. Interdependence was very high under the Soviet system, and the Ukrainian government reduced this interdependence intentionally following Ukraine's declaration of independence. This policy has now largely been reversed as the price of economic independence—that is, increased autarky—has proven high. It is therefore likely that Ukraine will tolerate and even seek a much higher level of interdependence with Russia in the coming years, as it tries to restore some of the economic efficiency that accompanied interdependence.

On the second issue of economic sovereignty, however, the nationalist position seems to be holding. Even many of the eastern ex-communists who support closer ties with Russia are wary of establishing any organs to govern those ties; many "national communists" are equally ardent in their support for reestablishing ties with Russia and their opposition to creating an "economic union" with central decision-making. On this second issue, Ukrainian opinion is still relatively unified, and is still jealous of Ukrainian sovereignty and suspicious of Russian intentions. Ukraine has remained highly protective of its sovereignty, even as the economic costs of that policy have become obvious, and even as it has become more realistic about accepting interdependence with Russia. This suggests that sovereignty is Ukraine's first priority in considering international cooperation and that the focus on sovereignty is a fundamental rather than a transitory phenomenon. Accepting interdependence with Russia while rejecting international management has created an additional dilemma, which is addressed in the following chapter.

6

Interdependence, Sovereignty, and the Commonwealth of Independent States

> Ukraine will no longer share even one percent of its power with anyone.
> —Leonid Kravchuk, *Izvestiya*

> Anyone who does not regret the disintegration of the USSR has no heart, anyone who hopes to revive it has no head.
> —Leonid Kuchma, *Trud*

In the two previous chapters, we have seen how two essential problems have become clear for Ukrainian leaders. First, high economic dependence on Russia creates a severe danger to Ukraine's political independence, as shown most vividly by the energy war. Second, Ukraine cannot offset this threat by severing relations with Russia, because the economic cost is too high. The problem therefore created by these somewhat inescapable parameters is how to be economically interdependent with Russia while remaining politically independent. The primary realm in which this problem has been addressed has been that of the CIS, and the fundamental question has been: How can international interdependence be managed in such way that maximizes the prosperity gains of trade while minimizing the sovereignty losses inherent in international management. A second question has been raised as well: What is the effect of international management on state autonomy. "Ukraine is obviously interested in both the reestablishment of severed economic ties and the etablishment of new ones with CIS countries and, above all, with Russia. But the main problem is this: what kind of ties should they be . . . ?"[1]

The first question is based on the trade-off between prosperity and sovereignty: If trade is to be as free and efficient as possible, states need to take coordinated, or even common, policies on a number of issues. While some issues, such as overall tariff levels, can be dealt with on an ad hoc basis, others can be made only multilaterally, by delegating some decision-making power to a supranational body. For example, a common currency, discussed in the previous chapter, would require some type of international monetary policy body to handle day-to-day administration of policy, even if overall goals were still the subject of direct negotiations between state leaders. The same is true of a payments union between states with separate currencies. State leaders can get together to set up the principles and basic rules of the union, but some organ must implement the policies and make technical decisions.

It is possible to cooperate without institutions, but such cooperation will be limited to simple issues where ad hoc decision making will suffice. For more complex issues, ad hoc decision making will either prove highly inefficient due to increasing transaction costs,[2] or will simply be impossible. To the extent that cooperation is limited by ad hoc decision making, interdependence and prosperity are curtailed for the sake of sovereignty. This has been the driving factor behind increased EU integration in recent years: The desire to further the gains from reduced trade barriers has required that an increasing range of decisions be made internationally.

The second question is based on the paradoxical trade-off between sovereignty and autonomy, which was elaborated in chapter 3. Bilateral trade relations exaggerate the power differential between large and smaller states. By entering multilateral organizations, small states may dilute or balance the power of the largest. Multilateral cooperation allows smaller states to overcome the divide and conquer strategy of the largest. Ukraine would then not find itself constantly bargaining alone with a much more powerful Russia. Some therefore argue that in return for accepting the leadership of a large state, the small can get the large to forego the naked coercion that can occur in an anarchical international system. Following this logic, Kriekemayer and Zagorski assert: "Even though most of the other member states are weak and their respective interests vary significantly, they nevertheless share a common interest in attempting to subordinate Russia to genuinely collective decision making within the CIS."[3] However, given its history of domination by Russia, Ukrainian leaders have tended to see joining an organization with Russia as a step to re-creating the Russian Empire or the Soviet Union. Participation in the CIS seems like a way to guarantee, not to prevent, Russian domination.

The problem in part is Russia's size. While Russia's size is an advantage in resolving collective action problems, it also makes other states wonder whether the CIS can be independent from Russia, regardless of the rules set up. Ukraine's trade of sovereignty for freedom from dominance will not work if the rules are made by Russia or cannot be enforced on Russia.[4] In such a case, neither bilateral nor multilateral cooperation is attractive, and the small state must find some way of making one option or the other more palatable. This, I contend, is the dynamic in the CIS, and it partially accounts for Ukraine's general resistance to strengthening the CIS. Ukraine therefore has not been the only state to oppose the CIS out of fear of potential Russian dominance. Even those states that have most sought cooperation with Russia (notably Kazakhstan) have often found the cost in terms of surrendered sovereignty too high.

There are three ways in which formation of an organization might be expected to enhance Russia's ability to control the others. First, the organization serves to link issues that are substantively unrelated, increasing the ways a hegemon can exercise leverage.[5] In the case of the CIS, the linking of economic, political, and military issues would assist Russia in using its economic power in other realms, an outcome that Ukraine seeks to avoid. Second, it legitimates the unilateral policies of the hegemon by cloaking them in the organization.[6] Drawing from Max Weber, G. John Ikenberry and Charles Kupchan show how dominant states use international institutions to achieve "legitimate domination."[7] As Mark Beissinger shows, this is a major problem in the former Soviet Union.[8] The primary threat in the early years of the CIS has been peacekeeping, where activities ostensibly carried out by the CIS have actually been used by Russia to pursue its goals in the region. Third, when the hegemonic state is much larger than the others, it is very difficult for the others to sanction it for transgressing the rules; this means that the hegemon has little to prevent it from abandoning deals it finds inconvenient.[9] Hedley Bull argues, "The most basic rules depend for their effectiveness on the principle of 'reciprocity.' Where one state is preponderant, it may have the option of disregarding the rights of other states, without the fear that these states will reciprocate by disregarding their rights in turn."[10] In such a situation, multilateral cooperation does not provide an escape from arbitrary rule by the powerful.

Thus Ukraine is faced with a difficult choice in dealing with the CIS. If Ukraine wants to minimize its economic vulnerability, bilateral relations with Russia are disadvantageous. But if Russia is to control the CIS, membership in the CIS may be equally disadvantageous. Either way, refusing to operate within the CIS has important costs for prosperity, as mutually beneficial interdependence is inherently limited by ad hoc, bilateral cooperation.

In addition to these theoretical arguments for and against CIS integration, there are more practical and historical arguments. The case for Ukrainian involvement is made not only by economic theory but by the lessons of international trade in the postwar era, which seem to demonstrate that isolation is not a viable economic strategy, and that international economic regimes increase the prosperity of their members without drastically threatening their sovereignty. The Bretton Woods system is widely interpreted as the exercise of U.S. power to set up a system that was responsible for the prosperity of the entire industrialized world. More recently, all the states of the European

Union have become more prosperous, and none has found itself taken over by Germany (despite Germany's aggressive record earlier in the century). Additionally, there has been the experience, documented in the previous chapter, of what would happen to the Ukrainian economy separated from that of the former Soviet Union. To many the lesson seems clear that economic integration is not an option but a necessity.

To Ukrainian nationalists, however, there are other examples, reaching further back into history, that are equally relevant and much more ominous. And they are much closer to home. The first is the treaty of Pereiaslav of 1654, in which Russia pledged protection of Ukraine against Poland, and ended up taking over most of Ukraine until 1991. The historical details of the treaty are still debated, but which view is correct is less relevant than the fact that in Ukraine, it is viewed by many as evidence of what can happen when entering treaty relations with Ukraine's much larger and much more powerful northern neighbor.

The second historical example cited is also from Ukrainian-Russian relations: the Union treaty of 1922, which in Taras Kuzio's estimate, "closely resembled" the 1993 CIS charter.[11] Following the rise of Bolshevik power in Russia and then in Ukraine, a separate Ukrainian Soviet Socialist Republic was constructed in 1919. In 1922, the Union of Soviet Socialist Republics was created as a union of states whose sovereignty was assured in the text of the treaty. While this *de jure* sovereignty continued to exist until 1991 in such forms as a separate Ukrainian parliament and representation at the United Nations, the reality, of course, was that Ukraine's independence, limited in 1919, was completely eliminated by the end of the 1920s. It is impossible to say whether the correct lesson concerning the CIS is to be found in the contemporary experience of the advanced industrial states or in the more chronologically distant (but geographically proximate) experiences of Ukraine and Russia.

In addition to these historical arguments against integration, opponents can also point to Russian intentions, which were highlighted in chapter 2. The steady stream of statements from Russian leaders concerning Russia's desire, need, and right to dominate the "near abroad" make it easy to believe that Russia does not intend for the CIS to bind it, but rather to use the CIS to bind the smaller states. And finally, there remains the symbolic import of Ukrainian sovereignty, which is an important priority for many Ukrainians. To the extent that such symbolism (including a flag and a national currency) is important, the value of having national authorities unlimited by any supranational grouping is considerable, and substantial loss in prosperity might be considered a reasonable price to pay for such symbolic goods.

In the first five years of Ukrainian independence, these two questions (Does integration bolster or undermine Ukrainian autonomy? and if it bolsters autonomy, how much sovereignty should be surrendered for this goal?)

have been the dominant themes of Ukraine's policy toward the CIS, and they will continue to condition relations between Ukraine and Russia in the future. In essence, Ukrainian policy makers have rejected the idea of using the CIS to bind Russia. It simply does not seem plausible, nor does it seem that Russia would tolerate it: "[T]ransforming the CIS into a civilized integrated grouping which would realize the idea of a voluntary unification of independent states is impossible."[12] Ukraine has, however, recognized that some regulation is necessary both for the purposes of autonomy and prosperity. The trick for Ukrainian leaders has been first, to minimize the amount of central coordination for a given amount of trade cooperation, and second, to isolate the effects of centralized economic management from the broader political realm. Because the goals it seeks are inherently in tension, Ukraine finds itself continuously making difficult and controversial decisions.

In practice, the following set of rough rules has developed: First, Ukraine will not participate in any agreement or organization that requires it to delegate authority for future decision making, even on minor issues. Second, within the first constraint, Ukraine will participate in coordination of economic activities. Third, whenever possible, such coordination will be carried out bilaterally rather than through the CIS. The CIS, because it is viewed as inherently dangerous, is to be relied on as little as possible. Most fundamentally, Ukraine will not surrender sovereignty for increased prosperity, and it will not surrender sovereignty for autonomy even if that leaves it vulnerable to future economic coercion.

Ukraine's policies on the CIS demonstrate that Ukraine still values its sovereignty very highly, even more than prosperity. They also demonstrate that the calculus of cooperation is different in the former Soviet Union than in the West, both because of the increased focus on sovereignty and because of the increased fear of international institutions. In the former Soviet Union, institutions are regarded not as cooperative ventures between sovereign states, but as manifestations of great power imperialism.

Linking Economic Cooperation to Political and Military Cooperation

The issues of political and military cooperation in particular have been at the center of debates over the CIS, and have often encroached on what might otherwise be strictly economic issues. There is a natural tendency for economic cooperation to overlap into the political sphere, because economic integration is facilitated by a widening of common decision making on a whole range of issues. Two additional factors are important as well. First, political cooperation, and especially military cooperation, has been at the top of Russia's priority list since the breakup of the Soviet Union. Political cooperation is sought by Russia because of the perceived instability in neighboring republics and the danger this causes to Russia. Military cooperation is sought also due to the integrated nature of the Soviet defense apparatus, the desire to control the Soviet nuclear arsenal, and the expense and inconvenience of rebuilding defenses along Russian borders.

These issues are manifested most clearly in the areas of border protection and air defense. Russia had no internal border patrols, barriers, or customs stations with the other members of the Union. To build them from scratch would be very expensive. To leave the borders open, however, would leave Russia subject to unwanted immigration, criminal movement, and smuggling. In the case of air defense, many air defense radar installations on the perimeter of the Soviet Union are now beyond Russian jurisdiction, leaving Russia with gaps in its air defense. The desire of Russia (and the West) to maintain unified control over the region's extensive nuclear arsenal was perhaps the most immediate motivation for the maintenance of common military structures, and the only rationale for which Ukrainian leaders had any sympathy.

Second, the formation of the CIS itself linked two issues that might otherwise have been kept separate. Following the collapse of the Soviet Union, plans for economic relations and military relations were discussed separately for the first few months. The formation of the CIS created a common framework for these two different issues. Doing so was necessary to legally dissolve the Soviet Union, the first priority, and it promised (potentially) more rationalized cooperation. Russian leaders hoped that the need for economic cooperation would force the other republics to accept a political union as well:[13] "It is natural that the creation of an effective economic union without fail will have an effect also in the political life of the Commonwealth."[14] But by linking economic integration, which Ukraine has embraced to a limited extent, with political integration, which Ukraine vehemently opposes, made both seem dangerous. Because increased economic cooperation implied a strengthened CIS, which in turn implied increased political and military cooperation, Ukraine opposed economic cooperation. This linkage made it possible for Ukrainians to believe that many plans for economic cooperation were plans to "restore the center." Vadym Beliaiev, head of the Administration of Bilateral Relations with CIS Counries at the Ukrainian Ministry of International Economic Ties and Foreign Trade summarized the problem: "The problem of Ukraine's entrance into the Customs Union is not in its essence economic, and is deeply connected with the problems of the strategic interests and policies of the Russian Federation in the Post-Soviet space and the problem of protecting the national security of Ukraine."[15]

Ukraine, Russia, and the CIS

The Commonwealth of Independent States is perhaps most emblematic of the different views of Russia and Ukraine concerning their relationship. Ukraine viewed the CIS from the beginning as a means of dismantling the Soviet Union in an orderly fashion, and as time has passed has become the least involved of the Commonwealth's twelve members. Russia, in contrast, has seen the CIS as a means of continuing the beneficial ties of the Soviet Union even as the republics became independent, and its pressure on other states to make the CIS a viable and active institution has increased over time.

Ukraine's relationship with the CIS can be broken up into three phases, in which different factors dominated. In the first, from the formation of the CIS in late 1991 until early 1993, two trends dominated. First, there was an immense problem distinguishing between Russia, the CIS, and the remains of the USSR. This made it appear unlikely that the CIS would be independent of Russia, and lent credence to the fears of Ukrainian nationalists. And while the dilemma between prosperity and autonomy was already felt, it was not yet a dominant theme in Ukraine. Second, although many of Russia's policies were viewed with suspicion in Ukraine, Russia's strategy of building the CIS was basically one of benevolence—of convincing others to join the CIS by providing economic benefits.

In the second phase, beginning roughly in January 1993, debate in Ukraine over the CIS increased as a result of the economic crisis. The economic crisis strengthened the perceived need to reintegrate economically, as discussed in the previous chapter, and the debate focused on the economic benefits versus the political dangers of integration. The dangers were emphasized anew by the increased use of coercion by Russia. The debate therefore intensified up through the 1994 presidential elections. Russia's attitudes and strategies concerning the CIS changed, consistent with its shift to a more aggressive energy strategy. At this time, rather than offering incentives to joining the CIS, Russia turned to coercion. The energy war was one form, but more directly linked to the CIS were efforts to destabilize Georgia, Azerbaijan, and Moldova, and pressure to force others out of the ruble zone, denying them the economic benefits of the Russian currency.

The third, current phase, began with the election of Leonid Kuchma in July 1994, and has seen the situation stabilized, though not in the manner anticipated. As with the energy and trade issues, Ukraine has reached a compromise position between its contradictory goals. Political integration with the CIS has been rejected, and the decision is likely a final one. At the same time, however, economic cooperation has been accepted. Ukraine has therefore focused on bilateral rather than multilateral cooperation, a theme expressed since independence, and has kept the fundamental limit of no delegated decision making on its cooperative activities. This policy has resolved the dilemma of prosperity versus sovereignty in a middle position and has resolved the dilemma between sovereignty and autonomy in favor of sovereignty. By focusing trade relations bilaterally, Ukraine has chosen to leave itself open to future Russian economic coercion.

Prologue: The Formation of the CIS

The ideal relationship between the republics of the Soviet Union was an issue even before the coup attempt of August 1991 that prompted the collapse of the Union; indeed it was the prospect of a new Union treaty greatly weakening the center that prompted the coup attempt. While most republics, including Ukraine, used the occasion of the coup attempt to declare their independence, many leaders (including Boris Yeltsin and Belarussian President Stanislau Shushkevich) continued through the fall of 1991 to envision some type of political union between the newly independent states, and Soviet President Mikhail Gorbachev continued his efforts to preserve the Soviet Union Those who realized that the Soviet Union was doomed advocated separate plans for military and economic cooperation.

As early as 12 September, only three weeks after the coup attempt, Russian Federation Defense Committee Deputy Chairman Vladimir Lopatin advocated a new defense organization similar to NATO, and Soviet Defense Minister Evgenii Shaposhnikov said that republic leaders agreed that military forces should remain unified. Plans for an economic union, modeled on the European Community's original 1957 Treaty of Rome, were advanced by reformist economist Grigrory Yavlinsky.[16] Ukraine remained aloof from most of these discussions, awaiting the outcome of its December independence referendum before taking any action, though Kravchuk spoke of the necessity of continued Union.[17]

Already, however, some Ukrainian leaders had other ideas, particularly regarding maintenance of integrated structures. Defense Minister Konstantin Morozov announced that Ukraine desired its own army, stating: "We reject the idea of a unified military command. Our approach will be step-by-step towards an independent Ukrainian army."[18] And while ten other republics agreed on the draft Economic Union Treaty, the Ukrainian Verkhovna Rada immediately denounced it. Dmytro Pavlychko, chair of the Rada's Committee on Foreign Relations stated that Ukrainian independence must have "top priority over all other issues."[19] This fundamental difference in Russian and Ukrainian views has characterized disputes over the CIS since even before its inception.

In the economic realm, Grigory Yavlinsky put forth a program in the fall of 1991 that was modeled on the EC's Treaty of Rome. The plan was debated, and most states intended to sign it, but the centrifugal forces in the region quickly made such deep cooperation impossible. The Yavlinsky plan was opposed in part because it was seen as providing Russia with as much control over the economies of the republics as the Soviet Union had possessed previously.[20] Here the dilemma between prosperity and sovereignty was most clear. Yavlinsky based his plan on economic rationality, and copied the most successful model to date: the EC. In Ukraine there was no opposition to the economics in the plan, but because the economic logic had a political logic as well, the plan was rejected without much hesitation. This tendency has persisted.

On 1 December 1991, Ukraine's populace voted overwhelmingly for independence. Four days later, the Ukrainian parliament annulled the 1922 Union Treaty, and Kravchuk reiterated Ukraine's unwillingness to sign a new Union Treaty. Kravchuk then left for Minsk to meet with Belarussian and Russian leaders, and on 8 December, the establishment of the Commonwealth of Independent States was announced. The treaty creating the Commonwealth had two significant features.[21] First, it dissolved in international legal terms the Soviet Union, accomplishing a goal sought by Yeltsin as much as by Kravchuk. Yeltsin was able to use this provision to force Gorbachev from office a few weeks later. Second, it stated the intention to coordinate policy on the whole range of government activities, from ecology to foreign policy.[22] The significance of these provisions was not their breadth, but the "intentional" nature of them. Nothing concrete was agreed on, and as the first phase of the CIS, the creation, was completed, the stage for the second phase was set: the states had destroyed the Soviet Union but reached no real agreement on what to do next.

Up to that point, Russia and Ukraine had a common interest regarding central structures: the existing central structure—the USSR—continued to have a powerful leader in Mikhail Gorbachev and control over most of the levers of authority in both states. The USSR and Gorbachev still posed a fundamental threat to the sovereignty of the Russian republic as much as to Ukraine. Boris Yeltsin and Leonid Kravchuk had a common threat to the legitimacy of their governments and their individual power, and they cooperated, at least implicitly, against the center. Many Russians shared Ukrainian opposition to the Yavlinsky plan, because they too opposed maintaining a central government that would be superior to their state.[23] Unlike Gorbachev, Boris Yeltsin supported Ukraine's right to secede, for he recognized that this would undermine the Soviet Union and Gorbachev, which were much more immediate problems. The agreement on the Commonwealth, to the extent that it dissolved the Union, was in the interest of both Yeltsin and Kravchuk, of the Russian Federation and Ukraine.

After the dissolution of the Soviet Union, however, the interests of its two largest successors diverged for obvious reasons. With the Soviet juggernaut dismantled, Russia found itself the dominant actor in the region with no threat to its existence or sovereignty. It therefore could pursue a reintegration without the threat that it would be dominated by a new center. If a new center was to be dominated by anyone, it would be Russia. Russia therefore had nothing to fear. Ukraine was relieved to see the Soviet Union gone, but still feared that it could be dominated by a new central structure. History and perceived Russian intentions did not help the matter, and the temporary coincidence of interests concerning the CIS evaporated. The period since has been one of seeking to find what, if any, further coincidence of interests remains regarding the CIS. Ukraine feared above all renewed domination, and Kravchuk stated repeatedly that "if there is any attempt [for one state to stand above others] then the commonwealth will fall apart, because Ukraine will never agree to be subordinated to anyone."[24]

An additional congenital problem of the CIS was that leaders in both Ukraine and Russia seemed to have unrealistic views regarding the compatibility of diverse objectives. In both states, leaders supported a strong union that would not limit the sovereignty of the individual states. This was a contradiction. It is unclear why leaders persisted in acting as though a strong union and complete state sovereignty were compatible. Perhaps they simply did not understand the implications of the two concepts, or perhaps they did not want to make the extent of their disagreement clear. Even in September of 1992, Kravchuk stated that the CIS would eventually be a strictly economic organization, like the EC, apparently unaware of the high degree of political coordination necessary for economic coordination in the EC.[25] In any event, it quickly became clear that for Russia (whose sovereignty was not in doubt) the priority was a strong union, and for Ukraine (whose sovereignty was shaky) the priority was sovereignty, and a strong union came to be viewed as a threat to that sovereignty.

The Identity Crisis of the CIS

Following its establishment, the CIS shifted rapidly from agreement to acrimony. From its formation in late 1991 into 1992, the initial problem regarding the CIS from the Ukrainian perspective was clarifying the relationship between the CIS, its predecessor the USSR, and its largest state, Russia, particularly in the military realm. Because Russia took over many of the institutions and functions of the USSR, it appeared to be a continuation of the USSR, which appeared ominous to the other states. Similarly, because many

USSR institutions became CIS institutions, the new organization was suspect. Finally, it was also difficult to distinguish between Russia and the CIS, because many USSR institutions had officially devolved to the CIS but were obviously controlled by Russia. Because it was difficult to distinguish the Russian Federation, the CIS, and the USSR, Ukrainian fears of a "new center" were easy to confirm, regardless of Russian intentions. When some Russians then advocated that the CIS be used to reestablish central authority, it was seen as a direct threat to Ukrainian independence.

The Soviet Union and Russia

The Soviet Union was dominated by Russia, whose position above the others was enshrined officially in myriad ways. After the collapse of the Soviet Union, Russia began building its own institutions as a sovereign state. In doing so, however, it simply took control of many of the Soviet ministries and renamed them. Doing this while the possibility of some political union was still being debated contributed to the notion that Russia was inseparable from "the center" that all the republics feared. It seemed logical for Russia to become, as it did, the "legal successor to the Soviet Union," but it is precisely this logic that made Ukraine leery of the CIS. While other states, within and outside the region, assented to the transfer of most Soviet assets, institutions, and international prerogatives to Russia, Ukraine protested every step of the way. Russian control over Soviet assets not only was a financial issue, but also implied that Russia had some status that the other successors did not, a status that nearly every state in the world except Ukraine recognized.

Problems regarding the assets of the Soviet Union arose just a month after the coup, when Russia unilaterally negotiated a loan for the entire Union (at this point it seemed likely that some sort of union, minus the Baltic states, would remain). Ukrainian Prime Minister Vitold Fokin protested the assumption of new debt without a firm agreement on who would get the money and who would pay it back.[26] On 2 December 1991, Russia announced that it was taking responsibility for the Union budget until the end of the year. The move broke a political deadlock, but further blurred the distinction between the old Soviet Union and the new Russia.

The trend took on more symbolic import later in the month, when Russia took control of all Soviet property on its territory, including the Kremlin, the Ministry of External Relations, and the former KGB. At the same time, Russia took control of all Soviet foreign currency accounts and Soviet embassies. By this time the Soviet Union did not need the assets, because it no longer existed, but the other successor states did. Russian dominance on the foreign diplomatic front was further asserted at the beginning of 1992, when, in formally taking control of Soviet embassies, Russia agreed to represent the diplomatic interests of the other CIS states.[27] In each case, Russia was asserting its logical position as "*primus inter pares*," but Ukraine did not accept the logic.

The dispute over repayment of the Soviet debt heated up in early 1992, and again here the issue was whether Russia would simply take over the role played by the Soviet Union. At a meeting in Kiev in late February, all the former Soviet republics except Russia and Georgia (neither of which sent representatives) recommended removing the Vneshekonombank (Foreign Trade Bank) from Russian control, relocating it from Moscow, and reorganizing it as an interrepublic bank with each successor state having a vote. Russia saw no need to revise the existing state of affairs in which Russia simply made the decisions that had been previously made by the Soviet government. This issue has continued to fester, particularly between Ukraine and Russia. The other successors have reached agreements with Russia whereby Russia would assume the entire Soviet debt and retain all Soviet assets. Ukraine has been unwilling to sign such a deal, but Russia has *de facto* control over most of the assets. A call by Ukraine for foreign governments to freeze former Soviet assets to allow for their division went essentially unnoticed in the West.[28]

This issue demonstrates how highly Ukraine valued its sovereignty relative to other goals: each of the other successors recognized that as a practical matter, division of Soviet assets and liabilities was impossible. Moreover, by consolidating the debt in one state, all of the states became eligible for further international lending, which was being help up pending assignment of the responsibility for previous debt. Ukraine chose not the practical solution, but the principled one, which focused on the simple argument that Russia did not have the right to act on the behalf of the other states in retaining Soviet assets, in negotiating with creditors, or in paying the debt. To delegate such authority to Russia, many felt, would accelerate Ukraine's return to subservience. Additionally, some estimated that when properly accounted for, joint Soviet assets abroad were worth far more than liabilities. If so, the Russian plan to look after the debts in return for the assets was really a clever ploy to gain wealth for Russia that rightly belonged to all the successors.

There was also a problem distinguishing Soviet from Russian armed forces in the period before the establishment of the Russian army in 1992. A month after the coup, Pavel Grachev asserted that Russia would build a separate defense ministry only if other republics did. The assumption that the USSR defense ministry was sufficient to organize the Russian military encouraged the belief that Russia was not distinct from any supranational organization in the region. The fact that Grachev at that time was both USSR First Deputy Defense Minister and Chairman of the Russian Federation State Committee for Defense only confused the question of whether there was any separation between the newly sovereign Russia and whatever central structures might remain.[29] Russia continued to oppose the construction of separate forces, and built its own only after it became clear that maintenance of the Soviet armed forces was impossible. Because the lines between the Russian and Soviet armed forces were blurred in the interregnum between the Soviet collapse and formation of the CIS, the attempt to transform the Soviet forces into CIS forces served to blur the lines between CIS and Russian forces, an ominous development from Ukraine's point of view.

Russia has been viewed as a continuation of the Soviet Union not only in the region, but in the West as well. Russia was given the Soviet seat on the UN security council, along with its veto. The support for continued union voiced by key western states, from U.S. President Bush's speech in Kiev prior to the coup, to German Foreign Minister Genscher's disapproval of Ukraine's independent course after the coup,[30] reinforced the notion that Russia is essentially a continuation of the Soviet Union, and that this is a desirable state of affairs. While the benefits of such continuity are obvious, the dangers are particularly noticeable to those states considering getting into a new integrative arrangement with Russia. The fact that western policy focused so heavily on Russia was deeply resented in Ukraine, and contributed to the notion that Ukraine had to be hypervigilant concerning its sovereignty.

The Soviet Union and the CIS

Separating the CIS from the Soviet Union was equally difficult. Many of the institutions of the Soviet Union that were not taken over by Russia were simply converted into institutions of the CIS. Hardly any of the institutions of the Soviet Union have actually been disbanded. The fear of a new or reasserted Soviet Union preceded the official demise of the old one, and opposition to strengthening the CIS has consistently been bolstered by the accusation that it represents a continuation of the Soviet Union, with its implied Russian dominance.

The problem has been most concrete in the military realm. When the CIS was formed in December 1991, the military forces of the Soviet Union were simply renamed to become the CIS forces. The Soviet defense minister, Yevgenii Shaposhnikov, became the Commander in Chief of the CIS forces. The plan to continue the Soviet Army as the CIS army was undermined by the process of non-Russian states taking control of Soviet Army forces and equipment on their territory, but at the top there was complete continuity between the Soviet Union and the CIS. Russian Foreign Minister Andrei Kozyrev asserted that a unified army was one of Russia's national interests.[31] The main goal of Ukraine in the fall of 1991 was to ensure the demise of the Soviet Union, so to the extent that the CIS represented a continuation of Soviet institutions, it represented an institution to be feared, not welcomed, for Ukraine.

Russia and the CIS

Continuity between the Soviet Union and Russia, and between the Soviet Union and the CIS, signaled the potential for Russia and the CIS to be so inseparable that Russia would control the CIS as it did the Soviet Union, rather than the CIS constraining Russia. This was most problematic in the military realm, where control of CIS forces and direction of "peacekeeping" missions has been blurred between Russia and the CIS. This was especially prevalent in the period before the creation of a separate Russian army in mid-1992. The problem is also evident in economics, where Russia has in some cases appeared to control CIS policy organs.

Russia's decision in September 1991 not to seek membership in the UN was based on the assumption that the new Union would remain a member of the UN and take the Soviet seat on the security council[32] (in the Soviet era, the Soviet Union had a seat in the UN and on the security council; Belarus and Ukraine were UN members; Russia itself was not). Presumably Russia and the new union would be so close that Russia did not need the separate representation that all the other successors sought. Russia sought and obtained the Soviet seat only when it became clear a tight union was not in the cards. Russia's belief that the union seat would serve its interests was as annoying to Ukraine as its subsequent insistence (and western acquiescence) that it deserved the Soviet permanent seat on the Security Council and its veto.

Militarily, it was often difficult to distinguish between CIS forces and Russian ones, even after confusion between Russian and USSR forces and commands was resolved with the dissolution of the USSR. The role of CIS Commander in Chief (former Soviet Defense Minister) Yevgenii Shaposhnikov was especially confusing. For example, while the dispute over the Black Sea Fleet has largely been a Ukrainian-Russian issue, Shaposhnikov was often involved in advocating the Russian position. His proposal in January 1992 that Ukraine receive 7 percent of the fleet cannot have increased Ukrainian confidence about CIS impartiality, nor did his statement in April 1992 that he was, above all, a Russian citizen.[33]

Shaposhnikov also advocated that Russia, rather than the CIS, control all the nuclear weapons of the former Soviet Union, even as he called for closer CIS military cooperation.[34] The distinction between Russia and the CIS became murkier in October 1992 when the CIS eliminated the position of commander of the CIS strategic forces and left jurisdiction shared between Shaposhnikov and the commander of the Russian Strategic Rocket Forces.

The move eliminated a redundant command and recognized the reality that except for forces in Ukraine, all the strategic nuclear forces in the FSU were under the operational control of Russia not the CIS.[35]

The delay in constructing a separate defense ministry confused lines of command and institutions, but the problem was somewhat temporary. The more significant and lasting issue involved the actual activities of the troops on the ground in some non-Russian republics. In April 1992, Boris Yeltsin issued a decree establishing Russian control over the Fourteenth Army and other units deployed in Moldova. At the same time, however, he put Colonel General Vladimir Semenov, commander of the CIS ground forces, in charge of the newly Russianized units.[36] Besides being confusing, the move was seen as aggressive, as the Fourteenth Army took a major role in establishing the *de facto* partition of Moldova. Moldovan President Mircea Snegur accused Moscow of using the CIS to gain control over the other newly independent states, precisely the scenario feared by Ukraine.[37]

The relationship between the Russian and CIS militaries became clearer when Yeltsin decreed the creation of a Russian army on 7 May 1992. In the short term, however, control of both the Russian and CIS forces was still exercised by the former USSR Defense Ministry and General Staff.[38] In discussions in 1993 over the implementation of the CIS collective security treaty (signed by six states) there was considerable opposition to the Russian suggestion that a Russian Deputy Defense Minister be CIS Commander in Chief. The issue was further resolved in mid-1993 when Russia seemed to recognize that there was little support for an integrated CIS military.

While the institutional confusion surrounding Russia, the USSR, and the CIS was largely resolved by the end of 1992, the broader issue it represented continued to engender wariness from Ukraine toward the CIS. Ukraine continued to oppose Russian attempts to assume a predominant role in the region either institutionally, via the CIS, or in other ways. The ongoing Ukrainian view that Russian dominance was a threat made the CIS an institution to be feared, not strengthened.

Due largely to this concern about re-creating the "center," the CIS remained weak for most of its first year. There were frequent meetings of heads of state, and a multitude of agreements was signed, but these only served to paper over more genuine differences. Most of the agreements were merely statements of intentions, and even those that contained firm commitments were often disobeyed. Ukraine in particular refused to sign 40 percent of the agreements and signed another 10 percent only with qualifications.[39] Ukraine refused to sign the agreements that were most important to Russia and other CIS enthusiasts, including those that focused on military political affairs and common governing organs such as the collective security pact, joint armed forces, and the interparliamentary assembly.[40] After the May 1992 summit in

Kiev, in which Kravchuk plainly expressed his lack of support for the CIS, there was speculation that the organization would collapse entirely at the Tashkent summit in May, but that did not occur, despite the fact that Kravchuk neglected to attend, and the Commonwealth's fortunes subsequently improved after the Yeltsin-Kravchuk agreements at Dagomys in June.[41]

Nonetheless, in September 1992, Kravchuk was still criticizing Kazakh President Nursultan Nazarbaev for his strong advocacy of deeper integration, stating that Ukraine opposed "all attempts to turn back the wheel of history and revive the old imperial center by camouflaging [these attempts] with deceptive slogans about a single economic or some such space, the need for more coordination of activities, and the like."[42] Until early 1993, this opposition commanded wide support among Ukrainian political groups, with only the Socialist party of Ukraine and the Ukrainian Society of War Veterans favoring signing the CIS charter at a meeting of political groups with Kravchuk in January 1993.[43]

Peacekeeping and Russian Expansion

Perhaps the CIS issue that has been most symbolic of Ukraine's fears of the organization has been that of "peacekeeping," the deployment of CIS or member state troops to quell conflict in the region. So far, the issue has arisen in Tajikistan, Moldova, Georgia, and between Armenia and Azerbaijan in the Nagorno-Karabakh conflict. While many CIS members have welcomed Russia's ability to stabilize certain situations, most notably that in Tajikistan, they have simultaneously feared that Russia would use peacekeeping provisions to undermine the independence of other states, and that CIS peacekeeping provisions would only facilitate this potential. Russian forces are widely recognized to have helped destabilize Moldova, Georgia, and Azerbaijan. The ability of Russia to unilaterally carry the burden of peacekeeping (benign hegemony) has been inseparable from its ability to unilaterally decide when and where to keep or make peace, and where to let conflict continue (coercive hegemony).

The situation in Moldova demonstrated Russia's ability to undermine its neighbors' independence, as well as its ability to disregard agreements that it no longer supported. An agreement on Transdniestria worked out by the Russian, Romanian, Moldovan, and Ukrainian governments in April 1992 was perceived to favor Moldova. Russia initially did not abide by the agreement and then renounced its support for the deal.[44] It then suggested that the Fourteenth Army become a peacekeeping force in Moldova, which signaled a shift from Yeltsin's previous proposal to remove the Fourteenth Army, and instead gave it a formal role. Ukrainian, Romanian, and Moldovan governments opposed this proposal, but only Russia could remove the troops.[45] When Russia and Moldova met to discuss the withdrawal of the troops, Russia added to the agenda "the prospect of military cooperation between the two states," implying that cooperation might be a prerequisite for Russian withdrawal,[46] a condition which became explicit in March 1993.[47] The other states had no ability to sanction Russia's reneging on the agreement. It is this fear that Russia can do what it wants due to its immense power that leads Ukrainian leaders to be skeptical that the CIS will genuinely restrain Russia in return for Ukraine surrendering some sovereignty.

The problems faced by Moldova were mirrored in Georgia's fight with its Abkhazian and South Ossetian separatists.[48] Georgia sought Ukrainian mediation to supplement the Russian troop involvement to resolve the conflict over Abkhazia in 1993.[49] Georgia's Ambassador to Russia was resigned to Russia's ability to control the region, saying, "Georgia will be independent if Russia wants it, and vice versa."[50] The problem of Russian dominance in peacekeeping was addressed explicitly in October 1994, when Ukraine abandoned its policy of abstention and agreed to send cease-fire monitors to Georgia to offset Russian partiality in the conflict.[51] The ability of Russia to destabilize Moldova, Georgia, and Azerbaijan is particularly ominous to Ukraine, given its potential separatist problem in Crimea, which could easily be stoked by Russia. It has been important therefore for Ukraine to deny the legitimacy of Russian military activity in other post-Soviet republics. Because the CIS legitimates such a role for Russia, Ukraine opposed economic agreements that would legitimate the CIS, even if the agreements might have economic merit, because they contributed to the reanimation of "the center."

The Russian diplomatic campaign in 1993 and 1994 to have Russia's "special status" in the former Soviet Union acknowledged only increased fears that Russia's ability to maintain the peace could be put to dangerous use if officially sanctioned. Ukrainian leaders reacted strongly to Yeltsin's suggestion in February 1993 that the UN recognize Russia's right to serve as peacekeeper throughout the former Soviet Union, which they regarded as evidence of Russia's intent to reassert its dominance.[52] Russian Foreign Minister Kozyrev asserted that international approval was not needed for Russia to engage in peacekeeping.[53] Similarly, a Russian campaign to have the CIS recognized by the UN as an "international organization" was vigorously opposed by Ukraine, because under the UN Charter, regional international organizations can engage in peacekeeping without the approval of the UN.

Ukraine's initial policy toward the CIS therefore directly paralleled its policy toward trade with Russia. Policy at this stage was dominated by one domestic group, the nationalists, and by one overriding preoccupation: establishing Ukraine's independence from Russia and the Soviet Union. The goal was sovereignty, the means was rejection of policy coordination, and there was little room for compromise. The lack of agreement on the role of the CIS has continued to the present day, and has caused the institution itself to be moribund. Russia has been able to convince the more recalcitrant states (Georgia and Moldova) to join the organization, but there remains no significant institutionalization, due primarily to Ukraine's unwillingness to tolerate any centralized decision making. Ukraine has remained opposed even to signing a CIS Charter that would lay out the basic foundations of the organization, on the grounds that such a charter would re-create central structures.[54]

It is impossible to measure directly the economic effects of Ukraine's refusal to participate in meaningful policy coordination, but some barriers to trade were certainly created or maintained as a direct result of this refusal. In October 1992, for example, Russia set up customs barriers with Ukraine and Azerbaijan because those two states did not sign the agreement on a customs union signed by others in March of that year.[55]

The Shift in the Debate in 1993

Both Russia's and Ukraine's positions on the CIS changed significantly in 1993. Russia still pursued CIS integration, but increased the use of coercion rather than offering incentives to persuade others to go along. And Ukraine, while maintaining its fundamental opposition to meaningful integration, became more willing to participate in economic agreements, and to acknowledge the utility of the CIS as something other than a mechanism for divorce.

In the spring, after almost eighteen months of promoting the CIS, Russia began to downgrade the importance of the organization.[56] The deemphasis was shown most clearly in a changed Russian policy toward CIS defense structures. Previously, Russia had advocated maintaining a strong joint military, even as other republics formed their own armies. In May 1993, however, Russia rejected two draft agreements proposed by the CIS joint command to increase integration and to form the joint forces that Russia previously advocated. In particular, Russia opposed creating standing CIS forces during peacetime, a significant reversal from its original goal of an "Eastern NATO." There appeared to be two reasons for the change. First, Russia may have simply given up on the hope of joint forces and decided to focus its efforts on strengthening its own military. Second, as noted by the Russian representative at the talks, Col. Gen. Boris Gromov, Russia would have to foot most of the bill for such joint forces, and was hesitant to do so at a time when money was short and the idea of joint forces was dead anyhow.[57] In June, Russia suddenly reassigned Shaposhnikov to the Russian Security Council, and four days later the CIS Defense Ministers agreed to give up the effort to maintain common military forces.[58] At this point, the problem of separating Russian from CIS forces largely ceased.

However, the reluctance to pay for joint CIS troops did not indicate that Russia was decreasing its military role in the region. Instead, Russia sought to have Russian troops take the role previously envisioned for the CIS as regional peacekeepers.[59] There was nothing other states could do (none had the money to keep the joint forces going) but this different form of hegemony may have appeared even more threatening, especially considering the activities of Russia's troops in the region's conflicts.

Meanwhile, important changes were taking place in Ukraine's position toward Russia and the CIS. Until 1993, nationalists basically controlled policy on these issues, and steadfastly refused to deal with the CIS or to undertake significant cooperation with Russia. Moreover, opposition to the CIS charter commanded the support of forces all across the Ukrainian political spectrum.[60] As the Ukrainian economy crashed, however, many Ukrainians, particularly in the east, began to call for closer ties with Russia, the perception being that the economic collapse was due in large part to the severing of ties with Russia following independence. "Whereas the main pressure on . . . Kravchuk had formerly come from nationalists demanding the withdrawal of Ukraine from the CIS, he now found himself under equally strong pressure from conservative deputies and the industrial lobby . . . who wanted Ukraine to reestablish economic links with the other CIS states and even to sign the CIS charter."[61]

Kravchuk continued at the Minsk summit in January 1993 to refuse to sign the CIS charter, a document aimed at specifying the functions of the CIS and turning it into an operating international institution, but he did seek to reestablish economic links. "As in the past, the major stumbling block was Ukraine's stubborn refusal to affix its signature to the document on the grounds that the proposed charter would reanimate centralized 'superstate' structures and encroach upon its sovereignty as an independent state."[62] Kravchuk's recognition of the importance of the CIS, as well as his lack of enthusiasm, were demonstrated when he said, "If there were no CIS things would be worse." The difference in priorities was noticeable at the summit, where Ukraine stated the first priority was to resolve the economic crisis while the charter focused on reasserting principles in previous agreements, including collective security, a nonstarter for Ukraine, and political coordinating bodies, a difficult sell at best.[63] Even Belarussian President Shushkevich, whose parliament had given him explicit instructions to sign the charter, declined to sign the collective security agreement on the grounds that it conflicted with Belarus's neutrality.[64]

However, the refusal to sign the charter was accompanied by a more accommodative stance in other areas. Ukraine's willingness to participate in central organs reached a new high when it signed an agreement on an Interstate Economic Bank that gave a great deal of control to Russia (50% of the votes, the use of the Russian ruble as a common currency, and control by the Central Bank of Russia). On the practical level, the bank was more significant than the charter because it promised to restore much of the interstate trade that broke down with the introduction of separate currencies, and that afflicted Ukraine particularly severely. In the end, the bank did not preserve the ruble zone, as many hoped, but Ukrainian agreement to participate in it demonstrated a significant realignment of Ukrainian policy at this time, as well as a rare degree of agreement between Kuchma (at that time Prime Minister) and President Kravchuk.[65]

The shift in Ukraine's policy was attributable to the changing domestic economic and political situation in Ukraine. The dominance of nationalists that followed independence was eroding as pro-Russian forces reorganized and economic isolation incurred hardship. Kravchuk admitted in January 1993 that the society was now divided, with the pro-Russian group, including many members of the Verkhovna Rada, advocating acceptance of the CIS charter and the nationalists advocating not only rejection of the charter, but a Ukrainian exit from the CIS as well.[66] At the Minsk summit, Kravchuk was still able to straddle the two camps, pleasing the first by signing a document that would allow Ukraine to sign the charter later and pleasing the second by not signing it immediately. This straddle became increasingly difficult to maintain as Ukrainian society polarized and Russian pressure increased.

Ukraine was largely unable in this period to participate in economic agreements without political ones in large part due to Russia's new strategy of coercion, which sought to use Ukraine's economic woes to bring it into a broader political agreement. This solidified the linkage between economic and political cooperation that was the main barrier to Ukrainian participation in an economic agreement once the nationalist tide in Ukraine had ebbed. In a significant sign of Ukraine's new openness toward the CIS, however, the agreement was not rejected outright. Instead, a declaration was adopted that would allow nonsignatories (Ukraine, Turkmenistan, and Moldova) to sign later if they wished (none did).[67] While many commentators at the time saw this summit as a turning point for the CIS, it turned out to be just another in a long series of "agreements to agree" that meant little in practice.

In particular, the Interstate Economic Bank Agreement became irrelevant later in the year when Russia forced out the remaining members of the ruble zone in an effort to stem the devaluation of the ruble. Previously, Russia had actively promoted the ruble zone, and had made considerable concessions, to maintain the zone, including letting other states emit inflationary credit. By implying that states remaining in the ruble zone could continue to receive subsidized energy, Yeltsin provided a considerable incentive for other states to agree to Russian monetary hegemony. The policy changed in mid-

1993 both because Russia could no longer afford it and because it became apparent that the others needed the ruble zone more than Russia did. Rather than giving states rewards for staying in the ruble zone, Russia began to demand concessions in order to remain. In particular, continuing participation was predicated on willingness to delegate monetary policy making to Russia. The new policy reflected the growing feeling in Russia since late 1992 that the other states needed Russia more than it needed them. In contrast to statements following the coup that a union without Ukraine was unthinkable, Boris Yeltsin stated in mid-1992 that the others were learning they could not survive without Russia, and his Vice-President Alexandr Rutskoi was more blunt, saying, "We shall see who depends on whom."[68]

When Russia decided to reform its currency by withdrawing old rubles in July 1993, it did not abide by a prior agreement that all ruble zone members would provide six months' notice before introducing a new currency. Instead, the government simply announced that Soviet-era rubles were being taken out of circulation to be replaced with a new Russian ruble whose circulation would be limited to states that agreed to Russian control of monetary policy. In effect, Russia itself left the ruble zone. While the basic policy was widely supported as constructive, its sudden and unilateral implementation was severely disruptive. The Belarussian ruble lost nearly half its value. Georgia left the ruble zone, giving its citizens one week to exchange rubles for Georgian coupons. Azerbaijan's national bank was given two days to work out a plan to introduce a national currency.[69] Russia's sudden action showed that it could not be bound by its own agreements. It also showed that common decision making was likely to be Russian decision making. While the former may have been an economic benefit, the latter was intolerable even to those states less recalcitrant than Ukraine.

Fear over Russian power was the direct cause of Kazakhstan's decision to leave the ruble zone in November 1993, despite its goal of economic integration with Russia and its membership in the economic union agreement reached that September. Kazakh Prime Minister Tereschenko cited the "unacceptable conditions" being insisted on by Moscow—including maintaining large hard currency and gold reserves in Moscow—to use the new Russian ruble.[70] Uzbekistan, Kyrgyzstan, and Turkmenistan, other members of the nascent economic union, also withdrew from the ruble zone citing the concentration of monetary power in Russia as the reason. By November 1993, only Tajikistan intended to remain a member.[71] In this regard, Ukraine's policy was mirrored (a bit later) by the region's other states.

Contrary to the expectations expressed at the Minsk summit, which were characteristically overoptimistic, the CIS did not become the functioning organ that many hoped, and Ukraine continued to be the primary brake on CIS integration. Ukraine was more willing in 1993 to interact with the CIS, but the bottom line remained that no abridgment of Ukrainian sovereignty would be permitted, and that cooperation would be strictly limited to economic affairs. Thus when the Economic Union of the CIS was negotiated in September 1993, Ukraine insisted on creating a special "associate membership" for itself. According to details worked out at the Moscow CIS summit in April 1994, Ukraine will take part in only the organs it finds useful, and will be bound only by agreements it signs, not by decisions made by CIS organs that are binding on full members. "The decisions of the Economic Union in which Ukraine does not take part will have for Ukraine the character of recommendation."[72] While Ukraine sought to participate in the economic union, it still refused to delegate authority such that Ukraine might be legally committed to something it opposed. The effect of Ukraine's reluctance is to seriously undermine the ability of the economic union to deal with any but the most trivial issues.

And even at this point, Ukraine's shift in policy was being slowed by a counterattack from nationalist forces. Kuchma's decision to sign the agreement was attacked in western Ukraine, where there were calls for strikes and for Kuchma's resignation. A L'viv newspaper headlined, "The agreement crucifies Ukraine and she will never be resurrected"; and the author, a local government official, complained: "We recall the former slogans about harmonious and dynamic development in the name of the people, and what came of this? Lagging technology and an indigent economy. We should proceed further on this path?" His opposition in particular was that "In the conditions of integrated interdependence, such coordinating structures will deprive Ukraine of its economic freedom. . . . Thus a deprivation of economic freedom will lead to a deprivation of political freedom."[73] A western trade union declared that the "treaty signals the final economic and political serfdom of Ukraine and the return by her to colonial status and a full surrender of the sovereignty of Ukraine as a state. . . . We consider this act an insidious betrayal of the interests of the Ukrainian nation on the part of the government of L. Kuchma."[74] This reaction shows how difficult it was for the government to restore the institutional structures that it saw as essential tools for increasing efficiency.

As was discussed in the previous chapter, the issue of CIS integration played an important role in the 1994 Presidential campaign, with Kuchma, who was responsible for signing the economic union treaty in September 1993, advocating full rather than associate membership, and Kravchuk adopting the nationalists' position. Kuchma's convincing victory seemed to assure that the second phase of Ukrainian-CIS relations would end with a complete reversal of the belligerent policy that characterized the first phase. Instead, Kuchma adopted a position on the CIS that was as close to that advocated by the nationalists as to that advocated by Russophiles.

Ukraine's Policy of Bilateralism

In particular, under Kuchma Ukraine has maintained its unwillingness to compromise on the sovereignty issue.[75] As President, Kuchma has adopted a much less friendly line toward the CIS than he showed during the campaign, stating his opposition to the creation of centralized organs, and refusing in September 1994, to play a full role in the new CIS Interstate Economic Committee, or to participate in a new payments union.[76] In this respect there has been a fundamental continuity in Ukrainian policy toward the CIS from Kravchuk in 1991 through Kuchma in 1998.

The third phase of Ukraine's relations with the CIS has entrenched a policy whose roots were seen much earlier: bilateralism.[77] Such a policy does not reject economic interdependence, and does not reject formal agreements to govern international trade. But it does limit the acceptable forms of such cooperation. In particular, it rejects an important role for international institutions, which become much more important in facilitating multilateral cooperation, due to its complexity. It also rejects the need for Ukraine to submit to the will of a majority of its neighbors, since majority voting is not required in bilateral negotiations. Bilateralism allows Ukraine to carefully pick and choose what agreements it wants to participate in. The cost of this policy is a certain reduction in efficiency and a potential reduction in autonomy, and the benefit is the guarantee of sovereignty against the slow encroachment from Russia that has plagued Ukraine in the past.

Leonid Kravchuk advocated bilateral cooperation as early as November 1991, stating that "there should be no center" and that "We shall not ratify any kind of agreement that is propped up by central bodies—to any extent, however slight."[78] In December 1991 he stated that Ukraine would participate only in "bilateral state agreements."[79] He and other Ukrainian leaders have repeatedly asserted the benefits of bilateralism. Despite the knowledge that coordinating bodies are necessary for effective multilateral cooperation, Ukraine has consistently sought to prevent the establishment of such bodies.[80] In mid-1992, when leaders were discussing creation of a CIS "coordination council," Ukrainian Prime Minister Vitold Fokin, by no means a nationalist, preferred to refer to a "consultative-coordinating council," because the word "consultative" implied that the group had no actual authority.[81]

Kravchuk opposed the creation of central institutions primarily because they threatened to re-create the Soviet Union, but an additional reason was that he did not believe that they were any more suited to solving problems than bilateral ties. As evidence, he cited the fact that in the final few years of the Soviet Union, central ministries existed but were unable to solve anything.[82] An additional problem was that as cooperation involved more countries, it became more difficult to find solutions amenable to all. Normally, this would simply involve compromise, but Ukraine, still heavily emphasizing sovereignty, viewed compromise within a central institution as abrogation of sovereignty. The way to minimize the need to compromise was to interact bilaterally.[83]

In the period following Kuchma's election, bilateralism has become ensconced as Ukraine's preferred means of trade cooperation with Russia. Bilateralism now has an organizational basis in the Ministry of International Economic Relations and Trade, which has an "Administration for Bilateral Relations with Russia" and an "Administration of Bilateral Relations with CIS Countries." Rather than having any particular virtue, it has prevailed as a policy because it is the least of three evils, and represents a political as well as an economic compromise. Economically, bilateralism represents a compromise between the most efficient policy of multilateralism and integration and the least efficient position of isolation. Politically, it represents a compromise between the nationalists' isolationist position and the Russophiles' integrationist view. Volodymyr Horbulin, Secretary of Ukraine's National Security Council, captured the prevailing view saying: "Ukraine is interested unconditionally in renewal of old, and establishment of new, economic ties both with the countries of the CIS and first of all with Russia. . . . On the other hand, the artificial acceleration of still incompletely formed market economic structures will lead to the rebuilding of the 'single economic complex' of the former USSR with all of its inherent consequences."[84]

As was shown in the last chapter, isolationism was eliminated on economic grounds, after it dominated the first period of Ukraine's independence. In this chapter, we have seen that multilateralism has been rejected on political grounds, after being seriously considered in the second phase of Ukraine's independence. Continuity in Ukraine's policy will arise in part because of the underlying balance of power in the country politically. The nationalists, even though out of power, continue to be powerful enough to prevent a complete surrender of their position. The continuity is also being supported, however, by a growing political center in the country's political spectrum. More and more Ukrainians are holding the position that interdependence is necessary, but integration dangerous. This previously vacant middle is gaining adherents as some in the west give up some of the more naive expectations they had about Ukraine's economic potential and others in the east recognize that Russia is a potential threat.

Conclusion

While Ukraine has readjusted its policy to end its economic isolation to increase prosperity, it has been unwilling to sacrifice sovereignty for that goal.

Despite a reconsideration of policy, and a vigorous debate within Ukraine, the bottom line has remained: Ukraine will seek economic cooperation with Russia, but only to the extent that supranational institutions are not required. In this respect, Ukraine's policy has continued to be driven by the sentiments its leaders expressed even before the formation of the CIS. For this reason, Russia and Ukraine continue to be at odds over the proper role of the CIS. By the Summer or 1994, about 500 agreements had been signed under the aegis of the CIS, and almost none were being implemented.[85]

The continuity in policy toward the CIS contrasts with the shift on economic interaction with Russia, discussed in the previous chapter. After deliberately isolating itself from trade with Russia in 1992, Ukraine largely reversed course in 1994 and 1995 after the costs became clear. Policy on the CIS was questioned at the same time, but did not undergo nearly as significant a modification, demonstrating that even powerful forces for change in Ukraine did not alter the opposition to supranational structures. Ukraine was willing to tolerate more interaction for the sake of prosperity, but it was not willing to tolerate any loss of sovereignty.

Together, these two decisions demonstrate that Ukraine is more concerned with its *de jure* sovereignty than its *de facto* autonomy. By agreeing to interact more with Russia, Ukraine again made itself more subject to Russian pressure, and in that manner sacrificed some autonomy. Some freedom from coercion could have been maintained if Ukraine was willing to join with other states to create rules to govern international trade, which would presumably limit Russia from some of the unilateral and coercive measures it has enacted. Ukraine chose not to do this, in part because it was skeptical that the rules would actually protect it, but also because they would encroach on Ukrainian sovereignty. By dealing with Russia bilaterally, Ukraine violates one of the primary rules on how small states can maintain their autonomy in an independent world. Theory and experience show that bilateral relations make it easiest for powerful states to control their smaller neighbors.

Ukraine has taken an extreme position, at least in the current international context, in favor of preserving sovereignty at the expense of the economic efficiency and autonomy that could be pursued through integration. The main reason is clear: after a long struggle for independence, Ukraine is very jealous of its sovereignty, and fears that any initial surrender of sovereignty could open the door to renewed dominance by Moscow. Ukraine's unorthodox policy does not, therefore, indicate a lack of wisdom by its leaders, but rather a caution bred by centuries of domination. Ukraine will make its sovereignty absolutely secure before it pursues other goals.

7

The Direct Economics-Security Connection

Nuclear Weapons in Ukraine

> The main threat to Ukrainian statehood can come only
> from Russia.
> —Anatoliy Zlenko, *Radianska Ukraina*

> I place primary importance on the internal threat, because
> there is currently no country or group of countries that could
> dare attack Ukraine militarily.
> —Boris Tarasyuk, "A New Concept of European Security"

Ukraine's policy on nuclear weapons and its policy on its economic vulnerability were closely intertwined, and understanding that relationship is important for understanding the dynamics of both issues. Nuclear weapons made Ukraine address a fundamental issue in its relations with Russia: Was it to deal with Russia's assertiveness by confronting it with countervailing military power (balancing), or by "bandwagoning"—submitting to Russian hegemony? Ukraine was unalterably opposed to bandwagoning, but in examining the nuclear relationship, realized that balancing Russian power was simply not feasible. Contrary to conventional wisdom, nuclear weapons would *not* guarantee Ukraine's security. Ukraine could not hope to prevail in a military competition with Russia, especially one carried out in the form of nuclear arms race. That direct confrontation was infeasible was admitted by Kravchuk when he stated: "Those who have quarreled with Russia have lost."[1] The recognition that the battle cannot be fought in the military arena has made the economic arena crucial to Russian and Ukrainian policy makers, and to Ukraine's fate.

At the same time, the economic struggle helps us understand why Ukraine adopted the nuclear stance that it did. In particular, the themes established in the preceding chapters, namely that Ukraine has been concerned with sovereignty above all else, and that prosperity, even if increasing in importance, remains a secondary goal, help us understand why Ukraine hesitated in its commitment to disarmament, and why it then went ahead. Having expected the world to readily respect its sovereignty, Ukraine balked when this turned out not to be the case, and began using the nuclear weapons as a way to force Russia and the West to acknowledge Ukraine's sovereign rights. It continued to do so even after the West applied significant financial pressure to disarm. Ukraine's internal economic collapse was much more important in the decision to disarm than Western pressure and promises of aid. The aid pledged was not nearly what Ukraine sought, and we have seen that Ukraine was not primarily concerned with prosperity. Acknowledgment by Russia and the United States of Ukraine's legal equality, and Russian commitment to respect of Ukraine's territorial integrity were prerequisites to any deal on compensation. Thus there were two obstacles to Ukrainian nuclear disarmament: the belief that nuclear weapons provided Ukraine both a diplomatic lever and an effective deterrent; and Ukraine's insistence that others respect its sovereign rights concerning the weapons, even if they were to be given away.

This chapter focuses on the links between Ukraine's economic vulnerability and its nuclear weapons policy. After a discussion of the Soviet nuclear legacy and the concerns of Ukraine, Russia, and the West, two important shifts in the Ukrainian nuclear debate are chronicled. First was a drastic shift from idealism to crude power politics. Ukraine originally rejected nuclear status due to the recent memory of Chernobyl and the state's self-image as a neutral. This position was questioned when the ideals of state sovereignty did not seem to obtain in the real world: Russia and the west questioned Ukrainian independence and did not respect its sovereignty. Ukraine's newly found realism was a crude one, which focused on the need to build military power to check Russian expansionism, and to use the nuclear weapons to bargain with the West.

This crude realism was then replaced by a much more pragmatic policy. As it became clear first that Russia was unlikely to attack militarily, and second that Ukraine could not possibly compete in an arms race, the military and political rationale for the weapons was reduced. At the same time the economic danger became abundantly clear. This second shift, accompanied by increased recognition by Russia and the United States of Ukraine's sovereignty, paved the way to agreement. Ukrainian leaders came to realize that military conflict was not the primary threat to their state's independence. Ukraine agreed to surrender the weapons only after it became clear that economic, not military warfare, was the main threat from Russia. The driving force behind the agreement was not the relatively small monetary compensation given to Ukraine, but the reality that Ukraine could not afford military competition with Russia or economic isolation from the west. Ukraine's nuclear disarmament was thus closely tied to its problems of economic vulnerability.

The Problem

The Soviet Legacy

The Soviet Union stationed nuclear weapons throughout the former Soviet Union and Eastern Europe. Those in most of the newly independent states were transportable, and were removed with the end of the Cold War and the demise of Warsaw Pact in 1989 and 1990. Nuclear weapons were on permanent station in four Soviet republics at the time of the coup: Belarus, Kazakhstan, Russia, and Ukraine. In addition, important missile construction facilities were located in Ukraine, most notably Yuzhmash (Pivden'mash) in Dnipropetrovsk, where the SS-24 was built under the management of Leonid Kuchma. When Ukraine became independent in 1991, it inherited a significant portion of the nuclear arsenal of the Soviet Union and instantly became the world's third-leading nuclear power.[2] The nuclear weapons located in Ukraine composed a large and diverse arsenal, including large land-based Inter-Continental Ballistic Missiles (ICBMs) with multiple warheads, smaller older generation ICBMs, tactical nuclear weapons, and strategic bombers. All of these were on Ukrainian territory, whether Ukraine wanted them or not, and only a small portion (the tactical weapons) could easily be removed. In the short term, the weapons had to stay.

But their presence in Ukraine did not mean that Ukraine had the ability to use the weapons. Launch control was much more tightly held in the Soviet Union than in the United States, and was held strictly in Moscow.[3] In the short term, Ukraine had a bizarre nuclear status—it owned the weapons but could not launch them. In the longer term, Ukraine had the technical capacity to establish launch control over the weapons. In that sense, Russia and the West had something of a grace period to convince Ukraine to give up the weapons before Ukraine could get them to be operational. From a strategic standpoint, the situation was highly unstable, because as Ukraine got closer to being able to retarget and launch the weapons at Russia, the incentive for Russia to strike preemptively would be immense.

Russia's Security Fears

If Ukraine considered keeping the weapons to deter Russian aggression, Russia sought to have the weapons removed to prevent Ukrainian irresponsibility. Russia already had one nuclear neighbor in China, which was perceived as dangerous, and did not want to face another in the West—especially one controlled by Ukrainian nationalists whose hostility toward Russia was documented and whose political experience, caution, and control were suspect. A fear raised continuously by Russian leaders, partly out of genuine concern and partly to help frighten the West into a tougher line on the issue, was that the weapons themselves would not be secure under Ukrainian control.

A second Russian security fear was broader politically, but perhaps equally unnerving: the idea of Ukraine as equal. Russia has made it a primary goal of its foreign policy to have the same status in its region that the United States has in its; to be declared first among equals. By attaining full-blown nuclear status, Ukraine would also be declaring its complete independence from Russia, and perhaps even seek to challenge it for regional dominance. Russia's position of dominance, built and maintained over half a millennium, was threatened.

Security Fears in the West

In the West, where opposition to Ukrainian nuclear policy was led by the United States, fears largely mirrored those of Russia. Having spent decades building up a stable nuclear relationship with the Soviet Union, and having seen the underlying political dispute evaporate, the United States was loath to see the rise of new nuclear powers in the region undermine the certainty so painstakingly created. Moreover, since the United States recognized the potential for a Ukrainian-Russian conflict, leaders were frightened that the region might become a "nuclear Yugoslavia." The United States put a much higher priority on ridding Ukraine of nuclear weapons than on preserving its independence, a policy that did not go unnoticed in Kiev. Nonproliferation was a major global foreign policy goal for the Clinton administration, and Ukraine was seen within this context as well. If it became nuclear, what was to stop near-nuclear powers from taking the final steps? Additionally, the priority in the United States on keeping Russia satisfied meant that if Russia found Ukrainian nuclear status unacceptable, then so by extension did the United States. In Western Europe, the Chernobyl factor played a more significant role, due to Europe's direct experience with that disaster. Europeans and Americans largely shared the Russian perception that Ukraine was simply not responsible enough to be trusted with such an immense power. The most popular concern over the weapons was perhaps the fear of "loose nukes"—the notion that because Ukraine was incapable of looking after the weapons, it would be easy for some terrorist group or rogue state to get hold of a nuclear device.

For the United States, the most immediately pressing problem was the danger that Ukraine presented for the overall arms control process. The START-I agreement had been the culmination of two decades of strategic arms control negotiations and was the first agreement actually to reduce the number of weapons. START-I had been negotiated between the United States and the Soviet Union, but the Soviet Union no longer existed, and many of the weapons involved were on Ukrainian, Kazakh, and Belarussian soil. Only with the agreement of these states could the reductions be carried out. The stakes were increased significantly in January 1993, when the United States and Russia signed the START-II agreement. That agreement required substantial cuts in the Russian arsenal, but its implementation was conditional on START-I being ratified by Ukraine. In this way, Ukraine had the ability to scuttle the entire strategic arms control process.[4] This was the immediate cause of U.S. impatience with Ukrainian hesitation on disarmament.

Security, Prosperity, and Sovereignty

In part, Ukraine faced a trade-off between autonomy—in this case security from military attack—and prosperity. By keeping control of its nuclear weapons, and then gaining launch ability, Ukraine could increase its ability to deter Russia from attack, thus engaging in the oldest of international political strategies, balancing power. Doing so, however, would incur significant economic costs in three ways. First, maintaining the weapons and the delivery systems, as well as gaining launch control would be costly. In that respect Ukraine faced a traditional "guns versus butter debate." Second, Ukraine faced an economic threat from Russia: if it did not surrender the nuclear weapons, Russia would exercise some of its economic weapons, as it did during the autumn of 1993. Third, the West, led by the United States, threatened to isolate Ukraine, both from the aid needed for reform and from the trade needed for a modern economy to be efficient. Ensuring its security through nuclear weapons would be costly.[5]

Ukrainian leaders, it seems, had to choose between maximizing their security through nuclear deterrence and maximizing prosperity through avoiding sanctions. On the surface, it seems that Ukraine simply decided to privilege prosperity over security. What actually happened, however, is that Ukraine reassessed the threats to its security, and concluded that increasing military security was not going to increase the state's overall security, because military attack was not the primary threat. Rather, the problem was economic security. The realization that the military threat was not the primary threat to Ukraine was behind the change in Ukraine's policy on nuclear weapons as well as the changes in trade policy described in the previous chapters.[6] Once Ukrainian leaders realized that balancing was neither possible nor necessary, it became clear to them that economics was the battleground on which Ukraine would contest its independence.

Underlying these military and economic issues, and equally important, was the question of sovereignty: Ukrainian policy was driven in large part by the leadership's assertion of Ukraine's sovereign rights throughout the negotiation, and a settlement was possible only when those concerns had been addressed. Insistence on preserving Ukraine's prerogatives, both in the final settlement and in the negotiating process, complicated the resolution of the problem.

Between 1991 and the Trilateral Agreement of January 1994, which finally resolved the issue, there were three issues from Ukraine's perspective. First, Ukraine was concerned throughout the process with asserting its sovereignty, a theme that has run through all of its policies. Second, following independence, Ukraine's fear of Russia increased due to a number of Russian demands and threatening actions. Third, economic security slowly came to replace military security as Ukraine's top concern. This shift in Ukrainian threat perception made disarmament an optimal strategy.

Sovereignty

Ukraine's fixation on asserting its sovereignty created two issues in the negotiations.[7] First, Ukraine consistently battled the notion that Russia was the sole legal successor to the Soviet Union. It therefore claimed a share of all Soviet assets, including embassies abroad and military forces and equipment on Ukrainian territory. Nuclear forces, in Ukraine's view, fell under this rubric, and though it intended to surrender the weapons, it insisted on its rights until that point. Initially, that meant insisting that Ukraine become a party to the START-I Treaty if that treaty were to bind Ukraine, and insisting that Ukraine participate in future negotiations concerning the weapons on its territory. Jack Snyder asserts that Ukraine's assertive policy on ownership of the weapons "stems not from confident swagger, but rather from its own self-doubts about the solidity of newly won sovereignty."[8] "The more Russia and the West ignored Ukraine while continuing to focus on nuclear disarmament, the larger the pro-nuclear lobby grew in Ukraine."[9]

Russia viewed the weapons as belonging to Russia and the CIS and sought to maintain unified ownership. Russia's offer of a security guarantee in January 1993 was conditioned by the key phrase "within the framework of the CIS," which Ukraine found unacceptable.[10] By focusing on its ownership rights, Ukraine unintentionally convinced many in Russia and the West that it intended to retain the weapons. The United States (and then Russia) acknowledged Ukraine's claim, agreeing to allow Ukraine, Belarus, and Kazakhstan to become parties to START-I via the Lisbon Protocol, signed in May 1992. This document had the virtue, from the view of the United States and Russia, of committing the three others to surrendering their weapons so that the next round of negotiations, for the START-II treaty, could be carried on bilaterally between the United States and Russia.

In addition to demanding a role in the treaty process, Ukraine, in its focus on sovereignty, insisted that because it owned the weapons, it should be compensated for getting rid of them. Again, the misunderstanding created was immense. Ukraine felt that it was simply getting its share of money out of the weapons, many of which were partially constructed in Ukraine. In light of its voluntary decision to surrender the weapons, Ukrainian leaders saw compensation not only as just, but as a small price for the other states to pay given their fears. In the West and Russia, the demand for compensation was seen as at best a cynical ploy to get some additional aid, and was viewed essentially as blackmail. It was seen at worst as another attempt to retract the earlier commitments to disarm. The West and Russia never viewed Ukrainian disarmament as a voluntary step, but as a compulsory one, and they were therefore less inclined to compensate Ukraine for it.

These two implications of Ukraine's focus on sovereignty were crucial in the process. Before they arose, Ukraine was willing to surrender the weapons without much discussion. Once these questions did arise, shortly after independence, the process became hopelessly bogged down, such that even the week before the final agreement, knowledgeable observers were predicting indefinite continuation of the impasse. Once Russia and the United States agreed to a compensation plan, implying that Ukraine did have rights to the warheads, agreement was relative straightforward. Both the amount of the compensation and the nature of security guarantees provided were much less than Ukraine hoped for, but its assertion of its rights was to a large degree vindicated.[11]

Security

Ukraine did not initially focus on its military security in its policy on the nuclear weapons. Had it done so, it probably would not have promised to give them up. From a strictly military strategic standpoint, the weapons could conceivably guarantee Ukraine's security much the way Britain's or France's weapons do. The problems in converting the Soviet arsenal into a usable asset for the Ukrainian military would be immense, but were not beyond Ukraine's technical ability.[12] And even in the short run, possession of the weapons would force Russia and the rest of the world to take Ukraine seriously. The fact that Ukraine initially disregarded this aspect of the weapons demonstrates that Ukraine initially did not fear for its security or political status. In this respect, Ukrainian policy was naive, and when the naiveté wore off, policy rebounded in the other direction, focusing on power and bargaining, and the threat of a nuclear Ukraine.

Ukrainian security fears evolved in their content. Initially, the threat was not from Russia (which had consented to Ukrainian independence) but from nuclear weapons themselves, which had the potential to create another Chernobyl. By early 1993, however, that memory had faded, and Russia's (and the world's) lack of respect for Ukrainian sovereignty and independence were much more dangerous. As claims on Ukrainian territory spread from the far right toward and then past the center of the Russian political spectrum, a policy of deterrence seemed necessary. This view faded only when Russian economic coercion of Ukraine in 1993, as well as Russian undermining of governments of Georgia and Azerbaijan, made it clear that military attack was not the primary threat to Ukraine's security.[13]

Prosperity

By mid-1993, the collapse of Ukraine's economy was leading to concern that the country might fragment. In this context, prosperity and security became closely related: only by stemming the economic collapse could civil unrest be prevented. Finally, Ukrainian policy focused on economic gain. If the focus on sovereignty, which implied that Ukraine was owed compensation, was one of principles, the concrete manifestation, the actual amount of compensation, was strictly a matter of economic interest. Once Ukrainian leaders shifted their security focus from weapons to economics, and the West and Russia made significant gestures to respect Ukrainian sovereignty, a deal on compensation was straightforward.

The Evolution of Ukrainian Nuclear Policy[14]

Ukraine's 1990 declaration of sovereignty asserted Ukraine's desire to become a neutral nonnuclear state. This statement, made a year before Ukraine declared independence and actually had to face the problem, was based on both idealistic and realistic factors. Among the primary motivations was the memory of Chernobyl,[15] and the desire to avoid all things nuclear. Politically, Ukrainian leaders recognized that, if the declaration of sovereignty and the subsequent drive for independence were not to be seen as extremely threatening to Russia and the world, Ukraine had to make clear that it did not aspire to nuclear status. The policy was idealistic in the assumption that nuclear weapons would be easy to surrender and that an independent Ukraine would have no security fears for which nuclear weapons might seem a reasonable solution. One commentator later attributed Ukraine's nonnuclear pledge to "idealism with respect to a nuclear free world that was introduced to the parliament by 'deputies from poetry and literature.'"[16] Given the fact that independence itself was a very idealistic notion in 1990, the lack of realism is not surprising.

This early policy shows that Ukraine had no inherent desire for nuclear status, and that the later consideration of retaining the nuclear weapons represented a significant shift in the debate. It also indicates that Ukrainian leaders recognized that a nuclear Ukraine would appear threatening to Russia and the West even before George Bush's 1991 speech in Kiev in which he urged Ukrainian leaders to support Mikhail Gorbachev in preserving the Soviet Union.[17]

When Ukraine declared independence in the summer of 1991, it continued to aspire to nonnuclear status. At this point, a series of misunderstandings began that obscured this point for the next two and a half years. The most fundamental misunderstanding was that in asserting its desire to be a nonnuclear state, Ukraine had not, in its view, made a unilateral commitment, or a commitment binding on it with the force of a treaty. Rather it was a statement of an intention, the details of which would be worked out later. As Ukraine later sought compensation and security guarantees, such requests were seen in Russia and the West as backtracking on an obligation, a view that only caused frustration in Ukraine.

The Rethinking of Ukraine's Disarmament Plans

The question of control of nuclear weapons arose during the August 1991 coup attempt even before Ukraine declared its independence. During the coup attempt, there was much speculation as to who controlled the Soviet nuclear "button."[18] The need to maintain unified command of Soviet nuclear forces was one of the main reasons cited for the need to continue some type of union arrangements after Ukraine declared independence.

The coup also highlighted, however, Ukraine's military vulnerability to Russia: On 19 August, one of the plotters, General Varrenikov, flew to Kiev and issued an ultimatum: if Ukrainian leaders did not follow the orders of the plotters, the Soviet Army would invade. A special forces unit was flown in from Brest and stationed outside Kiev, and helicopters hovered over the capital. Kravchuk stated afterward: "I realized that I had no one to defend me, [and] sensed that armed people could walk in at any time and take me away."[19] This episode began a lengthy process in which, having gained its independence, Ukraine and its leaders became concerned for their security and began thinking about repelling a Russian attack. The lessons of 1918, where the demise of the fledgling Ukrainian state was blamed on an inadequate military, were also prominent in the motivation to focus on the military aspects of security.[20]

The trend was reinforced throughout the first year as unpleasant reality repeatedly caused Ukraine to jettison the idealist principles of the independence struggle and shift to a much more power-oriented approach to politics. It was only later that this approach too was found inadequate. Ukraine had few experienced diplomats, and the learning process was a painful one. Ukraine reacted belligerently to two realizations in particular. First, it quickly became clear that despite Boris Yeltsin's approval of Ukraine's declaration of independence, Russia wanted to maintain some type of political control over Ukraine, and did not recognize Ukraine as an equal. All the problems highlighted in chapter 2—the Black Sea Fleet, Crimea, Russian citizens in Ukraine—and Russia's pursuit of those claims, were perceived in Ukraine as confirming that the new Russia was not much different from the old Russia. Therefore in late 1991 and 1992, Ukrainian leaders began focusing more on the need to attain sufficient military power to deter or defeat a Russian attack. Second, and much more disillusioning, was the realization that the West was not at all committed to Ukrainian independence, and that there as in Russia, power and interest seemed to be more important than the principle of sovereign equality.

Following independence, unanimity about nuclear policy evaporated rapidly, not so much due to deep divisions in the original policy of getting rid of the weapons, but over disagreements in the specifics of how such a policy was to be implemented. When Kravchuk reaffirmed that Ukraine would surrender its weapons, and that he was not concerned if they were moved to Russia, Vyacheslav Chornovil, his main opponent in the presidential election, advocated UN control instead. The irony of giving weapons to one's primary anticipated enemy continued to plague the debate for its duration. Chornovil's reservations about sending the weapons to Russia probably did not indicate a desire to keep them, as was thought in the West, but a perceived need to use the weapons issue as a way to deflect some of the increasing pressure coming from Moscow. Chornovil clearly believed that the continued presence of nuclear weapons on Ukrainian soil provided good incentives for Russia to come to terms on outstanding issues, as well as to other states to recognize Ukraine's independence.

His views were shared across the political spectrum in Ukraine: the leader of the banned (and since relegalized) Communist party of Ukraine, Oleksandr Moroz, stated in September 1991 that he supported nuclear disarmament in Ukraine, but that it would be "normal" for the weapons to remain in Ukraine for some time, and he suggested exploration of dual-controls such as those used by NATO.[21] The parliamentary opposition leader, Volodymyr Filenko, expressed the increasing concern with the balance of power most clearly: "Most MPs think we cannot just give weapons to Russia. It would upset the balance of power between Russia and Ukraine. We're afraid of Russia, if you like. We're fighting for independence from Russia. We cannot say there's a nuclear threat, but they did recently raise territorial claims."[22]

The situation festered toward the end of 1991, as Russia became increasingly frustrated with Ukraine's intention not to sign a new union treaty, and Ukraine felt increasingly threatened by Russian rhetoric. Ukraine's refusal to join a new union increased Moscow's concern about the nuclear weapons, but the resulting pressure from Russia only steeled Ukraine's resolve to be independent, and fostered the belief that the nuclear weapons were an important source of leverage. The possibility of a preemptive nuclear strike against Ukraine was apparently discussed by Yeltsin and his advisers in October.[23] Ukraine's adoption of a balance of power strategy had its roots in the October 1991 decision to nationalize the Soviet armed forces on Ukrainian territory. The primary motive for the decision was Ukraine's right to the Soviet assets on its soil, but underlying was the belief among some in Ukraine that Russia posed a military threat that could and should be met with countervailing military power. Plans for downsizing the Ukrainian military to 450,000 troops would still leave it with one of the biggest armies on the continent.

Even after the nuclear debate began in earnest, however, official Ukrainian policy still focused on disarmament. Discussing Ukraine's intention to build its own army, in late November 1991, the Presidium of the Verkhovna Rada recommitted itself "to become a neutral and nuclear-free state . . . that will adhere to three non-nuclear principles: not to receive, not to manufacture, and not to acquire nuclear weapons," and said that Ukraine would abide by existing treaties between the United States and USSR.[24] In meetings at Alma-Ata and Minsk in late December 1991, Ukraine agreed, despite disagreement with Russia on other issues, to transfer its stock of tactical nuclear weapons to Russia within a year and to transfer all of its strategic weapons by the end of 1994.[25] These policies were enacted by Kravchuk, who felt that complying with Western wishes would speed U.S. recognition as well as aid for destroying the missiles.

The question of recognition led to much misunderstanding between the West and Ukraine at this time. The West, hoping to see the Soviet Union preserved, withheld recognition until after the December referendum. This itself irked Ukrainians, who expected a much better reception, and the feeling was exacerbated by the tendency of Western leaders to make recognition conditional on Ukraine's accepting nonnuclear status. When Ukraine countered by trying to use the weapons to force recognition, it only increased fear and anger among Western leaders, and therefore the pressure to withhold recognition. The two sides managed to create a great deal of ill will over a relatively minor issue, and Ukraine at this point was unwilling to compromise.

The question of ownership was also driving the debate over Ukrainian policy. In a policy statement issued 10 September 1991, Chornovil reasserted his support for a nonnuclear Ukraine, but questioned transferring the weapons to Russia because Ukraine was "a rightful heir to all the material and technical resources, including weapons, of the former Soviet Union."[26] Transferring Ukrainian weapons to Russia would imply that Russia had a special status in the region, including sole rights to certain assets of the former Soviet Union.

At a time when, on another front, Ukraine was frustrated by Russia's assertion of ownership over other essential Soviet assets, including hard currency reserves, embassies, and the UN Security Council seat, the issue was a touchy one. In February 1992, Kravchuk protested Yeltsin's announcement that nuclear weapons would be cut further: "The strategic weapons belong to the Commonwealth of Independent States. So how can the Russian president cut weapons he does not have? . . . Our strategic potential may not be very great, but it is not up to him to decide its fate."[27] Because Ukraine was so focused on the principle of sovereign equality, the idea of denying ownership rights of any assets was difficult to accept.

Ukraine's assertion of ownership had major ramifications for the START-I Treaty. Ukraine insisted that further negotiations concerning nuclear weapons could not be conducted only by Russia and the United States, because that would imply that Russia was the sole successor of the Soviet Union and the owner of nuclear weapons in Ukraine.[28] U.S. and Russian negotiators feared this position because it meant trying to reconcile the position of five states rather than just two in the ensuing negotiations. The United States gave in on this question in early May 1992, and Russia opposed including Ukraine in the negotiations until the signing of the Lisbon Protocol later that month. The Protocol solved the problem by making Ukraine, Belarus, and Kazakhstan parties to START-I, and committing them to surrendering their weapons, which made their participation in future negotiations moot. When it signed the Lisbon Protocol, Ukraine appended a letter stating that Ukraine had "voluntarily renounced the right to possess nuclear weapons, to which it was entitled as one of the equal legal successor states of the former USSR."[29]

The ownership question was linked to a more practical one in the short term: control of the weapons for the time they remained in Ukraine. Again Ukraine asserted its sovereign rights, only to frighten the rest of the world with the appearance that it was becoming a full-fledged nuclear state. While Ukraine was willing to surrender the weapons, it would not allow another state even symbolic control of weapons on Ukrainian territory.[30] This position was elaborated by Kravchuk on 6 December: "We regard nuclear arms of the former Soviet Union on our territory as such which are stationed temporarily. Ukraine will insist that it should have political control over its non-use." In the same remark, he backed off from earlier categorical pledges to disarm, saying instead, "Ukraine should in the near future become a nuclear-free and neutral state," leaving open the possibility that it would not do so.

There was some tension between Ukraine's opposition to yielding control to Russia and its unwillingness to tolerate supranational organizations. The most immediate solution to the problem of controlling the weapons was to put them under international control. Thus the Alma-Ata declaration of 21

December 1991 provided for "single control over nuclear weapons."[31] This implied, however, that some supranational institution would exercise control over the weapons, and as shown in the previous chapter, this was viewed as intolerable due to concerns about sovereignty and about creating a "new center." As the contradiction became clear, joint control became unacceptable to Ukraine. Eventually, a third alternative that avoided this contradiction was examined: Ukraine would control the weapons itself.

The fact that the West supported Russia's position against Ukraine caused extreme disillusion among Ukrainian leaders, who had expected the West to see Ukraine as deserving of support both because of its role in destroying the Soviet Union and because of its potential to check Russia in the future. Instead, they found the West fearing Ukraine more than Russia. A Ukrainian commentator explained the new Ukrainian view: "We have to live without illusions. Nobody in the world is interested in [whether] we are free and independent . . . only one thing worries them—do we have the bomb? Nobody is interested in whether we are democratic or authoritarian. They are only concerned [about whether] we have the bomb."[32]

Nuclear Weapons as a Lever

The realization that the West was concerned primarily with Ukraine's nuclear weapons did not have the effect intended by Western leaders. Rather than recognizing that they had to surrender the weapons on the West's (and Russia's) terms to avoid a difficult conflict, Ukrainian leaders reached two conclusions: first, if Ukraine had no nuclear weapons, the West would have no concern about its fate. Second, the concern in Russia and the West about the weapons was so great that they should prove a useful bargaining resource. Thus Ukraine's period of naiveté ended rapidly and the period of power politics was ushered in. The new policy was based on a crude political realism: "The West only recognizes strength, and Ukraine intends to be strong."[33]

Although there remained little real desire in Ukraine to become a nuclear weapons state, the principle of nonnuclear status was abandoned, as Ukrainian leaders came to see how little their principles amounted to in the international political arena. A crude power politics was embraced in two ways. At the strategic level, nuclear weapons would now be used to prevent a Russian attack, either directly through nuclear deterrence or indirectly by extracting security guarantees from Russia and the United States in return for disarmament. At the tactical level of negotiations, Ukrainians worked on the assumption that they had something that everyone else wanted, and that others would have to meet their terms to get it. In this phase of Ukrainian policy, there were two primary demands, for security guarantees, and for compensation for the material in the warheads. The embrace of realpolitik led some to question whether Ukraine should surrender the weapons under any circumstances, now that their political value had been demonstrated.

By April 1992, the Kravchuk had adopted the position that Ukraine should receive guarantees in return for surrendering its nuclear weapons, saying in an interview:

> Let us assume that we remove all nuclear weapons from Ukraine and become a non-nuclear state. This is what we want. But what guarantee will there be for our security? Germany's security, for example, is guaranteed by NATO. Who will guarantee Ukraine's security? Russia? Perhaps. Perhaps we would agree, but Russia continually makes border claims on us.[34]

The United States and NATO immediately made it clear that no such guarantee would be made. Quite simply, the West was not going to go to war for Ukraine. Russia made a security guarantee contingent on Ukraine's remaining a member of the CIS. These positions only served to increase the feeling in Ukraine of threat. Russia implied that it did seek to retain a certain amount of political control over Ukraine, and the United States and NATO stated frankly that they were not overly concerned with Ukraine's survival. The demand for a security guarantee increased in importance in Ukraine. In a letter attached to the Lisbon Protocol, Ukraine stated that it "will insist on guarantees of its national security, including guarantees against the possible use of force . . . against Ukraine on the part of any nuclear state."[35]

By March 1992, Kravchuk had move further toward the hard-line position, halting the transfer of tactical weapons to Russia. By this time, 57 percent of Ukrainian tactical weapons had been moved to Russia. It appears that the shift in policy was due in part to a growing feeling in Ukraine that the country should get something in return for the weapons. Even more significant was Ukraine's frustration at Washington's uneven policy toward Ukraine and Russia, and the perception that following the agreement to ship the tactical warheads to Russia, the United States had focused its attention and aid more on Russia. These feelings tended to refute the theory that going along with Western wishes would yield more aid, and to confirm the belief that only the possibility of Ukraine retaining the weapons was getting Ukraine any help at all. However, the shipment of tactical weapons was soon continued and completed.

Reports began to circulate that Ukraine was studying the possibility of retaining part of its nuclear arsenal. Apparently the reconsideration was based on the desire to be taken seriously in the international arena and growing fear of Russia, as well as a sense that Ukraine must be paid for the weapons. Sergey Kolesnik of the Verkhovna Rada's committee on military affairs criticized Ukraine's naiveté: "Suppose America began sending its nuclear weapons to

Canada, and imagine what everyone would think. They are laughing at Ukraine in the Pentagon."[36] Nationalist Deputy Stepan Khmara concurred, stating: "Only strength can guarantee security. Agreements, guarantees are just paper, nothing more, they make us dependent on somebody else. Russia encroaches upon the Crimea and Sevastopol. Nuclear weapons [are] an efficient deterring factor."[37] But even as Ukrainians contemplated going nuclear, some did so with the thought of the value of the weapons, while others focused on the need to deter Russia.

On 6 May 1992, the CIS command announced that all the tactical weapons had been transferred to Russia.[38] Kravchuk acted without consulting the Verkhovna Rada, however, a move that made subsequent policy much more complicated, as the Verkhovna Rada opposed presidential policies in order to assert their authority as well as on the merits of the issue.[39]

The possibility of becoming a nuclear weapons state came to the top of the agenda in the middle of 1992 after the signing of the Lisbon Protocol. The center of activity shifted from Kravchuk, who as president had conducted the diplomacy, to the Verkhovna Rada, which had to ratify START-I and, in the process of adopting a military doctrine, determine Ukraine's nuclear policy. Chornovil, in evaluating the Lisbon Protocol, focused on the benefits of nuclear weapons, saying, "The fact that there are still nuclear weapons on Ukrainian territory is something that acts as a deterrent."[40]

Prior to September 1992, negotiations over aid to Ukraine for dismantling the weapons were relatively mild, and many in the West agreed that such aid was justified, although they were not eager to provide it. In September 1992, however, the United States and Russia reached a deal in which the United States would buy the enriched uranium from Russian warheads being dismantled under START-I. The goal of the program was to provide incentives for Russian arms reductions and aid for that process, but there was an unintended reaction in Ukraine. If the United States was going to pay Russia enormous sums of money for nuclear warheads, why should Ukraine give its warheads to Russia for nothing? The ownership issue was once again raised, and the U.S.-Russian deal unwittingly gave the Ukrainians much less reason to surrender the warheads without compensation. It was clear that U.S. money was available, at least for Russia. The deal not only reinforced Ukraine's sense of second-class status, but also made it feel that it had been naive in giving away its large stock of tactical warheads for nothing, for it now appeared that Russia would reap a substantial profit selling the materials to the United States.

The debate over nuclear status intensified during the discussion in the Verkhovna Rada of a military doctrine in the fall of 1992. One of the primary parliamentary advocates of nuclear status was Major General Tolubko, who adopted a somewhat logical but hard-line stance: unless Ukraine received serious security guarantees, it should not give up the weapons.[41] It is significant that even this position, which was considered extreme, continued to hold disarmament, under certain conditions, as the most desirable end. The position that Ukraine (and its neighbors) would be best off as a nuclear state was made persuasively by prominent American international relations scholars, including John Mearsheimer, Kenneth Waltz, and Barry Posen, but not by leading Ukrainian figures.[42] Many in Ukraine were considering that position, but it never gained widespread support.[43] Defense Minister Morozov asserted that the Ministry "considers the declaration of Ukraine as a nuclear state has no realistic basis and does not correspond with the current economic potential and strategic interests of our state."[44]

The policy of "going nuclear" continued to be considered by many and advocated by a few until the eventual resolution of the issue in January 1994. By late 1992, however, the Verkhovna Rada had reached the peak of its belligerence, and even at that peak continued to support disarmament, with conditions. In the end, despite frustration with the United States and Russia and fear of Russia, the basic belief in disarmament held, apparently for three related reasons. First, with the signing of the Lisbon Protocol, Ukraine received a good deal of satisfaction on the principle of sovereignty, by being recognized as an equal partner in START-I. Second, Ukraine's economic crisis raised much more immediate fears than the potential of a Russian attack. Third, as shown by the doctrine's focus on "reasonable sufficiency," Ukraine understood that to challenge Russia in the realm of armaments—nuclear or conventional—was a proposition that Ukraine could not win.

Pragmatism and the Economic Threat

In September 1992, the parliament forced out the Prime Minister, Vitold Fokin. Kravchuk had supported Fokin to the end, and the resignation was regarded as a defeat for Kravchuk and a victory for the parliament. When Leonid Kuchma, a candidate favored by the parliament, was chosen to succeed Fokin, it looked as though policy on nuclear weapons would take a more belligerent tone. The pronuclear parliament had gained power at the expense of the diplomatic president, and the new prime minister was the former director of the world's largest ICBM factory, Yuzhmash (Pivden'mash) in Dnipropetrovsk. Yurii Kostenko, who had led the campaign for a more recalcitrant policy on nuclear weapons, was appointed environment minister and was eventually put in charge of nuclear negotiations. The Verkhovna Rada's rejection of the military doctrine followed shortly.

The shift toward more belligerent policy, however, greatly slowed, even if it did not recede for some time. The crude realism that had replaced Ukraine's original idealism was itself replaced by a more restrained and pragmatic policy. Ukrainian leaders continued to insist on recognition of Ukraine's borders, security guarantees, and financial compensation, but they acknowledged that "going nuclear" was not a good option, and that nuclear weapons would do little good in a diplomatic conflict with Russia and the United States. Eventually, Ukraine achieved much of what it originally sought—recognition of its status and economic aid, though it did not end up with its most extreme demands—billions in aid and formal security guarantees.

Militarily, the realist policy was that Ukraine's security had to be guaranteed, and if it was not to be guaranteed by U.S. commitments, then it would be guaranteed by nuclear weapons. The more pragmatic policy accepted that neither guarantee was realistic. The United States was clearly not going to guarantee Ukraine's security, and converting the Soviet arsenal into a meaningful deterrent was much easier said than done. Moreover, it was likely that by inflaming Russian opinion and further decreasing Western support, going nuclear could make Ukraine less, not more, secure.[45]

This pragmatic line was espoused by those who focused on Ukraine's economic weakness, noting that weakness would be exacerbated by international isolation if Ukraine did not surrender its weapons. In late 1992, parliamentarian (and Army Colonel) Valeriy Izmalkov published a strongly worded attack on going nuclear in the government newspaper, *Holos Ukrainy*. He accused other deputies of seeking to blackmail the United States, and highlighted the weakness of Ukraine's position:

> For Iraq today [the Americans] have coined a definition: "a potentially aggressive country." If a corresponding definition is also found for us, then our international isolation will be guaranteed. . . . I want to recall that Ukraine's economic situation does not give us grounds to speak about a possibility to overcome the crisis on our own. Therefore we cannot do without help from the West.[46]

He made a second economic argument, that maintenance of the weapons was too costly while Ukraine was in an economic crisis: "What answer will ordinary people give after they learn what the possession of nuclear weapons involves? What will they say when they look at empty shelves of stores knowing the cost of strategic missiles?"[47] Other analysts focused on the irrelevance of nuclear deterrence for Ukraine and the unlikelihood of a Russian military attack:

> Of special importance to Ukraine are questions related to economic and ecological security, especially in light of the nation's objective circumstances. . . . *The classical military threat to Ukraine (invasion from Russia) is not a real one.* . . . Trying to reach the classical "balance of forces," and race for a relative military parity with Russia would result in the unnecessary economic and psychological exhaustion of

Ukraine and could very well lead to the nation's demise from an internal threat. . . . Ukraine has more than enough military potential to guarantee itself from any unexpected aggression from all other nations in the region. As for Russia, it will require a development of political relations and a special approach. . . . [48]

Deputy Prime Minister Boris Tarasyuk held a similar position in 1995: "Ukraine has two main security threats: the internal and the external. I place primary importance on the internal threat, because there is currently no country or group of countries that could dare attack Ukraine militarily."[49] This pragmatic line did not get much attention internationally, where observers tended to focus on advocates of nuclear status, but in Ukraine it continued to hold its ground against the more belligerent line. The Military Doctrine, finally adopted on 19 October 1993, acknowleged that economic and political blackmail were the chief threats to Ukrainian security.[50]

On becoming prime minister, Kuchma immediately took the more pragmatic line, making it clear that while Ukraine's policies would be dictated by its own interests rather than the West's, it would surrender the weapons given appropriate compensation. He stressed the importance of getting aid to pay for dismantling the weapons since Ukraine's economy was in shambles. This focus on economics first signaled Ukraine's recognition that economic woes were its primary problem. While pledging to get rid of the weapons, Kuchma continuously sounded the financial theme: "We removed the tactical nuclear weapons and what happened? Russia got a contract to supply the United States with nuclear fuel. Where is at least a minimal program of aid similar to Russia's? Our people are not fools. . . . What does Ukraine get in return? This is the question that troubles the Ukrainian people and parliament."[51] His Deputy Prime Minister, Ihor Yukhnovsky, pushed harder, suggesting that Ukraine would rid itself of its weapons by selling them to the highest bidder, whether it was Russia or not.[52]

This policy continued to be misunderstood in the West and Russia, where leaders accused Ukraine of breaking earlier vows to disarm, and of harboring ambitions of becoming a nuclear state. Ukrainian leaders, frustrated at these accusations, continued their efforts to explain their position. Ukraine's new pragmatism was still not appreciated in Russia or the West, which still sought to obtain unconditional—and uncompensated—disarmament from Ukraine, in which Ukraine would allow warheads to be removed and shipped to Russia and then use its own resources to carry out the other necessary measures, such as destroying missiles and silos.

The year 1993 was characterized on the nuclear front by a slow and unsteady progression toward an agreement and by continued recriminations.[53] Signature of START-II in January 1993 increased the importance of Ukrainian ratification of START-I, and increased U.S. pressure on Ukraine. Much of the struggle throughout the year concerned whether Ukraine was going to accede to Western/Russian wishes through the application of positive or negative incentives. Ukraine sought to be persuaded by positive incentives, hoping that a large aid package would bolster its flagging economy, and genuinely fearing having to pay for disarmament itself. The West, which still considered Ukraine to be violating earlier commitments, began to make thinly veiled threats of economic and political sanctions. These steps had the effect of infuriating Ukraine even more, but also probably had some role in convincing Ukraine of the need to reach a deal.

In September 1993, the situation seemed to be resolved at the Massandra summit, when Russia and Ukraine agreed on plans for Ukraine to be compensated for the warheads by the supply of nuclear reactor fuel. The agreement quickly evaporated when the two sides fought over the terms, and when it emerged that the signed version had a hand-written addendum by Kuchma on significant issues. While the Massandra summit ended up increasing, rather than resolving, the tension between the two countries, the aborted agreement on compensation served as a model for the final agreement in January 1994.

Similarly, when the Ukrainian parliament ratified START-I in November 1993, it did so with very significant conditions attached, including the assertion that START-I did not include the Ukrainian arsenal of SS-24 ICBMs, which most concerned other states.[54] The effect of this conditional ratification was to anger rather than appease Russia and the United States. In the end, however, this agreement solidified Ukraine's willingness to cut a deal and represented a stepping stone to the agreement reached just a few months later. In this way, the process was contentious and even rancorous, but was progressing incrementally toward an agreement.

The 1994 Trilateral Agreement

The Trilateral Agreement on Nuclear Weapons, signed by Kravchuk, Yeltsin, and Clinton in January 1994, essentially resolved the lengthy conflict over Ukraine's nuclear weapons. The treaty was "based on the documents signed at the Russian-Ukrainian summit meeting in Massandra in September 1993, but to which important provisions concerning compensation, security guarantees, and the timing of the warhead transfer have been added."[55]

The text of the agreement is concerned much more with what Ukraine is to receive than with its commitments. Ukraine committed itself under the agreement to "accede to the Nuclear Non-Proliferation treaty in the shortest possible time," effectively erasing the most important of the reservations made by the Verkhovna Rada in ratifying START-I. In addition, it explicitly agreed to "ensure the elimination of all nuclear weapons, including strategic offensive arms, located on its territory in accordance with the relevant agreements and during the seven-year period as provided by the START I Treaty." The treaty did not oblige Ukraine to anything it had not previously agreed to at one time or another, but did commit Ukraine to some actions (such as accession to the NPT) that it had been reconsidering.

In return, the agreement explicitly acknowledged the equality of the three states and their "respect for the independence, sovereignty, and territorial integrity of each nation."[56] This statement, while somewhat vague, was extremely important for Ukraine in symbolic terms, because it had initially reconsidered its nuclear position largely because of the perception that it was being regarded as Russia's inferior. The commitment to respect territorial integrity was also important strategically for Ukraine, as the situation in Crimea was becoming increasingly unstable. With this provision, Russia could not interfere in Crimea later without running the danger that Ukraine would claim it had violated the agreement and that Ukraine was no longer bound by it. In practical terms, the agreement therefore ameliorated one of Ukraine's most pressing problems.

The agreement also detailed compensation to Ukraine for its nuclear material. Essentially, Ukraine was to receive nuclear reactor fuel and a share of the proceeds from the sale on the world market of reactor fuel made from decomissioned warheads. The deal was expected to give Ukraine a billion dollars, and to provide Ukraine with a seven-year supply of reactor fuel.[57] Most significantly, perhaps, Ukraine received a series of vague security guarantees. All of these guarantees were made "in accordance with" the CSCE final act and the NPT (which pledges nuclear states not to attack nonnuclear states), and in that sense represented no new concession to Ukraine. But by getting these commitments reiterated in the context of the agreement, Ukraine was partially vindicated. The fact that these guarantees are somewhat vague is not important, since any security guarantee can be ignored when the chips are down. The significance of the commitments is not that they will prevent an attack or guarantee Western support in case of one, but that they will make it much less possible for Russia, alone or in the guise of the CIS, to use Crimea or some other pretext to interfere in Ukraine. Given the fact that this sort of problem was real, and that an all-out invasion seemed exceedingly unlikely, these assurances were of some benefit to Ukraine.

Conclusion

In many ways, Ukraine's position on economic vulnerability and military vulnerability moved in parallel to one another. In the earliest stages of independence, a somewhat belligerent policy was enacted, both due to Ukrainian domestic politics and to increasing perception of a threat from Russia. In time, however, Ukrainian leaders recognized that the threat from Russia was not primarily military, but stemmed instead from Ukraine's domestic economic weakness. After this realization, Ukraine retreated from its economic isolation and from its attempt to balance Russian power. The two shifts complemented one another, because both represented a growing understanding that to challenge Russia in power capabilities simply could not succeed. In economic terms, this meant ending isolation, and in military terms, it meant forgoing the futile attempt to match Russia's military capability. Once it was realized that challenging Russia was neither possible nor necessary, the economic plane of interaction became much more important.

Ukraine's policy on nuclear weapons was consistent with its international economic policy, and the two help explain each other. Ukraine's security dilemma between balancing and bandwagoning, and its search for a third alternative, shows why economic relations became the crux of Ukraine's complex relationship with Russia. As Ukraine contemplated becoming a nuclear power, its leaders recognized that in the realm of military power, it cannot hope to challenge Russia, and that to do so would likely be counterproductive. And Ukraine's focus on sovereignty above prosperity and autonomy helps explain why recognition of Ukraine's sovereign rights was at least as important as monetary compensation in negotiation over the terms of disarmament.

Ukraine is still attempting to find a way between balancing and bandwagoning. Isolation from Russia proved infeasible economically and politically. Balancing through alliance rather than through internal military power has proven equally infeasible. In one important way, however, agreeing on nuclear disarmament provided a substantial benefit to Ukraine: it eliminated the major obstacle to U.S. economic and political support just as momentum for such support was building in the United States More fundamentally, however, Ukraine realized that its internal cohesiveness is a major concern in its security policy. Russia is able to endanger Ukraine economically in large part because of internal problems in Ukraine itself, which make Ukraine less able to deal with the asymmetry of power between the two states. It is to this issue that we turn in Chapter 8.

Part III

The Bigger Picture

8

Internal Divisions and Ukrainian Economic Vulnerability

> Rarely can misguided policies and mismanagement have led
> so quickly to a country's collapse.
> —*The Economist*, "Warnings from Massandra"

Ukraine has faced a difficult situation in the early years of independence due to its vulnerability to Russia. Even if Ukraine made the best possible choices, the constraints inherent in its position would prevent a completely satisfactory outcome. But due to divisions within Ukraine, it is rarely possible to take the best possible policies. Indeed, Ukraine has in many cases been unable to adopt any policies at all. While the international situation presents Ukraine with a set of issues that are somewhat beyond its control, Ukraine's internal divisions place a different set of constraints on policy, by making certain policies untenable domestically, even if they would be beneficial in solving the problems associated with vulnerability. A prominent example cited previously is the inability to shift production away from energy-wasting industries, a necessary step to reducing energy vulnerability, due to the political power of the workers and the government's lack of unity. Simon Johnson and Oleg Ustenko contend that the blame for Ukraine's dismal economic performance lies primarily with "a lack of a government strategy of economic adjustment," rather than from external pressures.[1] Ukraine has been severely hindered in adopting a coherent strategy by divisions in its state and society. This lack of strategy means that Ukraine is at the mercy of Russia's actions rather than be being able to maneuver to counter them.[2]

Scholars of comparative foreign policies have noted that some states deal more successfully with dependence than do others:

> [I]n assessing the economic viability of new states, observers have tended to neglect the question of the policy-making competence of leaderships. Far too much attention has been paid to the natural resources and other physical attributes of the nations and not enough

171

to the quality of their leaderships. . . . Ukraine's vast territory and resources and Georgia's good climate amount to little if they are poorly
led; tiny and resource-poor Estonia and Slovenia seem able to do
quite well without such putative advantages.[3]

And while Hirschman and others have elaborated successful strategies for
minimizing vulnerability, states vary in their abilities to implement different
strategies. Stephen Krasner and Peter Katzenstein, among others, attributes
states' different abilities to cope successfully with interdependence to different state structures and state-society relations.[4] Ukraine's poorly defined state
institutions and the inability of the state to implement reform have prevented
it from adopting a successful strategy for political autonomy in the face of economic dependence. "Ineffective socio-economic policy and the nomenklatura-
tinged patriotism of the ruling elite made the country so weak that it has to
make new and dangerous concessions in its bilateral relations with Moscow,
bringing it closer to the Belarus status of a model 'younger brother.'"[5]

In order to understand why Ukraine has chosen the policies that it has,
and why Ukraine has had only limited success in coping with its dependence
on Russia, it is necessary to understand something about the nature of society
and the state in Ukraine. The divisions in Ukrainian society, along several axes,
limit the range of policies that are acceptable. The institutional divisions
within the Ukrainian government make it difficult to adopt any policy at all,
even within the narrow range of choices left by international and societal constraints. In short, Ukraine has a "weak" state, where weak describes not the
power of the state relative to other states, but the ability of the government to
adopt a policy and implement it in the society.[6] The goal of this chapter is to
show how Ukraine's societal and institutional divisions have eroded its ability
to cope with its economic vulnerability. The chapter aims to provide a view of
Ukraine's economic security that is fundamentally different from what domi-
nates the rest of the book, which focuses on constraints placed on Ukraine by
events beyond its borders, most notably by Russia.

Socially, Ukraine's historical division between the Russian and the Austro-
Hungarian empires has persisted. Society is divided along three axes that have
important impacts for foreign economic strategy. First, it is divided between
its Russophone east and its more Ukrainian west. Second, it is divided between
those who support rapid reform and those who do not. Third, it is divided
between nationalists and people with other primary values. There tends to
be some parallel between these axes, mostly corresponding to the east-west division: those who live in the east are more likely to speak Russian and favor
close relations with Russia, oppose rapid economic reform, and be less concerned with the Ukrainian nation compared to those in the west. There are
sufficient exceptions to this tendency, however, to merit treating the three axes
separately.[7]

Institutionally, Ukraine is also divided in two important ways. First, and related to the society's division, the parliament itself (and the political system more generally) is atomized, making it impossible for a single coherent strategy—regardless of its content or merits—to be adopted. No faction or coalition can muster a majority to advance a program. Second, there have been four major loci of authority at the top of the Ukrainian government, and until the adoption of a constitution in June 1996, no clear division of institutional responsibilities among them. The result is that none of them has been powerful enough to implement a program. Both of these problems are institutional, and stem from the institutional legacy of the Soviet Union. Ukraine's new constitution should eventually alleviate some of these problems, but for now, the Ukrainian state remains divided and ineffective.

Social Divisions in Ukraine

Most discussions of Ukraine's social divisions are focused on the question of which side will win, and what effects that victory will have. Predictions have often been dire, as when a U.S. intelligence report in early 1994 predicted that regional divisions would soon lead to civil war in Ukraine.[8] An equally important, but less widely examined effect of Ukraine's social divisions is that they have forced policy toward the middle, as politicians have tried to avoid angering the groups at the extremes. Often, these divisions have so constrained leaders' options that they have prevented any new policies at all from being adopted. The story is not of policy moving to extremes in support of one group or another, but of politicians walking a tightrope in the center to maintain a policy that is minimally acceptable to both extremes. These constraints have excluded from the realm of political viability many potential policies to overcome Ukraine's vulnerability. Whether those exclusions are good or bad depends largely on one's normative evaluation of the issues involved—How important is Ukraine's sovereignty and independence compared to prosperity? But the effect of excluding almost all potential policies has been to make Ukraine passive in its economic relations with Russia. As a pair of Ukrainian specialists puts it: "The profound and all-encompassing economic crisis is compounded by the political impotence of the ruling elite."[9]

On most political issues, one expects to see a normal distribution of opinion, with most people in the middle, and fewer people toward the extremes. In Ukraine, on many issues, opinion is sharply bifurcated, with most people close to one pole or another and few in the middle. It is this division that makes policy making so difficult. The tendency is especially true on questions relating to nationalism and relations with Russia. In a survey conducted in Donetsk and L'viv (archetypal eastern and western Ukrainian cities, respectively) in early 1994, answers to many questions have two modal responses, with respondents from L'viv gathered at one end of the spectrum and those from Donetsk at the other, and comparatively few in the middle.[10] It is important, however, not to exaggerate the dominance of the east-west divide. The same survey data show that Ukraine's cleavages are in many respects cross-cutting, rather than reinforcing.[11]

East versus West Ukraine[12]

The most commonly noticed effect of Ukraine's east-west split is the dispute over priorities between the regions. The division has raised concern that one region or the other would secede if it did not get its way, a concern that applied to Crimea as well. Thus Kuchma's win in the 1994 presidential election, as well as the results of the earlier parliamentary elections, was seen primarily as a victory of the Russophone east over the nationalist west. However, Kuchma's subsequent policies demonstrated that the west could not be ignored in defeat, and since his election, his standing has risen in the west while falling in the east.[13] Moreover, it has become clear that while regional differences are pronounced, the Ukrainian state is not likely to fragment territorially any time soon. Instead, Kuchma has found it necessary, as Kravchuk did before him, to tell both sides that they will not get what they want, but neither will they get an unacceptable policy. Pursuing such a policy is necessary, but limits the government's options considerably.

While 22 percent of Ukraine's population is defined as "Russian," that statistic refers to the nationality as defined in Soviet-era passports. A much larger percentage of Ukrainians speak Russian as their first language. Moreover, the Russophone population is concentrated in the eastern and southern parts of the country. In the west, the Ukrainian language is dominant, particularly in the regions that remained outside the Russian Empire/Soviet Union until 1939 and were spared the Tsars' assimilation programs and Stalin's war on the Ukrainian peasantry. Taken as groups, east and west Ukrainians differ in their opinions on a wide range of issues, in ways that are mostly predictable. More people in west Ukraine favor Ukrainian as the sole state language, while those in the east are more likely to favor Russian as a second language. West Ukrainians are more likely to take pride in the Ukrainian flag, and more likely to consider themselves Ukrainian. West Ukrainians are less likely to support close relations with Russia.

Large majorities in both regions voted for independence in December 1991,[14] and while evidence indicates that while there has been some fundamental requestioning of the decision to leave the union, support for an independent Ukraine is still widespread today. A January 1995 survey reported that 64 percent of Ukrainians continued to support Ukrainian independence, significantly down from the 90 percent of 1991, but up from 56 percent a year earlier.[15] However, after that fundamental agreement, policy preferences diverge on the key political issues for the state. For example, while there was consensus in 1991 on the independence referendum, east and west diverged sharply in the simultaneous presidential election: more than 60 percent voted for Kravchuk in most eastern oblasts, and a similar or greater share voted for nationalist candidate Vyacheslav Chornovil in many western areas. Kravchuk won easily because of the greater population of the east-south and because he carried the center as well. Kravchuk realized, however, that he had to placate the nationalists to remain in power, and the economic program adopted in early 1992 was authored almost exclusively by nationalists, as its content indicated. The same thing occurred in the 1994 presidential election, except that Kravchuk's support shifted from east to west. Again the candidate supported by the east won, and then disappointed his supporters by adopting many of the most important nationalist positions (in Kuchma's case, refusing to become a full member of the CIS economic union, a policy he had earlier advocated).

The primary issue relating to economic vulnerability has been how to order relations with Russia, and on this question the two sides of the country have differed drastically. Because it is so closely tied to Russia economically, historically, and culturally, eastern Ukraine has opposed breaking relations with Russia. In the west, where the costs of separation are lower, and resentment over Russian dominance is more widespread, the primary goal was separation. The effects of severing ties were felt more strongly in the east, which had the effect of driving opinion in the east even further away from that in the west.

Reform

The essential question for all of the former communist states has been what type of economy to create and how to move from the existing system to the desired one. Ukraine has been deeply divided on this question, and has been much slower than Russia in embracing reform. Thus the country that was regarded by many as having the most promising economy in the former Soviet Union at the time of independence was seen a few years later as having the worst.

Those who opposed reform did so for a variety of reasons. Many Ukrainians enjoyed the security in the old system, and feared what might happen in the new. Others focused on cynicism, arguing that reform would lead the old *nomenklatura* to enrich themselves at the public's expense. Others had positions of privilege under the old system that they did not want to give up. Many supported reform in theory, but not when the personal hardship involved became clear. Opinion on reform proposals was not as bifurcated as the east-west division would imply. Nonetheless, because opinion was spread over a wide spectrum it was impossible to come up with a policy that would command the support of a majority of Ukrainian citizens or policy makers. It was not that Ukraine had a policy not to reform, but rather that in the absence of a consensus on how to reform, inertia meant that the old system persisted even as it decayed.

Contrary to the image that the west was reformist and the east conservative, there was significant reformist sentiment among some groups in the east, and surprisingly little from some parts of the western nationalist movement. When the nationalists were ascendant in early 1992, and able to implement an economic program over the objections of eastern Ukrainian conservatives, that economic plan focused almost exclusively on separating the economy from Russia and not at all on economic reform.[16] The nationalists basically cut a deal with the *nomenklatura* to leave the system alone as long as they could get what they most wanted: independence from Russia. That plan was opposed largely by the "New Ukraine" movement, which had considerable support in the east. And it was Kuchma, the factory director from Dnipropetrovsk in the east, not Kravchuk, a neonationalist from the west, who advocated reform as prime minister and began to implement it as president.

Moreover, Western nationalists, as much as eastern communists, were very concerned with foreign economic penetration of Ukraine and the potential for neocolonialism. The nationalists therefore supported restrictions on foreign investment that made it nearly impossible. Only the bravest Western companies invested in Ukraine. Combined with the decision to cut off from Russia, obstructions to investment by Western firms left Ukraine isolated.

There is a wide range of opinion on what roles state and market should play in the Ukrainian economy. At one end of the spectrum, unreconstructed communists hold that the communist economic system should be retained, even if the political system is democratized. At the other end of the spectrum are those who support complete liberalization of the economy. Most support some degree of free enterprise, but there are still vast differences between those who want to privatize everything but the railroads and post offices, and those who see room for private ownership only in small cooperative ventures such as restaurants and small farming plots. On the question of land privatization in particular opinion differs between the Galicia in the west, where land was privately farmed until 1939, and never collectivized to the extent in the east, and eastern Ukraine where massive state and collective farms are a way of life and are powerful political actors. Many eastern Ukrainians continue to support state ownership of farmland. There is equally diverse opinion on the speed and methods by which reform should be implemented. In contrast with those Western-oriented economists that support the "shock therapy" approach, many argue that Ukraine, due to its uniqueness, should adopt a unique reform plan. Still others advocate gradual reform in order to prevent instability, for which they cite China as a relevant precedent.

This division of opinion on economic reform initially prevented reform entirely, and more recently, has hindered it considerably. Because complete reform of an economy requires extraordinary political will and consensus on goals and means, it has been nearly impossible to accomplish in Ukraine. There has never been a shortage of economic reformers in the Ukrainian government. Kravchuk's first government, one of the least reformist, contained the prominent reformers Viktor Pynzenyk and Ihor Yukhnovskiy. What has been lacking is the ability to pass and implement a reform package. Reform has been stymied by those in power under the Soviet system who retained powerful allies in the Verkhovna Rada (the Rada in power until the 1994 elections was elected in 1990). More fundamentally, because reform would create immense hardship on people, it required consensus that it was desirable as well as on how it should be implemented. These ingredients have existed in Ukraine only recently, and are still weak.

Nationalism[17]

In contrast to the view that Ukrainian foreign policy is dominated by stalwart nationalists, Andrew Wilson paints a more divided picture of nationalism in Ukraine:

> Ukraine's large Russian community . . . and a substantial number of ethnic Ukrainians do not share the nationalists' vision, and see Ukraine and Russia as intimately linked by a common history of mutual interchange as much as by colonial dependency. Moreover . . . the latter point of view is as much a part of the Ukrainian intellectual tradition as nationalism, with a pedigree stretching back to Gogol, Kostamarov, and beyond.[18]

The essential issue regarding nationalism in Ukraine is not whether individuals supported an independent Ukraine; this was basically resolved in December 1991. The issue has been what independence should mean and what it should entail. In this respect, economic relations with Russia became a crucial issue. Opinion was divided into three categories. The most expedient view was that there was no particular reason to sever economic relations with Russia, and that given the hardship it would entail, it was a bad idea. The nationalist position was that such relations were perilous for Ukraine, and should be avoided at any cost. Moreover some nationalists held that severing ties would improve Ukraine's economy. The intermediate position held that while it was desirable to reduce economic dependence on Russia, the cost of doing so should be taken into account in order to avoid excessive hardship.

As in the case of reform, nationalist sentiment in Ukraine divided only in part along east-west lines. A significant group of east Ukrainian conservatives, the "national communists" opposed reform but strongly supported severing ties with Russia. Ironically, their position was mirrored by some of the more ardent nationalists, to whom reform was either a secondary issue to establishing total independence or even undesirable, to the extent that it reduced the power of the state.[19] Western Ukraine was also the home of the most market-oriented reformers, who opposed the nationalist economic doctrine because they believed it would injure the economy. These individuals were steeped in Adam Smith rather than Taras Shevchenko, and understood that the disruption created by disconnection from Russia's economy would make reform impossible. But contrary to the prevailing trend, some of the most prominent supporters of a nationalist economic policy were in the east, and some of the most ardent opponents were from the west.[20]

> Ukrainian liberals and market-oriented political movements are more cosmopolitian, and take a neutral stance toward Russia, or even sometimes show loyalty concerning the Russian position. They consider in this situation that the main threat to the national security of the state is the delay of reform. In contrast to them, the national democrats and radical nationalists see the main threat in Russian pressure, membership of Ukraine in the CIS, and plans for federalization of the state.[21]

Political Divisions and Economic Strategy

The sharp divisions among Ukrainian citizens and leaders on fundamental issues and the regional division that to some extent underlies these divisions led to sharp debate on the issues involved, where opinion tended to divide quickly toward the extremes and abandon the middle. It was this division, and the regional problem in particular, that made many wonder if Ukraine would come apart at the seams. It seemed that when one side gained the upper hand, policy would swing rapidly to that extreme. However, if the effect on debate was divisive, the effect on Ukraine's policy makers was to force them to the center. Kravchuk and Kuchma, both pragmatists, found the only tenable policy was to hew to the middle of the road, such that, even if both sides opposed the prevailing policy, neither side could feel like that game was irretrievably lost. This need to satisfy widely disparate groups, however, placed significant constraints on policy options.

Initially, policy did not stick to the center. Following the coup, nationalism was on the rise, conservative forces were in disarray, and euphoria over independence allowed the nationalists to gain support for their policies, as long as they did not injure the interests of the *nomenklatura*. It was possible in early 1992, therefore, to implement the nationalist economic strategy that included cutting ties with Russia. By 1993, however, political forces in the east, and the former communists in particular, had reorganized themselves. Their demands for changes in policy, and threats of secession drove speculation that Ukraine might fragment.

Kravchuk managed to placate both sides. In doing so, however, he had to continuously vacillate on policy. Because the first priority was adopting a policy that would not lead to a major political crisis in the country, adopting a policy that would best deal with the economic situation was never the government's top priority, and while plenty of plans to overcome the economic difficulties were advanced, most were irrelevant because they were not politically feasible. Hence a number of ambitious privatization schemes have been advanced, but only a weak one was adopted, and even that has been implemented quite slowly.

A strategy of simply cutting trade with Russia was tried but found to be unacceptable in the east. A strategy based on increasing ties with Russia was not acceptable to the west, because it was perceived to endanger Ukrainian sovereignty. Reform would gradually strengthen the economy and engender aid from the west, but privatization and foreign investment were also widely opposed. Kravchuk found that he could keep the country together politically essentially by doing nothing. After the initial cutoff of trade failed, there were no new initiatives in economic strategy, economic reform, or administration. While this avoided the short-term political problem, it allowed the economic problem, and therefore the vulnerability problem, to worsen. While Ukraine was doing nothing, its energy debt to Russia was increasing and Ukrainian citizens' patience with their economic situation was eroding. Because opinion was too divided to adopt an economic strategy, Ukraine was unable to counteract Russian initiatives either by shifting trade elsewhere or restructuring the domestic economy.[22] The difficulty in navigating politically between east and west Ukraine was demonstrated by Kuchma's experience as prime minister in 1993. When he tried to placate increasingly restive eastern Ukraine by signing an economic treaty with Moscow, he was immediately attacked in the west and quickly forced from office.[23]

While Kravchuk managed to keep the country together and himself in power until 1994, the shift in the country's political spectrum made him base his support in the less populous west, and allowed Kuchma to dominate the east and south, and win the elections. The political spectrum had shifted markedly since 1991 toward the east and away from nationalism, but also toward reform, as stagnation had proven destructive. While the spectrum shifted, however, the problem remained the same: Kuchma could not exercise the "mandate" created by the election, but rather had to adopt a policy that would alienate neither side. Thus while he was able to take a less belligerent line toward Russia, it has only been slightly less so, as he moved quickly after inauguration to assure nationalists that Ukraine would not join any CIS supranational structures.

Economic reform would have been difficult to implement successfully even with political unity, but with such wide disagreement about the goals of reform and the means to attain them, no plan could be adopted. The lack of reform has been particularly important for economic vulnerability, both because the economic crash exacerbated the effects of economic isolation, and because the lack of foreign investment meant the absence of a potentially powerful antidote to Ukraine's economic woes. More recently, Kuchma has been able to begin implementing reform, although considerable opposition remains. More important, perhaps, Kuchma is much more committed to reform than was Kravchuk. If reform continues, it will ease the pressure on prosperity in the country, and create more room for maneuvering with Russia. However, there is still no strategy for dealing with Russia, and the regional and national divides may continue to prevent adoption of such a strategy.

Institutional Divisions

The divisions in Ukrainian society on various issues have had an important impact on what type of policies could be adopted, as well as on electoral politics. These societal divisions exist outside the government. Devising a coherent approach for dealing with Ukraine's economic vulnerability (and all its other problems) is hampered also by divisions *within* the government. These divisions are not so much differences of opinion, but division of authority in such a way that no one can get anything done. Just as the nationalists and pragmatists have fought each other to a stalemate within the society, the president and parliament have fought to a standoff in the government. Moreover, the parliament is itself badly divided and has had no working majority. In such a situation, decisive policies to overcome Ukraine's economic vulnerability cannot be adopted.[24] A new Constitution adopted in 1996 resolved much of the institutional debate in favor of the president, but parliamentary obstruction remains a problem.

The Ukrainian state was constructed under very difficult circumstances. While Ukraine had been gradually establishing greater independence from Moscow during the Gorbachev years, the coup presented an unexpected situation that was both an opportunity and a problem. The opportunity to break away from the Soviet Union was seized, but the problems of setting up an independent state could not be thought out in advance. The Ukrainian state was created almost spontaneously. "That Ukrainian independence came so abruptly and so unexpectedly has enormous consequences for the future of the country. Virtually no one in or out of the government was prepared for independence or its aftermath."[25] The government consists of a mix of institutions that were held over from the communist era because there was no time to create new ones (such as the Verkhovna Rada) and institutions that had to be devised in haste (such as the presidency and cabinet system) without sufficient consideration of how they might work. Most fundamentally, there was no time to adopt a new constitution at the time of independence, so government was initiated with a heavily modified version of the Soviet constitution. Ukraine adopted a post-Soviet constitution only in June 1996, and the lack of one created problems throughout the political system, including Ukraine's dealings with its dependence on Russia.

Politically, the establishment of independent Ukraine papered over a fundamental conflict of interest between the opposition nationalists and the government that existed in Ukraine at the time of the coup. Throughout history, Ukraine had been dominated from outside because it had been divided internally. So when the nationalists sought independence, they made a deal with the *nomenklatura* in Kiev. If the Kiev government broke with the Soviet Union, the nationalists would not try to remove the government from power in its drive for independence. The *nomenklatura* got their primary goal, remaining in power, and the nationalists got their goal, an independent Ukraine.[26] Thus the *nomenklatura* "managed to preserve real power and property quite easily after 1991 by means of a peculiar political deal—by recruiting to its ranks the most conformist leaders of the former counter-elite and by a timely change in its slogans for the sake of a new 'legitimacy.'"[27]

The consequences of this deal were significant. "Kravchuk's victory . . . in essence signified the retention of the dominant societal position of the *nomenklatura*."[28] By agreeing to let the communist-era government retain power under a new label, the opposition made political and economic change in the country extremely difficult. No one in this government had an interest in the changes that political and economic reformers sought. And if reformers thought the old guard would gradually be swept from power, they were mistaken. The old *nomenklatura* became known as "the party of power," because they had in common their positions of power and their primary interest was to stay there. The Ukrainian communist party had been at least as rigid and conservative as Russia's (some say that Ukrainian communists sought independence so Gorbachev would not force reform on them). And this group of people was responsible, along with a handful of transplants from the nationalist and reformist camps, for governing the new Ukraine.

The Lack of Political Parties

For a variety of historical, political, and institutional reasons, the Ukrainian political spectrum is atomized, such that, with the exception of the socialists in
the 1994 parliamentary elections, organized political parties in Ukraine play
an insignificant role in the political life of the country. The main result is that
there is no majority party in parliament, and consequently no group of deputies
that is able to put forward a coherent program and defend it before the opposition. More broadly, there is no focus to political debate in the country, because on any issue there are dozens of equally minor views put forward, rather
than a few major party positions to debate. As much as Americans enjoy
lamenting the existence of political parties, they play an essential role in struc-
turing the political debate in a country and allowing legislation to be formed
in a coherent manner. In Ukraine, "the absence of an institutionalized party
system means that . . . effective parliamentary rule is virtually impossible."[29]

There are two primary reasons for the absence of powerful parties in
Ukraine, one historical and one institutional. On the historical side, the identity of political parties with the Communist party has given them a bad name.[30]
Moreover, with Ukrainians only recently attaining their political freedom,
most individuals are not inclined to stick with a political party for the sake of
loyalty when they disagree on an issue. Instead, party leaders who fall out over
political issues create new parties with slightly different names. Party discipline, an important component of strong parties, is equated in Ukrainians'
minds with "democratic centralism," the principle by which communists were
expected to toe the party line. Thus in the 1994 parliamentary elections, many
prominent reformists in the west ran under the banner of the political movement "Nova Khvilya" (New Wave). This movement was not a party, the candidates emphasized, because it had no platform or set of principles that
candidates had to subscribe to. While this prevented the candidates from having to compromise their positions, it also meant that voters did not know what
the banner stood for and that the candidates were essentially independents.

The tendency of parties to fragment had its biggest effect on Rukh, the
primary organization promoting Ukrainian independence and reform. With
the ban on the Communist party following independence, it appeared that
Rukh would become a dominant force in the country, but it rapidly fragmented. The deal between the communists and the nationalists was successful in preventing Ukraine from dividing before independence was assured, but
it led in large part to the breakup of the nationalist movement after independence. The nationalists were unable to decide whether to continue in opposition, or to support the government, as well as whether to focus on nationalism
or economic reform.[31] Those who wanted to remain in opposition, led by
Rukh leader Chornovil, opposed the government of apparatchiks and insisted
on reform. Others argued that in the early stages of statehood, the national-

ists should support the government even if they disagreed with it.[32] In addition, they believed that by providing Kravchuk with support in the west, they could reduce his reliance on the "party of power" and wean him away. In mid-1992, Rukh split, as Mykhailo Horyn, Ivan Drach, and Larysa Skoryk, all prominent nationalists, left Rukh to form the Congress of National Democratic Forces.

> Formerly united in their opposition to Communism and in their pursuit of independence under the aegis of Rukh, the new elites have followed the path of all broad-based coalitions, such as Poland's Solidarity, Czechoslovakia's Civic Forum, and India's Janata Party, and split into a multitude of small, organizationally unsophisticated, and resource-poor parties. In turn, some of these have also split in a pattern uncomfortably reminiscent of 1917–1919, when party fragmentation prevented the formation of stable coalitions and the implementation of effective policies.[33]

Ukraine's two presidential elections have demonstrated the irrelevance of political parties in Ukraine. In December 1991, Kravchuk, who had recently abandoned the Communist party and ran as an independent, easily defeated Chornovil, who was at that time the leader of Ukraine's largest quasi party, Rukh. In 1994, none of the major contenders ran with political party backing. The closest thing to a party any candidate had was Kuchma's "Interregional Bloc for Reform," which had managed to win four seats in the parliament. In such a system, a situation where the head of government and parliamentary majority are in the same party, and therefore working together, is impossible. Such a situation precludes the sort of decisive action needed to cope with extreme economic vulnerability.

Institutional factors also play an important role in fragmenting Ukraine's political parties, and it is within the parliament that the problem is greatest. Under Soviet election law, candidates were elected by majority vote from single-member districts (much like the U.S. House of Representatives). The Communist party won all the seats until 1990, when nationalists were able to win many seats in the west under the Rukh umbrella. Because the candidates had only to win a majority in their districts, they did not need to rely on a national political organization for their positions. This independence from parties was reinforced when the Communist party was dissolved, but its members remained in the parliament, with no party affiliation or discipline. There was therefore no group that was able to advance a program to solve the state's problems. Similarly, the cabinet of ministers was able to operate without a coherent program.[34]

When, in the fall of 1993, new elections were scheduled for March 1994, the key question became the election method. Reformers advocated a party list system, such as that used in Germany. In that system, voters choose a party, rather than a candidate, and seats in the parliament are distributed to all parties receiving a certain minimum threshold (in Germany 5%) according to their percentage of the vote. The virtue of this system is that it puts the focus on parties, such that individual candidates can get nowhere by themselves. Because individuals rely on parties for their reelection hopes, the party can maintain discipline in the parliament. The majority party or coalition should then be able to present and pass its program, and stalemate is avoided. If the threshold to get into parliament is sufficiently high, there is a great incentive for small parties to join together, and for blocs within larger parties to negotiate their differences rather than split, because by splitting, both of the new parties may be short of the minimum required, or at best suffer reduced influence in the parliament.[35]

This plan for proportional representation was opposed on two grounds. First, many genuinely feared making individuals so dependent on their parties in a state where the Communist party was so recently defeated. More significantly, the new election law had to be passed by the old parliament, which meant that their interests were preeminent. All of these deputies had been elected from single-member districts, which meant that all had strong local support networks, either due to personal prestige or their positions as heads of large enterprises. In a system based on proportional representation and party lists, their local power bases would be much less important as political assets. Most were unwilling to surrender their most valuable asset in the hope of forcing a consolidation of Ukraine's political parties. Ukraine's new Verkhovna Rada was therefore elected under a law quite similar to the old Soviet law.

The 1994 parliamentary elections were therefore indecisive, and served to transmit Ukraine's atomized political spectrum into parliament.[36] The election law led to this fragmentation in two ways. First, it made parties largely irrelevant, because there was nothing they could do for candidates. Second, because party backing was not needed, anybody with some local notoriety and ambition could run. The result was that over 5,800 candidates ran for 450 seats (roughly 13 candidates per seat). Only 11 percent of these candidates came from political parties.[37] The result was chaos in the elections, as runoffs were still being held months later.[38]

The one group that came close to assembling a majority was the one strong political party in the country: the Communist party, which had retained its organizational network, and had its ban lifted. Together with its allies, the socialists and the agrarians, the communists controlled 118 seats after the first two rounds. The next largest coalition was the national democrats (Rukh and its allies) who together controlled just 35 seats. The largest "bloc" of candidates was the 163 unaffiliated candidates who had been elected solely on their local power base. This group was referred to in the Ukrainian media as "the swamp" due to its amorphous character.[39] Moreover, 113 seats, almost exactly one-fourth, remained unfilled.[40] Because few others were willing to work with the communists, no one was able to muster a working majority. The resulting parliament was ineffective because there was no group that could attempt to put forth a program. Instead, for any measure that one hoped to pass, a new coalition of support had to be assembled from scratch.

Because the communists were the only group potentially able to build a majority, the goal of the national democratic forces became to bloc any action (enacting their own plans was impossible) and stalemate became their objective.[41] This stalemate was achieved without much difficulty, especially since the communist bloc is not monolithic. There is no parliamentary majority, and little prospect of achieving one. There has been some coalescing of individuals and small groups into larger voting blocs, but these are unstable and show no signs of becoming formal organizations intent on establishing a program and trying to advance it.[42] Parliamentary activity is still defined more in terms of what one opposes than what one supports.

Opposition has therefore been the primary role of the parliament. Under Kravchuk, parliament opposed the president's policies on relations with the CIS and nuclear weapons. Kuchma has been much more active than Kravchuk, and has run into concerted opposition to his economic reform plans (e.g., control of privatization was moved from the State Property Committee to a parliamentary committee, and then an outright ban was passed). In the end, however, parliament's internal division has led to a partial resolution of another problem: the division of power between the president and parliament (see below). As parliamentarians recognized that their body was incapable of legislating coherently, more and more deputies were amenable to shifting power toward the president, and after a long struggle that has been done.

Despite this shift, the incoherence of the parliament and of Ukraine's political parties will continue to hamper policy making in the future. This will make it impossible for the country to devise a long-term strategy to deal with its economic vulnerability and to implement such a strategy domestically. Particularly in the key area of domestic economic reform, Ukraine will either need to create an electoral system that encourages formation of a parliamentary majority, or will have to continue to reduce the role of that branch of government.

Division of Power

In most Western governments, there is a constitution that defines which branches of government are allowed to perform which functions. Typically functions are divided between executive, legislative, and judicial branches. According to liberal theory, the three branches are supposed to check each other to prevent tyranny, but allow sufficient differentiation of authority so each can do its job unimpeded and the government can function. Executives have little legislative authority, and legislatures lack the power to implement the laws they enact. But the right of the legislature to enact laws and of the executive to enforce them is not in doubt.

Under the Soviet Union, a very different system existed in Ukraine. While all serious decisions were made in Moscow, Ukraine did have its own institutions, which focused not on the separation of powers, but on the monopoly of power in the Communist party, which controlled the government as the realization of Lenin's "dictatorship of the proletariat." The problem in Ukraine and in the other former Soviet states is moving from a system where power is monopolized to one where it is divided. In Ukraine, the situation has evolved in such a way that power is divided, but the powers of the various organs are not defined. Tyranny is averted, but effective policy making is nearly impossible. Ukraine has four centers of power at the top of its government: the parliament (Verkhovna Rada), the speaker of the parliament, the prime minister, and the president. Because each has had sufficient power to check the others, finding a policy that all approve of has been nearly impossible, especially as the four are struggling for power and have little incentive to do anything that might increase the prerogatives of their rivals.

The structure evolved due to the peculiarities of the disintegration of Soviet power. In the Soviet system, the organs of government were of secondary importance to those of the Communist party, which ceased to play a role at independence. The Verkhovna Rada was the main organ of government under communism, and the president and prime minister did not exist. As Ukraine moved toward independence prior to 1991, it became more and more necessary to have an individual figure who represented the embryonic state. This figure was created by the elevation of the speaker of the Verkhovna Rada, at the time Leonid Kravchuk. It was Kravchuk, who, by virtue of his position as speaker, took the lead in declaring independence in 1991, and it was his position of authority as speaker that made him a natural candidate for president. The speaker was the top figure in the Soviet system, and because that system of institutions has not been decisively overhauled, the speaker retained important authority (along with the inherent political power of the position) in post-Soviet Ukraine.[43]

As Ukraine became independent, the one branch of government that it already had was a parliament. This institution has continued in its previous form, and has adopted more or less the function of a western legislature. However, because there are no circumscriptions on its authority, it has often been involved in running the day-to-day affairs of the government, especially under Kravchuk, who tried to be apolitical and remain above the fray of daily political issues. This tendency is a holdover from the late Soviet era, when, "the [republic] Supreme Soviets, gradually accumulating power at the expense of the Union center . . . , in essence combined representative and executive functions."[44] The continuity in institutions was emphasized by a writer who stated in 1993 that "political conditions remain almost the way they were over two years ago."[45]

The institutions that Ukraine lacked were a head of government and a head of state. Ukraine created a head of government in the form of a prime minister and a head of state in the form of a president, but by failing to distinguish their powers, achieved only a watering down of leadership at the top of the state. The president was important to those (especially nationalists) who sought the presence of a strong symbolic leader of the Ukrainian state. In addition, the presidency ended the parliament's monopoly on power.[46] However, many members of the Verkhovna Rada were concerned about potential tyranny, and about diluting their own influence. They therefore maintained important levers of influence over the president, including the elimination of the position of vice-president (which was initially proposed), parliamentary right to veto executive decrees, simple majority vote to override a presidential veto (which in essence means no presidential veto), right to reject appointment of key ministers, and the right to dismiss the government. The president had no right to dissolve the parliament or call new elections.[47]

Neither office was made primarily responsible for policy (in contrast to the British and German systems, where the queen and president are symbolic figures and the prime minister and chancellor are responsible for policy). Some Ukrainians have compared the system to that of France, which it superficially resembles, a comparison that appeals to nationalists because of France's very strong state. In the French system, however, immense authority is vested in the presidency in order to prevent the system from stalemating. The Ukrainian parliament, in modifying the Soviet constitution, was unwilling to vest that much authority in the president, both because it would greatly reduce the relevance of the parliament and because genuine fear of authoritarianism remained. Quite unlike the French Fifth Republic, Ukraine has a system that is very prone to stalemate, and Italy is the more relevant analogy for the functioning, if not the structure, of the Ukrainian government.

Authority to make and implement laws, was therefore hopelessly diluted until the revisions of early 1995. The Verkhovna Rada had the primary authority to legislate, but both the president and the cabinet had prerogatives to issue decrees under certain circumstances. The president had the authority to appoint the prime minister and cabinet of ministers, but the parliament could reject his nominees. The cabinet of ministers was in charge of actually running the government, but there were no official limits on the ability of the parliament or the president to micromanage the bureaucracies. Because the cabinet of ministers and prime minister were dependent on both the president and the parliament for their continuance in office, there was no way to resist such encroachments. The speaker of the parliament retained little statutory authority by himself, but through his control of the legislative agenda he had significant ability to initiate and block legislation and to block executive decisions.[48] The kernel of the problem was that the prime minister and cabinet, who were presumably most responsible for devising a policy program, getting it enacted, and then implementing it, were at the mercy of both the president and the parliament.[49] Both the authority to legislate and the authority to execute laws were spread across the three primary institutions, and each of them and the speaker had a *de facto* veto over others' initiatives.

Gradually, power shifted from the president to the parliament, though its own division prevented much action.[50] "The majority of laws and resolutions adopted by the parliament stemmed from its own initiative, including those political decisions that were directly within the competence of the executive branch—above all, the president." Thus when the Russian parliament claimed Sevastopol in 1993, it was the Ukrainian Verkhovna Rada, not President Kravchuk, that directed Ukraine's diplomats to bring the issue up at the UN Security Council.[51]

This institutional fragmentation was most visible in policy making over nuclear weapons. It was never clear who had the authority to negotiate on behalf of Ukraine and what sort of ratification of agreements was necessary. Repeatedly, Kravchuk reached agreements on nuclear weapons only to find that he had no support in the Verkhovna Rada. Because he and other governments assumed he had the authority to negotiate for Ukraine, the repeated need to put previously reached agreements back on the bargaining table created the impression that Ukraine was reneging on its agreements, and finally had the effect of undermining Kravchuk's bargaining position, because he clearly could not deliver what he promised.[52] When the Trilateral Agreement was reached in early 1994, Kravchuk tried an end run by asserting that as a "statement" by executives, not a treaty, the deal did not need to be ratified by the parliament (American presidents have made similar attempts with "executive agreements").[53] Chornovil responded: "President Kravchuk has no authority to sign such an agreement. Nuclear policy is for parliament to work out."[54] Despite the gravity of the debate, there was no way to decide the issue on legal grounds.[55] In the end, the Verkhovna Rada won the war (it did get to vote on the agreement) but Kravchuk won the battle (the Rada ratified the treaty after Kravchuk left office).

The impotence of the prime minister and government was particularly important during 1993, when Ukraine was attempting to resolve its economic crisis and to solve its related problem with Russia. In 1992, the parliament had forced the resignation of prime minister Vitold Fokin because he was too closely allied with Kravchuk, and not responsive enough to parliament's desires. Kuchma was appointed because he was independent of Kravchuk, and hence more amenable to parliament. Instead of having a cabinet at odds with parliament, Ukraine now had a cabinet at odds with the president, which worked no better. The parliament-cabinet conflict was resolved further in November 1992 when Kuchma was granted special powers for six months to bring Ukraine out of its crisis. He was given the power to issue decrees that had the force of law unless vetoed by parliament. At the same time, however, the parliament extended its control over selection of ministers and renewed the cabinet's control over certain functions previously held by the president. In sum, the cabinet gained power, but more important the parliament gained power at the president's expense.[56]

When Kuchma began using the powers delegated to him as prime minister in late 1992, however, he quickly earned the opposition of the parliament, and because he had never had the strong support of Kravchuk, he was left isolated. The granting of special powers to the prime minister only increased Kravchuk's detachment from the prime minister and the details of governing.[57] The fact that his plans for reform endangered the interests of the well-entrenched *nomenklatura* only increased Kuchma's isolation. The parliament refused to renew the temporary powers, but also refused to allow Kravchuk to put his own team in charge of the government or to allow Kuchma to resign. Complete paralysis of the government ensued until September 1993, when the parliament finally accepted Kuchma's resignation after the Massandra fiasco.[58] The overall effect of this process was to weaken both the prime minister and the president to the benefit of the parliament. But since the parliament itself was stalemated, it could do nothing. "In this sense the Ukrainian Presidency has become something in the nature of a constitutional addendum to the Parliament rather than an attribute of the executive branch."[59]

The Massandra summit was indicative of the problems in Ukrainian government. First, it was not clear who had the authority to negotiate, Kuchma or Kravchuk (both of them signed agreements), or whether the agreements required parliamentary ratification. Related to this division of authority, the Ukrainians went to the summit without having prepared detailed negotiating positions. The Ukrainian negotiators were caught off guard by the Russian proposals on exchanging gas debt for fleet assets and on exchanging nuclear fuel for warheads. Kuchma was following what he viewed as a coherent plan in agreeing to the deal on nuclear weapons: he was primarily concerned with solving Ukraine's economic woes. The parliament had other priorities, and complained bitterly about the deals. Kravchuk immediately distanced himself from the agreements, even though he was as responsible as Kuchma for their existence. With no independent base of authority, both the Massandra agreements and Kuchma had to go.

One can debate whether Massandra was a good deal for Ukraine or whether Kuchma was a good prime minister, but the problem for Ukraine was deeper than the particular policy or prime minister. Because no actor was both able to implement a program and responsible for it, not only could policies never be made, but issues could never be resolved. In most states, the government is chosen based on a particular program, and is given some chance to govern, and survives or falls based on the results of those policies. This absence of a program was exacerbated under Kravchuk by his view of the president's role as that of an apolitical leader, above day-to-day policy conflicts. Thus the problem is not that Kuchma was rejected, but that when he was rejected, no particular set of policies was being rejected, and it was impossible therefore to move on. He was replaced with Yuchim Zviahilsky, and the same debates started all over again.

When Leonid Kuchma ran for president in 1994, one of his main themes, other than renewing economic ties with Russia, was the need to increase the power of the Ukrainian president. He had been frustrated at his inability to make policy as prime minister. He was not the only supporter of this view, and the need to reconstitute Ukraine's political institutions was widely recognized by other candidates, including Kravchuk and Ivan Plyushch, the speaker of the Verkhovna Rada. The stalemate that prevented government action, however, also prevented any agreement on restructuring the government. The Verkhovna Rada supported a shift to a parliamentary system, which would resolve the impasse by giving it primary power. Kravchuk and later Kuchma argued for a strong president, which would give one of them more power, and others continued to point to the French model.

The lack of concentrated power in the Ukrainian system was severe enough so that many advocated decidedly antidemocratic measures to solve the problem. Kravchuk put forth South Korea as an example in an interview in late 1993, and the example of Pinochet was cited so frequently that Ukrainians began speaking of "Pinochuk" as the solution to their political impasse. There is sufficient support for democracy in Ukraine that such sentiments have not gained wide support, but the belief that Ukraine needs a more unified and powerful state has had a significant effect. After his election, Kuchma made strengthening the presidency a priority issue:

> Without a doubt, the conditions, without which reforms or any movement forward are impossible, are the formation of a strong and effective state power. This envisages strengthening of a single executive vertical structure as the fundamental instrument for implementing statewide policy. At the same time, relations between all branches of power should be stabilized.[60]

Eventually he was able to succeed, but not without a fight. Even with a new president with a clear program and a strong electoral mandate, parliament was able to foil action, most notably when it passed a moratorium on all privatization in late 1994 in order to prevent Kuchma from initiating reform while parliament was in recess. The prime minister's power to check the president became a problem in early 1995 when, until he was forced out, Vitaliy Masol resisted many of the reforms that Kuchma was attempting to implement as president.[61]

Kuchma struggled with the parliament throughout early 1995 to change the system to grant more power to the president. His initial plan called for abolition of the prime minister's position, making the president head of government as well as head of state. There was significant opposition to giving the president this much power, so Kuchma advanced a plan that would tie the prime minister more closely to the president by removing the right of the parliament to a reject the president's candidates for prime minister and other key ministers. This would allow the president to put his own people in these jobs, rather than having the president attempt to placate the parliament (as Kravchuk had done in choosing Kuchma). This would make the prime minister more dependent on the president, and would give him only one master rather than two. Kuchma also sought the right to dissolve the parliament under some conditions.[62]

Much of the parliament was willing to allow the change in ministerial appointments, recognizing the need to make the government more unified. The large socialist contingent contended somewhat ironically that the system was moving toward dictatorship. More likely, the opposition can be regarded as a desire, not unique to Ukraine, to protect institutional prerogatives. There was widespread opposition to allowing the president to dissolve the parliament. Parliament asserted its power and expressed its discontent when it passed a motion of no confidence, removing the government, in April 1995.[63] Kuchma refused to appoint a new government, waiting until a new law was passed that would allow him to do so without parliamentary approval.

When the parliament resisted, Kuchma forced a showdown, threatening to hold a nonbinding referendum on the public's confidence in the parliament and the president, which Kuchma would likely win, strengthening his position.[64] The two sides finally reached a compromise that gave Kuchma his primary objective, the exclusive right of the president to form a government, but excluded provisions for the president to dissolve parliament or for the parliament to impeach the president.[65] Because sixty-nine articles of the existing constitution had to be suspended for the new law to go into effect, a measure requiring a two-thirds majority, communist deputies were initially able to block implementation of the new rules, forcing a second showdown.[66] Kuchma said he would implement the new law regardless of whether the constitution was suspended or not, and he again threatened to hold a referendum, this time going so far as to schedule a date (28 June, a month hence).[67] The parliament then vetoed the decree on the referendum, and Kuchma responded that he would carry it out anyhow, bringing the country to a major crisis.[68]

Again, a compromise was reached in which Kuchma got most of what he wanted: the relevant articles of constitution were suspended for a year until a new constitution could be adopted.[69]

By forcing the parliament to give in on this crucial issue, Kuchma was able to increase substantially the power of the president. This was one way (adopting a parliamentary system would have been another) to begin to clarify the separation of powers in the Ukrainian government. Kuchma quickly put his power to use, installing a government of reformers. In the foreign policy realm, Kuchma began developing a security strategy to deal with Ukraine's economic and security concerns and its precarious position between east and west.[70]

The institutional situation remained muddled, however. In order to resolve these questions finally, Ukraine needed to adopt a new constitution.[71] The repeatedly amended version of the Soviet-era Ukrainian constitution simply did not address many of the fundamental issues.[72] Lack of clarity over the parliament's right to treaty ratification was only one example. Does the chairman of the parliament's committee on foreign affairs have the right to conduct diplomacy, as he often does? It was not clear. More broadly, a constitution was necessary to end the governmental chaos that currently prevented Ukraine from dealing with any of its problems.

In the spring and summer of 1996, the standoff of 1995 was repeated over the new constitution. The constitutional commission's first draft gave Kuchma most of what he wanted—a strong presidency—but was widely opposed among parliamentarians. A subsequent draft gave more power to the parliament—especially over cabinet appointments—and looked much like the amended Soviet constitution that had been found unworkable. There was even conflict over how the constitution was to be adopted—by parliament, by referendum, or both—a crucial factor in what sort of provisions would prevail. A crisis was reached in early June, when the previous year's constitutional agreement expired.

Kuchma again seized the initiative and capitalized on his relative popularity over the parliament. He declared he would hold a put the constitution to the people in a referendum if the parliament did not approve one rapidly. In planning the referendum, he reverted to the previous draft (the one with greater presidential power). That draft was finally approved by parliament, and as of June 1996 Ukraine has a constitution that should resolve many of the problems that have plagued its institutions for the first five years of independence. How this constitution will function in practice remains to be seen, but it should be noted that one considerable shortcoming persists: the lack of a functioning court system. While Ukraine now has a constitution, it does not have an effective mechanism for resolving disputes over the constitution's provisions. Many of the same conflicts over prerogative have therefore continued even under the new document.

Kuchma's campaign to strengthen the presidency has represented an important shift in Ukrainian politics. Kuchma has transformed the presidency into a partisan position. Kravchuk saw himself as the leader of all Ukrainians, and saw his primary job as playing a unifying role in a divided society. This was perhaps crucial in the early stages of independence. But it meant that Kravchuk declined to take a firm stand on many issues of the day, because that would mean choosing sides rather than unifying. As a result, the lack of authority in the government was exacerbated. The one official who might have had the juridical authority and the political strength to try to advance a political program chose to stand aside.

Kuchma has taken a much more political role. He remains constrained by Ukraine's divisions, but he does not believe the president should stand above politics, as Kravchuk attempted. He has therefore put forth clear domestic and foreign policy plans, even if he has taken account of political necessity in doing so. By threatening referenda if he did not get the reforms he sought, he was committing himself to a policy and putting his prestige on the line. Whether Kuchma's reforms will succeed, and how long he will last as president, remain to be seen. The important point for this analysis is that Ukraine's institutional setting is changing, such that it might be more possible in the future than it has been in the past to devise and enact a coherent strategy to reduce economic vulnerability. Kuchma so far has at least a general strategy, which involves improving prosperity through reform and trading with Russia while keeping it at arm's length.

It should be emphasized, however, that while institutional confusion has been an important constraint on Ukraine's economic security policy, reforming Ukraine's institutional structure is not by itself a sufficient condition for reducing economic vulnerability. If Ukraine's other internal divisions, especially disagreement over economic reform and the relative priorities of prosperity, autonomy, and sovereignty, persist, stalemate will continue due to political rather than institutional reasons. Similarly, even if Ukraine does adopt a coherent strategy to deal with its economic vulnerability, the success of the policy will depend on the content of the policy. As indicated in chapter 3, some strategies are more likely to be more successful than others. Ukraine demonstrated this when the one somewhat coherent strategy it did adopt—economic isolation—proved to be immensely damaging.

Ukraine as a Weak State

Ukraine's institutional and political divisions help create a situation that places important constraints on Ukraine's ability to deal with its economic vulnerability: the state is very weak relative to the society. It is therefore limited in its ability to implement certain policies that might alleviate its economic vulnerability. Because the state is so divided, it is relatively easy for aggrieved societal actors to block policies that they oppose. Just as the weakness of the prime minister made it easy for the parliament to foil his program, the overall weakness of the government makes it easy for societal actors to obstruct certain policies. This is especially true when warring governmental actors adopt opposite positions to win an institutional battle.

This weakness can be divided analytically into two categories of issues in which the Ukrainian state is unable to reduce its vulnerability not because of external pressures or the inability to arrive at a policy, but because the policy in question cannot be implemented without the approval of the Ukrainian people. First, domestic efficiency and austerity measures have been nearly impossible to implement because people resist them. Second, the policy of economic isolation was unsustainable because of the domestic hardship created. In the first category, the status quo is on the side of society, and the state cannot overcome it; in the second, the people have been able to force the state to repeal a policy already enacted.

One of the primary ways to reduce economic dependence is simply to consume less, and therefore need to import and export less. Austerity is one way to approach this, and efficiency is another. These issues were crucial in the policy of economic isolation adopted in early 1992 and in the struggle over energy supplies. The government's success in implementing austerity and efficiency measures has been limited. Because the state continues its control of the energy supply and distribution, it was theoretically possible to cut off gas to certain consumers when times got bad. But the government could not withstand the inevitable unrest that would result. Because the state could not cut off its delinquent customers, Kravchuk sought to privatize much of the gas industry, in order to put it in the hands of an entity that might have the ability to force payment.[73] In promoting efficiency, the state was even less successful, because the interests it had to take on were well-organized and well-represented in Kiev. An energy austerity bill prepared by the Ministry of Power Engineering and Electrification during the energy crisis in November 1993 was "torpedoed" quickly in the Verkhovna Rada, apparently due to the opposition of "the directors' lobby," even as schools were being closed for lack of heat and light.[74]

It was therefore nearly impossible to close those factories that were the most profligate wasters of energy. In many cases, the factories were not only wasting energy, but losing money, but they could not be closed for two reasons. First, factory directors remained influential actors in the political system, able to deliver (or deny) large blocs of votes. "Top level executive official acknowledge that the Government does not even have control over the public sector of the economy, for enterprises which have separated from the State have no responsibilities to it."[75] Second, Ukrainians continue to believe that they have a right to a job. The need to reduce energy waste was widely acknowledged, and energy supplies were cut to many industries in the short term, but the government was unable to deal with the long-term issue by closing plants, even when they were not even profitable. Moreover, much administration is still conducted by the local Soviets, which have largely resisted efforts by Kiev to reduce their power, and which are largely unreformed since the Soviet era.[76]

The state's weakness was also a key issue in the retraction of the policy of isolation. While the policy was no doubt unwise in the first place, Kravchuk continued to support it even after widespread complaints began in eastern Ukraine. If the ability to extract sacrifice from the people is a measure of state strength, the Ukrainian government was proven to be weak. Protests from citizens and industries in eastern Ukraine caused Kravchuk to slowly back down on that policy, even as he moved toward the nationalist end of the political spectrum. At the same time however, the agreement to join the CIS economic union in 1993 had to be reconsidered due to opposition from nationalists. Kuchma's resignation was prompted by the public outcry caused by that decision and the Massandra agreements. The government's inability to resist being caught in the middle of this tug of war indicates its weakness in Ukraine, as well as the degree of political bifurcation within society. Together, those two characteristics (divided society, weak state) prevented action to deal with economic vulnerability and many other issues.

Conclusion

Ukraine's domestic political situation has had an important impact on how it has dealt (or rather, not dealt) with its economic security. Because the country is divided politically, and the state is divided institutionally, Ukraine has been unable to devise or implement a strategy to cope with economic vulnerability ever since its initial strategy of isolation failed. The inability to formulate a policy is not unique to economic security, but endemic to Ukrainian politics, and the inability to devise policies in other areas indirectly but powerfully affects Ukraine's economic vulnerability. This is most notable in the realm of economic reform, which would have entailed ending some of the practices that made Ukraine most dependent, especially in energy. The link between political reform, economic strategy, and Ukrainian independence was captured by Kuchma when he resigned as Prime Minister: "It is my belief that Ukraine badly needs substantial political reforms, without which economic reforms are impossible, and without which we risk losing our independence."[77]

Ukraine of course is not the only country in the world with a stalemated political system. However, as a state in dire economic and political straits, challenged both from within and outside the country, the political stalemate has magnified effects. Advanced industrial states, with economies that basically function, fundamental political questions resolved, and little external threat, can flourish with a relatively little adjustment in policy, and in some cases the continuity provided by such a system is beneficial. Ukraine's system did ensure a large degree of continuity in policy, in a way. But since previous political arrangements had been shattered, and Ukraine had no established patterns of government, the continuity provided was continuity of chaos.

Authors who write on the small states of western Europe explain their ability to be economically dependent but still politically autonomous by their ability to adjust to new conditions in the international political economy. In a sense, they survive along with large actors because their agility offsets their small size. Ukraine is in a similar or even worse position in terms of economic vulnerability, but is entirely lacking in agility. This explains why throughout the period covered by this book, Ukraine has scarcely responded to the challenges presented to it by Russia. There was unity of government for a short time in early 1992, but the action taken was in an unproductive direction. Had that unity persisted, the policy could have been reversed and a new plan implemented. Instead, chaos, both in the government and society, set in. Recent reforms have significantly increased the power of the president, and Kuchma will now have some ability to pursue his strategy. Whether his strategy will work is another question, but unlike previously, some action will be taken.

Since 1991, Ukraine has been paying the price for its sudden and unexpected need to declare independence. Doing so with no plan on how to govern and no constitution has forced the government to work in an ad hoc fashion that has not been successful. In the future, Ukraine's ability to function in every realm including security policy will rely in part on the degree to which the new constitution allows effective government.

It is equally unclear whether Ukraine's societal divisions will vanish anytime soon. Absent favorable societal conditions, it may be impossible to implement a strategy that will allow prosperity through openness and reduction of vulnerability. Katzenstein has shown that the small states of Western Europe have succeeded in large part because of corporatist arrangements that enable the state and elite representatives of key interests to hammer out agreed-on measures to deal with economic shocks from abroad. These arrangements, he argues, rely on "strong oligarchic tendencies. Political power is concentrated in the hands of few decision-makers and rests with strong parties or strong interest groups."[78] This chapter has shown that, contrary to these needs, Ukraine has no concentration of power and weak political parties (it has few organized interest groups[79]). There is no reason to believe that Ukraine will have such characteristics in the near future, even if political differences in the country narrow considerably.

If the essence of Russia's power over Ukraine is the ability to narrow Ukraine's range of feasible economic options, Ukraine's internal political situation narrows the range of possible choices even further. In the worst of times during the first few years of independence, these constraints have combined to prevent any real choices at all from being made. More recently, however, it appears that Ukraine's domestic ability to make choices to deal with its economic vulnerability is increasing. What the content of those choices will be and how successful they will be remains to be seen. With a weak state and a divided society, Ukraine will continue to find itself the passive victim of forces beyond its border.

9

Conclusions and Questions

Ukraine is pulled between two opposing forces. Politically, the state seeks to solidify the independence it has attained after three centuries of failed efforts, and this drive for independence pushes Ukraine away from Russia. Economically, however, Ukraine is pulled toward Russia by the interdependence that was established under the Soviet Union and by the dictates of economic efficiency. In struggling to find a stable position between these two forces, Ukraine has found that no truly secure or desirable position exists. It cannot assure both its independence and its prosperity simultaneously, and even one of these goals will be difficult to achieve. Since 1991, Ukraine's sovereignty and independence have been consolidated, reform has begun, and there are signs that the contraction of the economy may soon be replaced by growth. This progress, however, continues to rest on a shaky foundation, for Ukraine's economy still relies heavily on trade with Russia that is subject to manipulation. The fundamental dilemmas that Ukraine has faced since independence will continue to define its situation in the international political economy.

However, not all potential outcomes are equally bad. The primary task of the first years of independence has been for Ukraine to sort out its priorities: How important are sovereignty, autonomy, and prosperity, and how much of one should be sacrificed to provide for another? The evolution of Ukrainian policy described in the preceding chapters allows us to make some assessment of how Ukraine has ordered its priorities in this difficult situation. In pursuing those priorities, Ukraine has had to answer a host of questions concerning the relationship of means to ends, and the extent to which the goals are incompatible with one another: To what extent does economic isolation impede prosperity? To what extent does it protect autonomy? How much does trade with Russia endanger autonomy and sovereignty? Will the CIS help constrain or empower Russia? What role can nuclear weapons play in assuring Ukraine's security?

While it is early to make definitive judgments on recent events, some preliminary assessment is in order. In this concluding chapter, we first summarize the empirical findings of the issue studies in terms of the broad questions introduced at the beginning of the book. We then examine (cautiously) the outlook for future relations between Russia and Ukraine and for Ukraine's ability to continue to hold its ground between prosperity and independence. We then assess the relevance of this case for international relations theory. And finally we address the practical and theoretical implications of this case for the entire region.

The most significant conclusion of this study is that, despite improvement in Ukraine's strategic situation, there remains a contradiction in Ukrainian foreign policy priorities. Ukraine has yet to figure out how to protect all of its primary security goals—prosperity, autonomy, and sovereignty. The current policy of bilateralism has been able to provide an acceptable amount of prosperity and a nearly ideal degree of sovereignty, but because bilateralism maximizes Russia's capacity for coercion, it leaves a key Ukrainian goal, political autonomy, in jeopardy. The danger of economic coercion will continue to plague Ukraine for some time to come. Ironically, as Ukraine's economy improves, the situation could get worse. To the extent that economic recovery is predicated on free trade with Russia, it is vulnerable to the threat of cutoff. And unlike 1992–1993, when Ukraine's economy was in shambles and could not get much worse, as the economy strengthens Ukraine will have much more to lose. Any Ukrainian government intent on remaining in office will also be vulnerable. There will be considerable incentive for Ukrainian leaders to avoid anything that might prompt Russia to injure Ukraine's economy.

Four Questions

Chapters 1 and 3 introduced and developed a series of questions that Ukraine has had to address. The empirical chapters on energy, trade, the CIS, and nuclear weapons yield considerable insight into how Ukraine is dealing with the acute dilemmas it faces as a state that is economically dependent on a neighbor from whom it perceived a significant security threat. Ukraine has come to see the constraints inherent in its situation more clearly, and has begun to resolve some of the policy dilemmas created by those constraints. The evolving responses to these dilemmas can be seen in reconsidering each dilemma across the four issues covered.

Prosperity versus Autonomy

In choosing between autonomy and prosperity, Ukraine has undergone a fundamental shift in policy. Originally, its domestic and foreign policies were based on the perceived need to create a degree of economic independence to reinforce the state's political independence from Russia. Breaking the ties of interdependence, however, proved devastating to Ukraine's economy, and the policy of isolation has since been largely abandoned. Since the autumn of 1993, Ukraine has sought to reestablish many of the trade links that were severed after independence.

The decision to privilege autonomy over prosperity was made in the spring of 1992 when the Kravchuk government initiated and enacted Ukraine's economic plan, which focused on isolation from Russia rather than reform or economic performance. That policy signaled not simply a disregard for the wealth of Ukraine or the prosperity of its citizens, it signaled a fundamental misjudgment by the leadership concerning the prospects for economic development in isolation from Russia. When the policy was eroded and then reversed, it was not as much a reversal of priorities as of means: leaders had never intended to impoverish the country, and steered away once they saw where their policy was taking them. Since that time, prosperity has been reemphasized, but not to the complete exclusion of autonomy.

As chapters 5 (on trade) and 8 (on domestic divisions) showed, there has been no consensus concerning the relative importance of prosperity and autonomy in Ukraine. The policy of isolation was reversed because almost nobody was willing to tolerate such poverty. After that, however, there has been little agreement. The Kuchma government has managed to find, if not a consensus, at least a position that is minimally acceptable to a large majority of the population. Kuchma has guaranteed the interests of nationalists by maintaining limits on the *nature* of involvement with Russia, and pleased the nonnationalists by lifting much of the limit on the *amount* of involvement with Russia.

Having started at a very extreme position in favor of autonomy at the expense of prosperity, Ukraine has moved toward an intermediate position that makes significant concessions of autonomy for greater prosperity. The degree to which Ukraine has been willing to tolerate economic injury rather than surrender autonomy was demonstrated in the energy war, which also demonstrated how badly Russia can injure Ukraine economically. Despite the severe injury to Ukraine's economy, Ukraine did not budge on most of the issues that were the object of Russian coercion: the Black Sea Fleet, the CIS, and Ukraine's gas pipelines.[1] Compared to most other states in the world and in the region, Ukraine's policy is still a very nationalist one. Nonetheless, by renewing trade with Russia, Ukraine has increased its dependence on Russia, and its vulnerability to Russian pressure. This is one of the main effects of international trade: By making the state more prosperous (and therefore more stable internally), beneficial trade makes the state more vulnerable to external coercion. Having seen how badly Ukraine did when ties were severed, both Ukrainian and Russian leaders are aware of what difficulties might ensue if Russia cut trade in the future.[2]

However, Ukraine's shift toward a more moderate position may not be as damaging to its security as some Ukrainian nationalists have feared, for reasons developed in chapters 7 and 8. Because the society is so badly divided, internal divisions (Crimea, the east-west split, resurgent communism) have been as deep a threat to the security of the country as has been Russian imperialism. Moreover, Ukraine's disastrous domestic economy actually facilitated Russian pressure by making Ukraine weak and by sowing dissatisfaction with the meager fruits of independence. To some extent, then, the effect of increasing direct vulnerability to Russian pressure has been offset by increasing Ukraine's ability to resist such pressure.

While the problem of outright coercion has receded for now, it could reassert itself. As Ukraine finds itself highly dependent on Russia, but without any agreed means for governing trade relations, the potential for Russian unilateral action to either injure Ukraine, or simply compel Ukraine to adopt Russian policies, will increase. A May 1996 report by the Russian Council on Foreign and Defense Policy indicates that the issue is still very much on Russia's agenda.[3] Even if attempts to re-create a Union in the aftermath of collapse failed, long-term formation of a strong Russian sphere of interest is still very possible. It was Russia's unilateral price rise in 1992 that in part prompted Ukraine's decision to isolate itself from Russia. If the opposite happened, and Russia reasserted price controls on certain goods, Ukraine might again have to follow suit or face massive disruption. Ukraine will also be vulnerable to disruptions beyond the control of the Russian government, such as inflation.[4]

Sovereignty versus Prosperity

By reestablishing trade with Russia, the question of managing that trade returns to the agenda with renewed importance. If Ukraine has a great deal of trade with Russia, but no rules to govern it, two problems arise. First, the ability of trade to contribute to prosperity will be limited, both by the transfer of shocks from one economy to the other and by the trade barriers inherent in different and uncoordinated economic systems. These problems have had an important effect in driving the states of the EU and of NAFTA toward deeper integration, even when some of them have been very wary of the consequences for their sovereignty. In this way Ukraine's resolution of one debate, autonomy versus prosperity, has simply led to two new trade-offs: sovereignty versus prosperity and sovereignty versus autonomy.

While willing to sacrifice some autonomy for prosperity, Ukraine has steadfastly resisted surrendering sovereignty, no matter what the cost in domestic prosperity. Ukraine has been fixated on sovereignty, making it the dominant theme in negotiations over nuclear weapons and in dealings over the CIS. In the nuclear weapons case, Ukraine focused primarily on getting Russia and the United States to recognize its rights to equal participation in the negotiations and only secondarliy on receiving its share of assets that belonged to the Soviet Union, as well as on getting Russia to commit itself to respecting Ukraine's borders and territorial integrity. In the case of the CIS, Ukraine has been very consistent in refusing to allow the CIS any coordinating or decision-making role, regardless of the benefits to prosperity that might ensue from such coordination. This consistency stems from the principle of sovereignty as an unabridgeable state right, and from a perceived lesson of history that international coordination starts one on a slippery slope toward Russian domination. The tenacity with which Ukraine has clung to its sovereignty has been demonstrated not only by its unwillingness to give in to the dictates of free trade theory, but also by its unwillingness to give in during Russia's energy offensive in 1993–1994.

The contrast between Ukraine's behavior in protecting its autonomy and in protecting its prosperity has been remarkable. Ukraine was willing to reassess its focus on autonomy when the costs became clear. No such reassessment has taken place on the question of sovereignty, where Ukraine has not made a single notable concession. Kravchuk and Kuchma tried to make a concession in September 1993 in signing the CIS economic agreement, but that deal had to be scrapped when it was assailed for surrendering too much sovereignty. It remains true that the commitment to sovereignty is held unevenly throughout the population, but it has remained a powerful force. To the extent that there has been opposition to Ukraine's independent line, it has been met not by conceding sovereignty, but by conceding more genuine autonomy, as in removing restrictions to trade with Russia. The coalition of forces that sees sovereignty as preeminent goal is strong in particular because it cuts across Ukraine's other major political schisms. When the change in president from Kravchuk to Kuchma did not produce a major shift in this policy, it became clear that it is solidly entrenched.

This preoccupation with sovereignty stands in contrast to dominant trends among the advanced industrial states, as well as to the contention of many scholars that the nation state, and the Westphalian international system that is defined by state sovereignty, are coming to an end. If Ukraine's fixation on its sovereignty persists, and all indications are that it will, it may become the dominant limiting factor on Ukraine's foreign policy in the future. Attempting to resolve the challenges of interdependence while retaining such a heavy emphasis on sovereignty creates a policy puzzle that will not be easily solved. Other states, most notably those of the EU, have found it impossible to reconcile the goals of prosperity and sovereignty in a highly interdependent world.

Sovereignty versus Autonomy

Ukraine's unwillingness to cede any decision-making authority to the CIS has important implications for autonomy as well as for prosperity. The lack of international coordination of trade and monetary policies, combined with the decision to seek trade with Russia to pursue prosperity, guarantees that Ukraine will continue to face a threat to its autonomy in two important ways: unintended disruption and intended coercion. Ukraine originally isolated itself from Russia largely to protect its autonomy, but this safeguard was removed for the sake of repairing Ukraine's decimated economy. Given a deep trade relationship with Russia, only rules could prevent disruption or coercion from Russia. Rules would reduce disruption by creating established procedures to coordinate trade and economic policies and by creating stable expectations of future actions. Rules could also, if properly set up and obeyed by both sides, make economic coercion much less likely. Ukraine has forgone such rules, however, both because they would infringe on its sovereignty and because Ukraine is skeptical that they could be fairly set up and that Russia would obey them.

The crux of the problem for Ukraine is that it cannot deal with Russia successfully on the basis of power, but that other policies are even less acceptable. Not trading with Russia proved unworkable. Trading with Russia on the basis of internationally established rules has been unacceptable. That leaves Ukraine trading with a much more powerful Russia with no constraints on coercion. Ukraine thus appears doomed to face continued difficulties: It faces a much larger and more powerful actor on which it is heavily reliant, in an environment that is essentially anarchic. In such a situation, the only thing to prevent coercion is the interest or beneficence of the powerful, and Ukraine cannot be optimistic in this regard. Only a few Ukrainian leaders or scholars seem to appreciate this problem: "[T]he Ukrainian leadership's reliance upon bilateral relationships among CIS member-states (which was motivated by fears of Russia's domination in any interstate body) led in practice to an even greater Russian supremacy of each of its CIS partners in their relations with Russia."[5] The problem Ukraine has faced and will continue to face was made evident in the energy war. By joining the CIS, Ukraine could largely avert the danger of an energy war. Instead, Ukraine has chosen to stay out of the CIS and continue in a situation with no barrier to Russian coercion on energy or any other issue. There is nothing to prevent a repetition of the energy war, or more subtle forms of pressure.

This policy of safeguarding sovereignty to the exclusion of the pursuit of genuine autonomy (freedom from the threat of coercion) has tremendous implications for Ukrainian-Russian relations. Battles over economic policy are likely to continue, and Russia will continue to have the means to prevail in such disputes. More ominously, should Russia decide for one reason or another to attempt again to subjugate Ukraine, there remain no obstacles to Russia devastating the Ukrainian economy. This point is significant in light of the finding at the conclusion of chapter 4 concerning Russian and Ukrainian will in the energy war. Ukraine exhibited immense will and capacity for suffering in resisting Russian pressure. However, Russia was not severely strained in bringing Ukraine to that dire point. Having failed in winning a quick and easy victory, Russia relented. It remains to be seen, however, if Ukraine can withstand a protracted and concerted effort by Russia to destroy its economy—including an all-out embargo. Even though that eventuality is unlikely, Ukraine must make every decision in its relations with Russia with the awareness that Russia can destroy the Ukrainian economy at any time. The threat of a new trade war does not need to be explicit to have effect.

Ukraine's position thus seems to be an extreme one, and perhaps a very shortsighted one. In pursuit of *de jure* sovereignty, which has little practical significance, it is endangering its prosperity and its autonomy, which have a great deal of practical significance. However, the assertion that Ukraine is sacrificing the potential to protect itself from Russia by refusing to join the CIS relies on the crucial assumption that international rules and international institutions are capable of constraining Russian behavior and protecting Ukraine. And regardless of the experience of the small states of the EU or the arguments of liberal international relations theorists, Ukraine has no confidence that this is so. Ukraine's refusal to seek to protect its autonomy through international institutions is not at all mysterious in light of the belief by Ukrainian leaders that the institution in question, the CIS, would magnify not constrain Russian power, and therefore would endanger rather than protect Ukraine's autonomy. Ukrainian leaders have several reasons for believing this, and there is no way of knowing whether their arguments are any less valid than those that have prevailed in Western Europe.

First, the fact that Russia is so large compared to the rest of the CIS states (greater than half the population and GNP) means that there is nothing within the organization to check it. This is different from the relatively balanced situation between Germany, France, Italy, and Great Britain in the EU, and also contradicts the principle of internal balance enshrined in the United Nations and most Western constitutions. Second, Russian leaders have stated on many occasions that they hope the CIS will provide a means of reintegrating "the former Soviet space," and the assumption seems to be that Russia would dominate such an entity. Third, unlike the EU, the CIS contains a large military component as well as an economic component, increasing the potential for Russia to use the organization to legitimate aggressive activity.[6] Fourth, experience has already shown that while Russia does not get everything it wants in the CIS, no measure is approved over Russian objections. Moreover, Russia's ability to act unilaterally within the Commonwealth has proven considerable.

Fifth, more distant experience of the Union Treaty of 1922 and the Treaty of Pereiaslav of 1654 provide an uncomfortable precedent for Ukrainian independence in collaboration with Russia. Finally, and perhaps most significant, events since Ukraine's independence have not served to increase anyone's faith in the ability of international institutions to protect the weak. The spectacular failure of the UN, NATO, and the EU to halt Serbian aggression in the former Yugoslavia was highlighted to Ukraine, which had a group of peacekeepers held hostage for a time in mid-1995. The lukewarm reaction of Western governments to Ukraine's independence and the perception that they lacked respect for Ukraine's sovereignty has contributed to a widespread skepticism in Ukraine concerning the meaning of international commitments. Evidence of this was seen in the debates on nuclear weapons policy. In sum, Ukraine is convinced that participation in the CIS threatens its sovereignty and autonomy more than does the possibility of naked coercion by Russia. Ukraine is more concerned that the CIS will subtly undermine its independence than that Russia will openly and forcefully crush it.

Ukraine's Ongoing Dilemma: To Balance or Bandwagon?

Ukrainian leaders are unable to resolve the debate between autonomy and prosperity in part due to Ukraine's unfortunate situation as a state dealing with a much larger adversary, but also because they have been unable to resolve a fundamental strategic dilemma: that of balancing versus bandwagoning. As we have seen, neither of these strategies is feasible for Ukraine, nor has Ukraine been able to devise a suitable alternative. Bandwagoning is unacceptable in Ukraine to a majority of masses and elites alike. Indeed it is the fear of being forced to accept Russian hegemony that creates Ukraine's dilemmas in the first place. Internal balancing simply is not feasible given the relative size of the two states. Ukraine does not have the resources to compete militarily and economically with Russia. Nor is external balancing feasible, as Ukraine learned in some of its exploratory efforts. "Most of the other states in the region are certainly keen to see Ukraine remain independent but are probably fearful of incurring Russia's wrath by aligning against her."[7] Ukraine's neighbor to the north, Belarus, has elected to submit to Russian hegemony. Those with better links to the West, notably the Czech Republic, Slovakia, Poland, and the Baltics, have pinned their hopes on joining NATO, and therefore have little use for Ukraine. Moreover, Ukraine fears that NATO expansion will leave it to deal with Russia alone.[8] Links with NATO are reassuring, but fall far short of meeting Ukraine's needs.

Kravchuk's government tried to resolve this dilemma in early 1992 through its policy of isolation. While isolation would not protect Ukraine from a direct military attack, it would insulate Ukraine from economic and political pressure. To the extent that it was a solution to the balancing versus bandwagoning dilemma, the strategy of isolation was a reasonable one, but it was not feasible in terms of domestic economics any more than building an army to challenge Russia's would be. Having found that none of these strategies will work, Ukraine has yet to develop a strategy for dealing with its large neighbor. In the events since independence, however, one can see a policy emerging in fact even if it is not yet enshrined as doctrine. Ukraine's declarations of sovereignty and independence stated that Ukraine would be neutral. Exactly what that should mean in practice (and whether it should be the basis for Ukrainian policy) have been at the center of Ukrainian debates over developing a security strategy. In particular, the question is whether neutrality should be regarded strictly, such that it excludes joining most international organizations; or interpreted as "nonbloc" status, which would allow joining such groups as the EU but not NATO; or should be disregarded altogether to allow participation in NATO's Partnership for Peace and pursuit of eventual NATO membership.[9]

Ukraine is taking on the position of an armed neutral, in that it will do what it can to stay out of conflicts, but retain some capacity to fight if needed. This strategy retains minimal aspects of balancing, in terms of retaining significant potential to deter Russia, even if it cannot repel an all-out attack. It also makes a slight bow toward bandwagoning in its commitment not to undertake actions that might give Russia cause for aggression (i.e., retaining nuclear weapons or joining NATO). And it adopts aspects of isolationism, by making it a point to stay out of conflicts by dealing with its potential adversary as little as possible. Neutrality also has a strong, if ironic, domestic base of support: nationalists see it as an obstacle to joining the CIS, and Russophiles see it as an obstacle to joining NATO.

The strategy does not guarantee success, but then for the small state in an anarchic world, no strategy will. In the end, Ukraine's survival will depend to some extent on Russia retaining some limits on the costs it is willing to incur to reassert its dominance, as well as on some western pressure on Russia to behave peacefully. It will also depend on Ukraine's ability to marshal its own internal resources. This strategy is certainly not ideal in any sense, but it is realistic—perhaps the only realistic strategy—given the constraints inherent in the situation.

Potential Alternate Strategies

Initially, the Ukraine-Russia relationship was a regional one, but it is becoming more enmeshed in broader European security discussions. To the extent that the Ukraine-Russia relationship becomes tied up in larger European issues, two possibilities emerge. Balancing and institutions, two solutions that appear foreclosed in the current circumstances, could be reopened if, as now seems possible, the Ukrainian-Russian relationship becomes entangled in broader discussions of European security.

The main problem with the CIS is the potential for Russia to dominate it. It is possible that Ukraine's fixation with its sovereignty would not be so strong if the supranational organization under consideration were not the CIS. Ukrainian nationalists have not appeared nearly as concerned about joining the EU as they have about the CIS.[10] If Ukraine and Russia were both members of some larger security grouping, one large enough to allow other members to check Russian power, Ukraine might find it easier both to cooperate with Russia and to guarantee its security, a dilemma that is currently not resolvable. The Ukrainian campaign for a special relationship with NATO was aimed at this alternative.

The groups that one can imagine taking on such a role are the OSCE and NATO. The OSCE has fifty members, including the United States and all the major European states, and would not be dominated by Russia. It also is quite ineffectual, however, making it unlikely either that it will take on a larger role or that Ukraine would put a lot of faith in it. The inability of the OSCE to resolve any of the major conflicts of the post–Cold War era—Yugoslavia, Nagorno-Karabakh, Chechnya—leaves leaders unlikely to stake their security on its success. Indeed, Russia has been trying to give OSCE a larger role in the region, presumably because that organization is less capable of real action than NATO.

NATO expansion has been on the agenda since the fall of communism in Eastern Europe in 1989. The Partnership for Peace program, by including both Ukraine and Russia, creates some hope that eventually both will become members of NATO and that NATO will be transformed from a defensive alliance to a collective security system. Ukraine might be more willing to engage in supranational economic regulation if NATO were backing up its security. Again, however, the chances of this happening are slim.[11] While NATO will expand at least to include the Czech Republic, Hungary, and Poland, expansion to include Ukraine as a full member with security guarantees, is quite unlikely for the simple reason that few outside Ukraine want to risk war for Ukraine. Robert Cullen of the Atlantic Council notes that guaranteeing Ukrainian security "would commit the U.S. to fight a war . . . over a territory that Russia controlled, to no obvious detriment to the United States, for all but 3 of the last 340 years."[12] NATO's agreements with Ukraine and Russia have hedged the issue, making reassurances of tangible benefit to Ukraine while containing no complete solutions. More important, involvement in NATO focuses on the military threats to Ukraine's security, which this study has shown are less dangerous than the economic threats. Ukrainian membership in the European Union would do more to augment Ukraine's independence than membership in NATO, but is perhaps even less likely.

Ironically, the best chance for Ukraine to resolve its security dilemma may not be the enlargement of international organizations, but the rekindling of conflict between the West and Russia. This may already be happening: "A pattern emerges: as America becomes unhappier with the Russians, it gets chummier with the Ukrainians."[13] In such a situation, Ukraine would become strategically important to the West, as some commentators have argued it already is, and Ukraine might then have options for external balancing that it does not have now. Even if Ukraine were unable to gain a NATO security guarantee, a situation where the West viewed Ukraine as a crucial first line of defense would improve Ukraine's prospects for gaining aid in resisting Russian military or economic pressure. Because this scenario presupposes a renewal of the Cold War, it might not improve Ukraine's overall security (or anyone else's) but it would create for Ukraine strategic options that do not now exist. For this reason, Ukrainian diplomats have strived to convince Western leaders how strategically important their country is in thwarting potential Russia revanchism. Beginning with Zhirinovsky's strong showing in the December 1993 parliamentary elections, and increasing with the invasion of Chechnya, events within Russia have aided Ukraine in making this case. However, Ukraine is still a long way from being able to count on its link with the West to resolve the dilemmas it faces concerning Russia.

This discussion of alternative scenarios that might allow Ukraine to resolve its strategic dilemma has included several far-fetched possibilities that serve to highlight the intractability of Ukraine's current position. Because this basic situation is so unlikely to change, Ukraine will continue to face the same dilemmas that have characterized the first eight years of independence. Most important, this discussion emphasizes that Ukraine's current set of priorities and policies continue to leave its autonomy subject to Russian economic pressure.

Ukraine's Prospects

Having laid out several scenarios that appear unlikely, it is worth examining what we might expect to happen. Recent events in this part of the world warn us to make such predictions timidly and to read them with skepticism. Nonetheless the attempt is in order if for no other reason than to specify the implications of the analysis so far. Two points deserve emphasis. First, Ukraine's situation has improved substantially since early 1994, when either internal collapse or reabsorption into Russia seemed very possible. Second, despite the improvement since then, Ukraine's economic vulnerability remains largely undiminished, and so its political-economic dilemmas.

Prior to mid-1994, Ukraine was on a trajectory that apparently would have brought it back into the Russian sphere eventually. The economy was in shambles and there were no signs of any reform plan. Domestic strife was increasing. Crimea was moving toward secession. Many Ukrainians were demanding that the government cut a deal with Russia in order to reestablish some of the economic stability that had been lost. And in late 1993, both Kravchuk and Kuchma appeared to be willing to negotiate a deal, having seen no alternatives, and were halted only by nationalists in the parliament. When a conservative leftist parliament and then the pro-Russian Kuchma were elected in 1994, it appeared that Russia would reassert its dominant role, and Vladimir Zhirinovsky greeted Kuchma's election with hope.[14]

However, Ukraine's trajectory has changed since it began facing its domestic economic problems in mid-1994.[15] Ukraine is now on a path that, if maintained, will preserve its independence. Having withstood the worst of Russia's economic pressure in 1993–1994, and having started to resolve some of the internal divisions that make Ukraine more vulnerable to economic pressure, Ukraine will be able to maintain its current level of independence if there are no new shocks to its position. But while Ukraine will likely remain more independent than many of the other successors, it will need to maintain a high level of interaction with Russia, and hence a high degree of economic vulnerability.

Ukraine has solved many of its most divisive issues. Ukraine's regional division seemed to heal as Kuchma's leadership has proven acceptable to many in both regions. Crimean separatist sentiment has waned, and the Crimean constitution has been modified to accept Kiev's sovereignty.[16] The adoption of a Ukrainian Constitution in mid-1996 should enable Ukraine to react more responsively to the challenges that face it. Some of the pressure on the economy and on the government may be removed if economic reform slows the economic collapse. Most important, Kuchma has been able to reach what appears to be a working compromise on the relative importance of prosperity, autonomy, and sovereignty.

Moreover, Russian pressure has subsided to some degree, for three reasons. First, Ukraine's resistance made it clear that victory would not come easily. Second, the replacement of Kravchuk with Kuchma raised some hope of negotiated solutions acceptable to Russia. Third, and perhaps most important, Russia's Chechen fiasco has completely altered the strategic landscape. Russia is distracted, the West and Ukraine are vigilant, and encouraging Crimean separatism suddenly looks like a very bad precedent to set.[17] It also appears that some Russian leaders are resigning themselves to Ukraine's independence.[18] Finally, due to Ukraine's decision to disarm and its embrace of economic reform, its international isolation has ended, making it a much more difficult target.[19] Prior to the Trilateral Agreement, Western leaders were happy to have Russia put economic pressure on Ukraine, because they believed it would make Ukraine more desperate for a deal on nuclear weapons.

For all of these reasons, Ukrainian independence is becoming more secure. Rather than rejoining Russia or rejecting it, Ukraine is likely to persist in its current difficult mode: accepting the need for a great deal of trade with Russia, coordinating policy where necessary (but only bilaterally), moving forward with economic reform, and steadfastly refusing to engage in CIS rule-making. There is no reason why this set of policies cannot persist for some time to come if there is no significant shock. However, the region has not been characterized by the absense of shocks in recent years, and Ukraine's economy remains unsteady.

Most of the potential challenges to this new status-quo could originate in Russian, not Ukrainian, politics and policies, which emphasizes how much Ukraine's problems are framed beyond its borders. Russian politics are still highly volatile, and any number of factors could cause Russia to renew pressure on Ukraine: further gains by right- and left-wing parties, or the death of Boris Yeltsin followed by a power struggle. It is worth noting that the most liberal of the prominent potential successors to Boris Yeltsin, Moscow Mayor Yuri Luzhkov and Yeltsin Advisor Boris Nemtsov, both became vocal advocates in early 1997 of an assertive Russian policy toward control of Sevastopol. Luzhkov introduced measures in the Federation Council asserting Russian sovereignty over the city, and financed construction of housing for troops there out of the Moscow city budget. Nemtsov advocated having Russian firms buy up property and businesses in the city, saying "Historical justice should be restored by capitalist methods."[20]

It is difficult to predict what effect a harder Russian line might have on Ukraine. If Russia took an aggressive approach, and returned to energy cutoffs as a tactic, the situation for Ukraine would be difficult. At the same time, such aggression might steel the will of the Ukrainian government, forge greater unity among political groups there, and bring the West to aid Ukraine in some fashion. Some Russian policy makers seem to recognize this possibility, as did Andranik Migranyan, author of the so-called Russian Monroe Doctrine when he argued that Russian pressure on Ukraine would be counterproductive because it would strengthen Ukrainian nationalism.[21] In this respect the end of Ukraine's international isolation is a crucial factor. Western support could be decisive in helping Ukraine overcome a new economic offensive. Similarly, the narrowing of Ukraine's domestic divisions also has increased Ukraine's ability to resist outside pressure, but the Ukrainian state remains weak, and there is a long way to go in this regard.

The West and Ukraine's Economic Security

One significantly improved factor in Ukraine's economic security picture is the geopolitical role that Ukraine has taken on. While Ukrainian leaders and some Western analysts have argued since 1991 that Ukraine is a crucial piece in the European security puzzle, this belief has only recently motivated policy in the West. The reasons for the shift are straightforward: the need to pressure Ukraine over its nuclear weapons is gone, and Russia appears much more threatening. Nationalists did well in the December 1993 elections, and Communists did well in 1995. The Aldrich Ames spy case created feeling in the United States that the Cold War was not over. Russian recalcitrance on a whole range of issues, including NATO expansion, troop withdrawals from the Baltics, and Yugoslavia, has eroded the notion of Russia and the West as partners with only common interests. The Chechen conflict renewed fears of Russian imperialism.[22] Russia's peaceful expansion into the former Soviet Union, including military basing rights and an economic union treaty with Belarus, have further raised the specter of a renewed Soviet Union. Russian pressure on Azerbaijan and Kazakhstan to renegotiate important oil deals has injured powerful interests in the West.

For all these reasons, the impression was created that Russia posed at least a latent threat to important Western interests. In particular, the potential for Russian reassertion in the former republics of the Soviet Union renewed the prospect that Russian troops would again threaten major Western interests or simply create so much instability in Europe that the West would have to respond. The shift was acknowledged by *Nezavisimaya Gazeta*, which said in April 1995 that the West was now supporting Ukraine more than Russia, attributing the shift to the Chechen conflict and Kuchma's handling of the dispute over Crimea.[23] At least in terms of bilateral aid, Ukraine has indeed surpassed Russia in the calculations of the U.S. government.

In many places, the argument, made most convincingly by Zbigniew Brzezinski, that Ukraine holds the key to Central Europe, has caught on. This view that the region is in peril and that Ukraine is the key has changed Western assessments of Ukraine's role, and consequently Ukraine's political situation. For this reason, there is significant incentive in the West that Ukraine be able to resist Russian economic pressure. The rapid expansion of IMF and World Bank aid in 1994 and 1995 is emblematic of the heightened profile of Ukraine in Western eyes.[24] As discussed in chapter 4, this increased aid played a decisive role in enabling Ukraine to pay its energy bills to Russia, neutralizing Russia's most powerful economic lever. In this very concrete way, as well as in more symbolic ways, Western support has altered Ukraine's prospects. However, Ukraine's economic situation has not improved nearly as much as its international political situation, and it is the economic arena where Ukraine is most threatened. Western support has not extended to opening Western markets to Ukrainian exports, the one thing that would most allow Ukraine to reduce its economic vulnerability.

Ukraine's prospects for navigating the difficult waters between economic catastrophe and renewed colonial status have improved significantly since mid-1994. A combination of changed internal political factors and new international conditions have created this improved outlook. Ukraine is by no means safely through its difficult period, however. On the contrary, the dilemmas discussed here will continue to characterize Ukrainian policy for the foreseeable future. Only a fundamental shift in the geopolitics would actually remove the dilemma, and that does not seem likely. The key question then for Ukrainian leaders and for students of the subject is how well Ukraine will negotiate this difficult situation and what factors will affect its prospects for doing so. It looks as though Ukraine will stay off the rocks in the near term, but clear sailing is nowhere in sight.

Ukrainian-Russian Relations and International Relations Theory

Ukraine's experiences in the post-Soviet world provide us with a case that involves many of the theoretical issues that most concern discussions of international cooperation, but in a setting far different from those in which international cooperation is usually studied. This case therefore provides a useful ground for testing the breadth of applicability of important approaches to international politics. When the Ukrainian-Russian relationship is considered not as a case by itself, but as one of a large set of cases that theories of international interdependence attempt to explain, the most immediate questions that arise concern assumptions. Many of the assumptions on which interdependence theories and theories of cooperation are based simply do not hold for Ukraine and Russia. This finding does not necessarily impeach those theories, but rather makes us aware of the limits of their applicability, even if they are quite useful in other realms. Recognizing the ways in which the FSU differs from other regions will help us generate a conceptual understanding of politics in that region, while enabling us to refine our theories.

The case of Ukraine's relations with Russia raises three issues regarding prominent approaches to international interdependence. In each of these areas, this case highlights problems with conventional approaches, and presents insights into possible refinements. First, while many of the problems of interdependence in the Former Soviet Union (FSU) are captured by liberal international theory, important liberal assumptions do not hold, raising questions about how to make liberal theory more broadly applicable. Second, one particular factor that plays a crucial role in Ukraine but is downplayed by liberal theory is sovereignty. The importance of sovereignty indicates that arguments about the obsolescence of realism are a bit premature. However, this case also raises important questions for realism, in particular because sovereignty and autonomy have been found in this case to sometimes contradict one another. Realist theory, which does not distinguish between sovereignty and autonomy as state goals, will also have difficulty explaining the politics of the FSU. More broadly, the primacy of the economic field of conflict over the military contradicts a major tenet of some versions of realist theory. Third, perhaps the most important question that Ukraine has had to answer is one that international relations theory has largely glossed over: Under what conditions do international organizations bind their largest members, and under what conditions do they constrain them?

Liberal Assumptions and the Realities of the FSU

The basic problem that Ukraine faces in its foreign economic relations is similar to that focused on in liberal international theory: Ukraine seeks to maximize prosperity through trade while remaining invulnerable to external economic shocks. However, Ukraine's willingness to subjugate economic prosperity to concerns about sovereignty creates an anomaly from the perspective of liberal cooperation theory. This case does not refute liberal theory because it is not a situation in which one would expect the theory to succeed. Ukraine's nationalism and security concerns lead us to expect a lack of cooperation. This case does, however, demonstrate the limited applicability of liberal theory. Liberal theory is based on a series of assumptions, which include the primary importance of individual welfare (especially economic) and the nonproblematic nature of sovereignty.[25] The modern versions of the theory have been devised and applied primarily with reference to Western Europe in the post–World War II era, when the sovereignty of the member states has seemed largely guaranteed, both by the lack of territorial claims and by the presence of U.S. troops. That these factors are crucial to the theory's utility—and that they cannot everywhere be taken for granted—is demonstrated in the former Soviet Union, where, absent these factors, debates over cooperation are carried out in terms much more familiar to realists.

In the case of Ukraine's relations with Russia, several liberal assumptions do not hold. First, as Ukraine demonstrated consistently in its policy on energy, trade, and the CIS, the prosperity of its citizens is not the foremost goal of the state. While economic prosperity is an important criterion of the government's effectiveness, it appears not to be the primary one. This divergence from liberal assumptions seems rooted in a more fundamental one: Ukraine is very concerned for its security, and for its national identity. The liberal paradigm, particularly as it is applied to international political economy, is based on the assumption that economic welfare concerns have come to rival or even surpass security concerns on states' priority lists.[26] The liberal assumption is not that states do not care for their security, but that it is well enough established that they can pursue other goals. This is not the case for Ukraine. So while Ukraine's basic economic problem resembles that dealt with by liberal theory, its political situation does not.

This finding, while not shocking, indicates that future research (both theoretical and empirical) should focus on the conditions necessary for the liberal model to apply. In what types of cases are the political prerequisites for liberal solutions not present, even when the economic conditions—interdependence and a desire for prosperity—are present? If both the CIS and the EU are characterized by high interdependence that makes trade cooperation highly desirable, what accounts for the differences between them? Is it the stabilizing outside influence of the United States in the formative years of the EC? The relative balance of power there? The firm respect that those states have for each others' borders and sovereignty that is not present in the FSU? Theoretically, liberal and realist theories paint very different pictures of the world. Empirically, it appears that both those worlds exist. If so, what are the essential characteristics that distinguish one from the other? What modifications would be required to make liberal theory more applicable to the FSU?

These questions are not simply academic. Because the international politics of the EU are quite stable—and the international trade of the EU is so efficient, and because the states of the FSU so strongly desire to emulate their Western neighbors, it is important to ask which conditions in the FSU would have to change to make it resemble the EC of 1957, whose founding treaty the FSU states sought to emulate in the fall of 1991. An answer to these questions would be relevant not only to policy makers in the FSU, but also to those in the EU and other groups contemplating integration, by increasing understanding of the prerequisites for integration. It would also contribute to broader understanding of international cooperation, the study of which to this point has been concentrated in a small number of similar cases.

Realism in the Former Soviet Union

The focus of this book on issues of economic interdependence leads one to begin with liberal rather than realist theories, but the conflictive nature of the situation and the importance of power implies that the situation comes closer to meeting the assumptions of realist theory, which focuses on the struggle for power in an anarchical international system. But while realist theory provides many of the concepts needed to understand the situation, there are anomalies as well.

This study has made extensive use of Albert Hirschman's framework of analysis to examine Ukrainian-Russian trade relations. That this very realist framework has proven so useful is itself a significant theoretical statement. In many ways the FSU still operates in a realist political economy rather than in a liberal one, and has the characteristics prevalent in Europe prior to World War II rather than in the EU today. The prominence of realist characteristics in the situation and in state polices is evident in several ways: The states, rather than actors within them, have been the dominant actors. Coercion based on power, and resistance based on power, have been the normal modes of interaction in this relationship, and the states' ability to injure one another has been more important than devising solutions to collective action problems.[27]

More significantly, perhaps, Ukraine's focus on establishing and safeguarding its sovereignty indicates the relevance of realist theory in two related ways. First, by treating sovereignty as the paramount issue, Ukraine's policy (and that of other states in the region) indicates that sovereignty is still a crucial factor in international politics and a primary goal of states. The fact that Ukraine has focused on sovereignty even at the expense of domestic prosperity indicates that the ordering of state priorities hypothesized by realism remains relevant, at least in this part of the world. Second, the fact that Ukraine is continually seeing threats to its sovereignty from Russian policies indicates that sovereignty cannot be taken for granted—that Ukraine would lose its sovereignty if it did not jealously guard it. This implies that states in other regions that do not focus on sovereignty are able to neglect it not because they do not value it or cannot possibly lose it, but because other guarantees of it are in place. The Westphalian system is alive and well in the former Soviet Union.

However, Ukraine's focus on sovereignty raises another question that provides a bit more difficulty for realism. Because, at least in some ways, Ukraine can increase its sovereignty only at the expense of some autonomy, these two goals are in some degree of tension. In this respect, multilateral cooperation may have some of the qualities of alliances (the trade of sovereignty for increased security),[28] a proposition that needs to be examined more closely. That sovereignty and autonomy are not basically complementary goals seems paradoxical from the perspective of realist theory, which tends not to distinguish between the two, because both are subsumed under the rubric of "power" or "security." For Ukraine, however, it is not clear whether focusing on sovereignty or autonomy will most allow it to resist Russian pressure. The issue is a crucial one, but it is not clear how realist theory would answer it.

In the long run, the two goals are probably complementary, because a loss of sovereignty may allow another state to reduce one's autonomy or power (as Ukraine clearly fears), and because a decrease in power may leave one with a very narrow range of options, reducing sovereignty to a formality. If the two goals are complementary in the long run, resolving the short-term contradiction may be even more problematic. If Ukraine needs to be concerned in the long run both with autonomy and sovereignty, how can it order its policies in a short-term situation where these priorities may conflict with each other, and where both conflict with prosperity?

There is, however, a much more fundamental problem with realist theory as applied to Ukrainian-Russian relations. While realism is compatible with the basic facts of our story, some recent versions of the theory are largely incompatible with the finding that in Ukrainian-Russian relations, military power has taken on a relatively insignificant role, and the main field of struggle has been economic. Ukraine surrendered its nuclear weapons in part because it realized that they would not be of much use in preserving its independence against Russia. That nuclear weapons might not be useful, but that the ability to cut gas shipments is crucial, presents a major problem for the typical realist assertion that "clubs are trump." Prominent realist writers including Kenneth Waltz, John Mearsheimer, and Barry Posen have argued that the nuclear weapons guaranteed Ukraine's security and regional stability, and that Ukraine should therefore keep them.[29] While theoretically persuasive, these arguments did not capture the nature of Ukraine's problem. Russia cannot seriously contemplate a military conquest of Ukraine, but at the same time, Ukraine's independence tottered due to economic weakness. Given recent arguments about the disutility of force in the modern international system, and the somewhat convincing rejoinders offered by realist theorists, the case of Russia and Ukraine merits much deeper attention in this regard.[30] Versions of realism such as those of Hirschman, Gilpin, and Krasner, who find economics an important arena of international conflict, are more consistent with the findings in this case.

The importance of interdependence in the Russian-Ukrainian relationship is more in tune with liberal than realist theory, while the conflict itself fits much better with realist theory. This case therefore represents a challenge for both, and for the lines we have drawn between them. The challenge in particular to liberals is to specify more clearly the conditions under which their theory will apply. For realists the challenge is to sort out the links between sovereignty and autonomy, and the relation of both to the familiar realist concept "power." Overall, realism seems the more relevant theory. Ironically in a study of the former Soviet Union, one might conclude that Marxist theory, with its focus on economic power as a tool for dominance, merits another look as an explanation, even if it has been debunked as a political system.[31]

International Institutions: Friend or Foe of the Weak?

Hirschman's finding that bilateral trade favors the strong implies that multi-lateral cooperation would allow Ukraine to decrease its vulnerability to Russia.[32] This finding has been echoed by many advocates of the EU, including prominent realists, such as Joseph Grieco, who argues that the organization helps the smaller states bind Germany and prevent it from exploiting them. The argument that international organizations constrain the strong against the weak is made both by liberals and realists, but it is not believed by Ukrainian leaders. Are international institutions instruments for the weak to bind the strong? Or are they means by which the strong control the weak, as Marxists and most realists contend?

In the literature on international cooperation, this question is seen in the unresolved debate between the realist and liberal strands of hegemonic stability theory.[33] The liberal strand of this theory, exemplified by the work of Charles Kindleberger and Robert Keohane, views international order as a collective goods problem, and argues that hegemony of one state provides a benefit for all by providing collective goods to all. The realist strand of the theory, as presented by Stephen Krasner and Robert Gilpin, contends that great powers pursue hegemony in order to create a world order favorable to themselves, and often exploitative to others (this position is not at great variance with the Marxist view, which identifies "hegemony" with "imperialism").[34]

The CIS looks very different depending on which view one subscribes to, and it is clear that Ukraine subscribes to the realist view. The question here is not whether one view is superior to the other, but what characteristics of Ukraine's situation might make the realist analysis more appropriate here. Perhaps Ukrainian nationalism or paranoia is responsible for its wariness concerning the CIS. But it seems entirely possible that the EU does constrain Germany, while the CIS would, if given substantial authority, empower Russia. Why should the two organizations have different effects? The question points to a substantial lacuna in international relations theory. Several hypotheses are worth examining.

First, it is possible that the difference is in the actors' intentions. Following the World War II, Germany made a remarkable metamorphosis from a revisionist to a status quo state. Because Germany no longer sought to dominate the continent, it was willing to enter into institutional arrangements that constrained it to some degree. In return, Germany was welcomed back into the European community of states, and the stage was set for its economic recovery. Russia, in contrast, has not completely gotten over the loss of its empire, and at least a substantial portion of the leadership would like to revise the status quo that was established by the collapse of the Soviet Union. Even if they do not want fully to reintegrate the former republics, many wish to reestablish Russian hegemony. Russia is perhaps therefore only willing to enter into institutional arrangements that would further this goal, making a CIS that constrained Russia impossible.

Second, it is possible that the crucial difference in the two systems is the existence of an external enemy. Because the states of the European Community were driven together by a common threat (the Soviet Union) the primary threat to each state's autonomy came not from within the group in terms of German economic might, but from outside in the form of Soviet military might. The states of the EC were less concerned with constraining each others' power than with opposing the Soviet Union. In this respect, the EC was to some extent a defensive alliance, in which the trade of sovereignty for autonomy is straightforward. In the case of the CIS, the enemy is within the group, not outside, even if the threat is economic. The proper analogue is not a defensive alliance, therefore, but a collective security system, an institution that historically has an uninspiring track record for protecting the independence of small states.[35]

Third, it is possible that the problem is one of relative size within the group of states. It is a fundamental tenet not only of realist international theory, but also of liberal domestic theory, that stability relies on balancing power such that no one actor or group can oppress the rest. In the EC, Germany, the most powerful state, has never been so large and powerful that it could hope to take on the others in military or economic battle. The close involvement of the United States, a large but external actor in Western European politics, reduced the threat from Germany even further. In such circumstances, it was easy for the small states to delegate power to the EC, because they could be certain that a German bid for hegemony would be repulsed by a coalition of other states. Balance of power politics is therefore not irrelevant to international organizations. From this perspective, the problem in the CIS is that Russia represents over half the population, GNP, and military might in the region, and there is therefore no internal check on its power.[36] No state or coalition of states in the CIS could prevent Russia from using its power to bend the organization to its purposes.

These three hypotheses indicate the variety of explanations possible. The question is ripe for further study. While hegemonic stability theorists have debated the "truth" of one version or another of their model, new regional groupings have emerged that make it possible to study the different conditions under which each theory may apply. The CIS provides much fertile ground for such study. The states of Eastern Europe clamoring to enter the EU are another, and NAFTA still a third. Further research on this question, even if it did not provide definitive answers, would help build theoretical bridges between realist and liberal theory, and help make our theory as contingent and conditional as the real world. Moreover, it would give us some criteria with which to generate improved expectations about the expansion of regional institutions.

Summary: International Relations Theory and Ukrainian-Russian Relations

A prominent guide to research methods in political science states that theories are not falsified, but rather have the limits of their applicability specified.[37] Examination of dominant international relations theories in this new and different regional context can help us move toward that goal. The assumption that has underlined this theoretical discussion is that the former Soviet Union is an important realm for investigating the theoretical questions that drive the academic field of international relations, and that the same theories that are applied elsewhere should be applicable to this region. The extent to which these theories are in many ways not applicable—though they are highly relevant—indicates that the contingencies under which our theories will and will not apply need to be further specified. This is most obvious in a cursory comparison between the FSU and Western Europe. The theoretical tools that we have for understanding international cooperation— provided mostly by liberal institutionalist theory—are too narrow to understand the international politics of the former Soviet Union. A much older realist view is more appropriate here. This book has shown, not only in this conclusion but in the borrowing of concepts from existing theories throughout, that our mainstream theories can and should be applied to the FSU. They should either perform as well here as they do elsewhere, or else make explicit the limits of their applicability.

International Politics in the Former Soviet Union

Ukraine is facing a problem that is endemic to the non-Russian former Soviet states. It is worth considering, therefore, the extent to which the findings presented here are generalizable to the region as a whole. While the basic problem is the same, the various states of the region have dealt with it quite differently, in part due to different circumstances and in part due to different internal characteristics.

The dilemmas of interdependence that were elaborated in chapter 3 apply equally well to the other former Soviet states, and a cursory analysis shows that all have faced fundamental trade-offs between autonomy, prosperity, and sovereignty. They have not, however, dealt with those dilemmas in the same way. Georgia has sought independence as ardently as Ukraine, but found itself working closely with Russia. Belarus has never been greatly concerned with its autonomy and sovereignty, and it to has moved close to Russia. Kazakhstan has also sought close relations with Russia from the beginning. Explaining these differences would require another book, but the question is an important one: Why have these different states dealt with similar problems so differently?

Four broad classes of explanations for the differences can be advanced, two based on the states' different situations and two based on their internal characteristics. Externally, one can focus on the states' relative power: perhaps some have been more susceptible to Russian blandishments because, unlike Ukraine, they are so small that genuine independence is simply unrealistic. In the framework developed in chapter 3, these states would be even more vulnerable to Russian pressure than Ukraine. This explanation would seem to account for Belarus and Georgia, but is contradicted by the very small yet fiercely independent Baltic states, as well as by Moldova. An alternative external explanation is that some states may have other security threats besides Russia, such that close relations with Russia are seen as preserving autonomy against another actor. In the case of Kazakhstan, it seems that the presence of China makes Russia seem the better of two evils, and throughout Central Asia the presence of Iran changes the security picture. In contrast, the Baltic states have not an additional external enemy, but additional external allies that Ukraine does not have. Support for the Baltic states in the West increases their potential to find substitute trading partners. The Baltics have therefore been able to take a more independent line.

Internally, a clear difference between Ukraine and many other states in the region is the level of nationalism. Put simply, Ukraine values its autonomy and sovereignty more than do Belarus and Kazakhstan, two large states that have sought close ties with Russia. Belarus and Kazakhstan therefore privilege prosperity more relative to autonomy and sovereignty than does Ukraine.[38] The reasons for this are complex, and involve historical as well as ethnic and domestic political factors. A second important internal factor is the division of the society. Ukraine's domestic fissures have provided the primary leverage point for Russian pressure, but other states in the region are even more divided. Kazakhs are an ethnic minority in their own country, and 40 percent of Kazakhstan's population is Russian. Similarly, the Russian population in Belarus is larger and even more Russified than that in Ukraine. In Georgia, Abkhaz separatism was directly linked to Russia's increased role, as President Shevardnadze was forced to request Russian troops to defeat the movement.[39] The Russian minority in Moldova has played a similar role, as has the Armenian minority in Azerbaijan, where the war over Nagorno-Karabakh has led to increased Russian leverage over both states.

This list of potential explanations is not exhaustive, and in many instances, the differences in state policies toward Russia seem overdetermined.

Understanding why the states of the former Soviet Union are dealing so differently with the dilemmas of interdependence is the most important question for future research on the region, both practically and theoretically. By examining one bilateral relationship, this study has begun to delve into the international politics of the region, but more comparitive work is in order. Practically, understanding which factors are important will help us assess the future of the region's politics. A useful first question to ask is whether the factors causing different policies are static and beyond state control (i.e., relative size) or whether they are more amenable to change, such as levels of domestic conflict.

Theoretically, understanding the dynamics of cooperation in this region would allow comparison with other regions, such as the EU, East Asia, or North America, to assess what *regional* factors account for conflict and cooperation in the world. This analysis has built on the assumption that the same broad theories used to explain cooperation elsewhere can be applied, in somewhat modified form, to the former Soviet Union, but that assumption remains to be thoroughly tested. Do the problems with liberal theory discussed above imply that a completely new theory must be created to deal with this region? For example, must nationalism, a factor absent in conventional interdependence (as well as realist) theory, play an important role in any explanation of the politics of interdependence in the FSU?

The framework for analysis developed in this book should be applicable to the other small states in the region, for it is based on a series of problems that all these states share. This does not mean that they will all deal with their problems similarly, but it does mean that the approach used here will be useful for examining other states in the region. To understand why this region is or is not like other regions, however, a broader approach that questions more fundamental issues will be necessary. Most broadly, it must be recognized that the rise of liberalism that characterizes much of the politics of the advanced industrial states has not yet occurred in the former Soviet Union.

In this respect, the view from the former Soviet Union is a sobering one. Rather than integration, the last five years have been characterized by disintegration on a massive scale. Instead of a democratic peace, we see the widespread fear that unstable democracies will degenerate into aggressive authoritarian states.[40] International institutions are still viewed primarily as threats to independence rather than as solutions to problems. Ukraine has not viewed its trade concerns with Russia as a collective action problem, where both sides can gain through cooperation, but as a struggle for power, with the characteristics of a zero-sum game. Most important, in the former Soviet Union, most of the states are constantly concerned about their survival, and self-preservation preempts other goals. Realism pervades the politics of the former Soviet Union.

Ukraine: Where Now?

The Ukrainian state in its independence is trying to navigate a rather treacherous channel between the danger of economic collapse, on one side, and the renewal of Russian dominance on the other. At times, disaster has been averted only narrowly. After steering away from Russia with the nationalist economic policy of 1992, Ukraine quickly found itself in economic breakdown. Many then sought to steer toward the other extreme, finding it more acceptable. Ukraine was unable to chart a consistent course between these two perils, because the society and state have been divided about how best to do so. As of early 1999, Ukraine seems to have found a narrow and uncertain path between the dangers: neither complete economic collapse nor Russian dominance is imminent. This represents the high point for Ukraine so far, but the fundamental threats remain on both sides. Ukraine's economy is still weak, and its vulnerability will likely increase as economic reform begins. Russia has turned to other problems for now, but reducing Ukraine's autonomy may interest it again at any time. That threat remains real because Ukraine has developed a set of priorities and a strategy that leave it very little economic autonomy. Russia can still devastate Ukraine's economy at relatively little cost to itself.

The challenge for Ukraine's leaders in the future, therefore, will be to increase its autonomy within the constraints on sovereignty and prosperity it has set for itself. Doing so will not be easy, but there is hope on several fronts. Economic reform may eventually put Ukraine's prosperity on a more efficient internal footing, allowing more latitude externally. Ukraine's entry into the strategic calculations of Western policy makers is already giving it opportunities to find economic alternatives to Russia. Russia, which has in the short term accepted Ukrainian independence only reluctantly, may become resigned to it eventually. In the final analysis, this is the only development that will truly ease Ukraine's dilemmas. Given Russia's immense power, Ukraine will find itself between a rock and a hard place as long as Russia seeks to keep it there. While Ukraine can be more or less successful in dealing with the problems of economic interdependence, only Russia can actually remove those problems.

In this book we have examined only the beginning of what will likely be a very long story. Ukraine has attained political independence. But how genuine that independence remains—and how much Ukrainian citizens continue to revel in it—remains to be seen. The Ukrainian people and their government have found that, as hard as it was to gain independence, running and maintaining an independent state in a dangerous world will be equally challenging.

Notes

1. Introduction

1. *Nezavisimaya Gazeta*, 23 May 1996. The report is discussed, and excerpts translated, in Scott Parrish, "'Will the Union Be Reborn?'" *Transition* (26 July 1996).

2. Volodymyr Horbulin, "Nasha Meta, Nasha Dolia," *Polityka I Chas* 1 (1996): 6.

3. Deirdre Collings, ed., *Ukraine Human Development Report 1995* (Kiev: United Nations Development Program, 1995), cited in Taras Kuzio, "After the Shock, the Therapy," *Transitions* (28 July 1995): 38.

4. Taras Kuzio, "Ukraine and Chechnia Crisis," *Politychna Dumka/ Political Thought* 1 (1995): 178–182.

5. "Georgia: Hope at Last?" *The Economist*, 27 May 1995, p. 48.

6. Economic dependence of other republics on Russia is assessed quantitatively in Alexander Granberg, "The Economic Interdependence of the Former Soviet Republics," in John Williamson, ed., *Economic Consequences of Soviet Disintegration* (Washington, D.C.: Institute for International Economics, 1993).

7. Karen Dawisha and Bruce Parrott, *Russia and the New States of Eurasia* (New York: Cambridge University Press, 1994), p. 34; Martha Brill Olcott, "Sovereignty and the 'Near Abroad,'" *Orbis* 39, 3 (Summer 1995): 364; Alexander A. Pikayev, "The Russian Domestic Debate on Policy Toward the 'Near Abroad,'" in Lena Jonson and Clive Archer, eds., *Peacekeeping and the Role of Russia in Eurasia* (Boulder: Westview, 1996).

8. *Izvestiya*, 7 August 1992.

9. "Vozroditsia li soiuz?" *Nezavisimaya Gazeta*, 23 May 1996. The report is analyzed and excerpts translated in Scott Parrish, "'Will the Union be Reborn'" *Transition*, July 26 1996.

10. Granberg, p. 49.

11. A widely accepted estimate is that 50 percent–80 percent of the decline in GDP since the breakup of the Soviet Union is due to the disrup. on of interrepublic links (Granberg, p. 70).

12. Most analysts agree that disintegration has occured due to political considerations rather than economic rationale. For examples, see the contributions in Williamson, *Economic Consequences of Soviet Disintegration.*

13. Evgeni Yasin, "The Economic Space of the Former Soviet Union, Past and Present," in Williamson, ed., *Economic Consequences of Soviet Disintegration*, pp. 20, 24–25.

14. On Ukraine's problems with access to European and American markets, see Bartolomiej Kaminski, "Trade Performance and Access to OECD Markets," in Constatine Michalopoulos and David G. Tarr, eds., *Trade in the New Independent States*, Studies of Economies in Transformation #13 (Washington, D.C.: World Bank, 1994); F. Stephen Larrabee, "Ukraine's Balancing Act," *Survival*, vol. 38, no. 2 (Summer 1996): 154; and Anders Aslund, "Problem Is Pricing, Not Dumping," (letter to the editor) *Financial Times*, 1 May 1997, p. 10.

15. Larrabee, p. 156.

16. "Russia's Old Imperial Map Is Still Shrivelling," *The Economist*, 24 May 1997, p. 48.

17. Granberg 1993, 62.

18. For development of these concepts see Stephen M. Walt, *The Origins of Alliances* (Ithaca: Cornell University Press, 1987). They are applied to the former Soviet Union by James Goldgeier, "Balancing versus Bandwagoning in the Former Soviet Union," Paper Presented at the annual meeting of the American Political Science Association, 1992, Chicago. Here, I will use the concepts slightly differently. Walt's work concerns the formation of military alliances, while the issue between Russia and Ukraine concerns economic cooperation.

19. This dilemma is reflected in the debate between the realist and liberal versions of hegemonic stability theory, and is discussed in greater detail in the conclusion.

20. Quoted in Edward Mead Earle, "Adam Smith, Alexander Hamilton, Friederich List: The Economic Foundations of Military Power," in Peter Paret, ed., *Makers of Modern Strategy* (Princeton: Princeton University Press, 1986), p. 218.

21. Vladimir Lukin, "Russia and Its Interests," in Stephen Sestanovich, ed., Rethinking the Russian National Interest (Washington, D.C.: Center for Strategic and International Studies, 1994), p. 106. This view is documented more extensively in Roman Solchanyk, "Russia, Ukraine, and the Imperial Legacy," *Post-Soviet Affairs*, no. 9 (1993): 339–342.

22. Quoted in James Richter, "Russian Foreign Policy and the Politics of National Identity," in Celeste A. Wallander, ed., *The Sources of Russian Foreign Policy After the Cold War* (Boulder: Westview Press, 1996).

23. Zbigniew Brzezinski, "The Premature Partnership," *Foreign Affairs*, vol. 73, no. 2 (March/April 1994): 80.

24. In May 1995, Russian customs officers were being stationed on the Belarussian-Polish border (OMRI Daily Digest, part I, 22 May 1995). Russia has also attained the Georgia's consent to reestablish several bases on Georgian soil.

25. See Taras Kuzio, "Ukraine: The Linchpin of Eastern Stability," *The Wall Street Journal* (May 11, 1994).

26. On the potential of a new Russo-German Rivalry, see John J. Mearsheimer, "Back to the Future: Instability in Europe after the Cold War," *International Security* (Summer 1990): 5–56.

27. Roy Allison, *Military Forces in the Soviet Successor States*, Adelphi Paper, no. 280 (London: IISS, 1993): 36.

2. Ukraine and Russia

1. There is a brief discussion of Ukrainian history and its current significance in Alexander J. Motyl, *Dilemmas of Independence: Ukraine after Totalitarianism* (New York: Council on Foreign Relatiuons Press, 1993), chapters 2 and 3. For full treatments of Ukrainian history, see Michael Hrushevsky, *A History of Ukraine* (New Haven: Yale University Press, 1941); Orest Subtelny, *Ukraine: A History*, 2nd ed. (Toronto: University of Toronto: 1994); and Paul Robert Magosci, *A History of Ukraine* (Seattle: University of Washington Press, 1996). On Russian-Ukrainian Relations, see Peter J. Potichnyj, et al., eds., *Ukraine and Russia in Their Historical Encounter* (Edmonton: Canadian Institute for Ukrainian Studies, 1992).

2. This discussion is based on Jaroslaw Pelenski, "The Contest for the 'Kievan inheritance' in Russian-Ukrainian Relations: The Origins and Early Ramifications," in Potichnyj, et al., pp. 3–19.

3. Pelenski, p. 3.

4. Nikolai Travkin, "Russia, Ukraine, and Eastern Europe," in Stephen Sestanovich, ed., *Rethinking Russia's National Interests* (Washington, D.C.: Center for Strategic and International Studies, 1994), p. 36.

5. On the importance of the Cossacks to Ukrainian national identity, see Motyl, pp. 85–87.

6. Hrushevsky, p. 296.

7. The events surrounding the treaty of Pereiaslav are discussed in Subtelny, pp. 134–137; and in Hrushevsky, pp. 293–296 and 311–312. The original text of the treaty has been lost.

8. See Vasyl' Kremin', Borys Parakhons'kyi, and Petro Sytnyk, "Ukraina i Rosiia: Sfery Konfrontatsii i Spivrobitnytstva," *Rozbudova Derzhava*, 2 (February 1993): 3.

9. Jonathan R. Adelman, *Torrents of Spring: Soviet and Post-Soviet Politics* (New York: McGraw Hill, 1995), p. 248.

10. Motyl emphasizes that "the collapse of the Russian polity and economy, and not non-Russian nationalism per se, impelled Russia's constituent provinces and imperial possessions to opt for nationalism and pursue independence . . . the only option that offered them refuge from imperial collapse and Bolshevik takeover" (pp. 30–31).

11. William Henry Chamberlain, *The Ukraine: A Submerged Nation* (New York: MacMillan, 1944), pp. 43–44.

12. Chamberlain, p. 46.

13. Subtelny, p. 359, Chamberlain, p. 48.

14. The Soviet-Polish war ended in the Treaty of Riga, signed March 18, 1921. See Chamberlain, p. 51, and Adam Ulam, *Expansion and Coexistence*, pp. 105–109.

15. Hrushevsky, p. 557.

16. Hrushevsky, p. 558.

17. There is still debate about whether the famine was intentional and over the exact number of deaths. Robert Conquest has provided the most thorough and reliable analysis of the famine, and I have used his assessments here. See *Harvest of Sorrow*.

18. Sheptyt'skyi's pastoral letter of 30 June 1941, quoted in John A. Armstrong, *Ukrainian Nationalism*, 3rd ed. (Engelwood, Co.: Ukrainian Academic Press, 1990), p. 56. Armstrong covers the period 1939 to 1945 in great detail.

19. Dawisha and Parrott, p. 37.

20. See Armstrong, *Ukrainian Nationalism*, Chapter XIII for an account of the postwar Ukrainian resistance.

21. Nikolai Travkin, "Russia, Ukraine, and Eastern Europe," in Stephen Sestanovich, ed., *Rethinking Russia's National Interests* (Washington, D.C.: Center for Strategic and International Studies, 1994), p. 36.

22. The path to independence is detailed by Motyl and by Roman Solchanyk, "Russia, Ukraine, and the Imperial Legacy," *Post-Soviet Affairs*, no. 9 (1993): 348–358.

23. Gertrude E. Schroeder, "Regional Economic Disparities, Gorbachev's Policies, and the Disintegration of the Soviet Union," in Richard F. Kaufman and John P. Hardt, eds., *The Former Soviet Union in Transition* (Armonk, NY: M. E. Sharpe, 1993), p. 139.

24. Schroeder, pp. 139–140.

25. Motyl, p. 45.

26. Schroeder, p. 141.

27. I.S. Koropeckyj, "Introduction," in Koropeckyj, ed., *The Ukrainian Economy: Achievements, Problems, Challenges* (Cambridge: Harvard Ukrainian Research Institute, 1992).

28. Motyl, p. 46.

29. *Ukrainian Weekly*, August 5 1990, p. 12, as quoted in Paul Robert Magocsi, "A Subordinate or Submerged People: The Ukrainians of Galicia under Hapsburg and Soviet Rule," in Richard L. Rudolph and David F. Good, eds., *Nationalism and Empire, the Hapsburg Empire and the Soviet Union* (New York: St. Martin's Press, 1992), pp. 105–106.

30. Motyl, p. 47.

31. Motyl, p. 47.

32. The suddenness with which Ukraine was faced with independence, and the implications of its lack of preparedness, are emphasized by Oleksandr Dergachov and Volodymyr Polokhalo, "The Metamorphosis of Post-Communist Power," *Politychna Dumka/Political Thought* 1 (1996): 118–120.

33. Schroeder, p. 143.

34. James A. Duran, Jr., "Russian Fiscal and Monetary Stabilitzation: A Tough Road Ahead," in Kaufman and Hardt, p. 214.

35. Subtelny, p. 589.

36. See Jacob W. Kipp, *Ukrainian and Belarus Presidential Elections: Prelude to a Crisis in the Western Borderlands of Russia* (Ft. Leavenworth: Foreign Military Studies Office, 1994).

37. See James Mace, "Geopolitical Implications of Ethnopolitics," *Politychna Dumka/Political Thought* 1 (1995): 192–201. It is important to recognize, however, that the figure of 12 million Russians frequently cited paints a simple picture of a complex situation. That number reflects the number of people who were officially registered by the Soviet government as "Russian." Many citizens of Ukraine have "mixed" Ukrainian and Russian parentage, and identify with both nations, leading to a complicated national identity picture. Moreover, Russian ethnicity does not necessarily mean pro-Russian or anti-Ukrainian sympathies. See Paul S. Pirie, "National Identity and Politics in Southern and Eastern Ukraine," *Europe-Asia Studies*, vol. 48, no. 7, (1996): 1079–1104.

38. See Frank Umbach, "The Crimean Question," *Jane's Intelligence Review*, May 1994, pp. 195–198.

39. *Washington Post*, 16, 27 July 1993.

40. National Public Radio, *Morning Edition*, 14 March 1994; *OMRI Daily Digest*, part I, 6 June 1995.

41. Ustina Markus, "Black Sea Fleet Dispute Apparently Over," *Transition* (28 July 1995): 31.

42. *OMRI Daily Digest*, part I, 9 February 1995.

43. The widely repeated myth that Khrushchev gave Crimea away on a whim to commemorate the 300th anniversary of the Treaty of Pereiaslav is forcefully debunked in Roman Laba, "The Russian-Ukrainian Conflict: State, Nation and Identity," *European Security*, vol. 4, no. 3 (Autumn 1995): 457–487.

44. This argument is made by Oleh Olenyuk, "The Teeth of Crimean Privatizers Have Cut Through, and They Can Gnaw at the Branches of Power with Those Teeth," *Ukraina Moloda*, 16 September 1994, p. 3, translated in FBIS-USR-94–109, 6 October 1994, pp. 25–26.

45. *Moscow News* (U.S. Edition), 15 April 1995. The Crimean legislature also battled Kiev for control of the privatization process (*OMRI Daily Digest*, 13 January 1995).

46. G. John Ikenberry and Charles A. Kupchan, "Legitimacy and Power: The Waning of U.S. and Soviet Hegemony," in Henry Bienen, ed., *Power, Economics, and Security* (Boulder: Westview Press, 1992).

47. *OMRI Daily Digest*, part I, 19 April 1995; part I, 20 April 1995; part I, 21 April 1995.

48. Zhirinovsky, quoted in *OMRI Daily Digest*, part I, 1 March 1995.

49. Different, but essentially parallel typologies of the Russian foreign policy debate are offered by Solchanyk, "Russia, Ukraine, and the Imperial Legacy," pp. 342–348, and by Jeremy Lester, "Russian Attitudes to Ukrainian Independence," *Journal of Communist Studies and Transition Politics*, vol. 10, no. 2 (June 1994): 193–233.

50. For example, St. Petersburg Mayor Anatolii Sobchak was key force in turning back the coup attempt in August 1991, but within weeks had questioned the right of the non-Russian republics to secede and advocated Russian protection of Russian speakers in the "near abroad."

51. Pursuit of this right was evident in the campaign in 1994 first to have the CIS recognized by the UN as a regional organization, and then to have the OSCE recognize Russia's role as a regional peacekeeper.

52. "Council's Recommendations," *Nezavisimaya Gazeta*, 27 May 1994, pp. 4–5, translated in FBIS-USR-94–062, 13 June 1994, p. 71. The group included: Ambassador to the UN Yuli Vorontsov, Presidential Council member Sergei Karaganov, First Deputy Minister of Defense Andrei Kokoshin, and Deputy Minister of Foreign Affairs Sergei Lavrov.

53. Yevgeniy Ruter, "The New Abroad: Partners or a Burden? What Price Will Have to Be Paid for the Russian 'Monroe Doctrine'?," *Novoye Vremya*, no. 23, June 1994, p. 15, translated in FBIS-USR-94–070, 30 June 1994, pp. 93–96.

54. Umbach, "The Crimean Question," p. 195.

55. *OMRI Daily Digest*, part I, 27 January 1995.

56. Abraham S. Becker, "Russia and Economic Integration in the CIS," *Survival*, vol. 38, no. 4 (Winter 1996–97): 117.

57. Becker, p. 117.

58. *The Economist*, 8 April 1995, p. 45.

59. *The Economist*, 25 March 1995, p. 59; 27 May 1995, p. 48.

60. The unlikelihood of outright invasion helps explain why Ukraine was willing to surrender its nuclear weapons. The Ukrainian leadership understood that economic measures were the primary danger, and that while nuclear weapons were useless, good standing among Western governments was essential. See chapter 7.

61. *RFE/RL Newsline*, part II, 16 July 1997.

3. Trade and Power in International Politics

1. Jacob Viner, "Power versus Plenty as Objectives of Foreign Policy in the Seventeenth and Eighteenth Centuries," *World Politics*, I (1948): 1–29.

2. Prominent examples in the large literature on "neoliberal institutionalism" are Robert O. Keohane and Joseph S. Nye, *Power and Interdependence*, 2nd ed. (New York: HarperCollins, 1989); Robert O. Keohane, *After Hegemony* (Princeton: Princeton University Press, 1984); and Stephen D. Krasner, ed., *International Regimes* (Ithaca: Cornell University Press, 1983).

3. Joseph M. Grieco, "Understanding the Problem of Cooperation: Neoliberal Institutionalism and the Future of Realist Theory," in David A. Baldwin, ed., *Neorealism and Neoliberalism: The Contemporary Debate* (New York: Columbia University Press, 1993).

4. *Power and Interdependence*, p. 40.

5. Quoted in Taraz Kuzio, "After the Shock, the Therapy," *Transition* (28 July 1995): 38.

6. Susan Strange, "Protectionism in World Politics," *International Organization* (Spring 1985): 236.

7. Albert O. Hirschman, *State Power and the Structure of Foreign Trade* (Berkeley: University of California Press, 1945), pp. 14–15.

8. Keohane and Nye, p. 9; Klaus Knorr, "International Economic Leverage and its Uses," in Klaus Knorr and Frank N. Trager, eds., *Economic Issues and National Security* (Lawrence: Regents Press of Kansas, 1977), pp. 117–118.

9. Keohane and Nye, p. 12; Kenneth N. Waltz, *Theory of International Politics* (Reading, Mass.: Addison Wesley, 1979), p. 138.

10. Keohane and Nye, p. 12.

11. Keohane and Nye, pp. 44–45; David A. Baldwin, "Interdependence and Power: A Conceptual Analysis," *International Organization*, 34, 4 (Autumn

1989): 487. James Caporaso refers to the "intensity of demand for a particular good." See James A. Caporaso, "Dependence, Dependency, and Power in the Global System: A Structural and Behavioral Analysis," *International Organization* 32, 1 (Winter 1978): 21.

12. David Baldwin contends that "vulnerability" should be the sole meaning of interdependence ("Interdependence and Power," p. 490–491).

13. Waltz, p. 140.

14. Hirschman, pp. 18–20.

15. Baldwin, p. 487, 494–495. See also John D. Harsanyi, "The Measurement of Social Power," in Martin Shubik, ed., *Game Theory and Related Approaches to Social Behavior* (New York: John Wiley and Sons, 1964), pp. 186–187. The opportunity cost to the coercer of a cut in trade is also relevant, even if it is lower than that to the state being coerced.

16. Caporaso, p. 31.

17. Keohane, "Sovereignty, Interdependence, and International Institutions," in Linda B. Miller and Michael Joseph Smith, eds., *Ideas and Ideals: Essays in Honor of Stanley Hoffman* (Boulder: Westview Press, 1993), p. 91.

18. Keohane, "Sovereignty, Interdependence, and International Institutions," p. 92–93.

19. Richard Cooper, *The Economics of Interdependence: Economic Policy in the Atlantic Community* (New York: McGraw-Hill, 1968), p. 4.

20. Robert Gilpin, *U.S. Power and the Multinational Corporation: The Political Economy of Direct Foreign Investment* (New York: Basic Books, 1975), p. 38.

21. Hirschman finds that the conditions under which interdependence would neutralize power politics are "not merely unrealistic, but entirely fantastic. They presuppose, indeed, a multitude of states of approximately equal importance each with approsimately the same volume of foreign trade, the trade of each country being spread equally over all the other countries and no country possessing a monopoly with respect to any particular skill or natural endowment" (p. 75).

22. Keohane and Nye, p. 249.

23. Knorr, p. 114.

24. Ruggie therefore discusses strategies for the "negation of depency" ("Introduction," in John G. Ruggie, ed., *The Antinomies of Interdependence* (New York: Columbia University Press, 1982), pp. 11–13). Keohane and Nye are more categorical: "Interdependence restricts autonomy" (p. 9). Cooper (p. 4) agrees with Keohane and Nye.

25. Albert O. Hirschman, "Beyond Asymmetry: Critical Notes on Myself as a Young Man and on Some Other Old Friends," *International Organization*, 32, 1 (Winter 1978): 45–48.

26. Peter J. Katzenstein, "The Small European States in the International Economy: Economic Dependence and Corporatist Politics," in John G.

Ruggie, ed., *The Antinomies of Interdependence* (New York: Columbia University Press, 1982), p. 93.

27. Hirschman, p. 8.

28. Ferguson and Mansbach point out that the Austro-Hungarian empire made sense economically, if not nationally. Together, its constituent parts were large and less vulnerable. But when divided into smaller states with smaller weaker economies, they were easy prey for Germany economic penetration. See Yale H. Ferguson and Richard W. Mansbach, "Between Celebration and Despair: Constructive Suggestions for Future International Theory," *International Studies Quarterly*, 35 (1991): 381.

29. Katzenstein, p. 91

30. Hirschman, p. 31.

31. Zbigniew K. Brzezinski, *The Soviet Bloc: Unity and Conflict* (Cambridge: Harvard University Press, 1960), pp. 122–124.

32. The classic statement on bilateralism and the power of the strong is Hirschman's. See also Katzenstein, p. 103; Timothy J. McKeown, "Hegemonic Stability Theory and Nineteenth Century Tariff Levels in Europe," *International Organization* 37, 1 (Winter 1983): 73–91; Arthur A. Stein, "The Hegemon's Dilemma: Great Britain, the United States and the International Order," *International Organization*, 38, 2 (Spring 1984): 355–386; and Steve Weber, "Shaping the Postwar Balance of Power: Multilateralism in NATO," in John G. Ruggie, ed., *Multilateralism Matters: The Theory and Praxis of an International Form* (New York: Columbia University Press, 1993), pp. 235–236.

33. Grieco (fn. 4), pp. 331–332.

34. Hirschman, p. 58; Roman Szporluk, *Communism and Nationalism* (New York: Oxford University Press, 1988), p. 232.

35. Hirschman, p. 31. For these reason Caporaso (p. 32) emphasizes that analysis of economic dependence "cannot be limitied to dyadic relations."

36. In the case of Ukraine, this has been advocated by Vasyl' Kremin', Borys Parakhons'kyi, and Petro Sytnyk, "Ukraina i Rosiia: Sfery Konfrontatsii i Spivrobitnytstva," *Rozbudova Derzhava*, 2 (February 1993): 4.

37. Joanne Gowa and Edward D. Mansfield, "Power Politics and International Trade," *American Political Science Review*, 87, no. 7 (June 1993), p. 408.

38. On Ukraine's problems with access to European and American markets, see Bartolomiej Kaminski, "Trade Performance and Access to OECD Markets," in Constantine Michalopoulos and David G. Tarr, eds., *Trade in the New Independent States*, Studies of Economies in Transformation #13 (Washington, D.C.: World Bank, 1994); F. Stephen Larrabee, "Ukraine's Balancing Act," Survival, vol. 38, no. 2 (Summer 1996): 154; and Anders Aslund, "Problem Is Pricing, Not Dumping," (letter to the editor) *Financial Times*, 1 May 1997, p. 10.

39. Hirschman argues that by focusing one's trade on partners who urgently need one's goods, the state can increase its economic power.

40. Karen Dawisha and Bruce Parrott, *Russia and the New States of Eurasia* (Cambridge: Cambridge University Press, 1994), p. 180.

41. Hirschman, pp. 32–33.

42. *PlanEcon Report*, vol. VIII, nos. 9–10 (13 March 1992): 30–31. See also John Morrison, "Pereyaslav and After: The Russian-Ukrainian Relationship," *International Affairs*, 69, 4 (1993): 686, 692.

43. This finding, which Hirschman demonstrates in great detail, is directly contradictory to the recent finding by realist scholars of international cooperation that states seek "relative gains" in their trade, and are disadvantaged to the extent that their partners receive a disproportionate share of the gains from trade. If one is trying to create vulnerability, it pays to allow one's partner relative gains, because in doing so the partner becomes more dependent, and more vulnerable. Hirschman thus separates two contradictory effects of the gains from trade: favorable distribution of gains represent a gain in power as resources, but a loss in power as dependence. In the former Soviet Union, the latter is more significant, because the disparity between the power resources of the states is so great that no imaginable quantitative change can change the qualitative fact of Russian superiority.

44. Open Media Research Institute (Hereafter OMRI) *Daily Digest*, 25 May 1995; Dawisha and Parrott, 174.

45. When the disparity is size is great, the large state does not even need to offer extremely lopsided gains in order to take advantage of them. The large state can receive a larger share of the gains of trade, and still have leverage over the small states, as long as its share of the gains is a smaller proportion of its economy than the smaller state's share is in its economy.

46. Morrison, pp. 688–689.

47. Hirschman, p. 33.

48. Dawisha and Parrot, pp. 175–176.

49. Stephen D. Krasner, "Domestic Constraints on International Economic Leverage," in Knorr and Trager, eds., *Economic Issues in National Security*, p. 160.

50. See Katzenstein, "The Small European States."

51. Hirschman notes, however, that it is not necessary to assume state ownership of enterprises to conclude that the state can exert economic leverage. It is only necessary for the state to have control of tariff levels, which it can use to punish or favor trading partners.

52. Hirschman, p. 16

53. See Caporaso, pp. 16–17, for a discussion of the fundamental nature of this problem in contemporary international politics. A possible exception is domestic economic reform, which promises both increased prosperity and reduced dependence.

54. A fourth dilemma for Ukraine, that between "balancing" and "bandwagoning" is examined in chapter 7. It is excluded from this discussion because it does not stem primarily from interdependence and because it is essentially a question of military security, unlike the questions of economic security addressed here.

55. E. H. Carr, *The Future of Nations: Independence or Interdependence* (London: Kegan Paul, Trench, Trubner & Co., 1941), p. 27, quoted in Caporaso, p. 16.

56. Keohane, "Sovereignty, Interdependence, and International Institutions," pp. 92–93.

57. Cited in Oleh Havrylyshyn and John Williamson, *From Soviet dis-Union to Eastern Economic Community?*, Policy Analyses in International Economics 35 (Washington, D.C.: Institute for International Economics, October 1991), p. 6.

58. Robert H. Jackson and Carl G. Rosberg, "Why Africa's Weak States Persist: The Empirical and the Juridical in Statehood," *World Politics*, XXXV, No. 1 (October 1982): 1–24.

59. Hirschman, pp. 5–11.

60. Edward Meade Earle, "Adam Smith, Alexander Hamilton, Friederich List: The Economic Foundations of Military Power," in Peter Paret, ed., *Makers of Modern Strategy* (Princeton: Princeton University Press, 1986), p. 218. On Mercantilism and Smith's advances, see also Viner, "Power versus Plenty," Hirschman, chapter 1; and Richard Betts, Michael Doyle, and G. John Ikenberry, "An Intellectual Remembrance of Klaus Knorr," in Henry Bienen, ed., *Power Economics, and Security* (Boulder: Westview Press, 1992).

61. For prominent examples, see Cooper, *The Economics of Interdependence*, and Keohane, *After Hegemony* and "Sovereignty, Interdependence, and International Institutions"). All analyses of interdependence that use the Prisoner's Dilemma as a metaphor for the problem assume symmetrical interdependence.

62. Keohane and Nye, *Power and Interdependence*, p. 9.

63. On calls in Ukraine for Ukrainian economic isolation, see Dawisha and Parrott and Kremin' et al., p. 3.

64. Caporaso, p. 17.

65. See Caporaso, p. 17, on autarky as an extreme measure to combat dependence.

66. P. 249. See also John G. Ruggie, "Collective Goods and Future International Collaboration," *American Political Science Review* 66 (September 1972), 875.

67. Caporaso, p. 17.

68. Stanley Hoffman, *Janus and Minerva: Essays in the Theory and Practice of International Politics* (Boulder: Westview, 1987), p. 293.

69. The difference between the military alliance and the economic organization is the that the military alliance is aimed at protecting the members from an outside threat, while the economic organization protects against conflict *within* the group (and is thus roughly akin to a collective security organization).

70. See fn 33.

71. Donald J. Puchala, "Western Europe," in Robert H. Jackson and Alan James, eds., *States in a Changing World: A Contemporary Analysis* (New York: Oxford University Press, 1993), pp. 71, 86–87; Katzenstein, p. 103.

72. Keohane and Nye, *Power and Interdependence*, p. 270.

73. Stephen D. Krasner, "Economic Interdependence and Independent Statehood," in Robert H. Jackson and Alan James, eds., *States in a Changing World: A Contemporary Analysis* (Oxford: Clarendon Press, 1993), p. 310. More currently, the WTO is constraining the ability of the United States to use its bilateral power to coerce Japan. See the *Economist*, 27 May 1995, p. 18.

74. Krasner, "Economic Interdependence," pp. 301–302.

75. Richard Cooper defines autonomy as "the ability to frame and carry out objectives of domestic economic policy which diverge widely from those of other countries," and sovereignty as "the formal ability of countries . . . to make their own decisions, but not necessarily to achieve their goals" (*The Economics of Interdependence*, p. 4).

76. Puchala, pp. 86–87.

77. Ivan Lukinov, "Radical Reconstruction of the Ukrainian Economy: Reasons, Reform, Outlook," in I.S. Koropeckyj, ed., *The Ukrainian Economy: Achievements, Problems, Challenges* (Cambridge: Harvard Ukrainian Research Institute, 1992), p. 36.

78. Hirschman, p. ix.

79. The most notable expression of this sentiment was by British Secretary of State for Trade and Industry Nicholas Ridley, who envisioned a Fourth Reich achieved through the dominance of the D-mark. Cited in Simon J. Bulmer, "Germany and European Integration: Toward Economic and Political Dominance,' in Carl F. Lankowski, ed., *Germany and the European Community: Beyond Hegemony and Containment* (New York: St. Martin's, 1993).

80. Morrison, p. 679.

4. The Energy War, 1993–1994

1. On the energy situation in Ukraine, see Leslie Dienes, "Energy, Minerals, and Economic Policy," in I. S. Koropeckyj, ed., *The Ukrainian Economy: Achievements, Problems, Challenges* (Cambridge: Harvard Ukrainian Research Institute, 1992); *PlanEcon Report*, 15 September 1992, pp. 16, 21; and

Leslie Dienes, Istvan Dobozi, and Marian Radezki, *Energy and Economic Reform in the Former Soviet Union* (New York: St. Martin's Press, 1994).

2. The rise of oil in industry, and correspondingly in international politics, is chronicled in Daniel Yergin, *The Prize* (New York: Simon and Schuster, 1991).

3. Dienes, "Energy, Minerals and Economic Policy," p. 124.

4. Dienes, pp. 128–129.

5. Dienes, p. 129.

6. Dienes, pp. 125–126, has more detail on the situation in the Ukrainian coal industry.

7. Dienes, pp. 126, 129.

8. Dienes, p. 129.

9. Jeffrey W. Schneider, "Republic Energy Sector and Inter-State Dependencies of the Commonwealth of Independent States and Georgia," in Richard F. Kaufman and John P. Hardt, eds., *The Former Soviet Union in Transition* (Armonk, NY: M. E. Sharpe, 1993), p. 478.

10. M. Dabrowski, "Ukrainian Way to Hyperinflation," DP 94/12, Center for Social and Economic Research, Warsaw, cited in Oleh Havrylyshyn, Marcus Miller, and William Perraudin, "Deficits, Inflation, and the Political Economy of Ukraine," *Economic Policy* 19 (October 1994): 359.

11. Havrylyshyn, Miller, and Perraudin, p. 359.

12. A precise accounting of Ukraine's energy economy is impossible to provide, because comprehensive and uniform statistics are not available. However, it is possible to draw a picture of Ukraine's situation at the time of independence that demonstrates the nature and magnitude of the problem with sufficient accuracy for our purposes. More recent data are more difficult to assess, because many reports of imports and consumption are of government policies and intergovernmental agreements, which are often not actually carried out.

13. Dienes, Dobozi, and Radetzki, p. 184.

14. Ihor Yukhnovskiy, "How Can the State Be Supplied with Electric Power? An Inquiry into the Reorganization of the Production Structure in Ukraine," *Vecherniy Kiyev*, 22 September 1992, pp. 3–4, translated in FBIS-USR-92-136, 23 October 1992, pp. 84–89.

15. Yukhnovskiy, p. 85.

16. Dienes, Dobozi, and Radetzki, p. 184.

17. Dienes, Dobozi, and Radetzki, p. 184.

18. *PlanEcon Report*, 15 September, 1992, p. 21.

19. Schneider, p. 483.

20. Schneider, p. 485.

21. For a thorough analysis of the effects of energy price increases, see H. Quan Chu and Wafik Grais, *Macroeconomic Consequences of Energy Supply*

Shocks in Ukraine, Studies of Economies in Transformation #12, (Washington, D.C.: World Bank, 1994).

22. "Russia, Belarus Agree on Monetary Union," *Financial Times*, 13 April 1994, p. 2.

23. *Radio Free Europe/Radio Liberty Report* (Hereafter *RFE/RL*), 10 January 1994.

24. The power of debtors was demonstrated during the Latin American debt crisis in the 1980s, when U.S. banks were forced to reschedule debt and continue lending for fear that failure to do so would result on default on earlier loans.

25. *RFE/RL*, 5 May 1994.

26. Turkmenistan, Ukraine's other natural gas supplier, has been much more quick than Russia to halt deliveries of gas to force payment.

27. A Ukrainian analyst contends therefore that an immediate move to world market prices in 1991 would have been received much better by Ukraine, because it would have been seen as harsh, but fair treatment, in contrast with their view that in the current state of affairs they are being manipulated (Dmitriy Vydrin, "The Russian Bear and the Ukrainian Fox," *Obshchaya Gazeta*, 22 April 1994, p. 5, translated in FBIS-USR-94-052, 16 May 1994, p. 13).

28. The discussion that follows is largely based on Peter Rutland, "Russia's Energy Empire under Strain," *Transition* (3 May 1996): 6–11; Peter Rutland, "Russia's Natural Gas Leviathan," *Transition* (3 May 1996): 12–13, 63; and Ustina Markus, "Energy Crisis Spurs Ukraine and Belarus to Seek Help Abroad," *Transition* (3 May 1996): 14–18.

29. Poltoranin and Yeltsin are cited in Taras Kuzio, "Ukraine and Its 'Near Abroad,'" *Politychna Dumka/Political Thought* 3 (1994): 202.

30. Rutland, "Russia's Natural Gas Leviathan," p. 12.

31. Rutland, "Russia's Natural Gas Leviathan," p. 12; "Russia's Energy Empire," p. 7.

32. RFE/RL Newsline, 30 June 1997, Part I.

33. Markus, p. 14.

34. Rutland, "Russia's Energy Empire," p. 8.

35. Rutland, "Russia's Energy Empire," pp. 6–7.

36. Rutland, "Russia's Energy Empire," pp. 10–11.

37. Rutland, "Russia's Energy Empire," p. 11.

38. *RFE/RL*, 5 February 1992.

39. *RFE/RL*, 21 February 1992.

40. *RFE/RL*, 27 March 1992.

41. Russian oil production was falling even before the collapse of the Soviet Union, from 552 millions of metric tons (mmt) in 1989 to 462 in 1992.

By 1994, production had stabilized at 315 mmt (*PlanEcon Report*, 10 March 1993, pp. 16–20; 7 April 1995, p. 7).

42. *RFE/RL*, 9, 10 February 1993.

43. *RFE/RL*, 6–10 September 1993.

44. Kravchuk's news conference of 6 September 1993, the transcript of which is in FBIS-SOV-93-171, 7 September 1993, p. 72.

45. Yeltsin interview on Russian Television Network, 4 September 1993, translated in FBIS-SOV-93-171, 7 September 1993, p. 7.

46. *RFE/RL*, 24 November 1993.

47. Reuters, 6 September 1993, quoted in Morrison, "Pereyaslav and After," p. 695.

48. ITAR-TASS, 4 September 1993, translated in FBIS-SOV-93-171, 7 September 1993, p. 63.

49. Agence France Press, 3 September 1993, in FBIS-SOV-93-171, 7 September 1993, p. 61.

50. *RFE/RL*, 7 October 1993.

51. On Ukraine's dire energy situation, see Jill Barshay, "Ukraine Shivers as Energy Dwindles," *Financial Times*, 23 November 1993, p. 2.

52. *RFE/RL*, 12 October 1993.

53. John Lloyd, "Ukrainians Offered Debt Swap for Nuclear Deal," *Financial Times*, 13 January 1994, p. 2, citing "key U.S. officials." See also "Rosiys'ki exportery hazu vymahaiut' rozrakhunku za svoi postavky," *Post-Postup*, 17–23 February 1994, p. B5, which indicates that part of Ukraine's gas dept was transferred to the general state debt and subsequently paid off as part of the nuclear deal.

54. For an analysis of Russia's policy of expanding its control of the gas and oil industries in former Soviet states, most notably Kazakhstan, Azerbaijan, and in the Caspian Sea, see Steve LeVine, "The Great Game Revisited," *Financial Times*, 7 March 1994, p. 12. See also LeVine and Robert Corzine, "Russians Muscle in on Oil Deals," *Financial Times*, 21 January 1994, p. 2. There has been considerable speculation that Chechnya's position astride key oil transport routes was the main motive for the Russian invasion in December 1994. See *OMRI Daily Digest*, part I, 19 January 1995.

55. *RFE/RL*, 7 February 1994. See also, John Lloyd, "Gazprom Threatens to Cut Exports" *Financial Times*, 12–13 February 1994, p. 2.

56. *RFE/RL*, 7, 9 March 1994. See also "Russia-Ukraine Gas Row Talks," *Financial Times*, 8 March 1994, p. 2.

57. *RFE/RL*, 9 March 1994. Russia had tried the same approach previously with Latvia.

58. John Lloyd and Jill Barshay, "Ukraine Rejects Black Sea Fleet Deal in Gas Row," *Financial Times*, 7 March 1994, p. 20.

59. *RFE/RL*, 3 March 1994. The accusation that Ukraine was taking more gas than it was entitled, leading to shortages in western Europe, was repeated by Gazprom chairman Rem Vyakhirev in 1996 ("Energy Market Report: Natural Gas," *Energy Economist*, December 1996).

60. Rustam Narzikulov, "Ukraine Agrees to Pay Debts to Gazprom. It Can Only Pay in Property," *Segodnya*, 11 March 1994, p. 1, translated in FBIS-SOV-94-048, 11 March 1994, p. 35.

61. Serhiy Lavreniuk, "Iadernoi Zbroi Vzhe Nema. Mozhe ne buty i hazoprovodiv." *Holos Ukrainy*, 12 March 1994; *RFE/RL* 11 March 1994; Jill Barclay, "Ukraine Gas Supplies Resume," *Financial Times*, 11 March 1994, p. 2. Plans to transfer Ukrainian gas facilities to Russia are discussed in great detail in Hanna Lyuta, "Vyrishennia Problemy Hazozabezpechennia Ukrainy Lezhit' u Politychniy Ploshchyni," *Post-Postup* (17–24 March 1994), p. 4; "Postavky Rosiys'koho Hazu v Ukrainy Pokryvaiut' Pryblizno 80% Obsiahu Ochikuvanoho Importu z Turkmenystanu," *Post-Postup* (1–7 April 1994) p. B5.

62. *RFE/RL*, 23, 30 March 1994.

63. *RFE/RL*, 2 April 1994.

64. "Spil'ni Interesy Ukrains'kykh i Rosiys'kykh Hazovykiv Pom'iakshuyut' Problemu Rosiys'kykh Hazopostavok," *Post-Postup*, no. 10 (8–14 April 1994) pp. B1, B5; "U Spravi Vyplaty Ukrainuyu Zaborhovanosti RAT "Gazprom" Stalysia Pevni Pozytyvni Zrushennia," *Post-Postup* (22–28 April 1994), p. B3.

65. Abraham S. Becker, "Russia and Economic Integration in the CIS," *Survival*, vol. 38, no. 4 (Winter 1996–97): 123.

66. *OMRI Daily Digest*, part II, 14 March 1995. Gazprom was able, however, to negotiate such a deal with Moldova (*OMRI Daily Digest*, part II, 16 May 1995).

67. "Ukrainian Parliament Halts Oil and Gas Privatisation," *East European Energy Report*, 27 November 1995.

68. "Ukraine to Cut Gas Imports by 10 percent," *East European Energy Report*, 22 September 1995.

69. "Ukraine Diversifies and Gets Transit Agreement with Russia," *East European Energy Report*, 20 December 1996.

70. Anatoliy Gordukalov, head of the Russian Ministry of Fuel and Power Engineering, said that "all the issues of gas and oil deliveries to Ukraine can only be resolved after the Black Sea Fleet issue is settled." Cited by *UNIAN*, 21 December 1994, translated by FBIS-SOV-94-246, 22 December 1994, p. 34.

71. The plan apparently called for Iran to deliver 3 billion cubic meters of gas and 4 million tons of oil in 1992, and envisioned eventual supply of 75 million cubic meters of gas and 50–70 million tons of oil annually (FBIS, 6 February 1992). That amount of oil would make Ukraine completely inde-

pendent of Russian imports. Ukraine was to pay for the fuels with equipment of various types, apparently to include SCUD-B missiles (FBIS, 30 April, 1992). The deal also called for $7 billion pipeline from Iran to Azerbaijan and a supertanker terminal at Odessa. The question of getting the oil from Azerbaijan to the Black Sea (it would have to cross either Russia or Georgia) never seems to have been resolved. An additional problem was that near Eastern oil had a sulfur content that Ukrainian refineries were not equipped to remove. In April 1994, discussions were continuing amid recriminations in Ukraine over the failure of the deal to be implemented (*Interfax*, 20 April 1994, translated by FBIS-SOV-94-077, 21 April 1994, p. 57).

72. See "Anatoliy Zlenko Znovu Vyklav Ne toi Tovar v Irans'kiy Naftoviy Lavtsi, Ale Ne Rozhubyvcia na Indiys'komu Bazari" *Post-Postup* (29 April–6 May 1994), p. 2; and "Ukraina ta Nigeriia ukladaiut' uhodu pro postacheniia nafty," and "Khorvaty zaproponuvaly Ukraini investuvaty v naftoprovid," *Post-Postup* (17–23 February 1994), p. B1.

73. O. Musafirova and F. Sizyy, "Rivers of Oil, Foreign Shores: Ukraine Seeks Solution to Energy Crisis," *Komsomolskaya Pravda*, 24 April 1992, p. 2, translated by FBIS. FBIS-USR-92-051, 4 May 1992, p. 64.

74. *UNIAN*, 19 October 1993, translated in FBIS-SOV-93–201, 20 October 1993, p. 70.

75. "Ukraine Considers Azeri Imports," *East European Energy Report*, 18 November 1996.

76. In January 1995, the Verkhovna Rada revived plans to build a new oil terminal at Odessa. The measure appropriated the necessary land, but there remained no funding for the project (*OMRI Daily Digest*, part II, 20 January 1995).

77. *UNIAN*, 23 July 1993, translated in FBIS-SOV-93-141, 26 July 1993, p. 54.

78. *OMRI Daily Digest*, part I, 25 May 1995. Belarus, which had much closer relations with Russia, was paying slightly more than Ukraine ($53 per thousand cubic meters).

79. "Intehratsiia dlia Vzaiemnoi Vyhody," *Uryadoviy Kurier*, 22 June 1996, p. 5.

80. "Kiev Eyes Black Sea Gas Boost," *International Gas Report*, 25 October 1996.

81. *Holos Ukrayiny*, 21 January 1994, p. 4, translated in FBIS-SOV-94-016, 25 January 1994, pp. 46–47.

82. The Atlantic Council of the United States, *Basic Concepts for the Development of Energy Policies for Russia and Ukraine* (Washington, D.C.: The Atlantic Council, 1993), p. 31.

83. UT-1 Television Network, 28 January 1994, translated in FBIS-SOV-94-020, 31 January 1994, p. 43.

84. A detailed analysis of Ukraine's energy situation and a plan for self-sufficiency is advanced by Ihor Yukhnovskiy, "How Can the State Be Supplied with Electric Power? An Inquiry into the Reorganization of the Production Structure in Ukraine," *Vecherniy Kiyev*, 22 September 1992, pp. 3–4, translated by FBIS. FBIS-USR-92-136, 23 October 1992, pp. 84–89. Yukhnovskiy was at the time Ukrainian first vice-prime minister. A more recent, but less detailed, plan is that of O. Sheberstov, "Energetika Ukrainy: shliakhy vykhody z kryzy," *Ekonomika Ukraina*, 5 (1996): 4–6.

85. Konstantin Smirnov, "Ukraine Tries to Repay Debt to 'Gazprom.' Ukrainian Government Launches 'Gas' Attack," *Kommersant-Daily*, 15 September 1993, p. 3, translated in FBIS-SOV-93-178, 16 September 1993, p. 37.

86. *Basic Concepts*, p. 46. See also Dienes, et al., p. 5.

87. *Basic Concepts*, pp. 45–46.

88. Yukhnovskiy, p. 85. According to Yukhnovskiy, refining efficiency averages 50 percent in Ukraine, and is as high as 83 percent in Germany and 90 percent in the United States.

89. "Ukraine to Increase Gas Prices," *East European Energy Report*, 22 May 1995.

90. See Aleksandr Maliyenko, "Electric Shortage is Coming," *Pravda Ukrainy*, 15 September 1994, p. 2, translated in FBIS-USR-94-108, 4 October 1994, pp. 66–67.

91. Smirnov, p. 37.

92. INTERFAX, 19 May 1994, translated in FBIS-SOV-94-098, 20 May 1994, p. 53.

93. *RFE/RL*, 16 August 1994. This $320 million underestimates the actual value of the gas consumed or its cost to the state, because the government was still heavily subsidizing it.

94. *OMRI Daily Digest*, part II, 24 January 1995.

95. "Ukraine to Cut Gas Imports by 10 percent," *East European Energy Report*, 22 September 1995.

96. "Ukraine Diversifies and Gets Transit Agreement with Russia," *East European Energy Report*, 20 December 1996.

97. Hanna Lyuta, "Uryad namahaet'sya zmusyty promyslovi pidpryemstva braty uchast' u finansuvanni importnyx enerhnociiv," *Post-Postup*, 3–9 1994, p. B4.

98. "Ukraine to Increase Gas Prices," *East European Energy Report*, 22 May 1995.

99. According to Taras Freiuk, assistant director of UKRHAZ, Ukraine's state-run gas concern, Ukraine needs to produce 3 million meters for industrial enterprises and 9 million overall. See "'UKRHAZ' Vvodyt' Zhorstkyy Kontrol' za Vykorystanniam Hazu," *Post-Postup*, 25–31 March 1994, p. B5.

100. *OMRI Daily Digest*, part II, 20 June 1995.

101. "Dealing with Ukraine's Gas Arrears," *IMF Survey*, 1 July 1996, p. 227.

102. "Domestic User Prices Jump," *International Gas Report*, 2 February 1996; "Gazprom Gets Tough on Gas Debt," *International Gas Report*, 16 February 1996.

103. Jill Barshay, "Ukraine Shivers as Energy Dwindles," *Financial Times*, 23 November 1993, p. 2. Barshay reported in March 1994 that oil and gas costs were double foreign currency earnings ("Ukraine's Kravchuk Poses Dilemma for West," *Financial Times*, 3 March 1994, p. 3.

104. Lloyd and Barshay, "Ukraine Rejects Black Sea Fleet Deal," p. 20.

105. Hanna Lyuta, "Rosiia Dala Haz Ukraini, Bo Ne Dala Inshym," *Post-Postup* (3–9 February 1994), p. B4; "Out of Gas," *The Economist*, 12 March 1994, p. 35.

106. *RFE/RL*, 27 January 1994.

107. *RFE/RL*, 16 February 1994. See also John Lloyd and Leyla Boulton, "Russians in Oil Export Revenue Trap," *Financial Times*, 6 April 1994, p. 2.

108. *RFE/RL*, 23 March 1994; *The Economist*, 12 March 1994.

109. *OMRI Daily Digest*, 4 January 1995.

110. Prime Minister Chernomyrdin, who owns a significant portion of Gazprom stock, rumored to be valued at a billion dollars, has ample incentive to see that Gazprom's fortunes are not sacrificed to foreign policy goals. In Russia, Chernomyrdin's political party "Our Home Is Russia" is referred to by cynics as "Our Home Is Gazprom."

111. Dienes, et al., pp. 98–99. See also The Atlantic Council, *Basic Concepts*, p. 24 for details on interdependence in the oil and gas industries in the FSU.

112. Interview with Nikolay Gonchar, chairman of the Finance and Budget Committee of the Council of the Russia Federation, *Holos Ukrainy*, 20 July 1994, p. 4, translated in FBIS-USR-94-083, 2 August 1994, p. 4.

113. Ukraine did not hesitate to use this lever early on in the game, when on 27 March 1992, it threatened to close the pipeline to Western Europe if Russia did not persuade Turkmenistan to lower its prices (FBIS, 30 March 1992). In January 1995, the Czech republic underwent a brief energy scare when the flow of oil was cut as Ukraine tried to negotiate a fivefold increase in transit fees (*OMRI Daily Digest*, 10 January, 13 January 1995.

114. Ninety percent of Russian gas shipments to western Europe cross Ukraine (Viktor Shanyuk, "Russian Gazprom Shackling Terms for Ukraine: Landyk Team Transfers Pipeline Control to Russia and Undermines Ukrainian Independence," *Ukrainska Hazeta*, 31 March–13 April 1994, pp. 1, 3, translated in FBIS-USR-94-043, 21 April 1994, p. 38.

115. "Ukraine Steps Up 'Gas War,'" *Financial Times*, 3 March 1994, p. 3; Dmytro Kyblyts'kyi, "Rosiys'ky Gazprom khoche deshcho pryvatyzuvaty v

Ukraini. Todi my zmozhemo deiaky chas varyty isty," *Post-Postup* (17–24 1994), p. 1.

116. "Ukraine and Russia Fail to Agree on Gas Transit Rates," *East European Energy Report*, 18 November 1996. After Ukraine tried to force Gazprom to pay market rates for transit in late 1996, the two sides reached an agreement raising pipeline tariff rates, but allowing Gazprom to pay in gas at market prices, and allowing Ukraine to continue paying in goods for some of the gas it receives ("Ukraine Diversifies and Gets Transit Agreement with Russia," *East European Energy Report*, 20 December 1996).

117. Dmitriy Vydrin, "The Russian Bear and the Ukrainian Fox," *Obshchaya Gazeta*, 22 April 1994, p. 5, translated in FBIS-USR-94-052, 16 May 1994, p. 12.

118. Quoted in Lloyd and Barshay, "Ukraine Rejects Black Sea Fleet Deal."

119. "Dealing with Ukraine's Gas Arrears," *IMF Survey*, 1 July 1996, p. 227.

120. Kiev Radio, 20 March 1992 translated in FBIS-SOV-92-056, 23 March 1992, p. 65, V. Nikitenko, "Fuel Loans Needed," *Rabochaya Gazeta*, 3 April 1992, p. 1, translated in FBIS-USR-92-050, 1 May 1992, p. 89.

121. Olga Misafirova, "Mariya Devi Khristos Was Right—End of the World Is Nigh in Kiev," *Komsomolskaya Pravda*, 26 November 1993, p. 1; and *UNIAN*, 29 November 1993, both translated in FBIS-SOV-93-227, 29 November 1993, pp. 61–62.

122. Chrystyna Lapychak, "Quarrels over Land Reform," *Transition* (1 December 1995): 54.

123. Vasiliy Lys, "Kremenchug People Lend a Helping Hand to Poltava Grain Producers, *Rabochaya Gazeta*, 27 October 1992, p. 1, translated in FBIS-USR-92-147, 15 November 1992, pp. 78–79.

124. Ostankino Television First Channel, 28 June 1993, tranlated in FBIS-SOV-93-123, 29 June 1993, p. 59; *UNIAN*, 20 July 1993, translated in FBIS-SOV-93-138, 21 July 1993, p. 43. More detailed analysis of agricultural problems and fuel shortages is in a report by V. Tymoshenko, the deputy chief of agricultural administration in the Ministry of Agricultural Production, in *Silski Vesti*, 3 November 1992; and V. Onenko, "We Will Catch Up on Our Plowing in Spring?," *Silski Vesti*, 6 November 1992, both translated in FBIS-USR-92-166, 30 December 1992, p. 96.

125. L. Dayen, "Oil Kings Can Do Everything," *Demokratychna Ukrayina*, 22 September 1992, p. 2, translated in FBIS-SOV-92-192, 2 October 1992, p. 25.

126. Barshay, "Ukraine Shivers," p. 2.

127. UNIAN, 22 March 1994, translated in FBIS-SOV-94-055, 22 March 1994, p. 45.

128. Leonid Kapelyushnyy, "Ukraine: No Television in Afternoon or After Midnight," *Izvestiya*, 1 December 1993, p. 2, translated in FBIS-SOV-93-231, 3 December 1993, p. 45.

129. The other main causes of this shift were probably the domestic economic problems that stemmed from Ukraine's lack of reform and decision to cut trade with Russia.

130. *RFE/RL*, 5 December 1991.

131. Nataliya Balyuk, "One Does Not Shake His Fist after Elections," *Vysokyy Zamok*, 28 July 1994, pp. 1–2, translated in FBIS-SOV-94-149, 3 August 1994, p. 38.

132. Kravchuk's performances in 1991 and 1994 are broken down by oblast' and compared in Jaroslaw Martyniuk, "The Shifting Political Landscape," *Transtion* (28 July 1995): 10.

133. See Jacob W. Kipp, *Ukrainian and Belarus Presidential Elections: Prelude to a Crisis in the Western Borderlands of Russia* (Ft. Leavenworth: Foreign Military Studies Office, 1994).

134. The timing of events gives some support to the theory that the energy situation was crucial: In September 1993, after the Massandra summit, anti-Kravchuk opinion in the west was high. This was after two years of independence, but before significant energy shortages were felt, beginning in November. By the following spring, as the Presidential campaign picked up, Kravchuk became "the best hope" for nationalists, even if they remained unenthusiastic about him. To the non-Ukrainian observer, the shift in views of Kravchuk in western Ukraine was remarkable.

135. "Motives for Oil Deal with Iran Examined," *Izvestiya*, 12 February 1992, p. 5, translated by FBIS. FBIS-SOV-92-035, 21 February 1992, p. 78.

136. On Kuchma's campaign themes, see Maria Kara, "Rozkol 'Rosiyskoi' Ukrainy," *Post-Postup*, 17–24 March 1994, pp. 1–2, and "Leonid Kuchma: 'Vlady v Ukraini s'ohodni nemaye. Pravliat' bal zovsim inshi syly," *Vysokyy Zamok*, 12 April 1994, p. 2.

137. Quoted in Kyblyts'kyy, "Rosiys'kyy Gazprom," p. 1.

138. This backlash was predicted by Vitaliy Portnikov in *Nezavisimaya Gazeta* after the Massandra summit. See "Moscow Cannot Be Indifferent to Kravchuk's Fate . . . ," *Nezavisimaya Gazeta*, 7 September 1993, p. 1, translated in FBIS-SOV-93-172, 8 September 1993, p. 12. For an example of mainstream Ukrainian attitudes toward Russian pressure on energy, see Lavreniuk, "Iadernoi zbroi . . . ," p. 2.

139. Quoted in Vladimir Mayevskiy, "Economy Must Be Secure," *Pravda Ukrainy*, 29 January 1993, p. 2, translated by FBIS-USR-93-023, 3 March 1993, p. 79.

140. See chapter 7.

141. Vydrin asserts that Ukraine resisted the energy pressure because "Western Ukraine, for which the independence and sovereignty of the country have self-contained if not religious signficiance, is prepared for any hardship. In turn, Eastern Ukraine lacks the full-fledged institutions of a civic society (with the exception of strike commitees), due to which economic dissatisfaction with the economic decay is reflected in political demands only very slowly" (p. 13).

5. Trade and Currency

1. David G. Tarr, "How Moving to World Prices Affects the Terms of Trade of the Former Soviet Union," Country Economics Department, The World Bank, January 1993, p. 13. Tarr estimates Ukraine's terms of trade decline with the former Soviet at 27.2 percent, which is partially offset by a terms of trade improvement with the rest of the world. Overall, he estimates, Ukraine's terms of trade could be expected to decline 18.1 percent, leading to a 2.6 percent drop in GDP (p. 17).

2. Volodimir N. Bandera, "National Income Transfers and Macroeconomic Accountability from the Standpoint of Ukraine," in I. S. Koropeckyj, ed., *The Ukrainian Economy: Achievements, Problems, Challenges* (Cambridge: Harvard Ukrainian Research Institute, 1992), p. 386.

3. This literature is reviewed by Taras Kuzio and Andrew Wilson, *Ukraine: Perestroika to Independence* (Edmonton: Canadian Institute of Ukrainian Studies, 1994), pp. 39–41.

4. Constantine Michalopoulos and David Tarr, *Trade and Payments Arrangements for States of the Former USSR*, Studies of Economies in Transformation, No. 2 (Washington, D.C.: The World Bank, 1992), p. 3. See also Oleh Havrylyshyn, "Reviving Trade Amongst the Newly Independent States," *Economic Policy*, no. 19 (December 1994): 171–190.

5. On "the crisis of Ukraine's economic ties with ex-USSR republics" see Ihor Burkavsky, "The Economic Situation in Ukraine," *Politychna Dumka/Political Thought*, no. 1 (1993): 166–168. On the economic reasons for reintegrating post-Soviet economies, see Abraham S. Becker, "Russia and Economic Integration in the CIS," *Survival*, vol. 38, no. 4 (Winter 1996–97): 118–120.

6. Thus Constantine Michalopoulos acknowledges the need for a long-term adjustment of trade patterns, but continues: "But precipitous drops in trade volumes are worrisome because they contribute to the disruption of production and decline in incomes. The contraction of output has further negative multiplier effects on trade" (*Trade Issues in the New Indepen-*

dent States, Studies of Economies in Transformation, no. 7 [Washington, D.C.: The World Bank, 1993], p. 1. See also Oleh Havrylyshyn and John Williamson, *From Soviet disUnion to Eastern Economic Community,?* Policy Analyses in International Economics 35 (Washington, D.C.: Institute for International Economics, October 1991), p. 2; Evgenii Yasin, "The Economic Sphere of the Former Soviet Union, Past and Present," in John Williamson, ed., *Economic Consequences of Soviet Disintegration* (Washington, D.C.: Institute for International Economics, 1993); and Ivan Lukinov, "Radical Reconstruction of the Ukrainian Economy: Reasons, Reform, Outlook," in I. S. Koropeckyj, ed., *The Ukrainian Economy: Achievements, Problems, Challenges* (Cambridge: Harvard Ukrainian Research Institute, 1992), pp. 32–33.

7. Leonid Kravchuk, speech in Kiev, 5 December 1991, translated in FBIS-SOV-91-235, 6 December 1991, p. 73.

8. See David Marples, "Radicalization of the Political Spectrum in Ukraine," Radio Free Europe/Radio Liberty, *Report on the USSR*, 30 August 1991, p. 31.

9. The pros and cons of monetary independence are examined in detail in Michael L. Wyzan, "Introduction," in Michael L. Wyzan, ed., *First Steps Toward Economic Independence*, (Westport, Conn.: Praeger, 1995), pp. 6–9.

10. See Oleh Havrylyshyn, Marcus Miller, and William Perraudin, "Deficits, Inflation, and the Political Economy of Ukraine," *Economic Policy* (October 1994): 355, 357–359.

11. Havrylyshyn and Williamson, p. 8.

12. Serhey Alexashenko, "Comment," in Williamson, *Economic Consequences of Soviet Disintegration*, pp. 273–276. See also, Wyzan, "Introduction," p. 8.

13. "The Cost of Monetary Chaos," *The Economist*, 20 November 1993, pp. 77–78.

14. Barry Eichengreen, "A Payments Mechanism for the Former Soviet Union: Is the EPU a Relevant Precedent?" *Economic Policy* 17 (October 1993): 311.

15. Jozef M. Von Brabant, "The New East and Its Preferred Trade Regime," in Richard F. Kaufman and John P. Hardt, eds., *The Former Soviet Union in Transition* (Armonk, N.Y.: M. E. Sharpe, 1993), p. 149; Eichengreen, p. 313.

16. Eichengreen, p. 314.

17. Tim Snyder points out the irony that despite Lenin's excoriation of monopoly under capitalism, the Soviet Union became much more heavily monopolized than capitalist states ("Soviet Monopoly," in Williamson, ed., *Economic Consequences of Soviet Disintegration*, pp. 175–176).

18. I. S. Koropeckyj, "Introduction," in Koropeckyj, ed., *The Ukrainian Economy*, p. 10; Havrylyshyn and Williamson, p. 19.

19. Havrylyshyn and Williamson, p. 19; Nikolai Petrakov, "Political Prospects for Preservation of the Single Economic Space," in Williamson, ed., *Economic Consequences of Soviet Disintegration*, pp. 41–42; Snyder, pp. 176–177.

20. See Snyder, "Soviet Monopoly."

21. Havrylyshyn and Williamson, p. 19.

22. Havrylyshyn and Williamson, p. 19.

23. Koropeckyj, p. 11.

24. Bandera, pp. 400–401.

25. Yasin, p. 32; Ivan Lukinov, "Radical Reconstruction of the Ukrainian Economy: Reasons, Reform, Outlook," in Koropeckyj, ed., *The Ukrainian Economy*, pp. 32–33.

26. Ukraine's energy situation is detailed in Leslie Dienes, "Energy, Minerals, and Economic Policy," in Koropeckyj, ed., *The Ukrainian Economy*; and in chapter 4.

27. Yasin, pp. 20, 24–25.

28. Petrakov, p. 41.

29. Granberg, p. 48.

30. Koropeckyj, pp. 10–11.

31. Heiko Pleines, "Ukraine's Organized Crime Is an Enduring Soviet Legacy," *Transition* (8 March 1996): 12.

32. *OMRI Economic Digest*, 7 November 1996, citing the Ukrainian Ministry of Statistics.

33. Alexander Granberg, "The Economic Interdependence of the Former Soviet Republics," in John Williamson, ed., *Economic Consequences of Soviet Disintegration* (Washington, D.C.: Institute for International Economics, 1993), p. 70.

34. "Grigoriy Yavlins'kyy skazav, shcho Ukraina musyt' sebe porakhuvaty," *Post-Postup*, 17–23 February 1994, p. A3.

35. Barry Eichengreen, "A Payments Union for the Former Soviet Union: Is the EPU a Relevant Precedent," *Economic Policy* 17 (October 1993): 310–353.

36. Yuriy Vatalyevich Shishkov, "CIS Economic Union: Projects and Problems," *Rossiyskiy Ekonomicheskiy Zhurnal*, no. 9 (September 1994): 56–66, translated in FBIS-USR-94-109, 6 October 1994, p. 6.

37. The 1994 figure is from Open Media Research Institute (hereafter *OMRI*) *Daily Digest*, part II, 9 February 1995. Another estimate stated that Russia accounted for 59 percent of Ukraine's imports, mostly in energy supplies (*OMRI Daily Digest*, part II, 28 February 1995). The 1995 figure is for the first nine months of that year and is from O.S. Samodurov, "Z Nashym Stratehichnym Partnerom," *Polityka I Chas* (1996) p. 38.

38. Karen Dawisha and Bruce Parrott, *Russia and the New States of Eurasia* (New York: Cambridge University Press, 1994), p. 177.

39. Leonid Kravchuk, on Radio Kiev, 10 October 1991, in FBIS-SOV-91-198, 11 October 1991, p. 64.

40. N. Gorenko, "Some Favor Resignation, Others Deferment," *Krasnaya Zvezda*, 10 October 1993, p. 3, translated in FBIS-SOV-91-198, 11 October 1991, p. 64.

41. TASS International Service, 26 November 1991, translated in FBIS-SOV-91-229, 27 November 1991, p. 59.

42. ADN, 21 September 1991, translated in FBIS-SOV-91-184, 23 September 1991, p. 67.

43. Leonid Kravchuk, "Vystup na Urochystomu Zasidanni Verkhovnoi Rady Ukrainy," 5 December 1991, in Leonid Kravchuk, *Ye Taka Derzhava—Ukraina* (Kiev: Globus, 1992), p. 12.

44. Alexander J. Motyl, *Dilemmas of Independence: Ukraine after Totalitarianism* (New York: Council on Foreign Relatiuons Press, 1993), pp. 138–139.

45. In particular, Russia's unilateral reform appeared to contradict several parts of the agreement signed following the establishment of the CIS, "to conduct coordinated economic reforms . . . ; to refrain from any actions inflicting economic damage on one another . . . ; to pursue a coordinated policy of price liberalization." "Declaration by the Governments of the Republic of Belarus, the Russian Federation, and the Ukraine on Coordination of Economic Policy," TASS International Service, 8 December 1991, translated in FBIS-SOV-91-236, 9 December 1991, p. 48.

46. *RFE/RL*, 27 December 1991.

47. Postfactum, 26 December 1991, translated in FBIS-SOV-91-249, 27 December 1991, p. 57.

48. Simon Johnson and Oleg Ustenko, "Ukraine," in Michael L. Wyzan, ed., *First Steps Toward Economic Independence* (Westport, Conn.: Praeger, 1995), p. 61.

49. *RFE/RL*, 2 January 1992.

50. *RFE/RL*, 11 June 1992.

51. *RFE/RL*, 10 January 1992.

52. Wyzan, "Introduction," p. 8.

53. Becker, p. 122.

54. Duran, p. 214.

55. *Postfactum*, 26 December 1991, translated in FBIS-SOV-91-249, 27 December 1991, p. 57.

56. Leonid Kravchuk, "Todi My Skazhemo: Ye Mohutna Ukraina," (interview with *Nezavisimaya Gazeta*, 30 January 1992), in Kravchuk, *Ye Taka Derzhava—Ukraina*, p. 44. See also the interview with *Le Figaro*, 23 January 1992, in ibid., p. 36.

57. While the Russian reform explains the hasty introduction of Ukrainian coupons, it does not account for the establishment of a separate currency,

which Ukraine would have done anyway. Ukraine had already discussed plans to introduce coupons in September 1991. The unplanned introduction of the currency, however, guaranteed that it would be unstable, contributing to trade uncertainty as well as domestic inflation.

58. When prices were liberalized, electricity rates were raised twelvefold for rural customers, and sixfold for urban. Price rises on many basic food items were intially limited to three times their previous price (for a list of price rises in Ukraine, see Kiev Radio Network, 31 December 1991, translated in FBIS-SOV-92-001, 2 January 1992, pp. 87–89). By August 1994, wages had been increased 400 percent (*EIU Country Profile: Ukraine*, 1993–1994, pp. 13–14).

59. *PlanEcon Report*, 15 September 1992, p. 7. An additional requirement that purchases over 4,000 rubles be made in coupons was aimed at making it much more difficult for citizens of other states to purchase goods in Ukraine.

60. Steven J. Woehrel, "Political-Economic Assessments: Ukraine," in Kaufman and Hardt, eds, *The Former Soviet Union in Transition*.

61. This paragraph is based on Dawisha and Parrot, p. 177.

62. Alexander Motyl makes a similar argument, contending that given the chaotic nature of economies in the region, larger units of economic administration do not make sense (pp. 132–133).

63. *INTERFAX*, 4 May 1992, translated in FBIS-SOV-92-87, 5 May 1992.

64. Mykhaylo Stasiuk, "Nashi Vikhy," *Derzhavnist'*, no. 2 (February 1993): 14.

65. "L. Kravchuk's Report Was a Bombshell," *Komsomolskaya Pravda*, 26 March 1992, pp. 1–2, translated in FBIS-SOV-92-060, 27 March 1992, p. 54. For a trenchant critque of the plan, see Mikhail Leontyev, "Couponization at a Faster Rate: The First Concept of Ukrainian Economic Reform," *Nezavisimaya Gazeta*, 1 April 1992, pp. 1, 4, translated in FBIS-USR-92-045, 22 April 1992, pp. 45–47.

66. Woehrel, pp. 966–967, "L. Kravchuk's Report," pp. 54–55.

67. "L. Kravchuk's Report," p. 55.

68. Dmitriy Kornilov, member of the coordinating council of Donbass Internationalist Movement, quoted by *Postfactum*, 23 March 1992, in FBIS-SOV-92-060, 27 March 1992, p. 56.

69. "L. Kravchuk's Report," p. 55.

70. INTERFAX, 31 December 1992, in FBIS-SOV-93-001, 4 January 1993, p. 45.

71. Granberg, p. 62.

72. *EIU Country Profile: Ukraine*, 1994–1995, p. 26.

73. *PlanEcon Report*, 20 December 1994, p. 6.

74. Another reason for introduction of the Ukrainian currency is that the high inflation it engendered, combined with the limited reform of the Ukrainian economy, produced negative real interest rates and hence large rents for those with access to government credit and/or export licenses. See Oleh

Havrylyshyn, Marcus Miller, and William Perraudin, "Deficits, Inflation, and the Political Economy of Ukraine," *Economic Policy* 19 (October 1994): 356, 371. It is of course impossible to weigh this influence, but it is worth keeping in mind that some individuals gained immensely from the collapse of the Ukrainian economy.

75. Havrylyshyn, Miller, and Perraudin, pp. 357–359.

76. See John Lloyd and Steve LeVine, "West Sees Danger in End of Rouble Zone," *Financial Times*, 12 November 1993, p. 2; and "The Cost of Monetary Chaos," *The Economist*, 20 November 1993, pp. 77–78. *The Economist* contends that the dissolution of the ruble zone was to the advantage of Russia and the disadvantage of other republics, who could no longer export their inflation to Russia. Havrylyshyn, Miller, and Perraudin (p. 377) harshly criticize the IMF for supporting the ruble zone.

77. The Ukrainian Karbanovets' lost 46 percent of its value against the dollar in one day, 30 March 1993, and inflation throughout 1993 approached 75 percent per month. Inflation and the value of the currency against the dollar stabilized somewhat in the first half of 1994, as currency emissions were limited, but skyrocketed again in the fall, following an annual cycle in which government payments to farmers at harvest time lead to inflation. More prudent monetary policy, facilitated by IMF credits, has since stabilized the *karbovanets'* and its successor, the *hryvnya*.

78. Duran, p. 33.

79. Motyl, p. 136.

80. Ukraine's introduction of coupons also caused inflation in Russia, where rubles displaced in Ukraine accumulated.

81. "The Cost of Monetary Chaos," *The Economist*, 20 November 1993, pp. 77–78.

82. Union Bank of Switzerland, *New Horizon Economies*, February 1997; *Houston Chronicle*, 19 May 1997.

83. "Ukraine Over the Brink," *The Economist*, 4 September 1993, p. 4.

84. Nikolai Zabirko, "Mozhet Uzhi Zalozhilo?" *Donetskii Kryazh*, 11–17 February 1994, p. 1.

85. Zabirko, p. 1; see also "Na Granitsye s Rossiyei," *Luhanskaya Pravda*, 27 January 1994, p. 1.

86. *RFE/RL* 16 March 1994.

87. Jill Barshay and Leyla Boulton, "Poll Widens Ukraine's East-West Split," *Financial Times*, 29 March 1994, p. 2.

88. INTERFAX, 4 February 1993, translated in FBIS-SOV, 5 February 1993.

89. A document on ending the economic crisis published in late 1992, after several months of isolation, continued to advocate isolation as a means to improve Ukraine's economic situation ("How to Get Out of the Crisis: The Program Developed by Scholars and People's Deputies Is Offered as a Working

Blueprint for the Ukrainian Government," *Golos Ukrainy,* 18 November 1992, pp. 6–8, translated in FBIS-USR-92-161, 16 December 1992, pp. 34–35).

90. INTERFAX, 6 March 1993, in FBIS-SOV-93-044, 9 March 1993, p. 36.

91. ITAR-TASS, 10 July 1993, translated in FBIS-SOV-93-131, 12 July 1993, p. 1.

92. The CIS Economic Union is analyzed in detail in Shishkov, "CIS Economic Union."

93. *RFE/RL,* 23 August 1993. Plyushch's opposition may have been based not simply on the economic content of the treaty, but on some of the overtly political content that seemed to bode ill for Ukraine's independence: "The governments particularly stress that they will strictly protect the legal interests of their fellow countrymen who live outside their states" (ITAR-TASS, 10 July 1993, translated in FBIS-SOV-93-131, 12 July 1993, p. 1).

94. Kravchuk interview on Ostankino television, 24 August 1993, translated in FBIS-SOV-93-163, 25 August 1993, p. 32. It is difficult to know if this was Kravchuk's genuine opinion, for Kravchuk was quoted as saying on 7 September that "we should not be a party to anything the Russian Federation is involved in" ("Leonid Kravchuk: 'The Main Enemy is Russia,' We Await Denial," *Pravda,* 15 September 1993, pp. 1–2, translated in FBIS-SOV-93-178, 16 September 1993, p. 36).

95. Speech by Kravchuk to the Verkhovna Rada, 11 November 1993, Kiev Radio World Service, translated in FBIS-SOV-93-218, 15 November 1993, p. 67.

96. *PlanEcon Report,* 20 December 1994, p. 13. It is not clear how much of this recovery occurred before Kuchma took over, or as a result of policies enacted before he took over.

97. "Statement of the Third All-Ukraine Assembly of the Ukrainian National Movement Concerning the Economic Sitution in Ukraine," *Narodna Hazeta,* March 1992, p. 1, translated in FBIS-USR-92-045, 22 April 1992, p. 47.

98. Quoted in "Zastyv na meste, Ukraina priblizhaetsya k propasti," *Donetskii Kryazh* (11–17 February 1994), p. 4.

99. Kravchuk interview on Ostankino television, 24 August 1993, translated in FBIS-SOV-93-163, 25 August 1993, p. 32.

100. Kuchma Inauguration speech, 19 July 1994, Kiev Radio World Service, translated in FBIS-SOV-94-139, 20 July 1994, p. 35.

101. Kuchma Inauguration speech, p. 37.

102. *RFE/RL,* 13 September 1994. See also Jill Barshay, "'Twere Well It Were Done Quickly," *Financial Times,* 2 August 1994, p. 14; and Mykola Tkachenko, "Read My Lips: No New Soviet Union," *Krieble Institute Monitor,* vol. II, no. 18 (15 October 1994).

103. Volodymyr Skachko, "Market Supporter Plus Noncommunist Plus Nonnationalist Equals Reformer?" *Holos Ukrainy*, 19 October 1994, p. 3, translated in FBIS-SOV-94-206, p. 43.

104. For examples of this new, much narrower debate, see Volodymyr Sidenko, "Economic Independence or Economic Efficiency: Foreign Economic Strategies in the Economy of Transitional Period," *Politychna Dumka/Political Thought*, 2 (1994): 160–166; Sidenko, "Geoeconomic Problems of Social Development," *Politychna Dumka/Political Thought*, 1 (1995): 171–177; Volodymyr Horbulin, "Nasha meta, nasha dolia," *Polityka I Chas*, 1 (1996): 3–8; Serhiy Fomin, "Tema dlia serioznykh rozdumov," *Polityka I Chas*, 3 (1996): 19–30; Vadym Beliaiev, "Nehatyvni naslidky—nemynuchi," *Politika I Chas*, 3 (1996): 25–30, and the roundtable discussion "A nam shcho robyty z Rosiieiu," *Politika I Chas*, 3–4 (1996): 7–18; 12–25.

6. Independence Sovereignty, and the Commonwealth of Independent States

1. Mykola Kulinych, "Ukraine and the CIS," *Politychna Dumka/Political Thought*, 3 (1994): 191–192.

2. Robert O. Keohane, *After Hegemony* (Princeton: Princeton University Press, 1984).

3. Anna Kreikemeyer and Andrei V. Zagorski, "The Commonwealth of Independent States," in Lena Jonson and Clive Archer, eds., *Peacekeeping and the Role of Russia in Eurasia* (Boulder: Westview Press, 1996), p. 164.

4. Hedley Bull, *The Anarchical Society* (New York: Columbia University Press, 1977), p. 108.

5. Lisa L. Martin, "The Rational State Choice of Multilateralism," in John G. Ruggie, ed., *Multilateralism Matters: The Theory and Praxis of an International Form* (New York: Columbia University Press, 1993), pp. 105–106.

6. John G. Ruggie, "Multilateralism: The Anatomy of an Institution," in Ruggie, *Multilateralism Matters*, p. 23; Martin contends that this legitimation provides for "quasi-voluntary compliance" (p. 110). James A. Caporaso points out that what the rules are and what constitutes a violation are determined by the organization ("International Relations Theory and Multilateralism: The Search for Foundations," in Ruggie, *Multilateralism Matters*, p. 63). In the case of the CIS, Russia has attempted to have the UN designate the CIS as a regional international organization. Doing so would, under the UN Charter, allow the CIS to conduct regional peacekeeping at its own discretion. For Russia, this would legitimate much of its activity in the "near abroad." The proposal has been strongly condemned by many of the other states in the region.

7. G. John Ikenberry and Charles A. Kupchan, "Legitimacy and Power: The Waning of U.S. and Soviet Hegemony," in Henry Bienen, ed., *Power, Economics, and Security* (Boulder: Westview Press, 1992).

8. Mark R. Beissinger, "The Persisting Ambiguity of Empire," *Post-Soviet Affairs* (April/June 1995): 169.

9. Drawing a parallel from Kenneth Shepsle's writing on domestic legislatures, Miles Kahler argues that in an international organization, there is no mechanism to enforce agreements. Large states can therefore always exit from an agreement they dislike (Miles Kahler, "Multilateralism with Large and Small Numbers," in Ruggie, *Multilateralism Matters*, pp. 317–318). Limiting the power of the hegemon is important because, as Cowhey asserts, "multilateralism provides even fewer external checks on dominant powers than purely bilateral . . . orders do" (Peter F. Cowhey, "Elect Locally—Order Globally: Domestic Politics and Multilateral Cooperation," in Ruggie, *Multilateralism Matters*, p. 157). He finds no international checks at all on a hegemon's ability to renege. Instead, he contends, the other states must rely on the domestic structure of the hegemon to prevent it from reneging.

10. Bull, p. 108. See also pp. 106–107.

11. Taras Kuzio, "Ukraine and Its 'Near Abroad,'" *Politychna Dumka/Political Thought*, 3 (1994): 198.

12. Oleksandr Dergachov, "Geopolitical Constellations in the Postcommunist World," *Politychna Dumka/Political Thought*, 1 (1995): 167.

13. Vice-President Rutskoi stated that Russia would not complete an economic union agreement without an accompanying political union (TASS International Service, 10 October 1991, translated in FBIS-SOV-91-198, 11 October 1991, p. 63).

14. Anna Kozyreva, "An Economic Union May Arise within the Framework of the CIS," *Rossiyskiye Vesti*, 21 July 1993, p. 3, translated in FBIS-USR-94-083, 2 August 1994, p. 3.

15. Vadym Beliaiev, "Negatyvni naslidky—nemynuchi," *Politika I Chas*, 3 (March 1996): 28.

16. *RFE/RL*, 12, 15 September 1991.

17. See for example Kravchuk's speech, cited in the previous chapter, on Radio Kiev, 10 October 1991, in FBIS-SOV-91-198, 11 October 1991, p. 64.

18. *RFE/RL*, 17 September 1991.

19. *RFE/RL*, 18 September 1991.

20. *RFE/RL*, 24 September 1991.

21. The text of the treaty is printed in the *Washington Post*, 10 December 1991, p. A32.

22. *RFE/RL*, 12 December 1991.

23. *RFE/RL*, 1, 7, 10 October 1991.

24. *Financial Times*, 17 December 1991, quoted in Solchanyk, "Kravchuk Defines Ukrainian-CIS Relations," p. 9.

25. ITAR-TASS, 5 September 1992, quoted by Ann Sheehy, "The CIS: A Progress Report," *RFE/RL Research Report*, vol. 1, no. 38 (25 September 1992): 6.

26. *RFE/RL*, 30 September 1991.

27. *RFE/RL*, 7 January 1992. Russia's suggestion that it represent others' diplomatic interests abroad must have appeared ominous to Ukraine: Prior to the Union Treaty of 1922, the first major step in ending the sovereignty of the Ukrainian S.S.R. was an agreement for Russia to represent all the Soviet states at the Genoa conference.

28. *RFE/RL*, 3 June 1992.

29. *RFE/RL*, 19 September 1991.

30. *RFE/RL*, 21 October 1991.

31. *RFE/RL*, 27 February 1992.

32. *RFE/RL*, 23 September 1991.

33. *RFE/RL*, 8 April 1992. Shaposhnikov later modified his proposal to give Ukraine 20 percent of the fleet and Russia 80 percent, leaving none for the CIS forces which Shaposhnikov commanded (RFE/RL 24 April 1992). The issue was muddled even further when the newly appointed Russian Defense Minister, Pavel Grachev, contradicted Yeltsin by advocating that the fleet not be divided between Russia and Ukraine, but remain subject to CIS control (*RFE/RL*, 11 June 1992).

34. *RFE/RL*, 30 September, 1 October 1992. He reiterated his belief that Russia should control the nuclear weapons in November (*RFE/RL*, 18 November 1992).

35. *RFE/RL*, 13 October 1992.

36. *RFE/RL*, 3 April 1992.

37. *RFE/RL*, 3 June 1992.

38. *RFE/RL*, 8 April 1992.

39. Sheehy, "The CIS: A Progress Report," p. 2.

40. Sheehy, "The CIS: A Progress Report," p. 2.

41. Sheehy, "The CIS: A Progress Report," pp. 2–3.

42. *Molod Ukrainy* and *Nezavisimaya gazeta*, 22 September 1992, quoted in Roman Solchanyk, "Ukraine and the CIS: A Troubled Relationship," *RFE/RL Research Report*, vol. 2, no. 17 (12 February 1993): 24.

43. Solchanyk, "Ukraine and the CIS," p. 25.

44. *RFE/RL*, 26 May 1992.

45. *RFE/RL*, 29 May 1992.

46. *RFE/RL*, 17 August, 22 September 1992.

47. *RFE/RL*, 2 March 1993.

48. On the similarities in Russian/CIS peacekeeping in Moldova and Georgia, see Suzanne Crow, "The Theory and Practice of Peacekeeping in the Former USSR," *RFE/RL Research Report*, vol. 1, no. 37, 18 September 1992, p. 31.

49. *RFE/RL*, 28 June 1993.

50. *RFE/RL*, 29 September 1994.

51. *RFE/RL*, 29 October 1994.

52. *RFE/RL*, 1, 2, 4 March 1993. See Suzanne Crow, "Russia Seeks Leadership in Regional Peacekeeping," *RFE/RL Research Report*, vol. 2, no. 15 (9 April 1993): 28–32.

53. *RFE/RL*, 17 March 1994.

54. The issue of the CIS Charter is discussed in some detail in Solchanyk, "Ukraine and the CIS: A Troubled Relationship," pp. 23–27.

55. Ann Sheehy, "The CIS: A Shaky Edifice," *RFE/RL Research Report*, vol. 2, no. 1 (1 January 1993): 39.

56. See John Lloyd, "Russia Begins to Choose between Union and Empire," *Financial Times*, 18 April 1994, p. 2.

57. *RFE/RL*, 14 May 1993. It seems that Russia was confronting at this point "the hegemon's dilemma." See Arthur Stein, "The Hegemon's Dilemma: Great Britain, The United States, and the International Economic Order," *International Organization* 38 (1984): 355–86. A potential or actual hegemon, Stein argues, must pay a disproportionate share of the costs of cooperation, and thus must choose between maintaining hegemony and securing individual long-term economic power.

58. *RFE/RL*, 14, 16 June 1993.

59. *RFE/RL*, 16 June 1993.

60. Solchanyk, "Ukraine and the CIS: A Troubled Relationship," p. 25.

61. Sheehy, "Seven States Sign Charter Strengthening CIS," *RFE/RL Research Report*, vol. 2, no. 9 (26 February 1993): 11.

62. "Ukraine and the CIS: A Troubled Relationship," p. 23.

63. Sheehy, "Seven States Sign Charter," p. 12.

64. Sheehy, "Seven States Sign Charter," p. 12.

65. The shortcomings of the Interstate Economic Bank as created are discussed by Sheehy, "Seven States Sign Charter," p. 13.

66. Solchanyk, "Ukraine and the CIS: A Troubled Relationship," p. 26.

67. Sheehy, "Seven States Sign Charter," p. 12.

68. Yelsin is paraphrased by Sheehy, "The CIS: A Progress Report," p. 1. Rutskoi is quoted in *RFE/RL*, 18 November 1992.

69. *RFE/RL*, 26 July 1993.

70. *RFE/RL*, 4 November 1993.

71. *RFE/RL*, 12, 18 November 1993.

72. Mykhailo Maymeskal of the Ukrainian Foreign Ministry, quoted in Myroslav Levyts'kyi, "Prezidenty Radiat', A Chyny Hadiat'," *Za Vil'nu Ukrainu*, 13 April 1994, p. 1.

73. Valerii Kalyniuk, "Dohovir Ukrainy rozipne I vona vzhe nykoly ne voskresne," *Vysokyi Zamok*, 4 September 1993, p. 1. The author went on to

compare the economic union treaty with the Soviet union treaty of 1922, and concluded that "The similarities between the two documents are remarkable."

74. *Vysokyi Zamok*, 4 September 1993, p. 1.

75. On Kuchma's views prior to the election, see Maria Kara, "Rozkol 'Rosiyskoi' Ukrainy," *Post-Postup* (17–24 March 1994), pp. 1–2, and "Leonid Kuchma: 'Vlady v Ukraini s'ohodni nemaie. Pravliat' bal zovsim inshi syly,'" *Vysokyi Zamok*, 12 April 1994, p. 2.

76. *RFE/RL*, 14 September 1994. See also Mykola Tkachenko, "Read My Lips: No New Soviet Union," *Krieble Institute Monitor*, vol. II, no. 18 (15 October 1994).

77. On bilateralism in the former Soviet Union, see Paul D'Anieri, "International Cooperation among Unequal Partners: The Emergence of Bilateralism in the Former Soviet Union," *International Politics* vol. 34, no. 4 (December 1997): 417–448.

78. See Roman Sochanyk, "Kravchuk Defines Ukraine-CIS Relations, *RFE/RL Research Report* (13 March 1992): 7; Ukraine's preference for bilateral cooperation was discussed by Kravchuk in detail late 1992 (see Solchanyk, "Ukraine and the CIS: A Trouble Relationship," p. 25). It was elaborated more recently in an interview on Ukrainian Television, 2 April 1994.

79. Reuters, 2 December 1991, quoted in Solchanyk, "Kravchuk Defines," p. 7.

80. Sheehy, "Seven States Sign Charter," pp. 10–11.

81. Sheehy, "The CIS: A Progress Report," p. 4.

82. Solchanyk, "Ukraine and the CIS," p. 25.

83. Solchanyk, "Ukraine and the CIS," p. 25.

84. Volodymyr Horbulin, "Nasha Meta, Nasha Dolia," *Polityka I Chas* 1 (1996): 6.

85. Yuriy Vatalyevich Shishkov, "CIS Economic Union: Prospects and Problems," *Rossiyskiy Ekonomicheskiy Zhurnal*, no. 9 (September 1994): 56–66, translated in FBIS-USR-94-109, 6 October 1994, p. 7.

7. The Direct Economics-Security Connection

1. *RFE/RL*, 23 September 1993.

2. Ukraine's nuclear arsenal is detailed in Bhupendra Jasani, "Ukraine's ICBM Arsenal," *Jane's Intelligence Review*, March 1994, pp. 120–122.

3. See Stephen M. Meyer, "Soviet Nuclear Operations," in Ashton B. Carter, John D. Steinbruner, and Charles A. Zraket, eds., *Managing Nuclear Operations* (Washington, D.C.: Brookings, 1987).

4. On Ukraine's pivotal role in the broader arms control process, see Michael Mihalka, "Ukraine: Salvaging Nuclear Arms Control," *Transition* (12 May 1995): 30–35.

5. See Jason Ellis, "The 'Ukrainian Dilemma' and U.S. Foreign Policy," *European Security*, vol. 3, no. 2 (Summer 1994): 251–280.

6. A 1993 article enumerated six ways in which Russia could injure Ukraine. Direct military attack was not among them. Instead the list focused on the various political and economic ways Russia could destabilize Ukraine internally (Vasyl Kremin', Borys Parakhons'kyi, and Petro Sytnyk, "Ukraina I Rosiia: Sfery Konfrontatsii I Spivrobitnitstva," *Rozbudova Derzhava*, 2 (February 1993), p. 7.

7. The crucial role of sovereignty in Ukraine's security policy is discussed in Ustina Markus, "Foreign Policy as a Security Tool," *Transition* (28 July 1995): 12–17.

8. Jack Snyder, "Containing Post-Soviet Nationalism: International Substitutes for Impotent States," The National Council for Soviet and East European Research, contract no. 806–11, 6 July 1992, pp. 33–34, cited in Ellis, "The 'Ukrainian Dilemma,'" pp. 266–267. See also Serhiy Tolstov, "Heopolitychni Chynyky Natsional'noi Bezpeky," *Geneza* 2 (1994): 173.

9. Taras Kuzio, "From Parish to Partner—Ukraine and Nuclear Weapons," *Jane's Intelligence Review*, May 1994, p. 204.

10. Mihalka, p. 31.

11. Kuzio, "From Parish to Partner," p. 204.

12. "Speculation has surrounded the Kharkov-based Khartron plant where the nuclear expertise exists to enable Ukrine, if it so desired, to research retargeting and operational control of strategic nuclear missiles located on its territory" (Taras Kuzio, "Ukraine's Military Industrial Plan," *Jane's Intelligence Review*, August 1994, p. 352).

13. The reasons a Russian attack on Ukraine is unlikely are discussed in Charles Dick, "The Military Doctrine of Ukraine," *Jane's Intelligence Review*, March 1994, p. 119.

14. Two excellent chronological accounts of the evolution of Ukrainian thinking on nuclear weapons are Bohdan Nahaylo, "The Shaping of Ukrainian Attitudes Towards Nuclear Weapons," *RFE/RL Research Report*, vol. 2, no. 8 (19 February 1993), which I have relied upon heavily below, and Sherman W. Garnett, "The Sources and Conduct of Ukrainian Nuclear Policy," in George Quester, ed., *The Nuclear Challenge in Russia and the New States of Eurasia* (Armonk, N.Y.: M. E. Sharpe, 1995).

15. The importance of Chernobyl in Ukraine's nonnuclear policy was stated by Kravchuk after independence. See the interview with Kravchuk in *Izvestiya*, 2 January 1992, translated in FBIS-SOV-92-002, 3 January 1992,

p. 55. It was reiterated by Kuchma at the conclusion of Ukraine's disarmament in June 1996 ("Ukraine Free of Nuclear Weapons," *Transition* (28 June 1996): 62.

16. Professor Manzhola of the Ukrainian Center for International Research, quoted in Yuriy Lenov, "Russia and Ukraine—After the Fall of the CIS," *Nezavisimaya Gazeta*, 18 April 1992, p. 2, translated in FBIS-USR-92-056, 9 May 1992, p. 11.

17. George Bush, "Remarks to the Supreme Soviet of the Republic of Ukraine in Kiev, Soviet Union," August 1, 1991, in *Weekly Compilation of Presidential Documents*, vol. 27, no. 31 (5 August 1991): 1093–1096.

18. John W. R. Lepingwell, "Ukraine, Russia, and the Control of Nuclear Weapons," *RFE/RL Research Report*, vol. 2, no. 8 (19 February 1993): 1.

19. Nahaylo, p. 23.

20. "Given Ukraine's history of coerced and forced annexation, it is hardly surprising that on the day Ukraine's leaders declared absolute sovereignty and full independence from Moscow, they simultaneously moved to create an armed force capable of defending the new state" (Karen Dawisha and Bruce Parrott, *Russia and the New States of Eurasia* (New York: Cambridge University Press, 1994), p. 245.) Similarly, John Morrison states: "Ukraine's political elite has experienced the events of 1990–1993 as a replay of 1917–1920. It is this memory of military defeat that explains the absolute proirity given to the creation of independent armed forces at independence ("Pereyaslav and After: The Russian-Ukrainian Relationship," *International Affairs* 69, 4 [1993]: 680).

21. Nahaylo, p. 26. See Nahaylo, pp. 25–26 for a more detailed survey of Ukrainian views in the early autumn of 1991.

22. Quoted in Jonathan Steele, "Ukraine Will Retain Its Nuclear Arms," *The Guardian*, 30 September 1991.

23. Nahaylo, p. 27.

24. "Presidium Statement on 'Own Armed Forces,'" Kiev Radio Kiev Network, 26 November 1991, translated in FBIS-SOV-91-230, 29 November 1991, p. 45. This position was reiterated by Foreign Minister Anatoliy Zlenko shortly after the independence vote in December. See "Foreign Minister Zlenko Outlines Policies," Kiev Radio Kiev Network, 4 December 1991, translated in FBIS-SOV-91-234, 5 December 1991, p. 63.

25. Lepingwell, "Ukraine, Russia, and the Control of Nuclear Weapons," 5–6.

26. Quoted in Nahaylo, p. 25.

27. "Kravchuk: Yeltsin Failed to Consult on Arms," *Izvestiya*, 4 February 1992, p. 2, translated in FBIS-SOV-92-025, 6 February 1992, p. 59.

28. See Kravchuk's statement in an interview with TASS, 26 November 1991, translated in FBIS-SOV-91-229, 27 November 1991, p. 59.

29. *Arms Control Today*, June 1992, pp. 34–36, cited in Nahaylo, p. 36. For a Russian assessment, see Sergei Rogov, "Military Interests and the Interests of the Military," in Stephen Sestanovich, ed., Rethinking Russia's National Interest (Washington, D.C.: Center for Strategic and International Studies, 1994), p. 71.

30. See "Kravchuk Speech on Domestic, Foreign Policy, Kiev Radio, 5 December 1991, translated in FBIS-SOV-91-235, 6 December 1995, p. 73. This position was not inconsistent with Kravchuk's signing an agreement later that month committing Ukraine to sign the NPT as a nonnuclear state ("Agreement on Joint Measures on Nuclear Weapons," *Pravda*, 23 December 1991, p. 2, translated in FBIS-SOV-91–246, 23 December 1991, p. 30). Ukraine was willing to give up the weapons, but sought to control them while they remained in Ukraine.

31. "'Text' of Alma-Ata Declaration," TASS, 21 December 1991, translated in FBIS-SOV-91-246, 23 December 1991, p. 29.

32. Serhii Korotayevsky, Radio Kiev, 24 October 1991, quoted in Nahaylo, pp. 28–29.

33. Unidentified Ukrainian parliamentarian, quoted in "Ukraine May 'Attempt to Remain' Nuclear Power," ITAR-TASS, 30 March 1992, translated in FBIS-SOV-92-061, 30 March 1992, p. 1.

34. Quoted in Nahaylo, p. 34.

35. *Arms Control Today*, June 1992, pp. 34–36, cited in Nahaylo, p. 36.

36. "Ukraine May 'Attempt to Remain' Nuclear Power," ITAR-TASS, 30 March 1992, translated in FBIS-SOV-92-061, 30 March 1992, p. 1.

37. Quoted in Ellis, "The 'Ukrainian Dilemma,'" p. 260.

38. John W. R. Lepingwell, "The Control of Former Soviet Nuclear Weapons: A Chronology," *RFE/RL Research Report*, vol. 2, no. 18 (19 February 1993): 72.

39. Nahaylo, p. 31.

40. Quoted by Nahaylo, p. 37.

41. Nahaylo, p. 39.

42. John J. Mearsheimer, "The Case for a Ukrainian Nuclear Deterrent," Foreign Affairs (Summer 1993): 50–66; Kenneth N. Waltz, "Waltz Responds to Sagan," in Kenneth N. Waltz and Scott D. Sagan, *The Spread of Nuclear Weapons: A Debate* (New York: W. W. Norton, 1995), p. 112; Barry R. Posen, "The Security Dilemma and Ethnic Conflict," *Survival*, vol. 35, no. 1 (Spring 1993): 30.

43. For an analysis of the pronuclear lobby in Ukraine, see Arkadiy Moshes, "Nuclear Policy of a Non-Nuclear Country," *Novoye Vremya*, no. 5 (January 1993), pp. 8–10, translated in FBIS-SOV-93-026, 10 February 1993, pp. 1–3.

44. *Uryadovyi Kuryer*, 4 December 1992, quoted in Nahaylo, p. 39.

45. Ellis, "The 'Ukrainian Dilemma,'" p. 260.

46. Col. Valeriy Izmalkov, "A Nuclear Missile Is Not a Stone Ax," *Holos Ukrainy*, 22 December 1992, p. 7, translated in FBIS-SOV-93–005, 8 January 1993, p. 1.

47. Izmalkov, p. 1.

48. Oleg Dergachov, "Problems of National Security," *Politychna Dumka/Political Thought*, no. 1 (1993): p. 136. See also Tolstov, "Heopolitychni Chynyky," p. 176.

49. Monika Jung, "A New Concept of European Security" [interview with Boris Tarasyuk], *Transition* (28 July 1995): 21.

50. Charles Dick, "The Military Doctrine of Ukraine, *Jane's Intelligence Review*, March 1994, p. 117.

51. *The Washington Post*, 6 November 1992, quoted in Nahaylo, p. 41.

52. Nahaylo, p. 41.

53. The course of negotiations in 1993 and early 1994 is covered in great detail in John W. R. Lepingwell, "Negotiations over Nuclear Weapons: The Past as Prologue," *RFE/RL Research Report*, vol. 3, no. 4 (28 January 1994).

54. The text of the Verkhovna Rada's is in "Supreme Council START I Ratification Resolution," *UNIAR*, 18 November 1993, translated in FBIS-SOV-93-222, 19 November 1993, p. 45.

55. John W. R. Lepingwell, "The Trilateral Agreement on Nuclear Weapons," *RFE/RL Research Report*, Vol. 3, No. 4 (28 January 1994): 12.

56. The agreement and its Annex are printed in Lepingwell, "The Trilateral Agreement," pp. 14–15.

57. Lepingwell, "The Trilateral Agreement," pp. 13–14.

8. Internal Divisions and Ukrainian Economic Vulnerability

1. Simon Johnson and Oleg Ustenko, "Ukraine," in Michael L. Wyzan, ed., *First Steps Toward Economic Independence* (Westport, Conn.: Praeger, 1995), pp. 51–52.

2. Ihor Buryakovskyi describes Ukraine as a "passive" respondent to others' policies, due to its own lack of strategy. See "On the Way to 'Guided' Integration?" *Politychna Dumka/Political Thought* 3 (1994): 190–191.

3. Michael L. Wyzan, "Introduction," in Michael L. Wyzan, ed., *First Steps Toward Economic Independence* (Westport, Conn.: Praeger, 1995), pp. 2–3.

4. Peter J. Katzenstein, "The Small European States in the International Economy: Economic Dependence and Corporatist Politics," in John G. Ruggie, ed., *The Antinomies of Interdependence* (New York: Columbia University Press, 1982). It might seem odd to compare Ukraine to the small European states. The theory as constructed, however, is not meant to be limited to

a particular set of states, as Katzenstein emphasizes when he states: "The domestic structures of the small European states, far from being unique, can aid in the analysis of the domestic structures of other states. . . . the analysis of the structures . . . should shed light on the more general political correlates of successful economic strategies," and specifically cites the communist states in this regard (pp. 128–130). And while Ukraine is as large in population and area as the large Western European states, it is relatively small compared to its main trading partner, Russia.

5. Oleksandr Dergachov, "Geopolitical Constellations in the Postcommunist World," *Politychna Dumka/Political Thought*, 1 (1995): 168.

6. A brief analysis of the concept of state strength is in Stephen D. Krasner, *Structural Conflict: The Third World Against Global Liberalism* (Berkeley: University of California Press, 1985), pp. 38–39. He refers to a state's "internal capacity to modulate and adjust to the pressures emanating from an uncertain international environment."

7. On the degree of parallel between demographic and political differences in Ukraine, see Paul D'Anieri and Oksana Malanchuk, "National Identity in Ukrainian Foriegn Policy," paper presented at the meeting of the International Society of Political Psychology, Washington, D.C., 8 July 1995.

8. The report is cited in Jill Barshay, "Two Cities campaign for Soul of Ukraine," *Financial Times*, 25 March 1994, p. 3.

9. Oleksandr Dergachov and Serhiy Makeyev, "Three Years of Ukrainian Independence: Trends of Social Development," *Politychna Dumka/Political Thought*, 4 (1994): 105–110.

10. These observations are based on data collected by Oksana Malanchuk and her colleagues. I am very grateful to them for sharing this data with me.

11. On this point see Sherman W Garnett, "The Ukrainian Question and the Future of Russia," *Politychna Dumka/Political Thought*, 4 (1994): 173–174.

12. Several analysts have provided a more detailed analysis of Ukraine's faultlines, dividing the country into east, west, southern, and central regions according to political tendencies. I retain the east-west division for the sake of simplicity. Essentially, southern Ukraine, and especially Crimea, stands politically with the east, while central Ukraine occupies a political position analogous to its geographical position, in the middle between east and west Ukraine. See Jacob W. Kipp, *Ukrainian and Belarus Presidential Elections: Prelude to a Crisis in the Western Borderlands of Russia* (Ft. Leavenworth: Foreign Military Studies Office, 1994).

13. Ustina Markus, "Foreign Policy as a Security Tool," *Transition* (28 July 1995): 15.

14. Even in Donetsk, the most Russophone area of east Ukraine, 80 percent voted for independence, compared to 90 percent in L'viv. Data are from

"Preliminary Referendum Data Reported," in FBIS-SOV-91-232, 3 December 1991, pp. 75–76.

15. *OMRI Daily Digest*, 10 January 1995.

16. Similarly, when Kuchma began implementing austerity measures in early 1995, opposition came from a combination of left- and right-wing members of parliament (*OMRI Daily Digest*, part II, 16 March 1995).

17. On nationalism in Ukraine's foreign, see Charles F. Furtado, Jr., "Nationalism and Foreign Policy in Ukraine," *Political Science Quarterly*, vol. 109, no. 1 (1994): 81–104.

18. Andrew Wilson, Ukrainian Nationalism in the 1990s: A Minority Faith (Cambridge: Cambridge University Press, 1997), p. 173.

19. Following the 1994 parliamentary elections, Rukh leader Vyacheslav Chornovil stated that Kuchma's bloc (the Interregional Bloc of Reform) was more dangerous than the Communists'. Cited by Vladimir Malinkovich, "Dangerous Games," *Obshchaya Gazeta*, 27 May 1994, p. 7, translated in FBIS-USR-94-063, 14 June 1994, p. 69.

20. Perhaps the most bizarre such alliance was the support by the right-wing nationalist group UNA-UNSO, in agreement with Ukrainian Communists and Russian Nationalists, of a Slavic Union. The difference was that in UNA-UNSO's plan, the union would be centered in Kiev rather than Moscow. See Oleksandr Kryvenko, "UNA-UNSO, The Bearer of Everything," *Post-Postup*, No. 42, 24–30 November 1994, p. 4, translated in FBIS-USR-94-136, pp. 44–45.

21. Serhiy Tolstov, "Heopolitychni Chnnyky Natsional'noi Bezpeky," *Geneza* 2 (1994): 172.

22. The need for small states to be able to restructure their economies rapidly in the face of external economic shocks is discussed by Katzenstein.

23. On the western nationalist reaction to the economic union treaty, see the articles in *Vysokyi Zamok*, 4 September 1993, p. 1.

24. Scholars using a social choice approach have demonstrated that, in the absense of clear institutional rules, policy choices tend to be unstable, making a consistent policy impossible.

25. Alexander J. Motyl, *Dilemmas of Independence: Ukraine After Totalitarianism* (New York: Council on Foreign Relations, 1993), p. 50; see also his chapter 2. Voldymyr Polokhalo, "The Neo-Totalitarian Transformations of Post-Communist Power in Ukraine," *Politychna Dumka/Political Thought*, 3 (1994): 133–134.

26. Markov, p. 32.

27. Voldymyr Polokhalo, "The Neo-Totalitarian Transformations of Post-Communist Power in Ukraine," *Politychna Dumka/Political Thought*, 3 (1994): 133–134.

28. Markov, p. 32.

29. Motyl, p. 173.

30. After being elected president, Kuchma said, "It is good that not a single political party supported me during the elections, as I am going to serve the people and not the party." See Oksana Holovko, "The Economy and Law and Order Are in the Foreground," *Uryadovyy Kuryer,* 16 July 1994, p. 2, translated in FBIS-SOV-94-139, 20 July 1994, p. 37.

31. Steven J. Woehrel, "Political-Economic Assessments: Ukraine," in Richard F. Kaufman and John P. Hardt, *The Former Soviet Union in Transition* (Armonk, N.Y.: M. E. Sharpe, 1993), p. 964.

32. This view was characterized by one observer in terms of the following thesis: "To support the President of Ukraine, who was elected by the whole nation, is to support independent state building. . . . Opposition to the President would lead to destroying the independent state." See Valentyn Yakushyk, "Establishment of the Multi-Party System," *Politychna Dumka/Political Thought,* no. 1 (1993): 122.

33. Motyl, p. 166.

34. See Dmytro Tabachnyk, "A Team That Does Not Like Playing Politics: The Government of Leonid Kuchma in the Setting of Modern Ukrainian History," *Ukrayina Moloda,* 22 January 1993, p. 4, translated in FBIS-USR-93-019, 24 February 1993, pp. 101–103. The author considers the apolitical nature of Kuchma's government and the absence of a program a virtue, because "it is not restricted to a certain party program" (p. 102). In the absense of such a program, however, it has been unclear what the government is trying to accomplish, or what it means when its decrees are rejected.

35. If thresholds are established at a low level, as they were in Poland's first postcommunist election, the system encourages party fragmentation, because any group that can get a tiny share of the vote (such as the Polish Beer Drinkers' party) can be represented.

36. Ivan Besyada, "Pershyi Parlament Nezalezhnoyi Derzhava Obrano," *Za Vil'ny Ukrainu,* 12 April 1994, p. 1.

37. These statistics are from "Settling in for More of the Same," *The Economist,* 19 March 1994, pp. 36–38.

38. In Ukrainian, like Soviet, election law, a candidate must win 50 percent of the vote to be elected. The Ukrainian law also specified that 50 percent of registered voters had to turn out for an election to be valid. In the first round, with so many candidates, only the most prominent national politicians won a majority. In the second round, which had only the top two in each district, many elections were invalidated by low turnout. Successive rounds were held, but some seats have not been filled due to voter apathy and the election law.

39. Oleg Shmid, "Vybory Staly Pomstoiu," *Post-Postup,* 15–24 April, 1994, p. 1.

40. Data are from "Lonely at the Top," *The Economist,* 16 April 1994, pp. 32, 37. A slightly different breakdown is provided by John Lloyd and Jill

Barshay, "Moscow Starts Crisis Talks with Kiev," *Financial Times*, 13 April 1994, p. 2.

41. See Shmid, "Vybory Staly Pomstoiu," p. 1.

42. Coaltions in the Ukrainian parliament are discussed in the CSCE report, "Focus on Serious Challenges Facing Ukraine," May 1994; and in "The New Parliament: In Anticipation of Compromises? Some Thoughts After the Elections," *Narodna Armiia*, 28 April 1994, pp. 1, 3, translated in FBIS-USR-94-054, 23 May 1994, pp. 34–37.

43. In April 1994, a Ukrainian commentator called the speaker "the first person" in the Ukrainian state, saying "in today's conditions the speaker is half the parliament." See Oleg Shmid, "Ivan Plyushch zmushenyi vybyraty mizh synytseyu I zhuravlem. Obydva ptakhy v nebe," *Post-Postup*, 22–28 April 1994, pp. 1–2.

44. Markov, p. 31.

45. Volodymyr Polokhalo and Anatoliy Slyusarenko, "Political Process and Political Elite," *Politychna Dumka/Political Thought*, no. 1 (1993): 109.

46. Markov, p. 31.

47. Markov, p. 32. Kravchuk complained about his lack of power almost from the beginning, saying of the parliament: "You want to put the president in a position where he would be walking around like a puppet, consulting with everyone about what he should do. That is not appropriate." See Kravchuk's interview in *Pravda*, 11 February 1992, pp. 1–2, translated in FBIS-SOV-92-029, 12 February 1992, p. 71.

48. One commentator states that "the first microphone is better than the English crown" (Shmid, "Ivan Plyushch . . . ," p. 2).

49. Markov, p. 34.

50. Vladimir Skachko, "Three Centers of Power: Leonid Kravchuk Has Shared Power with the Government and He Is Now Prepared to Share It with Parliament and the Local Soviets," *Nezavisimaya Gazeta*, 7 November 1992, p. 3, translated in FBIS-USR-92-155, 4 December 1992, pp. 111–112.

51. Markov, p. 33.

52. This problem of "involuntary defection" is the subject of an increasing literature on "two-level games," in which a state leader must negotiate simultaneously with other states and with elements within his or her own state that can block an agreement. See Robert Putnam, "Diplomacy and Domestic Politics: The Logic of Two-Level Games," *International Organization*, 42: 3 (Summer 1988): 427–460.

53. The assertion that the Trilateral Agreement was a "statement," not an agreement or treaty, was made by Foreign Minister Zlenko. RFE/RL, 17 January 1994.

54. John Lloyd, "Ukraine Nuclear Pact in Doubt," *Financial Times*, 12 January 1994, p. 2.

55. Note that this discussion has not included a discussion of the third branch of government, the judiciary. At the criminal and civil levels, the Ukrainian judicial system is in shambles, and until the adoption of the current Constitution, there was no notion of judicial review in Ukraine nor any "supreme court" to try to assert that authority. The new Constitution provides for judicial review, but the system is not yet functioning.

56. Skachko, 111–112. See also Vladimir Buyda, "Government's Supplementary Powers Confirmed. Parliament's commissions Instructed to Enshrine Them in Current Constitution," *Nezavisimaya Gazeta*, 24 November 1993, p. 3, translated in FBIS-USR-92-162, 19 December 1992, p. 130.

57. Markov, p. 33.

58. Kuchma attributed his resignation to the lack of sufficient power to implement a reform program. See "'Text' of Leonid Kuchma's Resignation Statement," Radio Ukraine World Service, 9 September 1993, translated in FBIS-SOV-93-174, 10 September 1993, p. 42.

59. Markov, p. 35.

60. See "Inauguration Speech by President Leonid Kuchma at the Supreme Council in Kiev—live relay," Radio Ukraine World Service, 19 July 1994, translated in FBIS-SOV-94-139, 20 July 1994, p. 36.

61. *OMRI Daily Digest*, part II, 2 March 1995.

62. *OMRI Daily Digest*, part II, 17 February 1995.

63. *OMRI Daily Digest*, part II, 5 April 1995.

64. *OMRI Daily Digest*, part II, 18 April, 15 May 1995.

65. *OMRI Daily Digest*, part II, 19 May 1995.

66. *OMRI Daily Digest*, part II, 26, 31 May 1995.

67. *OMRI Daily Digest*, part II, 30 May, 1 June 1995.

68. *OMRI Daily Digest*, part II, 2, 5, 6 June 1995.

69. *OMRI Daily Digest*, part II, 8 June 1995.

70. The effects of the constitutional agreement on foreign policy making are discussed in Voldymyr Horbulin, "Nasha Meta, Nasha Dolia," *Polityka I Chas*, 1 (1996): 5.

71. See Vitaly Kryukov, "Is the Time Ripe for a New Constitution?" *Politychna Dumka/Political Thought*, no. 1 (1993): 179–185.

72. For an example of the nature of a constitutional amendment carried out, which has tinkered with nearly every section of the Soviet Constitution but not replaced its basic structure, see "Law of Ukraine 'On Changes and Additions to the Constitution (Fundamental Law) of Ukraine,'" *Pravda Ukrainy*, 7 April 1992, p. 3, translated in FBIS-USR-92-050, 1 May 1992, pp. 76–80.

73. See "Kravchuk Presents Economic Program to Parliament," Radio Ukraine World Service, 11 November 1993, translated in FBIS-SOV-93-218, 15 November 1993, p. 65.

74. Leonid Dayen, "Ukraine Is Freezing, but, It Seems, People's Deputies Couldn't Care Less," *Demokratychna Ukrayina*, 1 December 1993, pp. 1, 3, translated in FBIS-SOV-93-231, 3 December 1993, pp. 44–45; "Energy Famine Hits Schools," *Izvestiya*, 1 December 1993, p. 2, translated in FBIS-SOV-93-231, 3 December 1993, pp. 45.

75. Voldymyr Volovych and Serhiy Makeyev, "Social Stratification and Politics," *Politychna Dumka/Political Thought*, no. 1 (1993): 113.

76. On the struggle between Kravchuk and the local Soviets, see Skachko, p. 112.

77. "'Text' of Leonid Kuchma's Resignation Statement," p. 52.

78. Katzenstein, p. 121.

79. On Ukraine's lack of organized interests, see Polokhalo and Slyusarenko, p. 110.

9. Conclusions and Questions

1. The one issue on which Ukraine did give in on was nuclear weapons, but that was some time after the threat had been implied, leaving it doubtful as to whether the energy threat was a driving factor in Ukraine's agreeing to the Trilateral Agreement.

2. It should be noted that while the economic effects of a Russian-initiated cutoff would resemble those of a Ukraine-initiated cutoff, the political effects would be vastly different. In particular, such a blatant attempt to injure Ukraine would have a unifying effect in Ukraine (as did the energy war) instead of the division caused by the perceived arbitrariness of the Ukrainian government's policy.

3. *Nezavisimaya Gazeta*, 23 May 1996. The report is discussed, and excerpts translated, in Scott Parrish, "'Will the Union Be Reborn?'" *Transition* (26 July 1996).

4. This second type of disruption, however, would signal a shift in Russian-Ukrainian trade politics from the realm of power politics to that of interdependence more traditionally viewed, where coercion was not a main goal of disruption. The state's economic autonomy would still be threatened, but its security would not be as endangered as in the case where Russia is deliberately injuring it and making demands in return for a halt.

5. Yuriy Pavlenko, "Ukraine and Modern Civilizations," *Politychna Dumka/Political Thought*, 3 (1994): 188.

6. For detailed analysis of Russia's domination of CIS peacekeeping, and its role in pursuing Russian policy in the region, see the essays in Lena Jonson and Clive Archer, eds., *Peacekeeping and the Role of Russia in Eurasia* (Boulder: Westview Press, 1996).

7. Charles Dick, "The Military Doctrine of Ukraine," *Jane's Intelligence Review*, March 1994, p. 118.

8. See the interview with Ukrainian Deputy Foreign Minister Boris Tarasyuk, "A New Concept of European Security," *Transition* (28 July 1995): 118–122.

9. On the question of neutrality, see Serhiy Tolstov, "Heopolitychni Chynyky Natsional'noi Bezpeky," *Geneza* 2 (1994): 171–185; Oleksandr Dergachov and Serhiy Makayev, "Three Years of Ukrainian Independence: Trends of Social Development," *Politychna Dumka/Political Thought*, 4 (1994): 105–110; Volodymyr Brooz, "Departing from the Policy of Neutrality," *Politychna Dumka/Political Thought*, 4 (1994): 194–195; Volodymyr Horbulin, "Nasha Meta, Nasha Dolia," *Polityka I Chas*, 1 (1996): 3–8; Hennadi Udovenko, "Zovhishnia Polityka Ukraina: Realii ta Perspektivy," *Polityka I Chas*, 1 (1996): 9–13.

10. See for example Vasyl' Kremin', Borys Parakhons'kyi, and Petro Sytnyk, "Ukraina i Rosiia: Sfery Konfrontatsii i Spivrobitnytstva," *Rozbudova Derzhava*, 2 (February 1993): 3, 10.

11. See F. Stephen Larrabee, "Ukraine's Balancing Act," *Survival* (Summer 1996): 143–165.

12. Robert Cullen, "Ukraine, Ukrainian Minorities, and U.S. Policy," Atlantic Council *Bulletin*, September 1994, p. 3.

13. *The Economist*, 8 April 1995, p. 46.

14. RFE/RL, 12 July 1994.

15. See Taras Kuzio, "After the Shock, The Therapy," *Transition* (28 July 1995): 38–40.

16. See Chrystyna Lapychak, "Crackdown on Crimean Separatism," *Transition* (26 May 1995): 2–5.

17. Mikhail Leontyev, "Crimea as Victim of Political Cholera," *Segodnya*, 21 March 1995, excerpted in *Transition* (12 May 1995): 44–45.

18. First Deputy Prime Minister Oleg Soskovets stated in March 1995, that it was time for Russia to accept Ukrainian independence, and said this view would prevail in Russia regardless of the leadership. At the same time, however, a group of parliamentary factions, including the liberal Yabloko, was calling for a reassessment of Russia's relations with Ukraine because of their unhappiness with Kuchma's policy on Crimea (*OMRI Daily Digest*, part I, 27 March 1995).

19. The link between Ukraine's disarmament and international aid is discussed in Michael Mihalka, "Ukraine: Salvaging Nuclear Arms Control," *Transition* (12 May 1995): 30–35.

20. *OMRI Daily Digest*, part I, 19 February 1997.

21. *Nezavisimaya Gazeta*, 18 January 1994.

22. The European Parliament delayed its partnership agreement with Russia in early 1995 due to the Chechen invasion (*OMRI Daily Digest,* part I, 20 January 1995).

23. *OMRI Daily Digest,* part II, 27 April 1995.

24. The IMF played a key role in getting Russia to roll over Ukraine's debts by making that an implicit condition for the next loan to Russia (*The Economist,* 8 April 1995, p. 45).

25. For an excellent review of the variants of liberal international theory and their assumptions, see Mark W. Zacher and Richard A. Matthew, "Liberal International Theory: Common Threads, Divergent Strands," in Charles W. Kegley, Jr., ed., *Controversies in International Relations Theory: Realism and the Neoliberal Challenge* (New York: St. Martin's Press, 1995). Sovereignty is not a problem for liberal theorists for two reasons. First, most current empirical liberal studies are based on Western Europe, where the actors' sovereignty is not threatened from outside (it is only threatened if they choose to surrender some to the EU). Similarly, neoliberal institutionalist approaches that use a rational choice approach (e.g., Keohane) take the existence of sovereign states as a given, much as neorealist theories do. Second, from a normative perspective, economic liberals see little intrinsic value in state sovereignty. If anything, sovereignty is undesirable in the liberal view because it impedes rational economic arrangements.

26. To repeat a point made in chapter 3, Keohane and Nye premise their seminal analysis of interdependence on the assumption that economic welfare is states' highest priority. See *Power and Interdependence,* p. 40.

27. On the distinction between bargaining based on power (a realist construct), and negotiating to solve collective action problems (a liberal construct), see Stephen D. Krasner, "Global Communications and National Power: Life on the Pareto Frontier," *World Politics,* 43 (April 1991), pp. 336–366.

28. James D. Morrow, "Alliances and Asymmetry: An Alternative to the Capability Aggregation Model of Alliances," *American Journal of Political Science,* vol. 35, no. 4 (November 1991): 904–933.

29. Kenneth N. Waltz, "Waltz Responds to Sagan," in Kenneth N. Waltz and Scott D. Sagan, *The Spread of Nuclear Weapons: A Debate* (New York: W. W. Norton, 1995, p. 112; John J. Mearsheimer, "The Case for a Ukrainian Nuclear Deterrent," *Foreign Affairs* (Summer 1993): 50–66; and Barry R. Posen, "The Security Dilemma and Ethnic Conflict," *Survival,* vol. 35, no. 1 (Spring 1993): 38, 44.

30. John Mueller makes the case for the "obsolescence of major war," and is rebutted by Carl Kaysen, and Robert Jervis. See John Mueller, *Retreat from Doomsday: The Obsolescence of Major War* (New York: The Free Press, 1989); Carl Kaysen, "Is War Obsolete?" *International Security* 14, 4 (Spring

1990): 42–64; and Robert Jervis, "The Political Effects of Nuclear Weapons," in Sean M. Lynn-Jones and Steven E. Miller, eds., *The Cold War and After: Prospects for Peace* (Cambridge: MIT Press, 1993), especially pp. 75–76. One of Jervis' most convincing defenses of the utility of nuclear weapons is that even if not used, nuclear weapons have provided sufficient deterrent to prevent lower conventional conflicts as well. The absense of war, he contends, is evidence not of the irrelevance of weapons, but of the continuing utility of the threat of force. In this case, however, leading nuclear states have gone out of their way to deny Ukraine a "nuclear umbrella." Russia has neither attacked nor used the threat, implicit or explicit, of attack, to cajole Ukraine. Rather, it has used economic threats.

31. In this regard it is worth noting that Hirschman regards himself as the "founding grandfather" of dependency theory. See Albert O. Hirschman, "Beyond Asymmetry: Critical Notes on Myself as a Young Man and on Some Other Old Friends," *International Organization*, 32, 1 (Winter 1978): 45. The links between Marxist theory and realist theory, due to their common focus on economic power, are emphasized by Gilpin, in *The Political Economy of International Relations* (Princeton: Princeton University Press, 1986). Their differences are emphasized by James Caporaso, who argues that dependency theory focuses on the internal economic relations in the dependent state, and the links between these relations and the world economy, while realist theories tend to focus more on the bargaining power between states. See James A. Caporaso, "Dependence, Dependency and Power in the Global System: A Structural and Behavioral Analysis," *International Organization*, 32, 1 (Winter 1978): 13–43.

32. This argument is discussed in more detail in chapter 3.

33. See Duncan Snidal, "The Limits of Hegemonic Stability Theory," *International Organization* 39 (1985): 579–614.

34. See Robert Gilpin, *U.S. Power and the Multinational Corporation* (New York: Basic Books, 1975), and *War and Change in World Politics* (Princeton: Princeton University Press, 1981); and Stephen Krasner, "State Power and the Structure of International Trade," *World Politics* 28 (April 1976): 317–347.

35. The viability of collective security systems is critiqued by Richard K. Betts, "Systems of Peace or Causes of War? Collective Security, Arms Control, and the New Europe," *International Security* 17, 1 (Summer 1992): 5–43. Currently, NATO's refusal to shift from being a defensive alliance (against Russia) to becoming a collective security system (including Russia) is largely predicated on skepticism that the latter form of organzation is effective.

36. For a detailed exploration of this hypothesis and an examination of Russia's size and its role in the CIS, see Paul D'Anieri, "International Cooperation among Unequal Partners: The Emergence of Bilateralism in the Former Soviet Union," *International Politics* vol. 34, no. 4 (December 1997): 417–448.

37. Gary King, Robert O. Keohane, and Sidney Verba, *Designing Social Inquiry: Scientific Inference in Qualitative Research* (Princeton: Princeton University Press, 1994), p. 101.

38. On Belarus and Ukraine, see Stephen R. Burant, "Foreign Policy and National Identity: A Comparison of Ukraine and Belarus," *Europe-Asia Studies*, vol. 47, no. 7 (1995): 1125–1144. On Kazakhstan and Belarus, see Paul D'Anieri and Bryan Schmiedeler, "Ukrainian and Kazakh Foreign Policies after the Collapse of the Soviet Union." Paper presented at the meeting of the International Security and Arms Control Section of the American Political Science Association, Washington, D.C. 13 October 1995).

39. On Russia's peacekeeping, see Lena Jonson and Clive Archer, eds., *Peacekeeping and the Role of Russia in Eurasia* (Boulder: Westview Press, 1996).

40. Jack Snyder, "Averting Anarchy in the New Europe," *International Security* 14, 4 (Spring 1990): 5–41; Edward Mansfield and Jack Snyder, "Democratization and the Danger of War," *International Security* 20, 1 (Summer 1995): 5–38; and Snyder, "Democratization, War, and Nationalism in the Post-Communist States," in Celeste A. Wallander, ed., *The Sources of Russian Foreign Policy after the Cold War* (Boulder: Westview Press, 1996).

Index